CODING

THE McGRAW-HILL INTERNATIONAL SERIES IN SOFTWARE ENGINEERING

Consulting Editor

Professor D. Ince
The Open University

Titles in this Series

CODING IN TURBO PASCAL

David Sargent
Senior Lecturer
The Open University

McGRAW-HILL BOOK COMPANY

London · New York · St Louis · San Francisco · Auckland · Bogotá · Caracas
Lisbon · Madrid · Mexico · Milan · Montreal · New Delhi · Panama
Paris · San Juan · São Paulo · Singapore · Sydney · Tokyo · Toronto

Published by
McGRAW-HILL Book Company Europe
SHOPPENHANGERS ROAD · MAIDENHEAD · BERKSHIRE · SL6 2QL · ENGLAND
TELEPHONE 0628 23432   FAX: 0628 770224

British Library Cataloguing in Publication Data

Sargent, David
  Coding in Turbo Pascal. – (McGraw-Hill
  International Series in Software
  Engineering)
  I. Title   II. Series
  005.13

  ISBN 0-07-707958-2

Library of Congress Cataloging-in-Publication Data

Sargent, David
    Coding in turbo pascal/David Sargent.
        p.   cm. — (The McGraw-Hill international series in software
    engineering)
      Includes index.
      ISBN 0-07-707958-2
      1. Pascal (Computer program language)   2. Turbo Pascal (Computer
    file)   I. Title.   II. Series.
    QA76.76.P2S263   1994
    005.26′2 — dc20   93-33781
                                                           CIP

1234CUP9564

Typeset by the author
and printed and bound in Great Britain at the University Press, Cambridge

CONTENTS

PREFACE

This book continues the work of the author's book *An Introduction to Program Design*, published as part of this series on software engineering, by going to the next stage of the software engineering lifecycle, namely that part associated with coding. The philosophy of separating the process of design from coding is continued in this text and it is assumed that the reader is familiar with design either from having studied the above book or from some other source. Problems will be posed in the form of a natural language description of the task to be carried out together with a design for its solution. A major aim of this book is to teach how to convert a design into Pascal code. The book also has the more ambitious aim of enabling the reader to read and understand programming language syntax. This is a skill that is transferable to other languages.

The syntax described in the text will correspond to that of Turbo Pascal Version 5.5. This choice of compiler was made on several grounds. First, it is a very commonly used version which is readily available. Secondly, the version supports object-oriented programming – this is the subject of Chapter 16. In making the choice it was recognized that this version has deficiencies, particularly with its failure strictly to conform to Standard Pascal.

Organization of the chapters Most of the chapters of this book run parallel to those of *An Introduction to Program Design*. (The exceptions are Chapters 1, 2, 9 and 16.) The topics are introduced in the same order so that readers who have access to both texts can compare design development in parallel with its implementation. The early chapters will introduce the design language used in specifying solutions to the problems but a more detailed description is to be found in Appendix II. However, it is not the intention to teach design in these early chapters.

Exercises There are many exercises within the text which the reader must tackle. They are designed to check progress and understanding, and readers are expected to attempt them all. Solutions to the exercises form an integral part of the teaching material and should not be skipped.

Problems Most chapters have at least one problem section, the purpose of which is to give readers the opportunity of getting additional practice in the topics introduced previously. Most of the problems attempt to model a real situation, suitably simplified so that they can be solved using only the skills taught up to that point. Occasionally you may feel that the simplification leads to a slightly unrealistic scenario. Since the main aim of the book is coding, a design has been provided for every problem. The design may not be the best possible but your task is to implement it, warts and all! Problems will be presented in the following format:

Problem statement
This will be a description of the task to be carried out. Since this is an introductory text there is no attempt to present formal specifications.

Design
This will be in the form of a final algorithm presented as a sequence of numbered steps. The numbering system used will enable readers to determine the initial algorithm from which the solution was devised. Appendix II gives details of the design language used in the algorithms.

Data requirements
These are presented in the form of a table that is referred to as a data table. It lists all identifiers used in the solution together with their description and type. The description will identify those data which are problem inputs and those which are problem outputs.

Test data
All the problems have suggestions for suitable test data but the reader may well be expected to generate particular examples from the suggestions.

Coding
This is the subject area covered by this book. All the code presented is in Turbo Pascal Version 5.5.

Design language Below we give a brief account of some of the design language used in this book. Additional design language will be introduced in chapters as and when it is required. A complete description can be found in Appendix II. A design is expressed as a sequence of numbered steps as illustrated by the sequence below:

1	*anInt* := 10	{Assign 10 to *number*. Assignment is denoted by :=}
2	increment *anInt*	{This means by 1 unless stated otherwise}
3	decrement *anINt* by 2	{Subtract 2 from *anInt*}
4	write out 'Enter a real number '	{Text for output to the screen is in quotes}
5	read in *aReal*	{Request for data input from the keyboard}
6	*aReal*:= *aReal* + 2.5	
7	write out 'The value is ', *aReal*	{Variables are not in quotes in write out steps}

The comments, in braces, describe the purpose of each step in the sequence. These steps refer to two variables, *anInt* and *aReal*. Variables used by designs are specified in data tables in the style illustrated below and are printed in italics.

Data table

Identifier	Description	Type
anInt	An integer value	*integer* variable
aReal	A real value entered by the user	*real* variable

A design having integer numbered steps is referred to as a top-level design and identifies the major design components of the solution to a problem. Usually the top-level design will need refining. To reflect the fact that this process has been undertaken, the numbering system of the steps is adjusted as illustrated below:

1	step 1
2.1	first step in refinement of step 2
2.2	second step in refinement of step 2
2.3	third step in refinement of step 2
3	step 3

Here, those steps numbered 2.1, 2.2 and 2.3 are all refinements of step 2 of an original top-level design. The simple designs in this book will be presented as top-level designs whereas those that have required more design effort will be presented as refined designs using this numbering system. The step numbers also provide an easy way to reference an individual line of a design.

In this chapter we shall code some very simple designs into Pascal, a process that is referred to as **implementation**. The purpose of the chapter is to see the overall structure of a simple Pascal program and to illustrate the use of the design language.

The design constructs used in this chapter include the following: *read in*, *read*, *write out*, *if*, *increment* and assignment. A description of these constructs can be found in Appendix II. Both *write* and *write out* are the design constructs which output data to the screen, and the difference between them is that the latter generates a new line after the output whereas the former does not. An example of the way a problem will be presented is given below. Examine the presentation and then study the commentary that follows it for an explanation of some of the details.

Problem

Write a program in which a user enters one of the years 1990 to 1993 inclusive and which produces as output the number of days in the year. You may assume that the user enters the year accurately.

Design

1.1	write 'Enter a year in the range 1990 to 1993 inclusive '
2.1	read in *year*
3.1	if *year* = 1992 then
3.2	*days* := 366
3.3	else
3.4	*days* := 365
3.5	ifend
4.1	write out 'There are ', *days*, ' days in this year'

Data table

Identifier	Description	Type
year	A year entered at keyboard	*integer* variable
days	Number of days in year	*integer* variable

Test data
The program needs to be tested with two input values, one of which will require step 3.2 to be executed, and the other, step 3.4. The values 1992 and 1993 will suffice.

Problems will always be specified using natural language and will appear under the heading *Problem*. The *Design* corresponding to a specification will have two main components: an **algorithm** or sequence of steps to be executed and a data table that defines the variables used in the algorithm. The rationale for the numbering of each design step can be found in the preface. This design includes the use of an *if* construct that extends from step 3.1 to step 3.5. The word *ifend* is used to signify the end of an *if* construct. It will be important to recognize the difference between a design step and a design construct. So here, this *one* construct occupies *five* design steps. The condition *year* = 1992 uses the symbol = as the test for equality. The result of this test is one of the Boolean values true or false. Care must be taken not to confuse the assignment symbol (:=) with the = symbol whose purpose is to compare two values for equality.

Finally, there will be some suggestions as to the kind of data that should be used to test the implementation. Sometimes this will be in the form of a description but at other times might consist of a collection of test data values.

1.1 FIRST PROGRAMS

We begin this section by writing a program corresponding to the following problem.

Problem
Write a program that will write out the three messages, *Greetings*, *My first program* and *Done* on separate lines of the screen.

Design
1   write out 'Greetings'
2   write out 'My first program'
3   write out 'Done'

As there are no variables in this design a data table is not required.

Test data
This will just require the program to be executed.

This design can be implemented as the program below. Examine its details before reading the commentary that follows.

```
program hello;
begin
  writeln('Greetings');
  writeln('My first program');
  writeln('Done')
end.
```

We can immediately identify a structure from this example that is common to all Pascal programs, as follows:

(a) Every program must have a name.
(b) The implementation of the program *design* occurs between the words **begin** and **end**. We shall call this portion of the program the **program body** or **main body** of the program.
(c) The final character in the code is a full stop following the word **end**.

If we examine this code in more detail we can see that several typographical conventions have been adopted in its layout. The purpose of the conventions is to aid program clarity for readers and they make no difference to the program logic. The first convention is that some words are printed in bold. They represent the **reserved** words of the language and are so called because they have a special fixed meaning that cannot be altered by the programmer. Note that it is only in the text that bold characters are used: in programs *you* type into a machine bold, or other, styles are not available; the characters on the screen will all be in the same font style.

A second typographical convention is the use of italics. All words printed in italics in Pascal programs correspond to what are known as **identifiers**. In this program there are two identifiers: *hello* and *writeln*. The first identifier is a **user-defined** identifier which means that it is the invention of the programmer. The second identifier is a **predefined** identifier which means that it is supplied as part of the language. As more of the language is introduced so more predefined identifiers will appear. In Pascal, identifiers must adhere to certain rules. They must begin with a letter but thereafter may consist of either letters, digits or underscore characters. Upper and lower case letters are *not* distinguished, and in Turbo Pascal only the first 63 characters of an identifier are significant! In the unlikely event that two different identifiers are identical for the first 63 characters but differ thereafter then the two identifiers would be indistinguishable. However, such long identifiers would be almost impossible to read and so should not be used. It should also be borne in mind that the number of characters that are significant in identifiers varies from one Pascal implementation to another, and some compilers will only distinguish identifiers based on as few as the first eight characters. The following identifiers are all syntactically correct but would not be distinguishable:

```
firstnumber
FirstNumber
firstNumber
```

Here, the two words, *first* and *number*, have been used to convey the fact that the variable is representing a 'first number'. Because space characters are not allowed in identifiers the two words have been run together. These examples show some of the approaches that can be used when more than one word is required to obtain a meaningful identifier. Use of upper case letters, as in the last two examples, can help the eye pick out the separate words that form the identifier. An alternative method is to use an underscore character to *separate* the words as in:

```
first_number
```

Any of these methods is perfectly acceptable. Essentially, it comes down to what you think is most easily read. For some combinations of letters an underscore approach is good, for others just running the words together produces a pleasing look. We shall use whatever method seems most aesthetically pleasing for the particular combination of letters.

The final typographical convention is the use of indentation. It plays a major role in the readability of code, in the same way as it does in design. As programs become more complex, so good indentation makes them easier to read and therefore to understand. Of course, style of indentation is not of the least interest to a compiler. It ignores extra space characters between words and indeed lines that are totally blank. So the compiler would be perfectly happy to have the program written as follows:

```
program hello;begin writeln('Greetings');writeln('My first program');
writeln('Done')end.
```

It makes little sense to present it like this for human beings since it is much more difficult to understand. Just as good layout can help the clarity of a design so it can help the understanding of a piece of code. Careful use of extra space characters, of new lines and completely blank lines should be used to create an aesthetically pleasing piece of code.

We shall now examine the structure of the program identified in the list (a) to (c) above in more detail.

1. Every program must have a program name constructed as follows. First, there is the reserved word **program**, followed by the name by which the program is known and finally a semicolon. The name must be an identifier that conforms to the rules described above. This first line of a program is called the **program heading**.

2. Following this there is the **program body**. Its starting point is indicated by the reserved word **begin** and it extends as far as the reserved word **end**. This is the part that corresponds to the design; each step of the design has become a code statement. We need to analyse this program body in some detail. The first statement corresponds to the design step *write out*. What is to be written out is the word *Greetings*, and in both the design and code this word is enclosed in single quotes. We refer to 'Greetings' as a string but note that the quotes themselves do not form part of the output. The process by which this string gets to the screen need not concern us – the details are all handled by the step called *writeln*. In fact, *writeln* is the identifier of what is known as a Pascal procedure. We shall not be studying procedures until Chapter 8 but until then we can think of them as 'black boxes' which perform some specific task. The important point to note now is that the *writeln* procedure handles output to the screen in such a way that following the output of the final character the cursor is sent to the beginning of a new line. The *writeln* statements in this program are examples of **procedure calls**. Typically, procedures have one or more **parameters**; here each *writeln* call has one parameter that consists of a string. However, *writeln* is more flexible than this and it can have several parameters. These parameters can be strings, as above, or can be variable identifiers. The effect of including an identifier in a *writeln* is to have the value represented by that identifier written to the screen. We shall see an example of this in Section 1.2. This first statement is then followed by a semicolon. The second statement is also a call to the procedure *writeln* and is also followed by a semicolon. The last statement is yet another procedure call but this time there is no semicolon.

3. The final symbol in the program is a full stop, and this is the only place within a program where this punctuation symbol is used at the end of a line.

The correct use of semicolons can cause problems to students new to programming, so we shall be giving a sequence of programming guidelines that are intended to help overcome the difficulties. The observation above leads to the first such guideline.

- Guideline (end) A semicolon should never immediately precede the word **end**.

Finally, notice how the **begin/end** pair has the effect of bracketing together the program body. We shall see many examples of the use of **begin/end** pairs to bracket statements together.

Exercise 1.1 Write a complete program that will produce the following four lines of output:

```
The next line is completely blank

This is the third line
This is the last line
```

1.2 PROGRAMS WITH VARIABLES

The following design uses integer variables to store data values.

```
        {A design to add two integers and write out their sum}
1.1     FirstNumber := 5
1.2     SecondNumber := 8
2.1     sum := FirstNumber + SecondNumber
3.1     write out 'The sum is ', sum, ' exactly'
```

Data table

Identifier	Description	Type
FirstNumber	A variable holding the value 5	*integer* variable
SecondNumber	A variable holding the value 8	*integer* variable
sum	Sum of *FirstNumber* and *SecondNumber*	*integer* variable

The output generated by step 3.1 should be as follows:

```
The sum is 13 exactly
```

Study the code below and try to identify the program body corresponding to the design steps. Note the way that the comment describing the purpose of the program is written in exactly the same in Pascal as it is in the design. The use of comments in programs is another way in which information can be conveyed to the reader but which is totally ignored by the compiler. Any text appearing between braces, even if it is spread over several lines, is interpreted by the compiler as a **comment** and so is ignored.

```
program addtwo;
{A design to add two integers and write out their sum}
var
   FirstNumber  : integer;
   SecondNumber : integer;
   sum          : integer;
begin
   FirstNumber := 5;
   SecondNumber := 8;
   sum := FirstNumber + SecondNumber;
   writeln('The sum is ', sum, ' exactly')
end.
```

The major difference between this design and the previous one is that the latter makes use of variables. All variables used in a Pascal program must be declared explicitly. Here, there are three variables to be declared, so this program has a declarations part as well as a program body. It is the declarations part that is the implementation of the data table.

Examining the code more closely we can see that the first line consists of the program heading. Immediately following this are the variable declarations, these being indicated by the reserved word **var**. Each declaration has the form: identifier, colon, variable type. We have inserted extra space characters after two of the identifiers in order to align the colons. This makes them more legible, but it is not necessary to do this when you type in your own programs. All three variables here are declared to be of type *integer*. This is one of the built-in types provided by the language. Notice also that each declaration is separated from the next one by a semicolon.

● Guideline (declarations) Each declaration has the form: identifier, colon, variable type, and every declaration is followed by a semicolon.

The program body has the same structure as before but it introduces some new implementation details. The assignment symbol in both design and Pascal is := in which a space is not permitted between the colon and the equals sign. In this program the *writeln* statement is used to output text and the value held by a variable and so has three parameters: a string value, then an integer variable and finally another string value. Note how each of these parameters is separated from its successor by a comma.

We can summarize the general Pascal program structure as follows:

(a) Every program must have a name.
(b) Declarations must come immediately after the program name and must be preceded by the word **var**. They constitute the implementation of the *data table*.
(c) The **main body** of the program occurs between the words **begin** and **end**.
(d) The final character in the code is a full stop following the word **end**.

Exercise 1.2 Assuming the variables *FirstNumber*, *SecondNumber* and *sum* have the values given above, write down the *writeln* statement that would be required to produce each of the following as output:
(a) 13 is the sum of the inputs
(b) The number 13 is the sum of the inputs
(c) Inputs were 5, 8 and their sum is 13

When, as in the example above, a program uses variables all of the same type, then they can be declared in a single statement by using a comma separated list. This is illustrated in the next program, which uses the same variables as the program above but also has input and output.

Problem
Write a program that enables a user to enter two integers from the keyboard and produces their sum as output. A typical dialogue from the program, in which the user responses are underlined, would be:

```
Enter the first integer 4<ret>
Enter the second integer 8<ret>
The sum is 12
```

Design

{A design to input two integers from the keyboard and write out their sum}
1.1   write 'Enter the first integer '
1.2   read in *FirstNumber*
1.3   write 'Enter the second integer '
1.4   read in *SecondNumber*
2.1   *sum := FirstNumber + SecondNumber*
3.1   write out 'The sum is ', *sum*

Data table

Identifier	Description	Type
FirstNumber	First integer entered from keyboard	*integer* variable
SecondNumber	Second integer entered from keyboard	*integer* variable
sum	Sum of *FirstNumber* and *SecondNumber*	*integer* variable

Test data
This should be tested with positive, zero and negative integer inputs.

The design construct *write* in step 1 indicates that the cursor is to be left on the same line as the prompt as it awaits input of the integer value. The Pascal procedure *write* has the property of positioning the cursor immediately after the last character that it outputs. This enables the design to be coded as follows:

```
program sumtwo;
var
   FirstNumber, SecondNumber, sum : integer;
begin
   write('Enter the first integer ');
   readln(FirstNumber);
   write('Enter the second integer ');
   readln(SecondNumber);
   sum := FirstNumber + SecondNumber;
   writeln('The sum is ', sum)
end.
```

Here, all three variables have been declared in a single statement. This is permissible when, as here, all the variables are of the same type. Thus a modified guideline for declarations is:

- Guideline (declarations) Each declaration has the form: identifier list, colon, variable type, in which the list consists of identifiers separated by commas. Every declaration must be followed by a semicolon.

The Pascal statement, *readln*, is the equivalent of the design step *read in*. We shall have more to say about *readln* later, but for now notice that in this design it has one parameter. When the call to *readln* is executed the program halts and awaits the input of an integer value. This is done by the user typing the number followed by <ret> after which the cursor moves to the beginning of the next line. The statement that assigns the sum of the two values to *sum* is the same in both design and Pascal.

Exercise 1.3

Problem

Write a program that enables a user to enter two integers from the keyboard and produces their difference as output. The second integer entered should be subtracted from the first.

Design

{A design to input two integers from the keyboard and write out their difference}
1.1   write 'Enter the first integer '
1.2   read in *FirstNumber*
1.3   write 'Enter the integer which is to be subtracted '
1.4   read in *TakeAway*
2.1   *difference* := *FirstNumber* – *TakeAway*
3.1   write out 'The difference is ', *difference*

Data table

Identifier	Description	Type
FirstNumber	First integer entered from keyboard	*integer* variable
TakeAway	Second integer entered from keyboard	*integer* variable
difference	*FirstNumber – TakeAway*	*integer* variable

Test data

This should be tested to ensure the subtraction is done the correct way round.

1.3 PROGRAMS WITH AN IF STATEMENT

We shall now look at how to implement an *if* construct. To concentrate on the coding, the problem to be solved will be deliberately trivial (and serves no realistic purpose). Consider the design below which was given in the Introduction.

1   write 'Enter a year in the range 1990 to 1993 inclusive '
2   read in *year*
3.1   if *year* = 1992 then
3.2   *days* := 366
3.3   else
3.4   *days* := 365
3.5   ifend
4   write out 'There are ', *days*, ' days in this year'

Data table

Identifier	Description	Type
year	A year entered at keyboard	*integer* variable
days	Number of days in year	*integer* variable

This design consists of four design constructs: a *write*, a *read in*, an *if* and a final *write out*. Examining the *if* construct we can see that both its *then* and *else* clauses consist of single assignment constructs. The program corresponding to the design is:

```
program leapyear;
var
  year, days : integer;
begin
  write('Enter a year in the range 1990 to 1993 inclusive ');
  readln(year);
  if year = 1992 then
    days := 366
  else
    days := 365;
  writeln('There are ', days, ' days in this year')
end.
```

The first two statements of the program body are straightforward and are each followed by a semicolon. The implementation of the *if* construct requires a little more explanation. First, the words **if**, **then** and **else** are reserved words in Pascal and so are printed in bold. When we wish to refer to the design form of one of these words we shall print them in italics, thus *if*, *then* and *else*. This typographical distinction between design and implementation reserved words will be useful when we wish to examine the same statement in both its design and code form. The use of bold in the next sentence will enable you to deduce that it is code and not design to which it refers. The punctuation associated with the **if** statement also requires close scrutiny. The **then** clause consists of a single assignment statement, corresponding to the single construct in the design, but it is not followed by a semicolon. The **else** clause also consists of a single assignment statement but it *does* end with a semicolon. This is because the **if** statement as a whole is now complete. We can think of the *ifend* of the design as having been translated into the semicolon following the number 365.

- Guideline (if then else) When the *then* clause consists of a single design construct its implementation is a single statement not followed by a semicolon. When the design of the *else* clause consists of a single construct then its implementation is a single statement followed by a semicolon (provided the next word is not **end**).

Exercise 1.4 Why is the final *writeln* statement not followed by a semicolon?

The program *leapyear* will now be modified so that a message is output in addition to the value of *days*. The design below gives the details.

```
1       write 'Enter a year in the range 1990 to 1993 inclusive '
2       read in year
3.1     if year = 1992 then
3.2         days := 366
3.3         write out 'This is a leap year'
3.4     else
3.5         days := 365
3.6         write out 'This is not a leap year'
3.7     ifend
4       write out 'There are ', days, ' days in this year'
```

Steps 1, 2 and 4 are coded as before but step 3 requires more care. Here, the *then* and *else* clauses both consist of two design constructs – an assignment and a *write out*. The design is implemented as follows:

```
program leapyear2;
var
  year, days : integer;
begin
  write('Enter a year in the range 1990 to 1993 inclusive ');
  readln(year);
  if year = 1992 then
    begin
      days := 366;
      writeln('This is a leap year')
    end
  else
    begin
      days := 365;
      writeln('This is not a leap year')
    end;
  writeln('There are ', days, ' days in this year')
end.
```

To implement the two design constructs of the *then* clause it is necessary to enclose them in a **begin/end** pair. The two constructs in the *then* clause are coded as usual but note how the second one is not followed by a semicolon. Similarly, to keep the two design constructs of the *else* clause together another **begin/end** pair is used.

Each of the **then** and **else** clauses here is an illustration of what is known as a **compound statement**. Intuitively, a compound statement consists of two or more lines of code enclosed in a **begin end** pair.

Exercise 1.5 Why is neither of the *writeln* statements involving the text 'This is ... a leap year' followed by a semicolon? Why is the first **end** not followed by a semicolon whereas the second one is?

The solution to Exercise 1.5 leads to the following modified guideline:

• Guideline (if then else) When the *then* clause consists of two or more design constructs, then it must be implemented as a compound statement where the **end** is not followed by a semicolon. When the *else* clause consists of two or more design constructs, it must be implemented as a compound statement. The **end** corresponding to this compound statement should be followed by a semicolon provided it does not immediately precede the word **end**.

Care must be taken to distinguish between design constructs and design steps when using this guideline. It is the constructs that must be counted, not the steps. The process of counting constructs will be extended, so try to master it now. So in the design we have just coded there is a single *if* construct consisting of seven design steps, numbered 3.1 – 3.7, which extends from the word *if* to the word *ifend*.

If you are in doubt about whether a line of a design is a step or a construct, try to classify it as one of the following: an *if* construct, an assignment construct, a *write out* construct, a *read in* construct or, as we examine shortly, a *loop* construct. If it isn't one of these then you have a step, not a construct. For example, the *then* clause above consists of two constructs: an assignment construct and a *write out* construct. As more design constructs are introduced you will have to modify this advice appropriately, but you will soon get used to recognizing them. The next problem requires the use of a loop in its solution.

Problem

Write a program that will enable a user to input the initial value of a microcomputer and which will produce as output the value of the machine over the following five years under the assumption that it depreciates by 15 per cent per annum.

The output to be produced by this design for an input value of 100.00 should have the form illustrated below:

```
After year 1 depreciated value is 85.00
After year 2 depreciated value is 77.25
After year 3 depreciated value is 61.41
After year 4 depreciated value is 52.20
After year 5 depreciated value is 44.37
```

Design

1.1	write out 'Enter initial value of micro'
1.2	read in *value*
1.3	*year* := 1
2.1	loop while *year* <= 5
3.1	*value* := 0.85*value*
3.2	write out 'After year ', *year,* ' depreciated value is ', *value*
3.3	increment *year*
4	loopend

Data table

Identifier	Description	Type
value	Current value of micro	*real* variable
year	Number of years passed	*integer* variable

Test data

Executing the program with an input value of 100.0 should give the values above but you will have to wait until Chapter 3 before seeing how to output the numbers to two decimal places.

This design uses a real variable which is declared in a similar way to that of integer variables. Study the complete code of the program shown below and then read the commentary that follows.

```
program depreciation;
var
  value : real;
  year  : integer;
begin
  write('Enter initial value of micro ');
  readln(value);
```

```
  year := 1;
  while year <= 5 do
    begin
      value := 0.85*value;
      writeln('After year ', year, ' depreciated value is ', value);
      year := year + 1
    end
end.
```

The implementation of step 2.1 is new and it is translated as:

```
while year <= 5 do
```

This illustrates the general form of a Pascal **while** loop. The word **while** is a reserved word, as is the word **do**. Between them there is the condition that controls the loop. We can, if we wish, enclose the condition in brackets:

```
while (year <= 5) do
```

although when the condition is simple like this one we shall not do so. The design steps which form the body of this loop and which are repeatedly executed are those numbered 3 and are implemented by means of a compound statement. This leads to the following guideline:

- Guideline (while) When a *while* loop consists of two or more design constructs then it must be implemented using a compound statement. The statement preceding the **end** that terminates the compound statement should not be followed by a semicolon. Whether the **end** itself is followed by a semicolon is determined by what follows on.

1.4 PROGRAM FRAGMENTS

We shall not always want to write complete programs when illustrating details of some particular Pascal syntax. In situations like this we shall be content to write a **Pascal fragment**. Such a fragment will be a piece of code that would form part of a program. In nearly all cases the fragment will be part of a compound statement, but as it may be incomplete we shall not include the **begin** and **end** associated with it. Even when the fragment does correspond to a complete compound statement, the **begin** and **end** will be omitted for brevity. So, for example, the following are both fragments from the program *sumtwo*.

```
write('Enter the second integer ');
readln(SecondNumber);
sum := FirstNumber + SecondNumber
```

```
write('Enter the first integer ');
readln(FirstNumber);
write('Enter the second integer ');
readln(SecondNumber);
sum := FirstNumber + SecondNumber;
writeln('The sum is ', sum)
```

We shall adopt the convention that the final statement in a fragment will in general not be followed by a semicolon. This is because the inclusion of a semicolon would imply that another statement follows the final one of the fragment and this, as the second example shows, will not always be the case. By adopting this convention a fragment can more closely match the syntax of a complete program. One exception to the convention is when the fragment consists only of the declarations part of a program when of course every declaration is always followed by a semicolon.

An additional syntactic difficulty with program fragments is how to handle the declaration of the variables they use. Often the text will describe the variables and their type, but sometimes we shall want the fragment to include explicit declarations. In that case we shall declare them in the normal way, using a **var** declaration, but will follow it immediately with the Pascal fragment, thus:

```
var
    SecondNumber, SecondNumber, sum : integer;
    :
write('Enter the second integer ');
readln(SecondNumber);
sum := FirstNumber + SecondNumber
```

1.5 EXERCISES AND PROBLEMS

Exercises in sections such as these will be straightforward tests of your understanding of the text. The problems, which are to be found in Appendix I, will be more substantial and will consist of a problem statement together with a design. Your task will be to implement the design. Most of the problems have been derived from the author's book *An Introduction to Program Design*, which is in the same series as this text, and so if you wish to study the development of the designs you can refer to it. Problems that are new to this book will be marked with an asterisk. Problems 1.1 and 1.2 give you the opportunity of writing complete Pascal programs involving variables.

Exercise 1.6 Write down Pascal statements which will declare three integer variables, *one*, *two*, *three*, and two real variables, *first* and *second*.

Exercise 1.7 Write a complete program which will write out your name.

1.6 PROGRAMMING HINTS

The following guidelines have been developed in this chapter:

(a) Guideline (program) Every program must have a heading of the form
    program *identifier;*.
(b) Guideline (declarations part) Immediately following the program heading come the variable declarations (if there are any) indicated by the reserved word **var**. The declarations part corresponds to the implementation of the design data table.
(c) Guideline (declarations) Each declaration has the form: identifier list, colon, variable

type, in which the list consists of identifiers separated by commas. Every declaration must be followed by a semicolon.

(d)   The **main body** of the program occurs between the words **begin** and **end**.

(e)   The final character of a program is a full stop (following the final **end**).

(f)   Guideline (end) A semicolon should never immediately precede the word **end**.

(g)   Guideline (if then else) When the *then* clause consists of a single design construct its implementation is a single statement *not followed* by a semicolon. When the *then* clause consists of two or more design constructs, then it must be implemented as a compound statement where the **end** is not followed by a semicolon. When the design of the *else* clause consists of a single construct, then its implementation is a single statement followed by a semicolon (provided the next word is not **end**). When the *else* clause consists of two or more design constructs it must be implemented as a compound statement. The **end** corresponding to this compound statement should be followed by a semicolon provided it does not immediately precede the word **end**.

(h)   Guideline (while) When a *while* loop consists of two or more design constructs, then it must be implemented using a compound statement. The statement preceding the **end** that terminates the compound statement should not be followed by a semicolon. Whether the **end** itself is followed by a semicolon is determined by what follows on.

(i)   Guideline (comment) Any text appearing between braces is a comment and is ignored by the compiler. A comment may extend over many lines.

1.7 SUMMARY

In this chapter we have looked at the overall structure of a Pascal program and have translated some simple designs into Pascal. We have also seen illustrations of the use of compound statements. Guidelines have been given, including those to help you to decide when a compound statement is required and where semicolons should be placed.

2

THE SYNTAX OF A SIMPLE PROGRAM

In this chapter we shall begin the study of Pascal syntax by looking at the constituent parts of a simple program. These parts will be represented diagrammatically by what are known as **railroad** or **syntax diagrams** which, when understood, can be used to check the syntax of other programs. They will also show you why the informal programming guidelines in Chapter 1 pertain.

Syntax diagrams are referred to by a name enclosed in angled brackets, for example, < identifier >. To begin with, each such term will be described informally in the text and will then be presented more formally as a diagram. On many occasions the diagrams will not contain all the details associated with the term being defined. This is so as to enable the material to be more easily understood, but as we progress, many of the simplified diagrams will be extended until they more fully specify the term. It is not the intention of this book to give a full account of Pascal syntax, so few terms will be developed as far as a full definition. As more detail is added to a particular diagram we shall refer to it as a modified version of what has gone before. This does not mean the syntax has changed – it merely means that it more closely resembles the form of a full definition such as could be found in a technical manual for a particular Pascal compiler.

You may find some of this material rather challenging on first exposure, in which case you should come back to it later once you have developed your programming skills.

2.1 A FIRST PROGRAM ANALYSED

We start with the simple 'hello' program introduced in Chapter 1:

```
program hello;
begin
  writeln('Greetings');
  writeln('My first program');
  writeln('Done')
end.
```

We have already remarked that the first line of the code is called the **program heading**. All Pascal programs must begin with a program heading – it is a rule of the language. The body of rules that governs the construction of a program is known as the **syntax** of the language. The rules must be documented so that the language definition is precise and unambiguous. There are a variety of ways of documenting syntax rules, and the one we have chosen uses diagrams. Figure 2.1 below expresses the syntax of the term < program heading >.

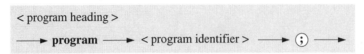

< program heading >

Figure 2.1 The syntax of < program heading >

We shall explain the notation of syntax diagrams by reference to Figure 2.1. The term being defined, here *program heading*, is enclosed in angled brackets. The definition of this term is read by entering the diagram through the arrow on the left, following the arrows and finally exiting through the arrow on the right. As you pass through a syntax diagram two possible kinds of symbol may be encountered: these are called **terminal** and **non-terminal** symbols. Terminal symbols are the words, punctuation marks and operations of the language and their meaning cannot be modified by the user. Figure 2.1 contains two terminal symbols, the first of which is the word **program** and the second a semicolon. In syntax diagrams, terminal symbols consisting of a word will be printed in bold and those which are punctuation marks or operations will be enclosed in a circle. The former is known as a **reserved word**. Reserved words may not be used by programmers as identifiers in their code – at least, if they are used a compilation error will result. So the word **program** is a reserved word and as a consequence may not be used as an identifier.

The second kind of symbol that can be encountered is a non-terminal symbol. These are enclosed in angled brackets to denote that their definition is to be found elsewhere in another syntax diagram. Thus < program identifier > is a non-terminal symbol and we need to look up its syntax diagram to determine what a valid program identifier is. If we were to do so we would find the following (Figure 2.2):

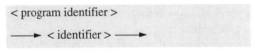

< program identifier >

Figure 2.2 The syntax of < program identifier >

This diagram may seem a little odd because all it appears to do is to define < program identifier > as an identifier! In fact there are other types of identifiers, such as variable identifiers, and it is useful to be able to distinguish them. The syntax of < identifier > itself, is given in Figure 2.3.

Figure 2.3 is more complex than hitherto because it includes a diverging branch to the right of the uppermost < letter >. Whenever a diverging branch is encountered either path may be chosen so here there is a choice between exiting the diagram altogether or turning right and going down the vertical path. Taking the latter route we encounter other branches giving a choice between < letter > and < digit > and an underscore character. The path then returns to rejoin the original one.

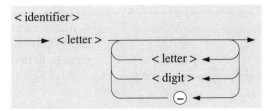

Figure 2.3 The syntax of < identifier >

Exercise 2.1 Using your intuition as to what constitutes a letter and a digit, determine which of the following are valid identifiers. For those that are not valid explain why they break the syntax rule.
(a) *hello2* (b) *second_program* (c) *3rdtry* (d) *_my2try* (e) *a_long_name*

Several questions arise from Exercise 2.1. What are the allowable letters and digits and can an identifier have as many letters, digits and underscores as you like? The answer to the second question cannot be ascertained from syntax diagrams as they do not contain information such as the number of times a given path may be traversed. Other methods of defining syntax do include such information but they tend to be harder to read than diagrams. We have already mentioned that in Turbo Pascal only the first 63 characters are distinguished. Unlike some other implementations, the underscore in Turbo Pascal is significant and so, for example, *a_long_name* and *alongname* are different identifiers.

To answer the first question the syntax diagram for < letter > and < digit > must be examined. That for < digit > is given in Figure 2.4 below.

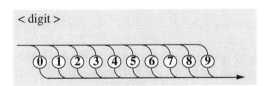

Figure 2.4 The syntax of < digit >

We can see from this diagram that all the digits are terminal symbols. This is indicated by their being enclosed in a circle. A similar syntax diagram for < letter > would show all the lower case letters a … z, together with the upper case letters A … Z. Each letter is a terminal symbol.

What we have done so far is to trace in detail through the syntax of the term < program identifier >. It has been a long route and has eventually led to diagrams consisting only of terminal symbols. This is true of any syntax diagram – by examining the definitions of the non-terminal symbols, eventually diagrams will be reached which contain only terminal symbols.

Syntax diagrams not only define the syntax of a language but also enable you to check that a given expression conforms to the syntax. The following exercise asks you to do this.

Exercise 2.2 Use the following syntax diagrams to answer the questions below.

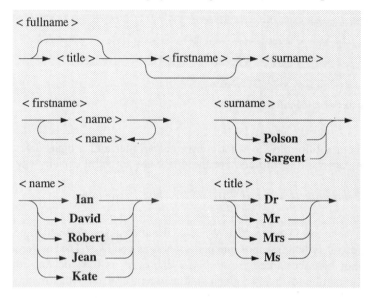

Which of the following are valid fullnames according to these syntax rules? Explain your answers.

(a) David Sargent
(b) Prof. Jean Polson
(c) Dr Polson
(d) Ms Kate
(e) Ian Robert Sargent
(f) David Robert Kate Sargent

The syntax for the whole of a Pascal program is expressed in Figure 2.5 below. Essentially, this lumps together everything other than the program heading and the final full stop into one syntactic term called a < block >. Thus, the first line of code corresponds to the program heading and all the remaining code, excluding the final full stop, is the program block. The importance of the term 'block' will not become apparent until Chapter 8.

< program > {simplified}

⟶ < program heading > ⟶ < block > ⟶ ⊙

Figure 2.5 The syntax of < program >

Exercise 2.3 Does the term < block > include the program declarations?

2.2 A PROGRAM WITH VARIABLES

To look at the syntax of a block we shall examine the code from Chapter 1 that sums two numbers input from the keyboard. The comments that have been included will be explained below.

```
program sumtwo; {<program heading>}
var               {<declarations>}
  FirstNumber, SecondNumber, sum : integer;
begin             {<compound statement>}
  write('Enter the first integer ');
  readln(FirstNumber);
  write('Enter the second integer ');
  readln(SecondNumber);
  sum := FirstNumber + SecondNumber;
  writeln('The sum is ', sum)
end.
```

A block corresponds to everything after the program heading and so includes the declarations and main program body. Figure 2.6 gives its syntax.

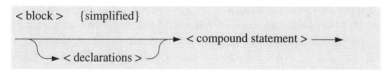

Figure 2.6 The simplified syntax of < block >

Figures 2.5 and 2.6 can be combined into one as follows:

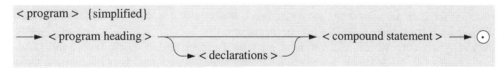

Figure 2.7 The expanded syntax of < program >

Each of the terms in Figure 2.7 has been identified in the code by means of a comment in the program *sumtwo* and the diagrams enable us to justify the general program structure that was presented in Chapter 1.

(a) Every program must have a heading.
    This corresponds to the term < program heading > and includes the word **program**, an identifier, followed by a semicolon.
(b) Declarations must come immediately after the program name and must be preceded by the word **var**.
    This is shown by the path going through < declarations >. Not all programs have variables to declare, the earlier program being an example – the path that avoids < declarations > shows that such programs are syntactically legitimate.

(c) The main body of the program occurs between the words **begin** and **end**.
The main body is the term called < compound statement > in Figure 2.6 and it will be examined in detail shortly.
(d) The final character in the code is a full stop following the word **end**.

Figure 2.6 also shows that when a design uses variables they are implemented by means of a declaration that must precede the start of the < compound statement > of the main program body. A simplified version of the syntax of declarations is as follows (Figure 2.8):

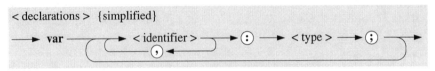

Figure 2.8 The simplified syntax of < declarations >

This is the most complex diagram so far in that there are two paths that branch back. Upon entry to the diagram the reserved word **var** is encountered and is therefore mandatory. The diagram shows that the word **var** must be followed by at least one occurrence of an identifier. Ignoring, for the time being, the branch that loops back under < identifier >, this identifier must be followed by a colon which in turn must be followed by a < type >. An instance of < type > is the built-in type *integer*. In this chapter the only allowable instances of < type > are the two built-in types we have encountered so far, namely *integer* and *real*. This is then followed by a semicolon and we can either exit or return to make another declaration by listing its identifier and type. This is precisely the way the declarations were made in the program *addtwo* of Chapter 1; the word **var** is followed by the identifier *FirstNumber*, then a colon, then the type, *integer*, and finally a semicolon. A traversal along the long loop back then accounts for the declaration of *SecondNumber* and so on. Notice how the syntax forces each declaration to have the form identifier, colon, type, semicolon. This explains Guideline (declarations) in Chapter 1 which stated that every declaration must be followed by a semicolon.
The syntax diagram also explains the modification to the guideline in which a declaration such as

```
var
   FirstNumber, SecondNumber, sum : integer;
```

which appeared in program *sumtwo* is also syntactically valid. It exploits the loop under < identifier > and so enables variables of the same type to be listed one after the other, separated by commas, prior to the colon, type and semicolon.

Exercise 2.4 Would the following declaration be a syntactically valid way of declaring these three variables? Explain your answer.

```
var
   FirstNumber, SecondNumber : integer;
   sum                       : integer;
```

Exercise 2.5 What is syntactically wrong with the following declaration?
var
    integer : first;

Exercise 2.5 illustrates the way in which syntax diagrams can be used to trace errors in code. When a compiler encounters a syntax error, compilation stops and an error message is produced. Because of the enormous number of syntax errors that can occur, the error messages are not always too helpful but the error occurs before the position at which compilation stops. The ability to read and understand syntax diagrams will greatly enhance your skills at locating and correcting syntax errors.

Having dealt with the syntax of declarations we can move on to the main program body, namely the term < compound statement > in Figure 2.6. In looking at its syntax it will become apparent why the penultimate line of the code in **program** *sumtwo* is not followed by a semicolon when all the other lines are. Indeed, this will justify the guideline from Chapter 1:

• Guideline (end) A semicolon should never immediately precede the word **end**.

The syntax for < compound statement > is given in Figure 2.9 below.

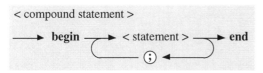

Figure 2.9 The syntax of < compound statement >

The start of a compound statement is indicated by the reserved word **begin**, so the first < statement > in *sumtwo* is *write*('Enter the first integer '), that is, the whole of the fifth line of code up to, but not including, the semicolon. The sixth line of the code is also part of this compound statement and corresponds to taking the path of Figure 2.9 that loops back under < statement >. But in so doing a semicolon is encountered, this being the one immediately following *write*('Enter the first integer '). This process repeats until the final statement *writeln*('The sum is ', *sum*). This time there are no following statements and so we exit from the diagram. In so doing the reserved word **end** is passed, rather than the semicolon, thereby explaining the punctuation associated with this last line. Thus, the guideline (end) above is justified.

2.3 THE SYNTAX OF A STATEMENT

Figure 2.9 introduced the term < statement >. In this section we shall make a start on examining its syntactic definition. The task will not be completed until Chapter 8 which should give you some idea of its complexity. We shall also make a start on the syntax of another complex syntactic term < expression >, although our approach to this will be somewhat more intuitive. The program below is reproduced from Chapter 1.

```
program leapyear;
var
  year, days : integer;
begin
  write('Enter a year in the range 1990 to 1993 inclusive ');
  readln(year);
  if year = 1992 then
    days := 366
  else
    days := 365;
  writeln('There are ', days, ' days in this year')
end.
```

This program illustrates the use of four different types of statement: a procedure call, an **if** statement, an assignment statement and a compound statement. We have also seen a **while** statement in Chapter 1. These observations enable us to appreciate a simplified version of the formal syntax of < statement >. Clearly, whatever a < statement > is, it must include an **if** statement, an assignment statement, a procedure call, a compound statement and a **while** statement. All of this information is summarized in Figure 2.10 below.

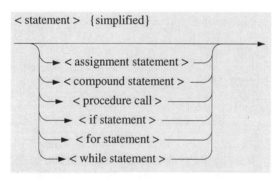

Figure 2.10 The simplified syntax of < statement >

One very strange property of this diagram is that it appears there is a path straight through it! This is indeed the case, and it gives rise to what is known as a **null statement**, which is the Pascal equivalent of the design step *do nothing*. The next most simple term in this diagram is that of < assignment statement >. Its syntax is shown in Figure 2.11 below.

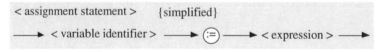

Figure 2.11 The syntax of <assignment statement >

In Figure 2.11, < variable identifier > is just an identifier corresponding to a variable and an < expression > is something which evaluates to a value that can be assigned to the variable. The important point here is that this diagram does not contain a semicolon. Semicolons are associated with compound statements and do not appear in any of the terms other than < compound statement > in Figure 2.10.

We can examine the syntax of < if statement > with reference to the program *leapyear*. The **if** statement extends from the reserved word **if** all the way to the 5 of the number 365. It is important to realize that both of the assignment statements in this code are part of the **if** statement, one being associated with the **then** and the other with the **else**. The syntax for an < if statement > is given in Figure 2.12 below.

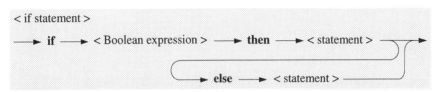

Figure 2.12 The syntax of < if statement >

For the time being we shall settle for an intuitive definition of < Boolean expression > which appears in this diagram. We shall take it to mean any collection of variables and symbols that evaluates to true or false. Here, the Boolean expression corresponds to (*year* = 1992) and this is either true or false depending upon whether or not *year* has value 1992. < Boolean expression > is followed by the reserved word **then** which in turn is followed by < statement >. In the program *leapyear* the latter corresponds to a single assignment statement. After this there are two possible routes in Figure 2.12, one that passes to the reserved word **else** and the other that passes straight out. The former corresponds to **if** statements that have **else** clauses, as in our example program. So an **else** clause is itself followed by < statement >, which again here is a single assignment statement.

What remains to be explained is the punctuation associated with the **if** statement in the program *leapyear* and in particular why the line containing 365 has a semicolon whereas that containing 366 does not. The program, as a whole, has one compound statement that starts with the word **begin** and terminates with the word **end**. The syntax of a compound statement informs us that each of the statements within it, except the last, is followed by a semicolon. The **if** statement is one of these statements and, as it is not the last one within the compound statement, it is followed by a semicolon. This explains the presence of the semicolon following the number 365. It also explains why the assignment involving the number 366 is not followed by a semicolon. This is because the **then** clause consists of a single assignment statement and, as Figure 2.11 shows, an assignment statement does not have a semicolon associated with it. The first version of the guideline for **if** statements given in Chapter 1 is reproduced below and expresses this in a more informal way.

• Guideline (if then else) When the *then* clause consists of a single design construct its implementation is a single statement *not followed* by a semicolon. When the design of the *else* clause consists of a single construct then its implementation is a single statement followed by a semicolon (provided the next word is not **end**).

Some *if* statements do not have an associated *else* clause. Here is an alternative program that has the same purpose as the *leapyear* program above:

```
program leapyear3;
var
  year, days : integer;
begin
  write('Enter a year in the range 1990 to 1993 inclusive ');
  readln(year);
  days := 365;
  if year = 1992 then
   days := 366;
  writeln('There are ', days, ' days in this year')
end.
```

Here, *days* is initialized to 365 but has its value updated in the event that the year is 1992. This code exploits the path in Figure 2.12 that avoids the **else** clause. To explain the existence of the semicolon following the number 366 we note again that the program as a whole is a compound statement consisting of: a *write*, a *readln*, an assignment, an **if** and finally a *writeln*. So each of these, except the last, must be followed by a semicolon. An easier way of looking at this is to use the following guideline for an **if** construct which does *not* contain an **else** clause.

- Guideline (if then) When the *then* clause consists of a single design construct its implementation is a single statement followed by a semicolon (provided the next word is not **end**).

We shall now look at the program *leapyear2* from Chapter 1 in which both the **then** and **else** clauses consist of two design constructs. The relevant parts of the design, the program and the guideline from Chapter 1 are reproduced below for ease of reference.

- Guideline (if then else) When the *then* clause consists of two or more design constructs, then it must be implemented as a compound statement where the **end** is not followed by a semicolon. When the *else* clause consists of two or more design constructs it must be implemented as a compound statement. The **end** corresponding to this compound statement should be followed by a semicolon provided it does not immediately precede the word **end**.

In order to explain the occurrence of the **begin/end** pairs in this program we shall need to examine what, at first sight, might appear to be a rather strange term in Figure 2.10. That is the fact that an instance of < statement > is the term < compound statement >. But we know that a < compound statement > includes the term < statement > in its definition. This would appear to be circular. To explain why it is not we shall examine the syntactic composition of *leapyear2* in detail.

The program body, as a whole, is a compound statement consisting of two procedure calls, an **if** statement and a final *writeln* procedure call. This accounts for the main program body **begin/end** pair and the semicolons on the lines marked {*}. All that remains is to examine the **then** and **else** clauses of the **if** statement. Figure 2.12 shows that the **then** clause must consist of a < statement >. But the syntax of < statement > includes the possibility that it itself can be a < compound statement >. Indeed, to reflect the fact that the two design steps 3.2 and 3.3 are both within the *then* clause, they *must* be implemented as a compound statement. The lines marked {+} correspond to this compound statement. Note that the punctuation associated with these lines is precisely that required by the syntax of a compound statement. There is a **begin/end** pair and the line involving 'This is a leap year' is not followed by a semicolon. This explains the first part of the guideline.

```
3.1    if year = 1992 then
3.2       days := 366
3.3       write out 'This is a leap year'
3.4    else
3.5       days := 365
3.6       write out 'This is not a leap year'
3.7    ifend
```

```
program leapyear2;
var
  year, days : integer;
begin                                     {start of main body compound statement}
  write('Enter a year in the range 1990 to 1993 inclusive ');    {*}
  readln(year);                                                  {*}
  if year = 1992 then
    begin                                                        {+}
      days := 366;                                               {+}
      writeln('This is a leap year')                             {+}
    end                                                          {+}
  else
    begin
      days := 365;
      writeln('This is not a leap year')
    end;                                                         {*}
  writeln('There are ', days, ' days in this year')
end.                                      {finish of main body compound statement}
```

Exercise 2.6 Explain in a similar way the punctuation and syntax of the **else** clause with reference to the program *leapyear2* and hence justify the second part of the guideline.

Exercise 2.7 Write a modification of the *leapyear* program based on the following design :

```
1.1    write 'Enter a year in the range 1990 to 1993 inclusive '
2.1    read in year
2.2    days := 365
3.1    if year = 1992 then
3.2       days := 366
3.3       write out 'This is a leap year'
3.7    ifend
4.1    write out 'There are ', days, ' days in this year'
```

The solution to Exercise 2.7 enables us to complete the guideline for implementing *if* design constructs which do not contain *else* clauses.

- Guideline (if then) When the *then* clause consists of a single design construct its implementation is a single statement. When the *then* clause consists of two or more design constructs, then it must be implemented as a compound statement. In either case a semicolon follows (unless the following word is **end**).

The syntax of a **while** loop also includes the term < statement >, which of course can be a compound statement (Figure 2.13).

Figure 2.13 The syntax of < while statement >

Guideline (while) in Chapter 1 stated that when a *while* loop body consists of two or more design constructs then it must be implemented using a compound statement. An example is provided in the program *depreciation* from Chapter 1.

```
program depreciation;
var
  value : real;
  year  : integer;
begin
  write('Enter initial value of micro ');
  readln(value);
  year := 1;
  while year <= 5 do
    begin
      value := 0.85*value;
      writeln('After year ', year, ' depreciated value is ', value);
      year := year + 1
    end
end.
```

Here, the **while** loop body consists of three design constructs and so has been implemented with a compound statement. This raises the question of how a *while* loop that has only one construct in its body is implemented. The design and implementation below which finds the smallest integer whose square exceeds 150 provides an example.

```
1   number := 1
2   loop while (number*number) < 150
3       number := number + 1
4   loopend
5   write out 'The smallest number whose square exceeds 150 is ', number
```

```
program squares;
var
  number : integer;
begin
  number := 1;
  while (number*number) < 150 do
    number := number + 1;
  writeln( 'The smallest number whose square exceeds 150 is ', number)
end.
```

There are two interesting points about this code. First, the Boolean expression controlling the loop requires a calculation to be performed before the evaluation of the inequality. Secondly, the loop body contains only one construct and so is not implemented using a compound statement. The semicolon that follows the incrementation of *number* arises by virtue of the fact that the **while** statement as a whole is just one in the sequence of the compound statement that forms the main body of the program. This enables us to extend the programming guideline for *while* loops to include those which have only one construct in their body.

- Guideline (while) When a *while* loop body consists of a single construct its implementation is a single statement followed by a semicolon (provided the next word is not **end**). When a *while* loop body consists of two or more design constructs then it must be implemented using a compound statement. The statement preceding the **end** that terminates the compound statement should not be followed by a semicolon. Whether the **end** itself is followed by a semicolon is determined by what follows on.

2.4 EXERCISES

Exercise 2.8 In this exercise the term < digit > corresponds to the definition in the text but the term < letter > should be taken to mean any upper case alphabetic character, that is, one of the characters A, B, ..., Z. Draw a sequence of syntax diagrams that define the term < registration > which represents the registration plate on a car. All registration plates conform to the following rules. They must begin with an upper case letter which is followed by a number in the range 0–999. This in turn is followed by at least one but at most three letters. For example, all the following are valid registrations: A845BGV, F6A, H056AB.

Exercise 2.9 Modify your answer to Exercise 2.8 so that the number component cannot begin with the digit zero.

Exercise 2.10 Given the syntax diagram below, describe in detail what constitutes a valid identifier.

< identifier >

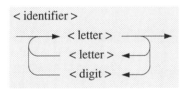

2.5 PROGRAMMING HINTS FOR FINDING ERRORS

We can distinguish two types of errors that can occur in programs – **semantic** errors and **syntactic** errors. A syntax error occurs when one of the grammatical rules of Pascal has been broken. For example, if a semicolon is omitted after a declaration or a **begin** has no matching **end**, then the result is no longer syntactically correct and so the code will not compile, let alone execute. The compiler will pick up syntax errors and report them together with a message that attempts to give the reason for the error. However, such is the variety of errors that we humans can make that the messages are not always too helpful, so don't rely on them to sort out your incorrect syntax. Furthermore, the compiler will often generate an error some time after the actual point at which the syntax is incorrect. The reason for this is that it may not be able to detect a syntax violation until it has examined the code that comes after the error. What you can say is that the error occurs at a point that precedes the place where the compilation stops. Often the error will be on the preceding line but it can be even further back. All syntax errors have to be corrected before compilation will be successful. Reference to syntax diagrams can help in determining compiler errors, but the programming hints at the end of each chapter are designed to help you avoid them in the first place.

In some circumstances there will be an error in coding which the compiler cannot detect and which leads to an erroneous program. Consider the following design that calculates the number of years it will take for an initial investment of £100 to reach £1000 at 8 per cent per annum. That is, the investment is increased by a factor of 1.08 per annum. In the design *balance* is a *real* variable and *year* an *integer* variable.

```
1    balance := 100.0
2    year := 1993
3    loop while balance < 1000.0
4       balance := balance*1.08
5       year := year + 1
6    loopend
7    write out 'The investment reaches £1000 in the year ', year
```

Suppose this was coded as follows:

```
program calcint;
var
  balance : real;
  year     : integer;
begin
  balance := 100.0;
  year := 1993;
  while balance < 1000.0 do
    balance := balance*1.08;
    year := year + 1;
  writeln('The investment reaches £1000 in the year ', year)
end.
```

This is a syntactically correct program but it is not a correct implementation of the given design. If compiled and executed, the program would produce the surprising result that the balance of £1000 is achieved in 1994, that is, after one year of investment. This is clearly wrong and we have a semantic error. What has happened is that the body of the loop has been incorrectly coded – step 5 should be within the loop body. The indentation here (deliberately incorrect) indicates that this is what the implementor had in mind but the compiler takes no notice of it.

Exercise 2.11 Write a correct implementation for the design above.

Semantic errors can also arise from faulty designs. In this case the corresponding program containing the semantic error either does not give the correct output or it fails during execution, when it is known as a **run-time** error. An example of a run-time error is when an attempt is made to divide a number by zero.

The programs we have seen so far have been simple so it has been easy to understand their algorithms. However, programs are usually sufficiently complex that it may be difficult to keep a mental track of the way the program behaves. It is no use running a program if you have no expectation of how it is meant to behave, as you will have nothing against which to check its actual behaviour. Generating data against which a design and subsequently a program can be tested is part of the design process and is an important part of program development. Generating data that test every aspect of a program is important, so that you are able to predict what ought to happen and test against it. Try to do this in the following example.

Exercise 2.12 The purpose of the code below is to find the largest power of 4 that is less than 200. Decide whether or not the code is correct.

```
program poweroffour;
var
   power, number : integer;
begin
   power := 1;
   number := 4;
   while number < 200 do
     begin
       number := number*4;
       power := power + 1
     end;
   writeln('Largest power of 4 which is less than 200 is ', power)
end.
```

There are various ways in which you can test the performance of a program when it does not give expected results. Most programming environments include utilities that simplify this task. They are often called **debuggers**. Generally they allow you to execute a program line by line and observe the values of the variables as execution continues. They tend to be rather sophisticated tools and therefore daunting for the novice. However, there are simpler tricks that can be used. One of the most useful is to include *writeln* statements in the code which either contain simple messages that a particular point in the program has been reached or output the value of some variables that are crucial for that section of the program. For the program in Exercise 2.12 *writeln* statements could be included as follows:

```
   power := 1;
   writeln('The initial value of power is ', power);
   number := 4;
   while number < 200 do
     begin
       number := number*4;
       power := power + 1;
       writeln('Value of power at end of loop is ', power);
       writeln('Value of number at end of loop is ', number)
     end;
   writeln('Largest power of 4 which is less than 200 is ', power)
```

For this simple problem all these insertions are probably not required but it shows what can be done without resorting to sophisticated debugging tools that may be difficult to learn. Of course, when all the errors have been corrected, any debugging code has to be removed.

The following hints and guidelines have been developed in this chapter:

(a)   When compiler errors are encountered, examine the syntax diagram of the statement that appears to be causing the problem to see if you have committed any obvious violations.

(b)   If a program compiles but does not produce the correct results with test data, then strategically placed *writeln* statements can help identify where the error occurs.

(c)   Guideline (while) When a *while* loop body consists of a single construct its implementation is a single statement followed by a semicolon (provided the next word is not **end**). When a *while* loop body consists of two or more design constructs then it must be implemented using a compound statement. The statement preceding the **end** that terminates the compound statement should not be followed by a semicolon. Whether the **end** itself is followed by a semicolon is determined by what follows on.

2.6 SUMMARY

In this chapter we have looked at the overall structure of a Pascal program and have examined the syntax of various terms. When coding a design, use the guidelines given in this chapter in order to determine where semicolons should be placed. Syntax diagrams can be used to check your coding and must be used when you are unsure of the syntax of a particular construct. More formally, the diagrams define the syntax of the language. Having studied the chapter you should be able to write the code corresponding to simple designs that include a single *if* construct.

3

FUNDAMENTAL DATA TYPES

In this chapter we shall examine five of the built-in data types provided in Pascal, *integer*, *real*, *char*, *string* and *Boolean*. These types are categorized in the following way (Figure 3.1):

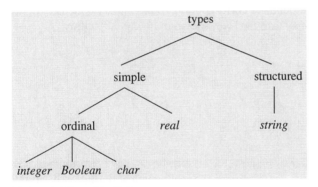

Figure 3.1 Pascal built-in types

In Figure 3.1 there are two main categories: **simple types** and **structured types**. A variable of simple type has only one element so it does not represent a collection of values. On the other hand, a variable that does represent a collection of values is called a structured type. For example, a string consists of a sequence of characters and so is of structured type. The simple type splits into two sub-categories: **ordinal types** and **real types**. The ordinal types are those whose values can be arranged in an ordered sequence with a first value, second value and so on. There are three ordinal types in this diagram: *integer*, *Boolean* and *char*. They are represented in a syntax diagram in Figure 3.2 below.

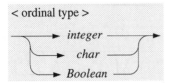

Figure 3.2 The syntax of < ordinal type >

In this chapter we shall give a more detailed description of each of these types and consider the operators defined on them. We shall also look at the ways in which they can be entered into and written out of the machine and consider whether a data value of one type can be assigned to a variable of a different type. Finally, we shall look at some error situations, including the run-time support that can be expected when a user makes a syntactic error when inputting data and what happens when a reference is made to an uninitialized variable.

Some of the descriptions contain much detail, particularly those dealing with the *read* and *readln* procedures, and you may prefer to skip over them on a first reading. If you do this then you should ensure that you are familiar with the sorts of values each type may assume and the operators that are defined on them.

3.1 THE DATA TYPE *INTEGER*

The identifier *integer* is the type identifier corresponding to the integer type used in design. In general, an unsigned integer may take the form shown in Figure 3.3 below.

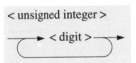

Figure 3.3 The syntax of < unsigned integer >

This syntax diagram would appear to suggest that an integer can have any number of digits. In fact, the type *integer* represents a subrange of the mathematical definition of an integer, and a variable of type *integer* can only assume integer values in the range:

    -maxint..maxint

where the identifier *maxint* is predefined and where the value is implementation dependent. Typically, its value is 32 767, although on some implementations it can be as large as 281 474 976 710 655. Integers can be positive, negative or zero, with a negative integer being defined as an unsigned integer preceded by a minus sign. We will not pursue the detailed syntax of a signed integer. The integer operators are:

   + − * div mod

The first three of these symbols correspond to addition, subtraction and multiplication respectively. The last two operators will be discussed shortly. The operators are called

binary operators because they take two integer values and form a third integer value as a result. For example, the expression 2*3 takes the numbers 2 and 3 and multiplies them to give the number 6. The numbers 2 and 3 in this expression are referred to as **operands** of the multiplication operator. They are the numbers upon which multiplication operates. Operands can be variables and we have already seen statements like

```
sum := FirstNumber + SecondNumber;
```

in which the value assigned is an expression involving integer variables. When an integer value appears in an expression it is sometimes referred to as an integer **literal**. This is to enable a distinction to be made between variables and values. So, for example, in the expression 2 + *FirstNumber* the number 2 is an integer literal and *FirstNumber* is an integer variable.

Any integer may be preceded by a plus or a minus sign (in which case the operators are known as **unary** operators) but care needs to be exercised when using unary operators in expressions. For example, the expression 2 multiplied by −3 must be written as 2*(−3). It would be an error to write 2*−3 because this places two operators side by side.

We now look at the definitions of **div** and **mod**. The standard definition for **div**, to which Turbo Pascal conforms, can be expressed informally as follows:

Perform the division, then truncate the result towards zero.

The operator is not defined for all integer operands. In particular, the expression *i* **div** *j* is not defined when *j* has value zero because this would attempt a division by zero. Care has to be exercised when negative arguments are involved because different Pascal implementations do not always use the same definition. The following examples illustrate some Turbo Pascal results:

> 5 **div** 2 has value 2
> 5 **div** 6 has value 0
> 5 **div** (−2) has value −2
> (−5) **div** 2 has value −2
> (−5) **div** (−2) has value 2

The standard definition for **mod** states that *i* **mod** *j* is only defined when *j* is positive and that in this case the result is an integer between 0 and *j* − 1 inclusive. The following examples illustrate standard values:

> 5 **mod** 3 has value 2
> 5 **mod** 6 has value 5
> (−5) **mod** 3 has value 1

Turbo Pascal violates this standard and for the last example would return the value −2. It also returns values for *i* **mod** *j* when *j* is negative. It is therefore recommended that use of **mod** is avoided for negative arguments.

Exercise 3.1 Assuming you are working to standard definitions, write down the values of the following expressions:

(i)   7 **div** 3   (ii) 7 **div** (−3)   (iii) (−7) **div** 3   (iv) (−7) **div** (−3)
(v)   7 **mod** 3   (vi) 7 **mod** (−3)   (vii) (−7) **mod** 3   (viii) (−7) **mod** (−3)

More complex expressions like 2∗3 + 4 can be built up using the binary operators. However, there is potential ambiguity in this example because it is not clear whether the multiplication is to be done before or after the addition. To overcome this, Pascal has operator precedence rules that determine the order. The operators ∗ **div**, **mod** have greater precedence than + −. The following examples are illustrative of their application:

2∗3 + 4 has value 10
13 + 10 **div** 5 has value 15
9 + 5∗3 **div** 2 has value 16
19 − 13 **mod** 3 has value 18

To override operator precedence, expressions must be grouped in parentheses. It is recommended that parentheses are always used in complicated expressions as they not only add clarity but they also ensure that the program states what the programmer intended.

Only integer values or expressions that evaluate to an integer can be assigned to an integer variable. Suppose *intnumber* is an integer variable, then all the following assignments are valid:

```
intnumber := 2 + 3;
intnumber := 2 - 3;
intnumber := (intnumber * intnumber);
intnumber := intnumber div 10
intnumber := 65 mod intnumber
```

It is an error to attempt to assign a real value, or an expression that evaluates to a real value, to an integer variable. This kind of error will be identified at compile-time and will give rise to the compiler error message that there is a type mismatch.

Type mismatches can also arise when integer data are being entered from the keyboard or from a file in backing store. Errors like these cause the program to cease execution at run-time. The cause will almost certainly be due to the input not conforming to the syntax of an integer. Trapping input errors like these can be quite complex, and are design problems in their own right.

Another error that can arise is the referencing of an uninitialized variable, that is, attempting to use the value of a variable before it has been assigned a value. Some implementations of Pascal provide compile-time support for identifying uninitialized variable references, but Turbo Pascal does not. This then raises the question of what happens at run-time if an uninitialized variable is referenced. The data stored at the memory locations reserved for the value of the identifier is interpreted as integer and is then used. You should not assume that uninitialized integer variables have a default value of zero.

In addition to the arithmetic operators there are six comparison operators defined on the integers. They are:

=   is equal to
<>   is not equal to
<   is less than
<=   is less than or equal to
>=   is greater than or equal to
>   is greater than

Values may be read into integer variables using the procedures *read* and *readln* and may be output to the screen using *write* and *writeln*. We shall illustrate these procedures using the following code in which *first* and *second* are integer variables.

```
write('Enter the first integer ');
readln(first);
write('Enter the second integer ');
readln(second)
```

A dialogue, in which the user response is underlined, resulting from the execution of this fragment is as follows:

```
Enter the first integer 23<ret>
Enter the second integer 45<ret>
```

It is possible for a single *readln* statement to include more than one parameter as illustrated by the following:

```
write('Enter two integers separated by a space ');
readln(first, second)
```

In this form *readln* expects the values input by the user to be separated by a space character. The following dialogue would assign the same values to the variables as that shown above:

```
Enter two integers separated by a space 23 45<ret>
```

To appreciate the way *readln* functions and to understand what *read* does, it is necessary to have a model of the way input is handled. Both procedures enable characters to be read from the keyboard and it is helpful to think of input as a stream of characters. The characters entered from the keyboard are immediately assigned to an area of memory called an **input buffer** that we shall represent as follows:

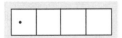

Each box represents a memory location and the dot denotes the end of the input stream so that this buffer is empty. The buffer represents a **file** and the end of the input stream marker is known as the **end of file** marker. We shall not be studying files until Chapter 9 and for the time being we do not need to know any details about the end of file marker. Processing of the input buffer begins when a <ret> is entered from the keyboard.

To help identify space characters the symbol □ will be used for a space. The input above can then be thought of as the character stream 23□45<ret> that can in turn be represented as:

2	3	□	4	5	<ret>	•

Notice the order of the characters in this diagram. The most recently entered character is next to the end of file marker whereas the first entered character is to the left of the diagram. When the <ret> is encountered, processing of the buffer begins at the left-hand end. The buffer is read one character at a time and we shall identify the character currently being processed by highlighting it thus:

The box is referred to as a **file window** and *readln* performs the following three tasks on the window:

(a) Positions the window.
(b) Examines the window content.
(c) Assigns a value, which depends on the outcome of (b) to the variable.

These tasks are carried out on each box in turn, so after three cycles the characters 2, 3 and □ have all been processed. The space character is interpreted as a separator between multiple inputs and so it indicates the end of the first input. Since the input here is to be assigned to an integer variable, *readln* interprets the characters 2, 3 as the integer 23 and assigns it to *first*. The file window then moves on to the 4 and the process continues until the file window is positioned over the <ret>. It also represents the end of an input and so the characters 4, 5 are interpreted as the integer value 45 which is then assigned to *second*.

Both *readln* and *read* will continue reading the input buffer until enough data have been read in to assign to the listed parameters. We shall now investigate what happens when too little or too much data are supplied by the user in response to the call above. Suppose, instead of providing two inputs as required, the user enters 23□45□67<ret>, that is, an extra integer is supplied. The first three characters are dealt with as before, with the result that 23 is assigned to *first*. The sixth character, being a space, indicates the end of an input and so 45 is assigned to *second*. This *readln* statement contained only two parameters so its task is now complete and the extra input is ignored. In fact, *readln* does more than just ignore the extra input, it flushes out the extra data from the input buffer leaving it in an empty state in preparation for the next keyboard entry.

An input of 23<ret> would correspond to too little input for this call. The number 23 would be assigned to *first* but *readln* would expect a second integer value and so would continue reading the buffer by positioning the file window over the end of file marker. From this, it recognizes that there are no more data ready to be read and so awaits further data entry. From the user's point of view nothing apparently happens; the program appears to have stopped. Indeed, it has, and will only continue when the user enters a second integer value, terminated with a <ret>, from the keyboard.

This description has assumed that the user separates the integer inputs with single space characters. Both *readln* and *read* will accept multiple space characters as separators and indeed will ignore initial space characters in the input. Other legitimate characters that a user can enter for integer values are + and − signs provided they are correctly positioned according to the syntax of an integer. A + sign will cause the value to be positive, a − sign will cause the value to be negative; absence of a + or − sign will be taken to mean positive.

The functioning of *read* is similar to that of *readln* but it differs in one major way. It is best illustrated by considering a *read* requesting two integer values but with the input sequence 23□45□67<ret>. We have already seen that for *readln* the extra input is discarded and therefore lost. This is not so with *read*. The extra data are kept in the input buffer and are used as soon as the next *read* or *readln* statement is encountered. We can see this in detail with the following fragment in which *third* is also an integer variable.

```
write('Enter two integers separated by a space ');
read(first, second);
writeln('Two inputs have been entered');
write('Enter a third value ');
read(third);
writeln('The first value is ', first);
writeln('The second value is ', second);
writeln('The third value is ', third);
```

As a result of the first *read* statement, *first* and *second* would be assigned the values 23 and 45 respectively. Having read in two values this *read* statement is completed and so processing continues. A *read* statement does not flush the input buffer whose state at this point is:

When the second *read* is encountered, the file window is positioned over the 6 and subsequently the value 67 would be assigned to *third*. This would happen without any intervention from the user who would see the following dialogue. (Note only the underlined characters are entered by the user.)

```
Enter two integers separated by a space 23 45 67<ret>
Two inputs have been entered
Enter a third value
The first value is 23
The second value is 45
The third value is 67
```

The prompt on the second and third lines would clearly be disconcerting, so you may well be wondering why *read* is used at all when *readln* automatically takes care of extraneous input. It tends to be used with files on backing store, which can be thought of as very long sequences in terms of our input model. We shall rarely be concerned with reading files in this way and so will tend to *readln* rather than *read*.

To output the value of an integer variable, all that is required is to include the identifier within the *write* or *writeln* procedure as we have already seen. The examples that follow use *writeln* but the comments are equally applicable to *write*. Furthermore, they only apply to Turbo Pascal; other implementations may differ in detail in the way values are formatted when output. Both procedures can include text in the form of a string literal or indeed, as we shall see, a string variable. For example, if *first* has value 23 then the statement

```
writeln('The number ', first, ' is not prime')
```

will produce as output

```
The number 23 is not prime
```

Note particularly the spacing in this output. Each character of the output occupies the same amount of space (unlike the text of this paragraph) and so occupies a particular *position* in the line. We shall often use the notion of position when discussing output. Note also that the space character following the word 'number' is part of the first string. The space following the digit 3 of 23 comes from the second string. Compare this output with that obtained from the statement

```
writeln('The number', first, 'is not prime')
```

which differs from that above in that the first string has had its final space character removed and the second string its initial space character removed:

```
The number23is not prime
```

This illustrates that when outputting values of integer variables *writeln* uses just enough positions for the integer and no more. So, if *second* has value 789 then the statement

```
writeln(first, second)
```

will produce as output

```
23789
```

with no space between the two values. This output can be improved by specifying a **field width** in which the output is to be placed. In the following statement the numbers following the colons are the field widths:

```
writeln(first:3, second:5)
```

When *first* is written out it is preceded by as many space characters as necessary to ensure that the output occupies *at least* three positions. Another way of saying this is to say that the output is **right justified** on a field width of 3. The output of *second* follows on immediately, but it too is right justified on its field width and so is preceded by as many space characters as necessary to ensure that it occupies at least five positions. This results in the output □23□□789, which will appear on screen as:

```
 23   789
```

Here, this output begins with a space and there are two spaces between the two numbers. The inclusion of *at least* in the above descriptions is important. Suppose *first* now has value 1234, then the statement would result in the output 1234□□789, that is:

```
1234   789
```

What has happened is that *first* has been output in the minimum field width required for all its characters, that is, a field width of 4. So if a field width specification results in too narrow a field for the number, the width is expanded until it is big enough. This has no effect on *second,* which is still output on a field width of 5 whose starting position is immediately after the first output.

Both *write* and *writeln* can be used to output integer literal values and expressions that evaluate to integer values as illustrated below:

```
writeln(9876:5, 2*first:3, second*second:5)
```

The following table provides a summary and shows the output of the integer constant 1234 in various formats. In order to see more clearly where it begins and ends it is surrounded by the letters X and Y.

statement	result	comment
`writeln('X', 1234, 'Y')`	X1234Y	No spaces between characters and number
`writeln('X', 1234:5,'Y')`	X 1234Y	Number right justified on field width
`writeln('X', 1234:3,'Y')`	X1234Y	Number occupies 4 spaces

Exercise 3.2 Write down a sequence of statements, which use only the integer constants 2, 4, 8, …, 256 together with appropriate field widths, which will produce the output below. The columns must have a minimum separation of 3 screen positions.

```
2    4    8    16
3    9   27    51
4   16   64   256
```

Exercise 3.3 Suppose *two*, *three*, *four* are three integer variables having values 2, 3 and 4 respectively. Write down precisely three statements that refer only to these variables but which will produce the same output as that in Exercise 3.2.

Turbo Pascal supports additional integer data types, each of which has a different range of values. They are:

Type	Range
byte	0..255
shortint	−128..127
word	0..65535
longint	−2147483648.. 2147483647

3.2 THE DATA TYPE *REAL*

The identifier *real* is the type identifier corresponding to the real type. Just as with integers, the number of digits of a real number that can be stored in a variable of type *real* is limited. As a consequence there is a limit both to the magnitude of real numbers that can be represented and to their accuracy. The magnitude typically ranges from 10^{-38} to 10^{38} with a precision of about 7–11 decimal digits, this being dependent upon the implementation. You are reminded that a number such as 5.9×10^{-3} can be written in the alternative decimal form of 0.0059 and that 3.4×10^3 can be written as 3400.0. The notation involving powers used in these two examples cannot be used in Pascal, which only permits real numbers to be expressed in one of two formats.

The first is the familiar decimal notation exemplified by numbers like 0.5 and 13.52. The decimal point must be preceded by and followed by at least one digit. The latter constraint is unlikely to cause a problem but it is quite common to see a number like .5 with no preceding 0. In Pascal this has to be written as 0.5. To represent a negative real value the number is preceded by a negative sign.

The alternative notation for reals is **floating point notation** which consists of two parts: a decimal number part called the **mantissa** and a power of 10, called the **exponent**, by which the mantissa is to be multiplied. So, for example, the notation 3.428E2 has mantissa 3.428 and exponent 2 and together they denote the number 3.428×10^2, that is, 342.8.

Exponents can contain a negative sign, as in the expression 7.5E–2, which has mantissa 7.5 and exponent –2 and which represents the value 7.5×10^{-2}, that is, 0.075.

Exercise 3.4 Convert the following real numbers into decimal notation:
(i) 439.4E2 (ii) 2.3E–3 (iii) 9E3

Exercise 3.5 Convert the following real numbers into floating point form in such a way that the mantissa lies in the range 1 (including 1 itself) to 10 (excluding 10 itself):
(i) 582.6 (ii) 0.00628   (iii) 10.23

The Pascal syntax defining an unsigned real number is as shown in Figure 3.4 below.

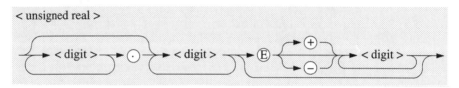

Figure 3.4 The syntax of < unsigned real >

As with all reserved words and identifiers the case of the characters is not significant and so a lower case e can be used in the exponent part. There are restrictions on the format of reals, some apparent from the diagram, others not. The constraint that the decimal point, if included, must be preceded by and followed by at least one digit is apparent. However, it is not mandatory for a real number to contain a decimal point. If the real number is expressed in floating point form then both the number and the magnitude of the digits in the exponent is restricted. Typically, the value must be an integer in the range – 38 to + 38. If the exponent notation is used then a digit must follow the character E. Reals can be positive, negative or zero, with a negative real being defined as an unsigned real preceded by a minus sign. We will not pursue the detailed syntax of a signed real.

Exercise 3.6 Which of the following represent valid Pascal real numbers?
(i) 3.45 (ii) .65E–8 (iii) –2E4 (iv) E10 (v) 2.45E (vi) 34

The real operators are:

    + – * /

where * and / have precedence over + and –. Note in particular that the integer operators **div** and **mod** are not defined on reals. However, the six comparison operators do apply to reals as well as integers, but equality should be used with extreme caution, particularly if one of the arguments results from a calculation. Indeed, it is recommended that equality is not used since the representation of real numbers can be very close in value without being identical. The following fragment illustrates the problem:

```
a := 0.44;
a := a + 0.01;
if a/15 = 0.03 then
  writeln('The values are the same')
else
  writeln('The values are different')
```

The message written out by this fragment would be that the values are different whereas, of course, they ought to be the same. The reason for this is that all the numbers are converted to their binary representations, which are then operated upon. The binary value resulting from the calculation is slightly different from the binary representation of 0.03. However, if you were to output the two values, the binary representations would be converted back into decimal floating point notation. For these data the decimal equivalents have the same value! This means that real numbers, which may appear to be the same when output to the screen, may well have slightly different binary representations. The issue is further complicated if the hardware has a maths co-processor, which will give yet more slightly different outcomes. To avoid all these difficulties never compare two reals for equality.

Values may be read into real variables using *read* or *readln*. Both procedures function in an analogous way to that described for integers, except that here the input data are converted into real values. The user must, of course, enter data that conform to the syntax of a real value. The output of a real value is achieved using the *write* or *writeln* procedures. For example, if *pi* is a real variable then the statements

```
pi := 3.142;
writeln('The value of pi is ', pi, ' approximately')
```

will produce as output

```
The value of pi is  3.1420000000E+00 approximately
```

In this format the output in Turbo always begins with a space (hence the two spaces after the s of the word *is*) which is followed by the mantissa and then the exponent. The exponent will always be in the form shown above and so will occupy four positions. To reduce the number of characters in the mantissa a field width can be specified. The minimum number of characters for the mantissa is three, this being enough space for two digits separated by a decimal point. Therefore, the minimum field width for a floating point number is 8, 1 for the leading space, 3 for the mantissa and 4 for the exponent. If fewer than eight spaces are allocated the field will be expanded to 8 positions. Field widths larger than 8 have the effect of increasing the number of digits appearing in the decimal part of the mantissa. The table below gives some illustrations of different floating point formats using the real constant value 123.4. It is surrounded by the letters X and Y so that you can see more clearly where the output begins and ends.

statement	result	comment
`writeln('X', 123.4, 'Y')`	`X 1.2340000000E+02Y`	Default format, note the leading space
`writeln('X', 123.4:6, 'Y')`	`X 1.2E+02Y`	8 spaces are used, not 6
`writeln('X', 123.4:8, 'Y')`	`X 1.2E+02Y`	Exactly 8 spaces required
`writeln('X', 123.4:9, 'Y')`	`X 1.23E+02Y`	An extra digit in the mantissa

To force the output to be in decimal notation the *writeln* statement has to contain formatting instructions that give both the field width and the number of decimal places that are required to be shown. In the example below, 3 decimal places on a field width of 5 have been specified (this being just enough for the five characters forming 3.142). The first integer in the formatting specifies the field width and the second integer the required number of decimal places.

```
pi := 3.142;
writeln('The value of pi is ', pi:5:3, ' approximately')
```

This would produce the following:

```
The value of pi is 3.142 approximately
```

In this style of formatting a leading space is not automatically output before the first digit of the real value. The spaces surrounding 3.142 arise from the spaces in the strings. Should a field width be chosen which is insufficiently large, then the output occupies as many positions as are required for the specified number of decimal places (dp). The table below illustrates different decimal number formats.

statement	result	comment
`writeln('X', 123.4:5:1, 'Y')`	X123.4Y	No leading space in this format
`writeln('X', 123.4:6:1, 'Y')`	X 123.4Y	Number is right justified on field width 6
`writeln('X', 123.4:6:2, 'Y')`	X123.40Y	Exactly correct width for 2 dps
`writeln('X', 123.4:3:2, 'Y')`	X123.40Y	Insufficient space is expanded
`writeln('X', 123.4:9:3, 'Y')`	X 123.400Y	Number is right justified on field width 9

Exercise 3.7 Write down a sequence of *writeln* statements which use only integer and real literals and which will produce as output the following table in which there is a minimum of two spaces between the columns:

```
 1   20.56
 2    3.67
20  127.56
```

Any expression that evaluates to a real number may be assigned to a real variable provided that its magnitude does not exceed that capable of being stored. Turbo Pascal supports other kinds of real numbers that differ in the range and precision of the values they hold. As their use depends upon hardware configurations we shall not be using them.

3.3 THE DATA TYPE *CHAR*

The data type *char* has 256 values that conform to the ASCII character set (see Appendix II). A particular value of type *char* is denoted by enclosing the character in single quotes; thus 'A', 'a', '?', '2' are all different examples of character constants. Note in particular that '2' means the character 2, which must not be confused with the integer 2. The apostrophe character itself requires special treatment and is represented by 2 quotes enclosed in single quotes, that is ''''. This can be confusing and it is perhaps better to avoid their use if possible. We shall continue to use the symbol '□' to denote a space character but note this is a typographical convenience and must not appear in program code as it is not a valid symbol of Pascal.

Variables of type *char* must be declared and may be assigned values using the usual assignment symbol. The program fragment below gives some examples of the declaration and assignment of a value to a *char* variable.

```
var
  ch : char;
begin
  ch := 'A';
  writeln(ch)
  write('Enter a character of your own choice ');
  readln(ch)
```

The operators defined on the data type *char* are the six relational operators for equality and inequality that apply to integers and reals. The result of a comparison is determined by the ASCII order. Each keyboard character has its own ASCII code and the code corresponding to 'A' is 65, that for 'B' is 66, and so on. Therefore we can see that, for example, 'A' <= 'A' is true but 'A' > 'B' is false. There are no operators that enable calculations to be performed on character values.

Characters may be written out using *write* or *writeln* and these procedures behave in the now familiar way. Entering *char* values using *read* or *readln* is a little bit more problematic. We suggest that until you become more skilled you just use *readln* as shown in the example above. This will mean that the user has to make two keystrokes to enter the character, one for the character itself and one for the terminating <ret> required by *readln*. This can be a minor disadvantage in situations where you want the user to make only one keystroke. A typical example of where this might be required is when selecting from a menu of options uniquely identified by a character. We shall see how to do this in Chapter 8 but you may be wondering why *read* would not achieve this objective. The text below explains why not but you may prefer to skip to the next subsection rather than struggle with the details.

To explain the way the Turbo Pascal function *read* works with *char* inputs there are two characters that need special mention. These are the characters with ASCII codes 10 and 13, which are referred to by the abbreviations LF, for linefeed, and CR, for carriage return. There is no single key corresponding to a linefeed although one can be generated using a combination of keystrokes. The key that is usually marked RETURN, ENTER or ↵ on your keyboard corresponds to the carriage return. It is variously identified as <ret> or <cr> in text, the former being preferred in this book.

The effect of a linefeed is to move the cursor vertically down one line. Thus, if the cursor is, say, 8 character positions in from the left edge of the screen then a linefeed will leave it 8 positions from the edge but will move it down a line. The effect of <ret> is to move the cursor to the leftmost position of the current line – note it stays on the same line. Your experience of using the <ret> key probably does not correspond to this. Most likely you would describe its action as performing *both* a linefeed and a carriage return. The reason for this apparent discrepancy between your experience and what carriage return actually does is that <ret> has a dual role – that of performing a carriage return and additionally indicating the end of a line of input. It is this detection of the end of a line that enables the system to issue a linefeed as well as a carriage return to that part of the system that is controlling the cursor.

We begin by looking at *readln* and shall expand the input buffer model already introduced when discussing integers. Suppose it was required to read in a character to the *char* variable *first* using the statement:

```
readln(first)
```

The system will await data entry into the buffer and will start processing the buffer on receipt of the first <ret> at which time the following tasks below are carried out. Note how task (b) is described in more detail than before; we shall see shortly what actions Turbo takes in the event that the character is an end of line or end of file marker.

(a) Position the window.
(b) Examine the window content to see if it is either an end of line or an end of file.
(c) Assign a value, which depends on the outcome of (b) to the variable.

The diagram below depicts the buffer after the file window has been positioned over the first input character.

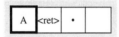

As the character in the file window is neither an end of line nor an end of file marker, task (c) is performed. Since the data that *readln* is expecting are of type *char* the value A is immediately assigned to *first*. As only one variable occurs in the *readln* parameter list the call is complete and the remainder of the data in the buffer are flushed, leaving it in an empty state.

Exercise 3.8 Describe in a similar way the processing of the input buffer when the statement *readln(first, second)* is executed with input data ABC<ret> where *first* and *second* are *char* variables.

Note in this example that *readln* only discards any extraneous data once the task of reading in the required number of data items has been achieved. Inputs in response to a *readln* must always be terminated with a <ret>. This can be thought of as the entry that starts off the buffer processing. The following exercise is a challenge!

Exercise 3.9 Describe the outcome when the statement *readln(first, second)* is executed with input data A<ret>. If a further <ret> was entered what then would be the outcome?

The action of *read* is similar, but with it the input buffer is not flushed once sufficient data have been processed. This leads to complications. Consider the following sequence of statements in which all variables are of type *char*.

```
writeln('Enter a character ');
read(first);
writeln(first);
writeln('Enter another character ');
read(second);
writeln(second);
```

The first *read* will only be activated upon receipt of a <ret>. So suppose the user responds A<ret> to the request for the first input. What happens? The input buffer at this stage is as follows:

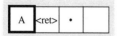

The buffer is processed by positioning the file window over the first character and examining its contents. This results in the value A being assigned to *first* which is then written out by the first *writeln* statement. The second prompt is then written out, but before the user has time to react to it the next *read* continues processing the input buffer. The file window is repositioned over the next character, thus:

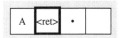

Examination of the file window contents reveals <ret> and so a carriage return character (ASCII code 13) is assigned to the variable *second*. This is then written out by the second *writeln* statement.

Exercise 3.10 What will appear on the screen if the following code is executed with the input values just described?

```
write('*', second, first, '!')
```

Suppose now that the user enters just a <ret> character in response to the first prompt for input. The act of entering <ret> starts the buffer processing so the file window is positioned over the <ret> thus:

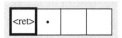

Examination of the contents of the window gives an end of line, and so ASCII code 13 is assigned to *first*. Again, processing continues to the second *read*. The input buffer is not registering an end of file condition and so the buffer continues to be processed. The file window is moved along so that it is now positioned over the end of file marker.

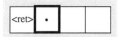

Turbo treats the end of file marker as a character, namely the character with ASCII code 10, which corresponds to a linefeed. Thus, a linefeed is assigned to the variable *second*. The fact that the window is now registering the end of file marker indicates to further *read* requests that the input buffer is empty. Processing of the next *read* would cause the system to await input from the keyboard. This entry would, of course, have to terminate with a <ret>.

Exercise 3.11 Assuming the execution just described, what would appear on the screen when the following code is executed and where will the cursor be?

```
write('**', second, '%%', first, '!')
```

Given the difficulties described above in the way Turbo handles <ret> and the end of file marker, it is perhaps as well to use *readln* to input *char* data values rather than *read*.

3.4 THE DATA TYPE *STRING*

A **character string**, or more briefly a string, is a sequence of zero or more characters from the ASCII character set. The start and end of a string are delimited by single quotes so that 'a short string' is an example of a string literal. A string can consist of any sequence of characters, but a single apostrophe must be represented as ''''. Therefore, the phrase Dave's book' would be represented by the string 'Dave''''s book'. The data type *string* is often referred to as a structured type. This is because strings are built up from sequences of individual characters.

Standard Pascal does not define a string type, which makes code involving strings implementation dependent. However, most implementations do support them, and in Turbo the declaration of string variables has the following form:

```
var
  medium : string[25];
  longest : string[255];
  shortest : string[1];
  name : string;
```

Here, the variable *medium* is declared to have **static length** 25, which means that it can be assigned a string value containing up to 25 characters. The variable *longest* has static length 255, this being the maximum allowable static length, and the variable *shortest* has static length 1, the shortest allowable static length. A string variable declared without a static length, such as the variable *name*, is given the default static length 255. Thus, there are essentially two ways of declaring a string variable. This is summarized in Figure 3.5 below.

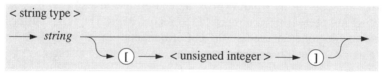

Figure 3.5 The syntax of < string type >

Once a string variable has been initialized, that is, has been assigned a value, then it has a **dynamic length**. This length is the number of characters in the assigned value. Here are some examples of assignments to the string variables above.

```
longest := 'Strings can contain space characters, punctuation and digit characters.'
medium := '6 Jun';
shortest := 'D';
name := 'Sargent'
```

Here, *medium* has dynamic length 5 and *shortest* dynamic length 1. A variable of type *string*[1] must not be confused with a *char* variable – they are not the same. All strings can be assigned the empty string value '', the string which has length 0 and consists of no characters whatsoever.

The operators defined on the data type string include the six comparison operators. For two strings to be equal they must have the same dynamic length and each pair of corresponding characters must be the same. The ordering between unequal strings is set by the ASCII ordering of the character values in corresponding positions. In two strings of unequal length, each character in the longer string not corresponding to a character in the shorter string takes on a higher value. So, for example, 'computes' has a higher value than 'compute'.

There is one further operator defined on strings and that is **concatenation** – the joining together of two strings. This operator is denoted by + and is used as follows:

```
fullname := shortest + ' ' + name
```

This would result in *fullname* being assigned the value 'D Sargent'. Note the order in which the concatenation is carried out. In most implementations of concatenation operator the arguments must all be of type *string* but Turbo also permits arguments of type *char*.

If, in the example above, *fullname* had been declared to have static length 8, then only the first 8 characters would have been assigned to it. This highlights the problem that string processing often requires knowledge of dynamic lengths. This information can be obtained by using the **function** *length*. A function is similar to a procedure and we shall study them in detail in Chapter 8. Functions, like procedures, have parameters which in the case of *length* is usually a string variable or a string literal. The following statements illustrate function calls:

```
number := length(name) ...
if length(name) < 6 then ...
if length(shortest + ' ' + name) < 8 then ...
```

Individual characters of a string are accessed by their position in the string using the notation illustrated below:

```
medium[3];
longest[10];
```

The first example refers to the third character of *medium*, that is, the character 'J', and the second example refers to the tenth character of *longest*, the character 'a'. The number appearing in this notation will be referred to as an **index**, and provided the index has a value within the current dynamic length of the string then it can be used to update individual characters. Thus, the statement

```
medium[5] := 'l';
```

would have the effect of updating the value of *medium* to '6 Jul'. In Turbo, if an index value bigger than the current dynamic length, but not exceeding the static length, is used in a string variable reference then no run-time error results and the string will maintain its original value. Other implementations detect such a run-time error and halt execution. The failure of Turbo to detect this kind of error means that it is possible to attempt to access characters beyond the dynamic length of a string. This should never be done because the value obtained will be arbitrary and will reflect the state of the memory location last time it was used. If the index exceeds the static length then a compiler error results. This individual character access method cannot be used to initialize a string variable because the system has to record the dynamic length when the string is initialized.

String variables may be initialized either by assigning string literals from within the program or by reading in the data from the keyboard, but only *readln* should be used for the latter. The reason for this will be explained at the end of this subsection but this is not essential reading.

The procedures *write* and *writeln* are very much simpler by comparison and have the same format as for other data types. In particular, a string variable can be output with a field width, in which case the string is right justified on that field. In the illustrations below, the first line should enable you to identify the field widths more easily.

statement	result
writeln('123456789')	123456789
writeln('Dave':5)	Dave
writeln('Dave':6)	Dave
writeln('Dave':7)	Dave
writeln('Dave':3, 'end')	Daveend

The reason *readln* should be used to enter strings from the keyboard is because it is essential to clear the input buffer before attempting to read another string. To see why, consider the following statements in which both variables are of type *string*:

```
read(mystring);
read(nextstring)
```

In response to this, the keyboard will be read into the input buffer until a <ret> is encountered. The buffer will then be processed. Suppose the characters AB<ret> are typed in. For strings, *read* processes all the characters up to, but not including, the first <ret> in the input buffer and assigns these characters to the input variable. The diagram below depicts the buffer just after the 'B' has been processed and the file window has been positioned over the <ret>.

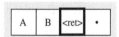

This indicates an end of line so the string 'AB' is assigned to *mystring*. Now, on the second call to *read* the file window is still positioned over the <ret>. This is because this character has not so far been read – remember that for the first string the knowledge that it was an end of line was exploited: the character value itself was not used. The current window position indicates an end of line, signalling the termination of this input. But no characters have been processed for *nextstring* and so it is assigned the null string. In fact, if this second *read* statement contained several string parameters, rather than just *nextstring*, all of them would be assigned the null string because the file window would never get past the <ret> character.

3.5 THE DATA TYPE *BOOLEAN*

Pascal's built-in data type *Boolean* has two possible values, true and false. Variables can be declared to be of type *Boolean* as illustrated below:

```
var
  flag : Boolean;
```

A Boolean variable can be assigned the value true or false or it can be assigned an expression that evaluates to true or false. In the following examples, which illustrate both methods, *response* is a *char* variable and *continue* a *Boolean* variable.

```
write('Do you wish to continue y/n ');
readln(response);
if response = 'y' then
  continue := true
else
  continue := false
```

An equivalent piece of code for this is:

```
write('Do you wish to continue y/n ');
readln(response);
continue := (response = 'y')
```

There are four operators in Turbo Pascal that are defined on Boolean values. They are **not**, **and**, **or** and **xor**. In expressions **not** has the highest precedence of any Boolean operator, followed by **and**, then **or** and finally **xor**. We shall study these operators in detail in Chapter 7 and will avoid their use until then.

3.6 COMPATIBLE TYPES

This section is concerned with issues such as assigning an integer value to a real variable. Assigning a value of one type to a variable of a different type is generally not allowed, but there are circumstances where it is necessary. At this stage you can rely on the programming hints at the end of the chapter, but this section is included here to complete the description of the data types introduced earlier. We recommend that you give it a quick read through now but use it for reference purposes once you have become more confident in coding.

Pascal is a strongly typed language. This means that the type of a value to be stored in a variable should be identical to the declared type of the variable, and expressions should contain only values of the same type. In this way the system is able to detect violations that attempt to assign to variables values of an inappropriate type, thereby improving the robustness of programs. So, for example, an attempt to assign a string value to an integer variable would be automatically detected and processing would halt. You may be wondering how such an error could be made. A simple example is to be found with personal identifiers, as used in employment or works numbers. These often have the form of a series of digits such as 9244. They are often represented as strings because arithmetic operators are normally not carried out on them. This enables works numbers like 0001 to exist. Now perhaps it is easier to see how the error above could arise – the works number, when written down, looks like an integer and yet is not one.

However, the rule that the type of a value to be stored in a variable should be identical to the declared type of the variable is unfortunately too simplistic. For example, if a real variable is to be used to hold the value 3.43, representing the sum of money £3.43, then it would be unreasonable not to be able to assign the value 2 to it, which would represent the exact amount of £2.

Similarly, limiting arithmetic expressions to values all of the same type is also too restrictive because it does not take into account the mathematical relationships that can exist between numerical data. Suppose you wanted to increment the value 3.5 by 2, then the expression 3.5 + 2 is the natural one that expresses this. But this expression consists of values of *real* and *integer* type respectively. We say it is an expression of mixed type.

The examples in the previous two paragraphs are both permitted. To determine what is and is not allowed there are rules called **compatibility** rules. Essentially, there are four compatibility rules: **expression compatibility**, **assignment compatibility**, **parameter compatibility** and **name equivalence**. Here we shall look at expression and assignment compatibility. In reading the rules you will need to bear in mind that they are implementation dependent and so may not be applicable in systems other than Turbo Pascal.

3.6.1 Expression compatibility

An **expression** is a combination of operators and operands that evaluate to a value. The expression is evaluated according to the appropriate operator precedence, taking into account any brackets in it. So at any one evaluation only one operator and two operands are involved. Expression compatibility therefore is only concerned with pairs of operand types. Two types are expression compatible when at least one of the following holds:

- Both are the same type.
- Both are integer types (this caters for the additional integer types mentioned in the text).
- Both are real types (this caters for the additional real types mentioned in the text).
- Both are string types (this means all strings are compatible regardless of static length).
- One type is a string type, the other of type *char*.
- If one of the operands of a +, − or ∗ operator is a real and the other an integer, then the result is real.
- For division the value of x/y is always of type *real* regardless of whether x or y are *integer* or *real*. (y must be non-zero, otherwise a divide by zero error occurs.)
- For all the comparison operators one operand can be of a real type and the other can be of an integer type.

The fifth rule says that a *char* type value is compatible with a string type value. This means that a *char* type value can be added to a string value (using the concatenation operator +). Also, when the two are compared the *char* type value is treated as a string type value with length 1. The examples below relate to the following definitions:

```
var
    int1, int2, int3: integer;
    real1, real2    : real;
    str1, str2      : string;
    shortstr        : string[10];
    ch              : char;
```

Assuming all these variables have been assigned values, then the expressions appearing in the following incomplete **if** statements are all valid:

```
if (int1 + int2) < 6 then      {bracket expression evaluates to integer}
if real1 < 6 then              {a real compared to an integer}
if (int3 + real2) < 2.5 then   {bracket expression evaluates to a real}
if shortstr = ch then          {string compared with char}
if (ch + 's') = 'as' then      {a char added to a char and then compared to a string}
if (ch + shortstr) = 'a' then  {a char added to a string and then compared to a char}
```

3.6.2 Assignment compatibility

The following are the assignment compatibility rules. They are expressed in the form of an assignment in which the left-hand side describes the type of the variable and the right-hand side the type of the value to which it may be assigned. The commentary below gives an explanation of each rule.

- T_type_variable   := T_type_value
- real_type_variable   := integer_type_value
- string_type_variable := any_string_type_value
- string_type_variable := char_type_value

The first of these rules says that assignments can be made between values and variables of identical types. The second says that an integer value can be assigned to a real variable. The integer value could, of course, be an expression that evaluates to an integer. Thus, integer values are said to be assignment compatible with real variables. The third rule says that any string value can be assigned to any string variable, no matter of what static length. If the static length is insufficient, then the assigned string is truncated to fit. The final rule says that a *char* value can be assigned to a string variable. Thus, *char* values are assignment compatible with strings. However, string values cannot be assigned to *char* variables.

Using the declarations in Section 3.6.1 the following are all valid assignments:

```
real1 := 2;
shortstr := 'averylongword';   {value assigned is truncated to 'averylongw'}
str1 := 'a';
```

Note that an error would result if an attempt was now made to assign *shortstr* to *ch* because they are not of assignment compatible types.

3.7 EXERCISES AND PROBLEMS

The problems in this section may involve any of the data types introduced in this chapter. Several of the problems may involve units of measure or currency values with which you are not familiar. You may like to read the appropriate section of the Preface should you be concerned about currency notations. Unless stated otherwise, you may assume that amounts of currency can be represented by real variables. The following exercises do not involve complete programs.

Exercise 3.12 This exercise uses the declarations in Section 3.6.1. Decide which of the following expressions are valid and give reasons for your choice.
(a) **while** (*int1**real1) < 20 **do**
(b) **while** *str1* <> 20 **do**
(c) **while** (*ch* + '1') < 20 **do**
(d) **while** (*ch* + '1') < '20' **do**

Exercise 3.13 Write down the dynamic length of the strings below after each of the assignments. The variables are declared in Section 3.6.1.

```
str1 := 'abcdefghijklmn';
str2 := str1 + str1;
shortstr := str1;
```

3.8 PROGRAMMING HINTS

(a) Use *writeln* when you want to generate a new line after the output.
(b) If you want the cursor to await input on the same line as the prompt for input use *write* followed by *readln*.
(c) Always use *readln* for input.
(d) Use field widths to align output in columns – the format of the command is exemplified by:

```
writeln(varid:6).
```

(e) For real values always include the number of decimal points in the output statement. The format is:

```
writeln(realid:6:2)
```

where the first number is the field width and the second the number of decimal places required.
(f) An integer value can be assigned to a *real* variable (but not vice versa).
(g) Strings may be declared with a given static length as in:

```
var
   mystring: string[10];
```

(h) Any string value (of whatever length) can be assigned to a string variable (of any declared static length). If the assigned string is too long it is truncated to fit.
(i) A character value can be assigned to a *string* variable (but not vice versa).
(j) Boolean variables can be assigned values using statements like:

```
continue := (response = 'y')
```

3.9 SUMMARY

In this chapter we have introduced the fundamental data types in Pascal. A data type consists of a collection of data objects together with the operators that are defined on those objects. In particular, we have looked at the simple types: the ordinal types *integer*, *Boolean*, *char* and the non-ordinal type *real*. We have also examined the structured type *string*. All of these types are predeclared in Pascal. Figure 3.6 below summarizes the data types introduced so far in which the term < ordinal type > refers to *integer*, *char* and *Boolean*.

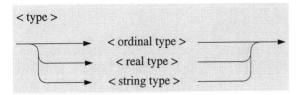

Figure 3.6 The simplified syntax of < type >

A variable of any of these types can be entered using one of the procedures *read* or *readln*, but for variables of type *char* and *string* the use of *readln* is recommended. The value of a variable may be output using one of the procedures *write* or *writeln*, each of which has optional commands that enable the output to be formatted. We also introduced the function *length* that returns the dynamic length of a string.

4

FUNDAMENTAL CONTROL STRUCTURES

This chapter is designed to give you more practice at coding designs, particularly those which have to be implemented using compound statements. The designs use simple sequences of control structures and exploit the data types introduced in Chapter 3. We also introduce the Pascal **const** definition and give some further details on controlling screen output.

4.1 AN INTRODUCTORY PROBLEM

Read through the following problem and its design and then read the commentary that follows.

Problem
This problem is concerned with working out how many years it takes for a fixed sum of £1000 to depreciate to half its value or less. The rate of depreciation is entered by the user as a positive real number between 0 and 100 and the output of the program is the number of years taken for the value to have decreased by half. For example, if the rate was 20 per cent then after one year the value would have decreased to £800, after two years to £640, and so on. A typical dialogue, in which the user response is underlined, would be:

```
Enter the depreciation rate as a number between 0 and 100
15<ret>
Original value will have halved in 5 years
```

Data table

Identifier	Description	Type
OriginalValue	Constant value representing £1000	*real* constant value 1000.00
year	Number of years passed	*integer* variable
value	Current value of micro	*real* variable
NewValue	Current depreciated value	*real* variable

Design

```
         {Calculate when depreciation halves value}
1.1      year := 0
1.2      NewValue := OriginalValue
1.3      write out 'Enter the depreciation rate as a number between 0 and 100'
1.4      read in rate
2.1      loop while NewValue > OriginalValue/2
3.1          NewValue := (100 – rate)*NewValue/100
3.2          increment year
4        loopend
5.1      write out 'Original value will have halved by the year ', year
```

Test data

This will require a calculation to be done by hand. It is suggested that a simple depreciation rate is chosen. For example, a value of 50 per cent should result in the answer one year, a value of 20 per cent should give four years.

This design includes references to integer literal values and to string literal values (in the prompts). What is new in this design is the use of an identifier to represent a constant value. The identifier is *OriginalValue* and it represents the real constant value 1000.0. Any reference to *OriginalValue* is taken as a reference to the value 1000.0.

The use of constant identifiers in designs helps to make them more readable and contributes to design and program documentation. When someone else reads this design the original amount on which the depreciation is being calculated is clearly identifiable throughout. In subsequent maintenance this amount could be changed, and all that would be required would be to redefine the value of the constant. The idea that a constant is defined leads us to describe the process of specifying its value as being a constant definition. Thus, we shall say that variables are declared and constants are defined. The code below shows how this would be implemented in Pascal.

```pascal
program depreciation;
{Calculate when depreciation halves value}
const
  OriginalValue = 1000.0;
var
  NewValue    : real;
  rate, year : integer;
begin
  year := 0;
  NewValue := OriginalValue;
  writeln('Enter depreciation rate as a number between 0 and 100');
  readln(rate);
  while NewValue > OriginalValue/2 do
    begin
      NewValue := (100 - rate)*NewValue/100;
      year := year + 1
    end;
  writeln('Original value will have halved in ', year, ' years')
end.
```

The definition of the constant identifier precedes the declaration of the variables. The reserved word **const** indicates the start of the constant definitions. Syntactically defining constants is all part of the syntax of < declarations >. Figure 4.1 shows an updated version of this term.

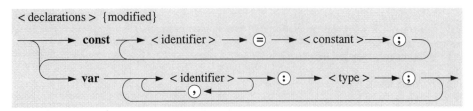

< declarations > {modified}

Figure 4.1 The updated syntax of < declarations >

This diagram shows that **const** definitions must precede **var** declarations. Turbo Pascal has an extension that allows declarations in other orders, but we shall only use the syntax as described by Figure 4.1. Notice that the path which includes **const** is optional, but if one exists then several different definitions can be made. All the constant definitions must be completed before the **var** declarations are made. An example of multiple constant definitions is given below.

```
program manyconsts;
const
   hoursinday  = 24;
   hoursinweek = 7*hoursinday;
   hoursinyear = 52*hoursinweek;
var
```

Here, the value of *hoursinday* is used to define the value of *hoursinweek*, which in turn is used in the definition of *hoursinyear*. It would be an error if the definition of *hoursinweek* preceded that of *hoursinday* because the former references the latter. This is an instance of a rule known as the 'declare before use' rule, which states that an identifier must be declared (or defined) before it is referenced.

Notice also how the value of the last two constants involves the evaluation of the constant expression that defines them. When constants are defined by expressions then all the operands in the expression must be of expression compatible types. The type of a constant can be deduced from the definition. Here, all the constants are integers whereas the constant *OriginalValue* was defined to be 1000.0 and so is real.

Constants can be defined to be of any of the types so far encountered.

```
program moreconsts;
const
   message   = 'Press any key to continue';
   star      = '*';
   twostars  = star + star;
var
```

The first constant is clearly a string constant but the second could be either *string* or *char*. Since *char* values and *string* values are compatible it does not matter which it is. The last constant uses the concatenation operator to define a string constant.

Exercise 4.1 Decide which of the following are valid constant declarations and determine their type. Explain why the invalid ones are syntactically incorrect.

```
const
  pi      = 3.14159;
  minsize = maxsize - 20;
  maxsize = 40;
  message := 'an unexpected error has occurred';
  pin     = '0' + maxsize;
  twopi   = 2*pi;
```

The values which constants represent can appear in expressions whose value is to be assigned to a variable. To do so, the variable must be declared to be of an appropriate type. An illustration is provided in the program *depreciation*, where *NewValue* is assigned the value of the constant *OriginalValue*. Constant values can also be written out, formatted as required.

4.2 CONTROLLING SCREEN OUTPUT

Turbo Pascal provides many facilities for controlling output on a screen, but they are extensions to Pascal that are restricted to this implementation and so are not available in other versions of the language. Most of the output in this book can be controlled by using appropriate formatting commands within the standard Pascal *write* and *writeln* calls, but one facility that we shall need is to be able to clear the screen completely. To achieve this requires us to use the Turbo Pascal extension procedure called *clrscr*. This procedure is stored in a library called *crt* along with similar procedures that manipulate the screen. Programs that use *clrscr* must inform the compiler that this library of procedures is required. The program fragment below shows how this is done and illustrates a call to *clrscr*.

```
program depreciation;
{Calculate when depreciation halves value}
uses
  crt;
const
  OriginalValue = 1000.0;
var
  NewValue   : real;
  rate, year : integer;
begin
  clrscr;
  year := 0;
```

The compiler is informed that *crt* is required by means of what is known as a **uses statement**. We shall be studying these in Chapter 8. Until then, if you wish to use *clrscr* then you must include the word **uses** followed by the identifier *crt* in your program. The uses statement must come before all other code (other than a comment which, as we know, is ignored by the compiler).

4.3 EXERCISES AND PROBLEMS

The problems in this section give you the opportunity to use **constant** definitions and **var** declarations. They also require the use of compound statements. The guidelines of Chapters 1 and 2 may be helpful in creating the implementations. For each problem in this section you clear the screen as an initial action. To simplify the problem statements this detail is not included in the specifications, but all the solutions contain the appropriate code.

4.4 PROGRAMMING HINTS

(a)   **const** definitions must precede **var** declarations.
(b)   **const** definitions use an equals sign.
(c)   **var** declarations use a colon.
(d)   Guideline (declare before use rule) An identifier must be declared (or defined) before it is referenced.
(e)   Constant definitions that reference other constants must obey the declare before use rule.
(f)   The screen may be cleared by calling the procedure *clrscr*, but this requires the inclusion of a **uses** *crt* statement immediately after the program heading.

4.5 SUMMARY

In this chapter we have looked at how a constant is declared in Pascal and how the screen is cleared. It has also given you the opportunity of coding many designs using compound statements.

5

FURTHER LOOP STRUCTURES

In this chapter we shall look at the implementation of *for* and *repeat* loops. A *for* loop is a loop that executes a fixed and therefore predetermined number of times whereas the continued execution of *while* and *repeat* loops is subject to a condition being satisfied. The design constructs for each type are *for ... loopend, while ... loopend, repeat ... until*.

We shall look at examples of the implementation of these loops and at their detailed syntax. All three are further examples of the syntax of < statement >. The revised diagram for this term is given in Figure 5.1 below.

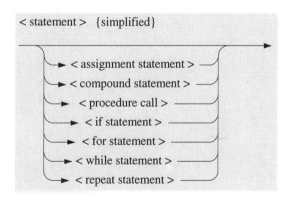

Figure 5.1 The updated syntax of < statement >

5.1 FOR LOOPS

Read the following problem specification and design and then compare the design and implementation before reading the commentary that follows.

Problem
Write a program that will find the average of 20 real numbers input from the keyboard.

Design
The design uses a *for* loop for the data entry part of the design.

1.1	*sum* := 0
2.1	loop for *count* from 1 to 20
3.1	write 'Enter number ', *count*, ' now '
3.2	read in *number*
3.3	*sum* := *sum* + *number*
4	loopend
5.1	*average* := *sum*/20
5.2	write out 'The average is ', *average*

Data table

Identifier	Description	Type
sum	The sum of the data values	*real* variable
count	A loop control variable	*integer* variable
number	A data value read in	*real* variable
average	The average of the 20 data values	*real* variable

Test data
Values should be chosen which can be averaged quite easily by calculator or by hand. You will need to check that exactly 20 values are read in and averaged. A data set consisting of 20 identical numbers could be used in addition to a non-identical set.

The code corresponding to this design is as follows:

```
program av20numbers;
var
   count                : integer;
   average, sum, number : real;
begin
   sum := 0;
   for count := 1 to 20 do
     begin
        write('Enter number ', count, ' now ');
        readln(number);
        sum := sum + number
     end;   {end of the for loop}
   average := sum/20;
   writeln('The average is ', average:5:2)
end.
```

Note the implementation details corresponding to step 2.1. The implementation involves the three reserved words **for, to** and **do** together with an assignment, which here assigns the value 1 to the variable *count*. The body of the loop consists of three design constructs and so it is implemented using a compound statement. The punctuation associated with this compound statement should, by now, be familiar.

Not all *for* loops have bodies that contain more than one design construct and so not all require a compound statement when implemented. In the code below, which produces a table of numbers and their squares, the body consists of a single construct.

```
program squares;
var
   count : integer;
begin
   writeln('Number  Square');
   writeln('--------------');
   for count := 1 to 20 do
      writeln(count:4, count*count:10);
   writeln('-------------')
end.
```

The single construct within this loop is followed by a semicolon. This has the effect of terminating the loop, which leads to the following analogous guideline to that for implementing *while* loops.

- Guideline (for) When a *for* loop body consists of a single construct its implementation is a single statement followed by a semicolon (provided the next word is not **end**). When a *for* loop body consists of two or more design constructs then it must be implemented using a compound statement followed by a semicolon (unless the following word is **end**).

In both of the examples above the loop executes for each integer value in the range 1 to 20 inclusive, that is, when *count* has values 1, 2, 3, ..., 20. Each execution of the loop automatically increments the value of *count* by 1 prior to the next execution. The counting mechanism of a **for** loop can be based on decrementing the control variable by 1, as in the following example which writes out the squares in reverse order:

```
Number  Square
--------------
  20       400
  19       361
  18       324
   :         :
   1         1
--------------
```

```
program reversesquares;
var
   count : integer;
begin
   writeln('Number  Square');
   writeln('--------------');
   for count := 20 downto 1 do
      writeln(count:4, count*count:10);
   writeln('--------------')
end.
```

We shall refer to a loop like this as a **downto** loop. The syntax of a < for statement > covers both the **for** loop and the **downto** loop and is shown in Figure 5.2 below.

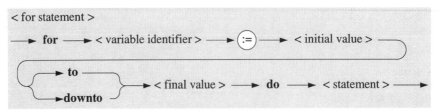

Figure 5.2 The syntax of < for statement >

In this diagram the term < variable identifier > is just an identifier representing the loop control variable. It must be of ordinal type, which, for the time being, means it must be either *integer* or *char*. The terms < initial value > and < final value > are expressions which have a value that is assignment compatible with the loop control variable. An example of the initial and final value being given by expressions is:

```
number := 10;
for i := (number + 2) to (number + 20) do
   writeln(i:4, i*i:10)
```

If, in a **for** loop, the initial value is not smaller than the final value then the loop does not execute at all and execution continues with the statement following the loop. Similarly, in a **downto** loop, if the initial value is not greater than the final value then the loop does not execute and execution continues with the statement following the loop. Upon completion of execution of a loop, the value of the control variable is undefined. Referencing the control variable will have unpredictable run-time consequences unless it is first re-initialized after loop execution. It is also an error for a statement within a **for** loop to alter the control variable. The compiler will not pick up this error and serious run-time errors can occur as a consequence.

Pascal does not contain a facility whereby the loop control variable can be incremented in values other than 1. The programmer is left to do this in other ways. For example, suppose we wanted a program fragment to write out all the odd integers between 1 and 100. Some languages would enable this to be done with a loop such as:

loop for *i* from 1 to 100 step 2
    write out *i*

This would write out the value 1 and then increment *i* to 3 before writing out its value. Then *i* would be incremented to 5 and written out and so on. The last value written out would be 99 because *i* would then be incremented to 101 and the loop would cease. The same result can be achieved in Pascal with the following:

```
for i := 1 to 49 do
   writeln(2*i + 1)
```

When faced with situations like this particular care must be taken to ensure that the loop executes with the required values and for the required number of times. The exercise that follows gives you the opportunity to practise this technique.

5.2 EXERCISES AND PROBLEMS

Problems 5.1–5.5 give you the opportunity of implementing designs that involve *for* loops.

Exercise 5.1 Write program fragments that will write out each of the following:
(a) All perfect squares in the range 1 to 64 inclusive.
(b) All the multiples of 4 from 100 down to 36 inclusive.

5.3 PRE- AND POSTCONDITIONED LOOPS

We have already seen several designs that use a *while* loop. We shall now look at *repeat* loops, and to compare them we reproduce the depreciation problem from Chapter 4.

Problem
Write a program that calculates the number of years it takes for a known sum of money to halve in value at a rate of depreciation, assumed to be non-zero, entered by a user.

Design

	{Calculate when depreciation halves value}
1.1	*year* := 0
1.2	*NewValue* := *OriginalValue*
1.3	write out 'Enter the depreciation rate as a number between 0 and 100'
1.4	read in *rate*
2.1	loop while *NewValue* > *OriginalValue*/2
3.1	*NewValue* := (100 − *rate*)*NewValue*/100
3.2	increment *year*
4	loopend
5.1	write out 'Original value will have halved by the year ', *year*

The data table and test data remain as described previously. Execution of the loop is determined by the condition in step 2.1. This condition is at the beginning of the loop, and gives rise to the loop being described as a **preconditioned** loop. A consequence of the condition being at the beginning of the loop is that the loop may not execute at all. This would happen if the condition evaluated to false on its first execution.

Exercise 5.2 Under what conditions would the loop in the design below not execute at all? What would be the purpose of this design fragment? The variable number is of type *real*.

1	read in *number*
2	loop while *number* <= 0
3	read in *number*
4	loopend

A *repeat* loop has its condition at the end of the statements that are to be repeatedly executed. For this reason *repeat* loops are known as **postconditioned** loops. The design below is an alternative solution to the depreciation problem and uses a postconditioned loop.

{Calculate when depreciation halves *OriginalValue* using repeat loop}
1.1   *year* := 0
1.2   *NewValue* := *OriginalValue*
1.3   write out 'Enter the depreciation rate as a number between 0 and 100'
1.4   read in *rate*
2   repeat
3.1   *NewValue* := (100 − *rate*)*NewValue*/100
3.2   increment *year*
4.1   until *NewValue* <= *OriginalValue*/2
5.1   write out 'Original value will have halved by the year ', *year*

The significant difference between a preconditioned loop and a postconditioned loop is that the former must execute the loop statements at least once. We can see why from this design. After step 1.4 has executed, step 2 and hence steps 3.1 and 3.2 are executed. Whether steps 3.1 and 3.2 get executed again is then determined by the outcome of the evaluation in step 4.1. But by this stage steps 3.1 and 3.2 have been executed at least once.

Implementing a *repeat* loop is much easier than implementing a *while* loop because a *repeat* loop never requires a compound statement. (Note that whether a *repeat* or *while* loop is appropriate in a particular problem is a design issue. Here, we are merely stressing the simplicity of the *implementation* of a *repeat* loop as compared with a *while* loop.) The reason for this is that the loop body is delimited by the words **repeat** and **until**. The syntax diagram for < repeat statement > (Figure 5.3) shows this more formally.

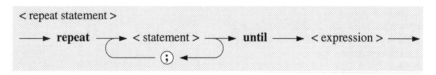

Figure 5.3 The syntax of < repeat statement >

Using this diagram, the design above can be coded as follows:

```
program depreciation;
const
  OriginalValue = 1000.0;
var
  NewValue   : real;
  rate, year : integer;
begin
  year :=0;
  NewValue := OriginalValue;
  writeln('Enter depreciation rate as a number between 0 and 100');
  readln(rate);
  repeat
    NewValue := (100 - rate)*NewValue/100;
    year := year + 1
  until NewValue <= OriginalValue/2;
  writeln('Original value will have halved by the year ', year);
end.
```

Note how the final statement of the loop body is not followed by a semicolon. This is because the path through the syntax diagram goes from < statement > to the reserved word **until**. This is analogous to the situation for a compound statement. A guideline for implementing *repeat* loops is thus:

- Guideline (repeat) All the construct(s) in the implementation of a *repeat* loop are followed by a semicolon except the one that immediately precedes the word **until**. The line containing **until** is also followed by a semicolon unless it is the penultimate statement of a compound statement.

5.4 EXERCISES AND PROBLEMS

Each of Problems 5.6–5.8 have two alternative designs, one using a preconditioned loop and the other a postconditioned loop. This will give you the opportunity to code and compare implementations of both types of loop.

Exercise 5.3 Write a program to implement the following design to find the smallest positive integer whose square exceeds 150. The variable *number* is of *integer* type.

```
1    numbe := 0
2    repeat
3        numbe := number + 1
4    until (number*number) > 150
5    write out 'The smallest positive integer whose square exceeds 150 is ', number
```

5.5 NESTED CONTROL STRUCTURES

Pascal permits any of the statements that we have introduced so far to be nested, one inside another, to any level. Several of the problems have already exploited this facility but at a fairly low level of complexity. In this section we shall look at more problems, the solution of which requires statements to be nested to quite complex levels. To explain how Pascal enables structures to be nested we need to refer to the syntax of < statement >, which is reproduced in Figure 5.4 below.

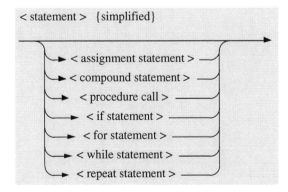

Figure 5.4 The updated syntax of < statement >

We begin with an example in which a *while* loop is nested within a *repeat* loop.

Problem

Write a program that enables a user to average sets of 20 numbers input from the keyboard. At the end of each batch the user should be asked if the program is to continue to average another set of data.

Design

```
        {Averaging program for sets of 20 numbers}
1       repeat
2.1       count := 1
2.2       sum := 0
2.3       loop while count <= 20
2.4          write 'Enter number ', count, ' now '
2.5          read in number
2.6          sum := sum + number
2.7          increment count
2.8       loopend
2.9       average := sum/20
2.10      write out 'The average of this set of 20 numbers is ' average
3.1       write 'Do you wish to process another 20 numbers? y/n '
3.2       read in ch
4.1     until ch = 'n'
```

Data table

Identifier	Description	Type
count	Inner loop control variable	*integer* variable
sum	Running total of input values	*real* variable
number	An input value	*real* variable
average	Average of the 20 inputs	*real* variable
ch	Outer loop control variable	*char* variable

Test data

The design exploits the averaging program developed in Section 5.1 and so here all that is required is to check that the outer loop functions correctly.

A program to implement this design is given below. Study the code and then read the commentary following it, which analyses the program in terms of syntax diagrams.

```
program MultipleAverages;
var
  count              : integer;
  sum, average, number : real;
  ch                 : char;
begin                                    {main body compound statement}
  repeat                                 {start of the repeat statement}
    count := 1;
    sum := 0;
    while count <= 20 do
      begin                              {inner loop compound statement}
        write('Enter number ', count, ' now ');
        readln(number);
        sum := sum + number;
```

```
      count := count + 1
    end;                                    {end of inner loop compound statement}
  average := sum/20;
  writeln('The average of this set of 20 numbers is ', average:5:2);
  write('Do you wish to continue y/n ');
  readln(ch)
until ch = 'n'                        {end of the repeat statement}
end.                                  {end of main body compound statement}
```

The program block consists of the declarations together with the main body compound statement, which here contains only one statement – a **repeat** statement. This accounts for the fact that the line of code containing **until** is not followed by a semicolon. Examination of the syntax of < repeat statement > in Figure 5.3 shows that it starts with the word **repeat** and then has occurrences of < statement >, each separated by semicolons until the one just preceding the **until**. But each such occurrence of < statement > can be any of the terms in Figure 5.4. Identifying them explicitly they are, in order, two assignments, one **while** loop, an assignment and finally three procedure calls (two *writeln*s and a *readln*). We could now go on to analyse the **while** loop by reference to its syntax diagram.

Exercise 5.4 Analyse the **while** loop in a similar way using the syntax diagram of Figure 2.13.

The explanation in Exercise 5.4 is rather complex, so it is probably easier to use the programming guidelines for implementing designs and to use the syntax diagrams when you want to check some syntax detail. The guidelines have to be applied with some care on certain designs. For example, consider the following design fragment that writes out the points of a compass corresponding to the value of a *char* variable:

```
1    if compass = 'N' then
2       write out 'Compass points North'
3    else
4       if compass = 'S' then
5          write out 'Compass points South'
6       else
7          if compass = 'W' then
8             write out 'Compass points West'
9          else
10            write out 'Compass points East'
11         ifend
12      ifend
13   ifend
14   write out 'End of fragment'
```

Before it is coded, it needs to be analysed rather carefully. It consists of two design constructs – an *if* which extends from step 1 to step 13, followed by a *write out* construct at step 14. So this outermost *if*, when implemented, will be followed by a semicolon. The *else* clause beginning at step 3 consists of a single design construct – namely the *if* that extends from step 4 to step 12 inclusive. Thus this clause will not be implemented as a compound statement. The *else* clause that begins at step 6 also consists of a single design construct (extending from step 7 to 11 inclusive) and so will not involve a compound statement. The design may be coded as follows:

```
if compass = 'N' then
  writeln('Compass points North')
else
  if compass = 'S' then
    writeln('Compass points South')
  else
    if compass = 'W' then
      writeln('Compass points West')
    else
      writeln('Compass points East');
writeln('End of fragment')
```

Notice how there is only one semicolon. Now consider the following modification to the design:

```
1    if compass = 'N' then
2        write out 'Compass points North'
3    else
4        write out 'Compass is not pointing North'
5        if compass = 'S' then
6            write out 'Compass points South'
7        else
8            if compass = 'W' then
9                write out 'Compass points West'
10           else
11               write out 'Compass points East'
12           ifend
13       ifend
14   ifend
15   write out 'End of fragment'
```

This time the first *else* clause at step 3 consists of two constructs: a *write out* and the *if* construct which extends from step 5 to step 13. This will need to be implemented using a compound statement.

```
if compass = 'N' then
  writeln('Compass points North')
else
  begin
    writeln('Compass is not pointing North');
    if compass = 'S' then
      writeln('Compass points South')
    else
      if compass = 'W' then
        writeln('Compass points West')
      else
        writeln('Compass points East')
  end;
writeln('End of fragment')
```

Exercise 5.5 Suppose an error of implementation was made to this design that failed to use a compound statement so that the code read as below (in which the indentation is deliberately wrong and expresses the intended semantics rather than the semantics that actually prevail). Would the code be syntactically correct and, if so, what would be the outcome if compass has value 'N'?

```
if compass = 'N' then
  writeln('Compass points North')
else
  writeln('Compass is not pointing North');
  if compass = 'S' then
    writeln('Compass points South')
  else
    if compass = 'W' then
      writeln('Compass points West')
    else
      writeln('Compass points East');
writeln('End of fragment')
```

Designs that involve *if* statements which do not have *else* clauses can be difficult to code. We shall illustrate the problems by writing design fragments whose purpose is to distinguish between positive and negative integers. You are reminded that neither the positive nor the negative integers include zero, in other words, zero is neither positive nor negative. If you are unsure of these descriptions, try the following exercise.

Exercise 5.6 From the list 'positive', 'negative', 'non-positive', 'non-negative', choose the word that best describes each of the following:
(a)   The number of coins in a purse.
(b)   The number of planets in the Solar system.
(c)   The integers −2, −1, 0.
(d)   The temperature in degrees Celsius at the South Pole.

The following design fragment, in which *number* is an integer variable, identifies a non-negative integer as either positive or zero.

```
1    if number >= 0 then
2      if number > 0 then
3        write out 'The number is positive'
4      else
5        write out 'The number is zero'
6      ifend
7    ifend
8    write out 'End of fragment'
```

Here, negative numbers are distinguished by step 1. In the event that a number is negative, processing goes straight to step 8. Otherwise the distinction between positive and zero is identified by steps 2 – 7. This may be coded as follows:

```
if number >= 0 then
  if number > 0 then
    writeln('The number is positive')
  else
    writeln('The number is zero');
writeln('End of fragment')
```

An alternative design to do the same thing is:

```
1    if number <= 0 then
2        if number = 0 then
3            write out 'The number is zero'
4        ifend
5    else
6            write out 'The number is positive'
7    ifend
8    write out 'End of fragment'
```

In this version step 1 distinguishes the non-positive integers so that the *else* at step 5 corresponds to the positive integers. It is quite clear from this design that the *else* at step 5 is associated with the *if* at step 1 (because the *if* at step 2 is paired with the *ifend* at step 4) and not with the *if* at step 2. We shall refer to this again shortly. If we try to code this according to the guidelines the argument would be that the *then* clause from step 1 contains one construct and so does not need a compound statement. A similar argument would apply to the *then* clause of step 2 and the *else* of step 5. This would lead to the following code (in which the indentation reflects the intended semantics):

```
if number <= 0 then
  if number = 0 then
    writeln('The number is zero')
else
  writeln('The number is positive');
writeln('End of fragment')
```

Here, we intend the **else** to be associated with the first **if**. Unfortunately, Pascal does not do this – it always associates an **else** with the nearest preceding **if**, and so the semantics of this fragment are better suggested by the following indentation:

```
if number <= 0 then               {line 1}
  if number = 0 then              {line 2}
    writeln('The number is zero') {line 3}
  else                            {line 4}
    writeln('The number is positive');
writeln('End of fragment')
```

Exercise 5.7 What would be output by this fragment if *number* had value 10? What would be output if it had the value –4?

This difficulty is caused by Pascal associating the **else** with the **if** at line 2 instead of that at line 1. To overcome this we must force the **else** to be associated with the **if** at line 1. At first sight it would be tempting to place a semicolon at the end of line 3 because then we know the fragment

```
  if number = 0 then              {line 2}
    writeln('The number is zero'); {line 3}
```

does not have an **else** part (the semicolon signals that the whole statement is finished). Unfortunately, so doing would also terminate the first **if** for exactly the same reason. That is, lines 2 and 3 now form a single construct followed by a semicolon and so this terminates the first **then** and indicates to the compiler that line 1 cannot have an **else**. When it subsequently encounters the **else** it has to report a syntax error.

The only way to overcome the problem is to enclose lines 2 and 3 within a **begin/end** pair, that is, to implement them as a compound statement.

```
if number <= 0 then
  begin
    if number = 0 then
      writeln('The number is zero')
  end
else
  writeln('The number is positive');
writeln('End of fragment')
```

Although we have stated up to now that a compound statement consists of more than one construct there is nothing in its syntax to say it cannot comprise a single construct, as here. The following guideline is a modification of that given in Chapter 1. The modification consists of the text in the second pair of parentheses.

- Guideline (if then else) When the *then* clause consists of a single design construct its implementation is a single statement *not followed* by a semicolon. When the *then* clause consists of two or more design constructs (or is a single *if then* construct without an *else*) then it must be implemented as a compound statement, where the **end** is not followed by a semicolon. When the design of the *else* clause consists of a single construct then its implementation is a single statement followed by a semicolon (provided the next word is not **end**). When the *else* clause consists of two or more design constructs it must be implemented as a compound statement. The **end** corresponding to this compound statement should be followed by a semicolon provided it does not immediately precede the word **end**.

It is worth remembering that a compound statement consisting of just one construct is a very rare occurrence. If you find your programs have many of them then you are probably not implementing the designs correctly.

5.6 EXERCISES AND PROBLEMS

Problems 5.9–5.14 are concerned with nested loop and *if* constructs. Of particular importance is the correct positioning of **begin/end** pairs and semicolons. The guidelines should be helpful in this regard.

Exercise 5.8
Problem
An agency is commissioned by an airline company to conduct some market research into the usage of its services. It is decided to set up a computer terminal at a main airport and to interview passengers as they arrive to catch planes. A keyboard operator inputs data according to each interviewee's response to the screen prompt:

```
Do you fly with us regularly?
Enter Y (for yes) or N (for no).
```

When the response is Y a second question is asked:

```
Do you fly first class?
Enter Y (for yes) or N (for no).
```

After 250 passengers have been interviewed two totals are written to the screen together with appropriate descriptive messages, namely the total number of users and the total number of these who travel first class.

Design

1.1	*regcount* := 0
1.2	*firstcount* := 0
1.3	*number* := 0
2	loop while *number* < *surveysize*
3.1	write out 'Do you fly with us regularly?'
3.2	write 'Enter Y (for yes) or N (for no). '
3.3	read in *answer1*
4	*number* := *number* + 1
5	if *answer1* = 'Y' then
6.1	*regcount* := *regcount* + 1
6.2	write out 'Do you fly first class?'
6.3	write 'Enter Y (for yes) or N (for no). '
6.4	read in *answer2*
6.5	if *answer2* = 'Y' then
6.6	*firstcount* := *firstcount* +1
6.7	ifend
7	ifend
8	loopend
9.1	write out *regcount*, ' passengers were regular users.'
9.2	write out *firstcount*, ' of these fly first class.'

Data table

Identifier	Description	Type
surveysize	Constant definition	*integer* constant value 250
regcount	Number of regular users	*integer* variable
firstcount	Number who travel first class	*integer* variable
number	Current count of number interviewed	*integer* variable
answer1	Response to first question	*char* variable
answer2	Response to second question	*char* variable

Test data

To test this program the constant value 250 can be reset to a smaller, more manageable value. Test data would need to check that the individual counts were correct and that the user is asked to interview precisely *surveysize* people. It should not require the input of a 251st response to the question of step 3.1. Responses of 'N' should not require the user to enter any further responses for that interviewee.

5.7 ADDITIONAL PROBLEMS

The problems in this section provide additional practice on the coding of designs involving the use of nested loops and nested *if* constructs.

5.8 PROGRAMMING HINTS

(a) Guideline (for) When a *for* loop body consists of a single construct its implementation is a single statement followed by a semicolon (provided the next word is not **end**). When a *for* loop body consists of two or more design constructs then it must be implemented using a compound statement followed by a semicolon (unless the following word is **end**).

(b) Guideline (repeat) All the construct(s) in the implementation of a *repeat* loop are followed by a semicolon except the one that immediately precedes the word **until**. The line containing **until** is also followed by a semicolon unless it is the penultimate statement of a compound statement.

(c) Guideline (if then else) When the *then* clause consists of a single design construct its implementation is a single statement *not followed* by a semicolon. When the *then* clause consists of two or more design constructs (or is a single *if then* construct without an *else*) then it must be implemented as a compound statement, where the **end** is not followed by a semicolon. When the design of the *else* clause consists of a single construct then its implementation is a single statement followed by a semicolon (provided the next word is not **end**). When the *else* clause consists of two or more design constructs it must be implemented as a compound statement. The **end** corresponding to this compound statement should be followed by a semicolon provided it does not immediately precede the word **end**.

5.9 SUMMARY

In this chapter we have looked at the implementation of *for, while* and *repeat* loops. When the latter has more than one construct in the loop body it does not require the use of a compound statement in its implementation. This is in contrast to the first two, which must use a compound statement. The chapter also looked at designs that involved the nesting of loop and *if* constructs. Again, care has to be exercised when coding such designs to ensure that compound statements are used in appropriate places.

6

FURTHER DATA TYPES

This chapter is mainly concerned with the structured data types arrays and records and their implementation in Pascal. Structured types are so called because they are built up from the simple types and thus have a structure that the user defines. Figure 6.1 shows how they relate to the other types we have seen.

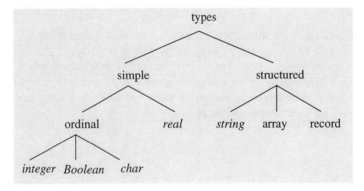

Figure 6.1 Data types in Pascal

To exploit these new types we shall look at applications based on searching. This is not intended to be a comprehensive introduction to searching algorithms.

6.1 THE DATA TYPE ARRAY

An array consists of a fixed number of **elements**, all of which must be of the same type. The elements are accessed by means of an index and both the index and the type of the element stored must be declared in a Pascal **var** declaration.

```
var
  first, second : array[1..25] of integer;
```

In this declaration both arrays are indexed 1 to 25 and both have base type *integer*. The first index, 1 in this example, is referred to as the lower index bound, or simply the **lower bound**, and the second index as the **upper bound**.

There are no operators defined on arrays as a whole, but Section 6.9 will discuss this further. This implies that arrays have to be processed on an element by element basis using the operators that apply to the base type. For the arrays above, the base type is *integer* and so the integer operators are the ones by which elements are processed. An individual element is referenced by the name of the array followed by an index surrounded by square brackets. Thus *first*[10] would reference the 10th element of the array *first*. The use of an index value that is less than the declared lower bound or greater than the declared upper bound will result in a run-time error. So, for example, it would be an error to attempt to reference *first*[26] because the array has an upper index bound of 25. A value can be assigned to an element in the following way:

```
first[10]:= 100
```

In general, an array is initialized by assigning a value to each of its elements. In the following illustration, in which *i* is an integer variable, this is achieved by entering values from the keyboard.

```
for i := 1 to 25 do
  begin
    write('Enter the value for element ', i);
    readln(first[i])
  end
```

Retrieving values from an array, for example when writing them to the screen, or when copying them to another array, or processing them in some other way, must be done element by element. In the following program, values are assigned to an array, then they are output to the screen and copied to a second array.

```
program arrayex2;
const
  maxsize = 5;
var
  realnos, copy : array[1..maxsize] of real;
  i             : integer;
begin
  for i := 1 to maxsize do
    realnos[i]:= 17.5*i;
  for i := 1 to maxsize do
    begin
      writeln(realnos[i]:5:2);
      copy[i]:= realnos[i]
    end
end.
```

A constant definition is used in the array declarations here so that whenever it is encountered in the program it is interpreted as the constant value 5. Its use significantly simplifies program maintenance. For example, if we were required to modify this program to allow for 10 elements, then only the definition of the constant would need updating. This is because the definition of the array itself and its manipulation by the program only refer to *maxsize* and not the value that it represents.

Figure 6.2 shows a simplified version of the syntax of an array type.

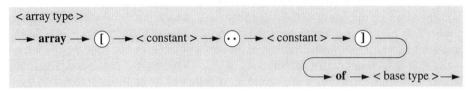

Figure 6.2 The syntax of < array type >

For the time being you can interpret the term < constant > as meaning either an integer constant value or an identifier that represents a constant. What is not apparent from this diagram is that the lower index bound must not exceed the upper index bound. A compiler error will be generated if this constraint is violated. The base type of the array is given as < base type > which for the time being means *integer*, *real*, *char*, *Boolean* or *string*. Later we shall give a more general version of the syntax that will show that both the index range and base type can be other than shown here.

Exercise 6.1 Which of the following declarations is valid and which is invalid? For any which is invalid give the reason why.

```
const
    lowbound = 10;
    highbound = 25;
var
    one    : array[1..lowbound] of real;
    two    : array[10..lowbound] of real;
    three  : array[20..lowbound] of real;
    four   : array[highbound..100] of real;
```

The introduction of an array type has expanded the variety of data types available to us, a fact which is reflected in Figure 6.3 below. We remind you that < simple type > represents *integer*, *char* or *Boolean*. This diagram will be refined as more data types are introduced.

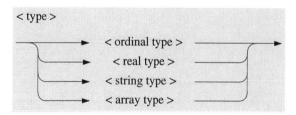

Figure 6.3 The updated syntax of < type >

Exercise 6.2 In this exercise *team* is an array indexed 1 to 22 that holds the names of football teams. The design below will produce a fixture list in which every team in the array will play every other team on a home and away basis. Write down a Pascal constant definition for the upper index bound *maxsize* and Pascal variable declarations for the array *team* and the *integer* variables *firstindex* and *secondindex*. Also write a Pascal fragment that implements the given design.

1.1	loop for *firstindex* := 1 to *maxsize* −1
2.1	loop for *secondindex* := *firstindex* + 1 to *maxsize*
3.1	write out *team*[*firstindex*], ' v ', *team*[*secondindex*]
3.2	write out *team*[*secondindex*], ' v ', *team*[*firstindex*]
4	loopend
5	loopend

In all the examples above, the index used to reference an element has either been a fixed value or a variable. This will not always be the case. Sometimes the index value will be calculated from some expression. A simple example is given by *team*[2 + 4], but in general an index expression will include one or more variables. Whatever form the expression takes it must evaluate to a value that lies within the index range of the array. Figure 6.4 below gives the details.

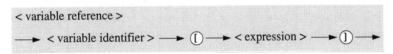

Figure 6.4 The syntax of < variable reference >

The use of an index expression is particularly useful when a **for** loop is to be used to access non-consecutive array elements as illustrated in the following exercise.

Exercise 6.3 Using the declarations resulting from Exercise 6.2, write a fragment of code that will output the names of the teams stored in the elements with odd numbered indexes.

Index expressions can be quite complex and can include references to array elements themselves. Study the following code before doing Exercises 6.4 and 6.5.

```
program indexes;
var
  power : array[1..8] of integer;
  i     : integer;
begin
  power[1]:= 2;
  for i := 2 to 8 do
    power[i] := 2*power[i - 1];
  for i := 1 to 3 do
    writeln(power[power[i]])
end.
```

Exercise 6.4 What values are stored in the array as a result of the first loop and what values are written out as a result of the second?

Exercise 6.5 Which of the following variable references is valid?

(a)   `power[7]`

(b)   `power[3*8 - 20]`

(c)   `power[power[4]]`

(d)   `power[power[power[1]]]`

In the examples above, the variables were declared by specifying the array structure within the **var** declaration. Pascal offers the opportunity of giving a structure like that above a name, thereby enabling the user to define new types. The definitions and declarations below illustrate this.

```
program arrayex;
const
  maxsize = 5;
type
  numlist = array[1..maxsize] of real;
var
  realnos : numlist;
  i       : integer;
```

Here a new type, called *numlist*, is defined and is used in a similar way to that of the predeclared types *integer*, *real*, *char*, *Boolean* or *string*. An extended definition of < type>, which includes this addition, is given in Figure 6.5 below in which < type identifier > conforms to the usual rules for identifiers.

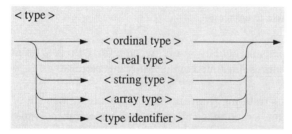

Figure 6.5 The updated syntax of < type >

The order in which the constant and type definitions and variable declarations come is important. Constant definitions precede type definitions which in turn precede variable declarations. This is summarized in the refinement of < declarations > in Figure 6.6.

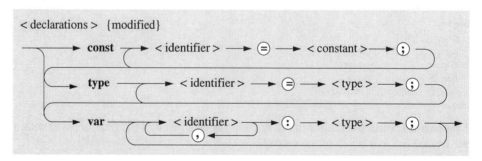

Figure 6.6 The updated syntax of < declarations >

We can deduce from Figure 6.6 that several type definitions can be made in a program, each separated by a semicolon. Indeed, we shall see shortly that type definitions are not restricted to defining types corresponding to array structures.

Exercise 6.6 Write down **const**, **type** and **var** statements to declare two arrays, *numbers* and *names*. The array *numbers* should be indexed 1 to 10 and be of base type *integer* and *names* should be indexed 10 to 100 of base type *string*[20]. The upper and lower index bounds should be defined as constants.

The declaration of *names* in Exercise 6.6 gives us the opportunity of seeing array notation alongside that for strings. You will recall that individual characters of a string can be accessed using the same index notation as for arrays. Suppose *names*[10] has been initialized to the string value 'Pascal'. Then the first character of this string would be referenced by the expression

> *names*[10][1]

When referencing characters from an array of *string*, it is important to get the indexes in the correct order. Note that the first index refers to the array and the second to the character position within the string.

6.2 EXERCISES AND PROBLEMS

Problems 6.1–6.4 give you the opportunity to practise implementing complete programs that involve the use of arrays. All of them involve a constant and type definition, and the statements of the problems illustrate how type definitions are represented in data tables. The exercises below concentrate on the use of expressions as indexes. The variables used are those declared in the text.

Exercise 6.7 Write a single **for** loop that will output the elements of *team* that have indexes 3, 7, 11, 15 and 19.

Exercise 6.8 Write a single **for** loop that will output the elements of *team* in reverse odd number index order, that is, in index order 21, 19, 17, …, 1.

Exercise 6.9 Given the declarations of Exercise 6.6 and the following initializations, what would be the values of:
(a) *names*[10][11]   (b) *names*[11][10]?

```
names[10] := 'ABCDEFGHIJKLM';
names[11] := 'NOPQRSTUVWXYZ';
```

6.3 THE LINEAR SEARCH

Searching an array for a particular value is a quite common activity and many algorithms have been developed to this end. In this section we shall look at some simple linear searches, that is, searches that examine successive elements in turn, to gain more practical experience of defining arrays and coding designs that involve them.

For data which are not stored according to some order, such as alphabetically or numerically, a very efficient design is one which uses an extra array element as a dummy item. The following problem illustrates the technique.

Problem
Write a program to search the array team defined in Section 6.1 for the index at which a team whose name is entered from the keyboard is stored.

	{Linear search}
1.1	write 'Enter the team whose position is sought'
1.2	read in *searchitem*
1.3	*team*[0] := *searchitem*
1.4	*index* := *maxsize*
2.1	loop while *team*[*index*] <> *searchitem*
3.1	decrement *index*
4	loopend
5.1	if *index* = 0 then
5.2	write out 'Item is not in the array'
5.3	else
5.4	write out 'Position of ' *searchitem,* ' is ', *index*
5.5	ifend

Data table

Identifier	Description	Type
maxsize	Array index upper bound	*integer* constant value 22
team	Array of team names	array[0..*maxsize*] of *string* variable
searchitem	Name being sought	*string* variable
index	Loop control variable	*integer* variable

Test data
Both successful and unsuccessful searches need to be tested. In addition, tests should be carried out to ensure the first and last items in the array can be sought as well as items in the middle of the array.

Exercise 6.10 Code the design given above. You will need to include some code that initializes the array.

6.4 PROBLEMS

Problems 6.5–6.7 give you practice at implementing some simple linear searches. Problem 6.6 uses the notion of two arrays to hold parallel information. We shall see that a record is a more efficient way of storing data that has components of different types but parallel arrays provide a useful source of exercises. In Problem 6.7 there is an array of base type *string* that requires individual characters within its elements to be accessed.

6.5 MULTIDIMENSIONAL ARRAYS

Two-dimensional arrays can be used to store data such as those illustrated in Figure 6.7.

	1987	1988	1989	1990
1	38	36	39	35
2	31	30	30	32
3	42	40	44	37
4	46	44	47	42
5	28	30	31	32
6	31	30	29	34
7	24	27	26	24
8	29	29	32	27
9	33	31	31	30
10	36	35	36	37
11	27	30	31	27
12	35	31	36	34

Figure 6.7 Birth data from a maternity ward for each month of the years 1987 – 1990

The array can be declared in Pascal as follows:

```
var
    births : array[1..12, 1987..1990] of integer;
```

Exercise 6.11 Declare the same variable *births* but this time use constant definitions for the upper and lower index bounds and a type definition for the array.

Arrays having more than two indexes are called multi-dimensional and can be declared in a similar way by specifying each index range separated by commas. Figure 6.8 below defines an array in this more general multi-dimensional situation.

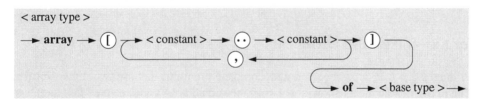

Figure 6.8 The updated syntax of < array type >

Two-dimensional array elements are referenced by enclosing both index values, separated by commas, within square brackets. Figure 6.9 below extends the earlier definition of a variable reference to include two-dimensional arrays.

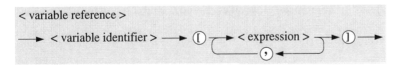

Figure 6.9 The syntax of < variable reference >

When all the elements of a two-dimensional array are to be referenced then two *for* loops are appropriate, but care has to be taken to nest them in the correct order. For example, suppose we wanted to enter the above data in *births* year by year so that all 12 entries for 1987 are entered first, then all 12 for 1988 and so on. An appropriate fragment of code, in which *year* and *month* are integer variables, would be:

```
for year := 1987 to 1990 do
  for month := 1 to 12 do
    begin
      write('Enter the data for month ', month, ' year ', year, ' ');
      readln(births[month, year])
    end
```

Figure 6.8 shows that the base type of an array must be < base type > and we have so far seen that this can be one of *integer*, *real*, *char*, *Boolean* or *string*. The base type of an array can be of any type other than *file*. This will include all the new types introduced in later sections, with the exception of *file*, and means that an array can be declared whose base type is an array! Here is an example:

```
var
  strange : array[1..12] of array[1987..1990] of integer;
```

The element of this array that has first index 10 and second index 1989 is then referenced as:

```
  strange[10][1989]
```

The index ranges in this example should be familiar – they are the same as for the array *births* above. What we have here is an alternative way of declaring and referencing a two-dimensional array. You may use either method, but we prefer to use the former, in which the indexes are listed one after the other separated by commas, as it is somewhat easier.

Two-dimensional arrays can be generalized to three, four and higher dimensions. The declarations must list each index range separated by commas. When referencing them the indexes must be in the correct order and must be separated by commas.

6.6 EXERCISES AND PROBLEMS

Problems 6.8–6.10 are concerned with complete programs that use two-dimensional arrays. The problem statements show how two-dimensional arrays are declared in data tables. The exercises below refer to variables declared in the previous section.

Exercise 6.12 Write a fragment of code that will produce as output the table of Figure 6.7. You should not try to include the lines given in the diagram but you should include the row and column headings.

Exercise 6.13 Why is the reference below an error and would it be identified at compile- or run-time?

```
  readln(births[year, month])
```

6.7 RECORDS

A **record** is a structure that enables a collection of values of different types to be stored. More precisely, a record is a data structure that contains several fields in a predefined fixed order, where each field contains data of a predefined type referenced by a distinct identifier.

Author	Title	Price	Copies
D Sargent	An Introduction to Program Design	£16.95	10

Figure 6.10 An example of data that can be represented as a record

If the information in Figure 6.10 is to be stored as a record, then the four fields need to be assigned identifiers of appropriate types. A record, *entry*, suitable for storing the data, could be declared as follows:

```
type
  booktype = record
               author : string;
               title  : string;
               cost   : real;
               copies : integer
             end;
var
  entry : booktype;
```

Although the use of a type definition is not mandatory when declaring a record variable, it is the form we shall always use. Record type definitions must conform to the syntax shown in Figure 6.11 below.

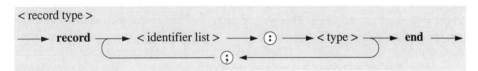

Figure 6.11 The syntax of < record type >

From this it can be seen that the type of any field must conform to the definition of < type >. Figure 6.5 gives the current version of this term, but to that diagram we must add < record type >. The implication of this is that a record can declare a field of type record. We shall not use such a complex structure yet, but the following update to the definition of < type > (Figure 6.12) formally notes that this is permissible.

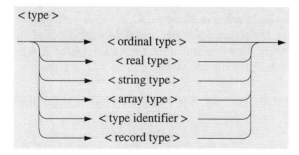

Figure 6.12 The updated syntax of < type >

A record is initialized by assigning values to each of its fields. The individual fields can be referenced using the 'dot notation' illustrated below.

```
entry.author := 'D Sargent';
entry.title := 'An Introduction to Program Design';
entry.cost := 16.95;
entry.copies := 10
```

The form of each of these references is *record identifier* followed by a full stop followed by a *field identifier*. This is expressed more formally in Figure 6.13 which extends the syntax for < variable reference > from the previous version.

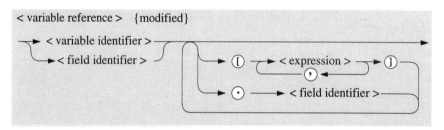

Figure 6.13 The syntax of < variable reference >

The operations on a field of a record are those that are appropriate to its type but the only operators that are defined on a record as a whole are the equality and inequality comparison operators. However, use of these comparison operators is restricted to records that are expression compatible. This will be discussed further in Section 6.9, but essentially it means that the two records must be declared by means of the same record type identifier. Errors can arise if this is violated. This is because Pascal implementations differ in the way they decide whether two records are expression compatible and in the way comparisons are made. Therefore, it is highly recommended that great care is exercised when making whole record comparisons and, if portable code is required, a field by field approach should be adopted. Having said that, two records are equal only if all their fields contain identical values.

The same proviso holds when one complete record is assigned to another. The two records concerned must have been declared using the same record type identifier. So if *newentry* is a record of type *booktype* then the assignment

```
newentry := entry
```

is valid, and it will assign all four field values of *entry* to *newentry*. The assignment compatibility of records will be discussed further in Section 6.9.

A field reference involves both the record identifier and field identifier and the two parts together form the overall identifier. This means that different record structures can use common field identifiers. The example below illustrates this.

```
type
  booktype = record
               author : string;
               title  : string;
               cost   : real;
               copies : integer
             end;
```

```
magtype = record
              title : string;
              cost  : real
          end;
var
  book     : booktype;
  magazine : magtype;
  cost     : real;
begin
  book.author := 'D Sargent';
  book.title := 'An Introduction to Program Design';
  book.cost := 16.95;
  book.copies := 10;
  write('Enter the price of the magazine ');
  readln(cost);
  magazine.title := 'Practical Computing';
  magazine.cost := cost
end.
```

Here the identifier *cost* appears three times, but the compound references associated with the fields ensure that they are distinct. However, the use of common identifiers in different record structures can be confusing and so is perhaps best avoided.

Assigning values to fields in the way described above can become quite tedious. The **with** statement provides a shorthand to the dot notation that avoids the need to specify the record identifier for each field reference. It takes the following form:

```
with entry do
  begin
    author := 'D Sargent';
    title := 'An Introduction to Program Design';
    cost := 16.95;
    copies := 10
  end
```

The following guideline can be used when using a **with** statement:

- Guideline (with) If a **with** construct contains a single design construct then a compound statement is not required – otherwise it is.

The syntax of the **with** statement is:

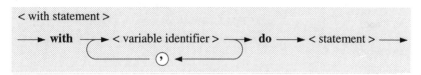

Figure 6.14 The syntax of < with statement >

Figure 6.14 shows that one or more record variables can be listed in a **with** statement, but care has to be exercised if the records have a field with a common identifier. In such an instance, use of the common identifier on its own is not permitted and the full record and field identifier is required. Furthermore, a simple variable also sharing a field name, such as the *real* variable *cost* in the example above, cannot be referenced at all within the **with** statement. The program fragment above would be rewritten as:

```
with book, magazine do
  begin
    author := 'D Sargent';
    title := 'An Introduction to Program Design';
    book.cost := 16.95;
    copies := 10;
    writeln('Enter the price of the magazine ');
    readln(magazine.cost);
    title := 'Practical Computing'
  end
```

We shall now look at records where the field type is more complex than in the examples given so far. To illustrate what is possible we shall use the same example throughout. We shall construct a record that can hold a person's name, address and date of birth. In each example we shall change the way we model the date of birth field.

A simple way of modelling a date is to use a string as follows:

```
type
  dobtype    = string;
  persontype = record
                 name    : string;
                 address : string;
                 dob     : dobtype
               end;
var
  person : persontype;
```

It may look a little strange to define an identifier *dobtype* to represent *string*. We could have used *string* directly in the declaration of *dob* but we shall return to this in Section 6.9. Calculations involving dates of birth would be quite difficult with this representation of the date. An alternative approach is to use an array indexed 1..3 of base type *integer* in which index 1 stores the day, index 2 the month and index 3 the year. With this model the declarations would be:

```
type
  dobtype    = array[1..3] of integer;
  persontype = record
                 name    : string;
                 address : string;
                 dob     : dobtype
               end;
var
  person : persontype;
```

Values could then be assigned to the date of birth field as follows:

```
person.dob[1] := 30;
person.dob[2] := 3;
person.dob[3] := 1993;
```

Note the form of these references. The two identifiers separated by a dot reference the date of birth field. Since this field is an array, array index notation is used to reference its elements. This representation makes calculations easier to do, but it does have the disadvantage that we have to remember that the first index represents the day, the second the month and the last the year. In Chapter 7 we shall see a way whereby this can be improved. The next representation overcomes this criticism.

```
type
  dobtype = record
                day  : integer;
                month: integer;
                year : integer
              end
  persontype = record
                  name    : string;
                  address : string;
                  dob     : dobtype
                end;
var
  person : persontype;
```

Here, the date of birth is represented using a record. So we have a record one of whose fields is a record! Reference to the field of *person* is either by repeated use of the dot notation or by use of a **with** statement. The fragment below illustrates both methods of referencing.

```
person.name := 'Henry Cotton';
person.address :='10 Downing Street';
person.dob.day := 30;
person.dob.month := 3;
person.dob.year := 1993;
```

or

```
with person, dob do
  begin
    name := 'Henry Cotton';
    address :='10 Downing Street';
    day := 30;
    month := 3;
    year := 1993
  end
```

Records like those we have just been considering rarely occur on their own. Usually there are many different records, all of the same type. One example, which uses the record structure above, is a register of student names. This might be manually stored as a table as illustrated in Figure 6.15 below.

Name	Address	Date of birth
Henry Cotton	10 Downing Street	30/3/1993
Edward Hodge	243 Lunsford Lane	13/4/1993
David Pollard	26 Hanover Close	12/3/1993
Margaret Smith	54 Blackman Avenue	1/4/1993

Figure 6.15 A register of personal details

To represent a table we need to define each row as a record and then to store the records in an array. The definitions and declarations below show one way in which this can be done. The index range of the array would enable 25 records to be stored.

```
type
   dobtype    = array[1..3] of integer;
   persontype = record
                   name    : string;
                   address : string;
                   dob     : dobtype
                end;
   tabletype = array[1..25] of persontype;
var
   person : persontype;
   table  : tabletype;
```

Finally we note that when several fields of a record are all of the same type then they can be declared simultaneously. For example:

```
type
   entrytype = record
                  author, title : string;
                  cost          : real;
                  copies        : integer
               end;
var
   book : entrytype;
```

This record type definition has identifiers of the same type as those of *booktype*, which appeared earlier. A problem which can arise with record variables that are declared in this way is when they are saved on file. Some implementations will store *author* data before *title* data and others may do the reverse, thereby rendering the data file non-portable. To avoid these complexities it is recommended that fields are listed individually, in which case the field order is uniquely determined.

6.8 EXERCISES AND PROBLEMS

Problems 6.11–6.16 are concerned with programs that use records. The specifications of the problems show how records are declared in a data table. The exercises below assume the definitions in the text.

Exercise 6.14 Using these definitions, write down a sequence of Pascal statements that will assign the details of Hodge (in Figure 6.15) to the element of *table* with index 2.

Exercise 6.15 Assuming that *person* has already been initialized, write down a single statement that will assign its field values to the record at index 3 of *table*.

Exercise 6.16 Rewrite the definition of *table* so that the date of birth field is represented by the record used in the text. Then assign the details of Hodge (in Figure 6.15) to the element of *table* with index 2.

Exercise 6.17 Write down type and variable declarations to declare an array indexed 1 to 100 of base type *booktype*. Write a fragment of code that will enable a user to initialize the array using data entered from the keyboard.

6.9 COMPATIBLE TYPES

In this section we shall extend the work of Section 3.6 to the new data types introduced in this chapter and look at compatibility rules with respect to arrays and records. Again, you may prefer to skip over this section and use it for reference once you have become more familiar with the language. This section is Pascal implementation dependent and expresses the situation that pertains in Turbo Pascal. To help explain the rules we first introduce some new terminology.

6.9.1 Name equivalence

The data types introduced in this chapter have been of structured type. This raises the question of what rules exist to determine when two structures can be thought of as being identical. Essentially, two data types are the same when they are declared using the same type identifier. When this happens the data types are said to be **name equivalent**. However, the requirement that a type identifier be used is crucial in this description. Consider the following declarations.

```
var
   a : array[1..10] of integer;
   b : array[1..10] of integer;
```

These two arrays are not of identical types since **array**[1..10] **of** *integer* is not a type identifier. The arrays are therefore said to be of anonymous type.

Anonymous variables can be made name equivalent, albeit with an anonymous name, by declaring them at the same time, as in the following definition:

```
var
   c, d : array[1..10] of integer;
```

Use of a type identifier to declare variables means that they are no longer anonymous and that all declarations involving the type identifier will be of name equivalent type, no matter in what order the declarations appear. For example, all three variables in the declaration below are of name equivalent type:

```
type
   arraytype = array[1..10] of integer;
var
   c, d : arraytype;
   e    : arraytype;
```

By contrast, the two arrays in the next declaration are not name equivalent even though the structure of each type definition is the same.

```
type
  firsttype  = array[1..10] of integer;
  secondtype = array[1..10] of integer;
var
  f : firsttype;
  g : secondtype;
```

These two variables can be made to be name equivalent by defining *firsttype* to be the same as *secondtype* as follows:

```
type
  firsttype  = array[1..10] of integer;
  secondtype = array[1..10] of integer;
  firsttype  = secondtype
```

although circumstances where this might be appropriate are hard to determine.

Although these examples have been expressed in terms of one-dimensional arrays, the ideas extend to multi-dimensional arrays and records. The following exercises give you the opportunity of testing your understanding of them.

Exercise 6.18 The definitions below lead to two variables that are not of name equivalent type. Explain why not and rewrite the definitions so that they are.

```
var
  strange : array[1..12] of array[1987..1990] of integer;
  births : array[1..12, 1987..1990] of integer;
```

Exercise 6.19 Determine the variables of name equivalent type in the following definitions:

```
const
  maxsize = 7;
type
  first = record
            cost       : real;
            deliveries : array[1..7] of integer
          end;

  second = record
            cost       : real;
            deliveries : array[1..maxsize] of integer
          end;
var
  rec1       : first;
  rec2       : second;
  rec3, rec4 : first;
```

Exercise 6.20 The last paragraph of Section 6.7 defined a record type *entrytype* that had the same structure and field names as that of *booktype*, which was defined earlier in the section. Would a variable of type *entrytype* be name equivalent to a variable of type *booktype*?

6.9.2 Assignment compatibility

The assignment compatibility rules given in Chapter 3 are reproduced below.

- T_type_variable   := T_type_value
- real_type_variable   := integer_type_value
- string_type_variable := any_string_type_value
- string_type_variable := char_type_value

The first of these rules says that assignments can be made between values and variables of identical types. More precisely, we can now say that two variables are assignment compatible if they are name equivalent or have the same anonymous type.

   If two variables have the same structure but are not name equivalent nor are of the same anonymous type, then assignment has to be carried out on a component by component basis. So, for example, if two arrays have the same index range and base type then one array can be given the value of the other array by assigning the individual array element values appropriately. In this way, whether they are assignment compatible as a complete structure does not matter. Similar remarks apply to records.

6.9.3 Expression compatibility

In Chapter 3 the first expression compatibility rule was that two types are expression compatible when they are of the same type. This can now be interpreted as meaning that they must be of name equivalent type.

   This can be illustrated using the records variables declared in Exercise 6.19. If *rec1* and *rec3* are initialized then both the statements

if *rec1* = *rec3* **then**
  :
if *rec1* <> *rec3* **then**

would be valid because both variables in the expressions are of the same type, *first*. However, if *rec3* was replaced by *rec2* then an error would occur because *rec2* is of type *second*.

   Because of the difficulties with expression compatibility and the fact that the rules are implementation dependent, it is best to avoid any type of comparison on structured data as a whole. It is much better and safer to perform the comparison on an element by element basis.

6.10 PROGRAMMING HINTS

(a) If a problem involves many items of related data, all of which have the same structure, then consideration should be given to modelling it using an array.

(b) If all elements of an array are to be examined a **for** loop should be used.

(c) The use of **const** and **type** definitions simplifies programs and their maintenance.

(d)   Definitions and declarations must be in the order **const, type, var**.

(e)   A record type is defined using the reserved word **record** and terminates with the word **end** (for which there is no matching **begin**).

(f)   Fields of the same type are best defined individually rather than using the comma-separated method.

(g)   The use of the same identifier for fields of different record types is permitted but is best avoided.

(h)   One record can be assigned in its entirety to another, but to do so the two records must be name equivalent.

(i)   Guideline (with) If a **with** construct contains more than one design construct then a compound statement is required – otherwise it is not.

6.11 SUMMARY

In this chapter we have introduced variables of array and record type. Arrays are used to store data that are all of the same base type whereas data that consist of collections of different types require the use of a record. We have seen how arrays can be exploited in search algorithms. Finally, we looked at the problem of compatibility. In order to copy a variable of one structured type, in its entirety, to another variable then both variables must be of name equivalent type.

7

AIDS TO DESIGN

In this chapter we shall look at the **case** statement, which gives more flexibility to selection. This will extend our knowledge of Pascal statements to the following (Figure 7.1):

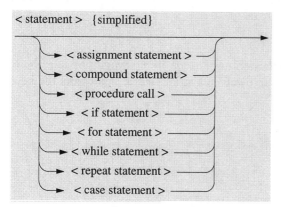

Figure 7.1 The updated syntax of < statement >

One of the things that a case statement is used for is to represent a sequence of nested *if* statements by a single construct, thus simplifying the code. In other words, it generalizes an *if* statement so that rather than selecting between two possibilities it can select one from many possibilities. We shall also introduce two new data types that extend our knowledge of < ordinal type > to include subranges and enumerated types as in Figure 7.2 below.

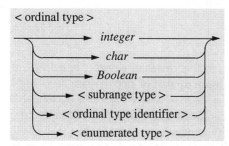

Figure 7.2 The updated syntax of < ordinal type >

Finally, we shall introduce a new type called 'set' that will extend the definition of < type > as shown in Figure 7.3 below.

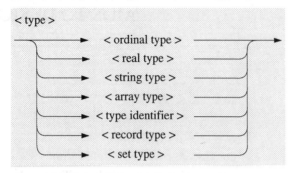

Figure 7.3 The updated syntax of < type >

7.1 THE CASE STATEMENT

A case construct enables a single selection to be made from several possible choices. A design to count the number of distinct vowels in a string, *word,* input from the keyboard would be:

```
1.1     write 'Enter a word '
1.2     read in word
1.3     i := 1
1.4     acount := 0
1.5     ecount := 0
1.6     icount := 0
1.7     ocount := 0
1.8     ucount := 0
2       loop for i := 1 to length(word)
3         select case depending on word[i]
4.1          'a', 'A'  :   acount := acount + 1
4.2          'e', 'E'  :   ecount := ecount + 1
4.3          'i', 'I'  :   icount := icount + 1
4.4          'o', 'O'  :   ocount := ocount + 1
4.5          'u', 'U'  :   ucount := ucount + 1
4.6          default  :   othercount := othercount + 1
5         selectend
6       loopend
7       write out results
```

The variable that controls the case statement, in this instance *word[i]*, is called the **case selector**. The two characters 'a' and 'A', which make up part of step 4.1, are an example of a **case label list** or, more briefly, a **case label**. The value of the case selector is compared with each case label list in turn until either a match is found or the default is encountered. When a match is found the construct associated with the match is executed. In the event that no case labels match the selector then the default clause is executed. The overall construct is

referred to as a case construct, each of the steps 4.1 to 4.5 is referred to as *a* case and step
4.6 is referred to as the case **default**. The case construct above can be implemented in
Pascal as the following case statement:

```
case word[i] of
  'a', 'A'  : acount := acount + 1;
  'e', 'E'  : ecount := ecount + 1;
  'i', 'I'  : icount := icount + 1;
  'o', 'O'  : ocount := ocount + 1;
  'u', 'U'  : ucount := ucount + 1
else
  othercount := othercount + 1
end
```

In Pascal a case statement begins with the reserved word **case** and terminates with the word
end. One oddity about case statements is that they terminate with **end**, yet there is no
corresponding **begin**. In this example, there are five cases, each of which has the format: a
case label list followed by a colon followed by an assignment. Each case, except the last,
terminates with a semicolon. The **else** statement corresponds to the design *default* construct
and is a Turbo Pascal extension. The **else** clause of a case statement must conform to
exactly the same syntax as the **else** clause of an **if** statement. This includes the possibility
that the **else** part may be left out entirely. From these observations we can give a guideline
for coding case statements.

- Guideline (case statement) A case statement begins with the word **case** and terminates
  with the word **end**. Each case, except the last one listed, has the format: case label list,
  colon, statement, semicolon. The last case in the list has the format: case label list,
  colon, statement. The default case, if present, is implemented using **else**, which has the
  same syntax as the **else** of an **if** statement.

In the example above, the case selector was a character value, but in general the case
selector can be an expression that evaluates to an ordinal type value. This means that neither
string variables nor real variables can be used as case selectors. Typically, a case selector
will be a single variable rather than an expression. The case labels must match the type of
the case selector – failure to comply with this will result in a compiler error. Case labels can
be single values, a list of values separated by commas or a subrange of values. This is
illustrated in the following example in which the case selector is an integer variable and
there is no default clause.

```
case i of
  0               : writeln('Zero');
  2, 4, 6, 8      : writeln('An even single digit');
  1, 3, 5, 7, 9   : writeln('An odd single digit');
  10..99          : writeln('A two digit integer')
end
```

Here, the case labels show the variety of formulations that are possible. The first label
is the literal integer value 0. The second label is the list 2, 4, 6, 8. The third is also a list. The
fourth is what is known as a **subrange**, and it denotes all the integers between 10 and 99
inclusive. The notation is familiar from that used in declaring array indexes and we shall be

studying it in detail in Section 7.5. You should note that the use of a subrange in a case label is a Turbo Pascal extension. A subrange can be used in combination with a list of values.

The values that appear in case labels should be unique. The following example shows the two ways in which this can be violated.

```
case i of
  0, 5, 0 : writeln('The label 0 is repeated in this list');
  1..9    : writeln('The label 5 has been used in the previous statement')
end
```

In the first case label list, the value 0 occurs twice and this is an error. The second error is more subtle because it is not immediately apparent that the value 5 appears in both the first and second labels. The Turbo Pascal compiler does not pick up either of these errors. At run-time it will execute the statement which first matches the case selector, ignoring any other occurrences. These observations lead to the following guideline for case labels:

• Guideline (case labels) Case labels must be of ordinal type and must match the type of the case selector. They can consist of single items, multiple items separated by commas, subranges or a combination of all three. The labels should be unique and non-overlapping.

We can now give a more formal definition of the term < case statement > (Figure 7.4).

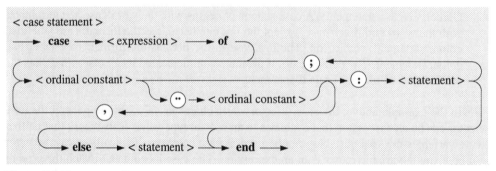

Figure 7.4 The syntax of < case statement >

It is worth examining this rather complex diagram to identify the parts we have described informally above. Initially there is the word **case** followed by the case selector, which must conform to the syntax of an < expression >. Following the word **of** there are the case labels, the first of which is indicated by the term < ordinal constant >. Taking the lower branch immediately after this term shows that a subrange is allowed, going straight on gives rise to a single constant. A list is obtained by looping back underneath the portion of the diagram that we have just traversed. In so doing, a comma is required before < ordinal constant > is encountered again. A list of constant values and subranges can therefore be built up in this way. When the list is complete we exit from the case label part through a colon. Following this is the < statement > associated with that case. After this there are two possible paths: the loop back for further cases, which passes to a semicolon, or straight on. The latter choice shows why the last case is not followed by a semicolon whereas all the others are. This path then splits, giving the possibility of there being a default clause as indicated by the word **else**. This implies that the **else** clause is optional. When the **else** clause is omitted and no matches to the selector are found in the case labels, then the whole case statement is by-passed. Execution then resumes at the statement following the case statement.

In all the examples above, the < statement > to be executed by each case has consisted of a single *writeln* statement. On most occasions there will be many. The code below illustrates this.

```
case i of
  0..9   : writeln('A single digit');
  10..99 : begin
             write('A two digit integer');
             sum := (i mod 10) + (i div 10);
             writeln('whose digits sum to ', sum)
           end
else
  if i > 0 then
    writeln('A positive integer with at least three digits')
  else
    writeln('A negative integer')
end
```

We can see why the case 10..99 is syntactically correct because < statement > must follow the colon that follows this subrange. But an instance of a < statement > is a < compound statement > and that is precisely what we have here.

* Guideline (case) If more than a single construct is to be executed corresponding to a particular case label then they must be implemented using a compound statement.

We conclude this section with a note of a difficulty that we have seen before but which is not apparent from the syntax of a case statement. Care has to be taken when implementing a case statement that has both a default and a final case that consists of an *if* without an *else*. This is because, if incorrectly coded, the **else** corresponding to the case default will be associated with the nearest preceding **if**. Problem 7.2 gives an example and explains the difficulty in full.

7.2 EXERCISES AND PROBLEMS

Problems 7.1–7.3 involve the use of case statements and are based on selectors of type *integer*. The exercises below use other ordinal types as selectors. The solutions to both the exercises and problems give guidance on the implementation details.

Exercise 7.1 This exercise is concerned with creating an output that describes the length of a word entered from the keyboard. A word containing between 1 and 5 characters is to be described as 'short', one of 6–8 characters as 'medium' and one exceeding these values to be 'long'. In addition, if no characters are entered a suitable message should be produced. Write a Pascal program, which includes a case statement, for this problem. You are reminded that if *word* is a string variable then the function call *length*(*word*) returns the number of characters in *word*.

Exercise 7.2 This problem is concerned with the processing of a user response to the menu shown below. You should assume that the user has already entered two real numbers and that they are stored in the real variables x and y. The purpose of the menu is to enable the user to perform arithmetic operations on these inputs. Write a case statement that will accept either the number or the initial letter of a menu option and will then carry out the appropriate calculation on x and y assigning the answer to the variable *result*. If division by zero is attempted, then a warning should be written out and no value should be assigned to *result*. You will need to decide the type of the case selector and to include a statement to read in its value from the keyboard.

    1 : Add to form $x + y$
    2 : Subtract to form $x - y$
    3 : Divide to form x/y
    4 : Multiply to form $x*y$

Exercise 7.3 In this exercise *ch* will be a value corresponding to one of the alphanumeric or punctuation characters on the keyboard. Write a Pascal fragment that will write out an appropriate message which identifies whether the character is an alpha, a digit or a punctuation character.

Exercise 7.4 Code the following design fragment into Pascal.

```
1       select case depending on number
2          0         :  write out 'The units digit is zero'
3          1..9      :  write out 'The units digit is ', number
4.1        10..99    :  write out 'The tens digit is ', number div 10
4.2                      write out 'The units digit is ', number mod 10
5.1        100..999  :  write out 'The hundreds digit is ', number div 100
5.2                      write out 'The tens digit is ', (number mod 100) div 10
5.3                      write out 'The units digit is ', (number mod 100) mod 10
6.1        default   :  if number < 0 then
6.2                         write out 'Negative numbers not catered for'
6.3                      else
6.4                         write out 'Number is too large'
6.5                      ifend
7       selectend
```

7.3 COMPOUND BOOLEAN EXPRESSIONS

The Turbo Pascal Boolean operators are **not, and, or** and **xor**. The latter operator is a Turbo Pascal extension. In expressions **not** has the highest Boolean operator precedence, followed by **and**, then **or** and finally **xor**. Figure 7.5 gives a truth table for these operators. Note in particular that associated with **xor**. It evaluates to true only in the event that one of x or y is true. This operator is an extension to standard Pascal.

x	y	**not** x	x **and** y	x **or** y	x **xor** y
true	true	false	true	true	false
true	false	false	false	true	true
false	true	true	false	true	true
false	false	true	false	false	false

Figure 7.5 The truth table for Boolean operators

Care has to be taken over the use of brackets in Boolean expressions. For example, if *number* and *total* are integer variables then the expression

```
(number > 5) or (total < 5)
```

is syntactically valid. If the brackets are inadvertently omitted then the resulting expression

```
number > 5 or total < 5
```

is invalid. This is because the system evaluates *number* > 5 and then tries to perform an **or** with the next variable *total*. But this variable is of type *integer* and so is a type mismatch for this operator. Furthermore, if an expression involves several Boolean operators then brackets may be required to override the normal operator precedence. For example, the two expressions

```
not (number > 5) or (total < 5)
not ((number > 5) or (total < 5))
```

are not equivalent.

Exercise 7.5 Evaluate these two expressions when *number* and *total* both have value 0.

In Exercise 7.5 the expressions were evaluated by working from left to right. This is not the case for all Pascal implementations so the programmer needs to be aware of this situation. Furthermore, of those implementations which do operate from left to right, some will cease evaluation as soon as the result of the entire expression becomes evident. For example, if *number* has value 10 then the overall value of the expression

```
(number > 5) or (total < 5)
```

is known to be true after just the evaluation of (*number* > 5) – there is no need to go on to evaluate the part after the **or**.

This is called **short circuit evaluation** and is the method adopted by default in Turbo Pascal. Short circuit evaluation should not be relied upon if program portability to other Pascal implementations is a possibility. Indeed, there are other complications which can arise. Consider the problem of searching an array for the occurrence of a particular value. Chapter 6 considered this problem and presented a design that extended the index range of the array by including an index 0. This leads to a very efficient simple design. A Pascal fragment to search an array *data* indexed 1 to *maxsize* which does not exploit index 0 is as follows:

```
index := 1
while (index <= maxsize) and (data[index] <> searchitem)
  index := index + 1;
if index > maxsize then
  writeln('Item is not in the array')
else
  writeln('Index of ' searchitem, ' is ', index)
```

This code would fail on some Pascal implementations and work on others. The reason for this is the way in which the evaluation of the expression controlling the loop is carried out. If the search item is not in the array, then *index* eventually assumes the value *maxsize* and is then incremented. The loop condition is then evaluated again. The condition (*index* <= *maxsize*) evaluates to false. If short circuit evaluation is operative, no further evaluation is required as the outcome of the overall expression is now determined. It is false. Therefore the loop does not execute and processing continues with the output stage.

However, if short circuit evaluation is not operative, a run-time error occurs because both parts of the compound expression controlling the loop are evaluated and the second part involves accessing the array *data*. Unfortunately, the value of *index* exceeds the upper index bound and so an index out of range error occurs. We would recommend that designs, and therefore code that relies on short circuit evaluation in the way illustrated by this example, are avoided.

7.4 EXERCISES AND PROBLEMS

Problems 7.4–7.10 involve complete program designs that require the use of compound Boolean expressions. The exercises below are concerned with program fragments only.

Exercise 7.6 Rewrite the following expression using the single operator **xor**:
```
if ((i = 2) or (j = 2)) and (i <> j)
```

Exercise 7.7 A computer game played between two players requires them to press a button on their consoles in response to an event on the screen. The first player to press his or her button is credited with a point. In the event that both players press their buttons simultaneously, both get a point. Criticize the following Pascal code fragment in which *button1* and *button2* are *Boolean* variables that are set to value true when the corresponding button has been pressed. The variables *player1total* and *player2total* are integer variables representing the points scored. Modify the code to take account of your criticism.
```
if button1 then
  player1total := player1total + 1
else
  player2total := player2total + 1
```

7.5 SUBRANGES

We have already encountered subranges in array index declarations and in case labels. In this section we shall extend their use. A subrange of any ordinal type can be defined. So far the ordinal types have been restricted to *integer*, *char* and *Boolean*, but this is about to be extended. A variable or type can be defined to be a subrange of an existing ordinal type. The result is a new ordinal type. The following type definitions define subranges of *integer* and *char*:
```
type
  DigitType = 0..9;
  LowerType = 'a'..'z';
var
  digit     : DigitType;
  letter    : LowerType;
  uppercase : 'A'..'Z';
  small     : array[0..9] of LowerType;
```

Here, two new ordinal types have been defined, *DigitType* and *LowerType*, both of which are subranges. Each one is an example of an < ordinal type identifier >. The variable *uppercase* is defined to be of subrange type directly. The format of a subrange definition is: first ordinal value followed by two dots followed by the second ordinal type value. This is represented more precisely in Figure 7.6.

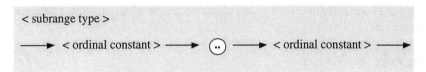

Figure 7.6 The syntax of < subrange type >

Both < subrange type > and < ordinal type identifier > are themselves ordinal types and so the definition of < ordinal type > can be updated to reflect this (Figure 7.7).

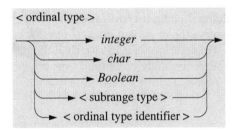

Figure 7.7 The updated syntax of < ordinal type >

The operators defined on a subrange are those of the underlying type. However, care has to be taken that the result of an expression lies within the subrange. For example, only a number in the range 0 to 9 inclusive can be assigned to the variable *digit*. An attempt to assign a value outside this range would result in a type mismatch error. Similarly, *letter* can only be assigned lower case characters. The variable *uppercase* is declared to be of subrange type directly, that is, without using a type definition. It can legally be assigned one of the upper case values 'A' to 'Z' inclusive. The values of the elements of *small* can only be assigned lower case characters.

The example also shows that the notation used in the declaration of an array index range is that of a subrange. A subrange is precisely what is being specified when the index range is being declared. This often leads to confusion over the notation for a subrange. Remember that subrange definitions do not include square brackets – the square bracket notation is associated with the array. The type identifier *DigitType* could have been used in place of the explicit index range 0..9 in the declaration of *small* as follows:

```
var
   small : array[DigitType] of LowerType;
```

With this method of declaration the identifier represents the subrange that is to be used for the index values. In Section 7.7 we shall extend the current definition of < array type > to reflect this alternative way of declaring an array.

Use of a subrange can improve the robustness of a program because it enables the system to detect assignments of values outside the subrange. For example, suppose a program had a variable that represented the number of days in a month. If that variable is declared to be of type *integer* then assignments of values like 100 and –34 are legal but clearly nonsensical. Declaring it to be of type 28..31 would enable the machine to detect assignments outside this range. Although this would not detect the error of the variable being assigned 31 days for the month of February it at least is an improvement on the *integer* declaration.

7.6 PROBLEMS

Problem 7.11 asks you to redefine the array *directory* of Problem 6.16 using subrange types. It also illustrates how subranges are defined in a data table.

7.7 ENUMERATION TYPES

Enumeration types are also known as **user-defined ordinal types**, **enumerated types** or **scalar types**. The first alternative certainly conveys the important information that it is the user who defines the type and that it is ordinal. However, for brevity, we shall use the more usual term enumeration type. This will complete our study of ordinal type whose final syntax diagram will then be as follows (Figure 7.8):

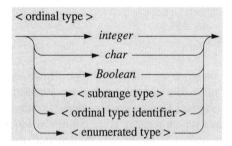

Figure 7.8 The updated syntax of < ordinal type >

Typically, enumeration types are used to aid program clarity and to enable programmers to create better models of certain types of data. Enumeration types are very useful for modelling data that naturally are described by a name – for example, the colours of the rainbow, the names of the suits in a pack of cards, subjects studied by pupils in school, days of the week, months of the year, the seasons, and so on. In some of these examples there is also a natural ordering of the values, and enumeration types can model this as well. Up to now we have usually modelled such data by using integers – for example, Problems 3.6, 3.7, 5.9 and 7.1 were all concerned with working out on which day of the week a given date falls. The designs used an integer variable *daycode* in which 0 represented Sunday, 1 Monday, and so on. This representation relies on the correct association of the values 0 – 7 with the names of the days of the week. An alternative approach would be to define an enumeration type to represent the days of the week. In the following declarations we have used a type definition to do this although it is permissible to declare variables to be of some enumeration type directly.

```
type
    weekdays = (sunday, monday, tuesday, wednesday, thursday, friday, saturday);
var
    day, anotherday : weekdays;
```

The choice of lower case initial letters in this example is deliberate and is done to emphasize the fact that the enumeration type values are not strings. This emphasis is important because enumeration type values can neither be read in from the keyboard nor written out to the screen. This constraint lessens their usefulness, but we shall see how to minimize the problem shortly. The great benefit is that references to a value like *monday* is quite clearly and unambiguously a reference associated with Monday. The syntax of enumeration type is given in Figure 7.9 below.

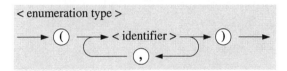

Figure 7.9 The syntax of < enumeration type >

Each identifier in the list must be unique and the order in which the identifiers are listed applies throughout the whole of the program. So, for the example above, *sunday* is first in order, *monday* is second, and so on. From this we can deduce that for this enumeration type *sunday* precedes *monday*. In the same way, *sunday* precedes *saturday*. This is analogous to the ordering of *char* values or of integer values.

The definition of an enumeration type determines the ordinality of its identifiers. The ordinality is not something of which the user has to be aware, but for the record the ordinality of the identifier *sunday* is 0, that of *monday* is 1, and so on. It is more important for the user to know the order in which the identifiers are listed than to know the ordinality.

The variables *day* and *anotherday* can be assigned any of the values listed in the definition of *weekdays*. For example:

```
day := monday;
anotherday := tuesday;
```

The operators defined on enumeration types include the comparison operators =, <>, <, >, <= and >=. These have their usual meanings, with the result being determined by the ordering within the enumeration type definition. With the assignments above, the expression *day < anotherday* evaluates to true because *monday* precedes *tuesday* in the definition of *weekdays*. In addition, there are two built-in functions, called *pred* and *succ*, which enable the predecessor and successor of an enumerated type to be found. For example, if we assume the assignments above then the two statements

```
day := pred(day);
anotherday := succ(anotherday);
```

would have the effect of updating the value of *day* to *sunday* and of *anotherday* to *wednesday*. Care has to be taken when using *pred* and *succ* because *sunday* has no predecessor and *saturday* has no successor. An attempt to find either of these will result in a run-time error.

7.7.1 Enumeration types in action

Enumeration types can be used to index arrays, as base types for arrays, as selectors in case statements and to control loops. The syntax of < case statement > given in Figure 7.4 already allows for this possibility and we shall look at an example shortly. The syntax of < array type > does not currently reflect the fact that index ranges can be specified with enumeration type values. Nor does it cater for the method of declaration used in Section 7.5 where a subrange type identifier was used. We rectify that now as shown in Figure 7.10 below.

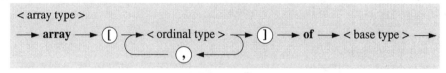

Figure 7.10 The updated syntax of < array type >

This is somewhat different from the earlier version of the syntax because it is not immediately obvious how the familiar index definition of *constant..constant* derives from this diagram. It does, however, confirm that the definition of the index range can be done with an ordinal type identifier. The declarations below include one which uses a subrange type identifier and also a declaration of an array with index range defined by *weekdays*.

```
type
  DigitType = 0..9;
  weekdays  = (sunday, monday, tuesday, wednesday, thursday, friday, saturday);
var
  small : array[DigitType] of integer;
  week  : array[weekdays] of real;
```

The variable *small* will be indexed from 0 to 9 and *week* will be indexed *sunday* to *saturday*. The explanation for the correctness of the following array declarations which use the more familiar method of declaring the index range requires the use of three diagrams from this chapter.

```
var
  large   : array[0..100] of integer;
  midweek : array[monday..friday] of real;
```

Both of these declarations use the *constant..constant* method of declaring the index range. From Figure 7.10, an index declaration must be an < ordinal type >. Examination of this figure shows that < subrange type > is an instance of < ordinal type >. Now referring to Figure 7.6 we can see that the syntax of < subrange type > is the familiar notation we have been using all along.

Figure 7.10 would seem to suggest that any ordinal type can appear in the definition of an array index. In particular, the definition

```
var
  big : array[integer] of real;
```

appears to be a syntactically valid declaration. This is indeed so! However, on most implementations this gives rise to an array that exceeds the maximum size of any structured type within the system. The compiler has to allocate space for structured types and so would recognize this structure as being too large and would report an error. However, it is worth noting that the declaration is syntactically valid.

Exercise 7.8 Determine which of the following declarations are valid. You may ignore size constraints but you should explain in what way an invalid declaration violates the syntax.

```
type
   lettertype = 'a'..'z';
   weekdays  = (sunday, monday, tuesday, wednesday, thursday, friday, saturday);
var
   first  : array[char] of weekdays;
   second : array[lettertype] of lettertype;
   third  : array[2.5..6.5] of char;
   fourth : array[friday..wednesday] of (half, third, quarter);
   fifth  : array[(red, amber, green)] of integer;
```

We shall now examine some program fragments that use enumeration types. We shall use the following declarations:

```
type
   weekdays  = (sunday, monday, tuesday, wednesday, thursday, friday, saturday);
var
   day    : weekdays;
   week   : array[weekdays] of real;
   daystr : array[weekdays] of string;
```

Assuming that the variable *week* has been initialized, the following code would write out its contents:

```
for day := sunday to saturday do
   writeln(week[day])
```

Here, the enumeration type variable *day* is controlling the loop and acting as an index for the array. The initial and final values for the loop statement could be any of the values in *weekdays*.

There are no facilities available for the input or output of enumeration type identifiers. So if this output is to be improved by providing the user with the name of the day for which the output corresponds, some method of generating the prompt must be devised. Essentially, there are two possibilities. The first is to use a case statement as shown below.

```
for day := sunday to saturday do
   begin
     case day of
        sunday    : write('The output for Sunday is ');
        monday    : write('The output for Monday is ');
        tuesday   : write('The output for Tuesday is ');
        wednesday : write('The output for Wednesday is ');
        thursday  : write('The output for Thursday is ');
        friday    : write('The output for Friday is ');
        saturday  : write('The output for Saturday is ')
     end;
     writeln(week[day])
   end
```

This is fine provided that the program only requires this to be done once. If there is input and output which both require the associated string values, then it is better to declare an array in parallel to *week* that contains the equivalent string values. This then needs to be initialized before it can be used.

```
daystr[sunday]    := 'Sunday';
daystr[monday]    := 'Monday';
daystr[tuesday]   := 'Tuesday';
daystr[wednesday] := 'Wednesday';
daystr[thursday]  := 'Thursday';
daystr[friday]    := 'Friday';
daystr[saturday]  := 'Saturday';
for day := sunday to saturday do
  begin
    write('Input the data for ', daystr[day]);
    readln(week[day])
  end;
for day := sunday to saturday do
  writeln('The output for ', daystr[day], ' is ', week[day])
```

7.8 EXERCISES AND PROBLEMS

The exercises below are in addition to Problems 7.12 and 7.13. Problem 7.13 illustrates how enumeration type definitions are made in data tables.

Exercise 7.9 This exercise is concerned with storing the days on which the first of each month falls in any given year. (The examples used refer to 1992.) You should assume the definitions *weekdays* and the declarations of *day*, *daystr* and *weekdays* from the text. In addition, you may assume the following definitions and declarations:

```
type
  months = (jan, feb, mar, apr, may, jun, jul, aug, sep, oct, nov, dec);
var
  month    : months;
  monthstr : array[months] of string;
  startday : array[months] of weekdays;
```

You may further assume that *daystr* is initialized as in the text; that *monthstr* has been initialized, so that *monthstr[jan]*:= 'January', *monthstr[feb]*:= 'February', and so on; and that *startday* has been initialized in such a way that each element represents the first day of the month corresponding to its index. So, for example, *startday[jan]* would be initialized to *wednesday*, which would indicate that 1 January fell on a Wednesday, *startday[feb]* to *saturday*, which would indicate that 1 February fell on a Saturday, and so on. Write a fragment of code that will produce the output for a whole year, part of which is illustrated below.

```
The 1st of January fell on a Wednesday
The 1st of February fell on a Saturday
   :
```

Exercise 7.10 This exercise uses the data from Exercise 7.8. Write down whether or not each of the following statements is valid. If so, write down its value.

(a) `startday[pred(mar)] = saturday`

(b) `startday[pred(mar)] = 'Saturday'`

(c) `startday[pred(mar)] = pred(sunday)`

(d) `wednesday = startday[wednesday]`

7.9 THE DATA TYPE SET

A **set** is a collection of distinct objects, all of which are of the same type. The objects which a set contains are called its **elements**. A set is defined by listing all its elements. The order in which the elements are listed is not important, but an element must be listed once and once only. Pascal imposes the restriction that the elements must be of ordinal type. Thus, to be more precise, we can say that a set consists of a unique unordered collection of elements, all of ordinal base type. Sets can be declared and initialized as illustrated below.

```
type
    weekdays    = (sunday, monday, tuesday, wednesday, thursday, friday, saturday);
    daysettype = set of weekdays;
var
    numberset : set of 1..20;
    dayset      : daysettype;
    lowerset   : set of 'a'..'z';
    allalpha  : set of char;
begin
    numberset := [3, 6, 1];
    dayset :=[friday, monday];
    lowerset := ['y', 'a'..'f'];
    allalpha := []
```

These declarations disguise some subtleties that must be observed when declaring set variables. The base type must not have more than 256 possible values so, for example, it is an error to declare a variable or define a type to be **set of** *integer*. This is because the integers contain more than 256 possible values. By contrast **set of** *char* is permitted because there are only 256 *char* values. The syntax of set type is shown in Figure 7.11 below in which < base type > is defined to be < ordinal > subject to the constraint just described.

< set type >

⟶ **set** ⟶ **of** ⟶ < base type > ⟶

Figure 7.11 The syntax of < set type >

In the initialization statements above, the set [3, 6, 1] could equally well have been listed as [1, 3, 6]. This is because elements are not ordered in sets. The initialization of *lowerset* makes use of a subrange to avoid having to list all the elements in this range explicitly. Finally, note also that *allalpha* is initialized in such a way that it does not contain any elements. This special set, having no elements, is called the **empty set**. The syntax relating to the creation of sets is called < set constructor > and is shown in Figure 7.12 below.

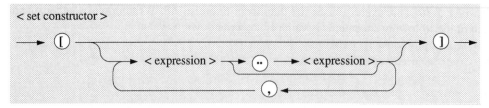

Figure 7.12 The syntax of < set constructor >

The operations defined on sets are somewhat different from those we have encountered so far. First, there is a test for membership. A given value either is, or is not, an element of a given set. For example, 6 is a member of the set *numberset* but 5 is not. The operator **in** is used to test for set membership. The statement below illustrates its use:

```
if 6 in numberset then
```

This operator used in conjunction with the Boolean operator **not** can be used to test whether an element is not in a set. However, care has to be exercised to ensure this is expressed in the correct way. Thus, we would write

```
if not (6 in numberset) then
```

Note that the **not** must be applied to an expression that evaluates to a Boolean value – the English expression 'if 6 is not in *numberset*' cannot be translated directly.

Exercise 7.11 Assuming the declarations and initializations above, decide whether each of the following is valid. If it is, write down its value.

(a)   *friday* **in** *dayset*
(b)   'g' **in** *lowerset*
(c)   5 **not in** *dayset*
(d)   **not** 5 **in** *dayset*

The **in** operator is often used in data validation processes where the list of allowable responses is represented as a set. The following is an example, in which *response* is a *char* variable.

```
if response in ['y', 'Y', 'n', 'N'] then...
```

The other set operators fall into two categories: those for manipulating sets and those for comparing them. We shall look at the former first. The **union** of two sets is the set consisting of all values of both sets. The union operator is denoted by +.

```
var
  A, B, C : set of char;
begin
  A :=['a', 'b'];
  B := ['b', 'c'];
  C := A + B
```

As a result of executing this fragment of code, *C* would be the set ['a', 'b', 'c']. The **intersection** of two sets is the set of all values common to both sets and is denoted by *.

```
  C := A * B;
```

As a result of executing this statement, *C* would be the set ['b']. The **difference** *A – B* of two sets is the set of elements which are members of *A* but which are not elements of *B*. Thus:

```
C := A - B;
```

would result in *C* being the set ['a'].

Exercise 7.12 Write down the values of the following expressions where all sets are of type *char*.

(a)   `['a'..'m'] + ['n'..'z']`
(b)   `['a'..'m'] * ['n'..'z']`
(c)   `['a'..'e'] - ['c'..'z']`

     Two sets can be compared for equality using the = operator and for inequality using the <> operator. The symbol <= is the operator for set inclusion. A set *A* is included in a set *B* if every element of *A* is also a member of *B*. If this is so, *A* is said to be a subset of *B*. For example:

```
if A <= B then
  writeln('A is a subset of B; every element of A is in B')
else
  writeln('A is not a subset of B')
```

The symbol >= is the superset operator. A set *A* is a superset of a set *B* if every element of *B* is also an element of *A*.

```
if A >= B then
  writeln('A is a superset of B, every element in B is also in A')
else
  writeln('A is not a superset of B')
```

Exercise 7.13 For each of the following Boolean expressions, decide whether it is true or false. All sets are of type *char*.

(a)   `['a'..'d'] = ['a', 'b', 'c', 'd']`
(b)   `['x'..'z'] <= ['x', 'y', 'z']`
(c)   `['m'..'p'] <> ['m', 'n', 'p']`

7.10 EXERCISES AND PROBLEMS

Problems 7.14–7.18 draw on ideas from the whole of this chapter. The exercises below are concerned with sets.

Exercise 7.14 Write a program fragment to read in a character from the keyboard until one of the characters 'y', 'Y', 'n' or 'N' has been read in. Your code should make use of a set.

Exercise 7.15 A computer dating agency keeps records of its clients' taste in music. The definitions and declarations associated with this are incompletely specified as follows:

```
const
  maxclients = 100;
type
  indexrange   = 1..maxclients;
  musicaltastes = (pop, funk, country, jazz, classical, folk);
  clientrecord = record
                   tastes : set of musicaltastes;
                   number : {the number of tastes in the previous field}
                 end;
var
  client : {an array for 100 client records}
  taste  : musicaltastes;
  count  : {a temporary variable which counts the number of tastes}
  i      : {a variable used to access the elements of client}
```

Complete the missing declarations and assuming that the *tastes* fields have already been initialized write a fragment of code that will count the number of elements in the set of *musicaltastes* and assign the result to the *number* field.

7.11 COMPATIBLE TYPES REVISITED

The compatibility rules of Section 6.9 extend to the new types that have been introduced in this chapter. Name equivalence is a direct extension of what has gone before. The assignment compatibility and expression compatibility rules have to be extended to cover subranges, enumeration types and sets.

7.11.1 Expression compatibility

Two types are expression compatible if one of the following holds:

- They are name equivalent
- One type is a subrange of the other
- Both types are subranges of the same host type
- Both are set types with expression compatible base types

Exercise 7.16 Determine which of the following are expression compatible.

```
type
  first    = 0..100;
  second   = 20..30;
  third    = 0..10;
  lower    = 'a'..'z';
  upper    = 'A'..'Z';
  weekdays = (sunday, monday, tuesday, wednesday, thursday, friday, saturday);
  midweek  = monday..friday;
  lateshop = thursday..friday;
  dayset   = set of weekdays;
  lowset   = set of third;
  bigset   = set of first;
```

7.11.2 Assignment compatibility

The following rules are in addition to those already given in Section 6.9.2. A value of type T_2 is assignment compatible with a variable of type T_1 if any of the following holds:

- T_1_ordinal_type_variable := T_2_ordinal_type_value

  where T_1 and T_2 are expression compatible and the value of T_2 falls within the range of possible values of T_1.

- T_1_set_type_variable := T_2_set_type_value

  where T_1 and T_2 are expression compatible and the members of the value of T_2 fall within the range of possible values of T_1.

A precondition of assignment compatibility is expression compatibility. So, for example, a variable of type *first* cannot be assigned a value of type *lower* because *first* and *lower* are not expression compatible. The types *first*, *second* and *third* are expression compatible and so we can consider assignment compatibility between variables and values from these types. Clearly, a variable of type *first* can be assigned a value of type *first*. Analogous statements hold for *second* and *third*. We shall express them as:

- *first* variable := *first* value
- *second* variable := *second* value
- *third* variable := *third* value

The following assignments are valid because the values being assigned all fall within the range of values of type *first*.

- *first* variable := *second* value
- *first* variable := *third* value

It would not be legitimate to assign a variable of type *second* a value of type *third*. This is because the values are 0..10, whereas the type of the variable only includes the values 20..30. Assigning a value of type *first* to a variable of type *second* is more problematic. Provided the value lies in the range 20..30 all is well, but values outside this range will cause errors. Despite this, the first rule tells us that these two are assignment compatible. A similar argument applies to assigning a value of type *first* to a variable of type *third*, and so we get:

- *second* variable := *first* value
- *third* variable := *first* value

Exercise 7.17 Complete the task of determining those types in Exercise 7.16 that would lead to assignment compatibility.

7.12 PROGRAMMING HINTS

(a) Use a case statement to distinguish between one of many ordinal type possibilities.

(b) Guideline (case statement) A case statement begins with the word **case** and terminates with the word **end**. Each case except the last one listed has the form: case list, colon, statement, semicolon. The last case listed has the form: case list, colon, statement. The default case is implemented using **else** which has the same syntax as the **else** of an **if** statement.

(c) Guideline (case labels) Case labels must be of ordinal type and must match the type of the case selector. They can consist of single items, multiple items separated by commas, subranges or a combination of all three. However, the labels should be unique and non-overlapping.

(d) Guideline (case) If more than a single construct is to be executed corresponding to a particular case label, then they must be implemented using a compound statement.

(e) Including the optional **else** clause of a case statement is good programming style.

(f) Use brackets round the separate components of a compound Boolean expression.

(g) Do not rely on left to right short circuit evaluation of compound Boolean expressions if program portability is important.

(h) Use subranges to model data which can only assume a range of ordinal type values.

(i) Enumeration type identifiers can neither be read in nor written out. Use a case statement or a suitably initialized array to overcome this difficulty.

(j) The first identifier of an enumeration type definition list has no predecessor and the last has no successor.

(k) Use a set constant to check that an ordinal type value has one of several allowable ordinal type values.

7.13 SUMMARY

In this chapter we have looked at case statements and compound Boolean expressions. We have also introduced the new data types: subrange, enumeration type and set type. The compatibility rules have been extended to cover these new types.

8

PROCEDURES AND FUNCTIONS

This chapter is concerned with designs that have been developed in a modular way using procedures and functions. The reader is assumed to be familiar with the notion of a procedure and function, but we shall briefly introduce the method whereby they will be presented in terms of design. We shall then see the facilities available in Pascal for their implementation.

8.1 PROCEDURE SPECIFICATION AND DESIGN

The purpose of this section is to introduce the notation used for specifying procedures and their designs. Section 8.3 will complete the task by introducing the notation used in designs for procedure calls. It is not the intention to teach the design of procedures here.

A procedure can be thought of as a subtask whose purpose is to compute results from some given source data. Thus, a specification of a procedure requires not only a description of its purpose but also a list of its **source data** and **results**. Because of this close link between the data and the process description we shall adopt a diagrammatic approach to procedure specification that combines the problem statement with these data requirements. This will take the form illustrated in Figure 8.1 below.

monthdays

month	Month in numeric form	*integer* parameter
{Assign to *days_in_month* the number of days in *month*. If *month* does not lie in the range 1..12 then set *valid* false else set it to true. The year is assumed not to be a leap year.}		
days_in_month *valid*	number of days in the month flag to denote success of process	*integer* parameter *Boolean* parameter

Figure 8.1 Specification of the procedure *monthdays*

First note the following points:

- The procedure is given a name – *monthdays.*
- The first boxed section contains the source data, that is, the data required for the procedure to carry out its task. Effectively, this box is a data table defining each source data item. We shall explain the word parameter that appears in the type definition shortly. This procedure has one source data item. Procedures can have zero, one or more source data items.
- The next boxed section contains the description of what the procedure is to do to the source data.
- The final box defines the results. Again, it takes the form of a data table, and a procedure can have zero, one or more items of results. However, some procedures with only one item of results can be treated differently; these will be discussed in Section 8.6.
- Collectively, the source data and results are called the **formal parameters** of the procedure. This procedure has three formal parameters: *month, days_in_month* and *valid.*

A design for a procedure follows the conventions used so far, except that in its layout explicit mention is made of the parameters. The algorithm for this procedure does not require the use of any variables and so a data table is not required. Thus, a design for the procedure *monthdays* is:

---

monthdays

---

month

1	*valid* := true	
2	select case depending on *month*	
3.1	2	: *days_in_month* := 28
3.2	4, 6, 9, 11	: *days_in_month* := 30
3.3	1, 3, 5, 7, 8, 10, 12	: *days_in_month* := 31
3.4	default	: *valid* := false
4	selectend	

---

days_in_month, valid

8.2 IMPLEMENTING A PROCEDURE

There are two parts to the implementation of procedures. Firstly, there is the **procedure heading**, which serves to inform the program of its existence and associates an identifier with it. Secondly, there is the **procedure body** which implements the detailed design. The two parts taken together are called a **procedure declaration**. We shall look shortly at where, in a program, a procedure declaration must be made, but for now we shall concentrate on the declaration itself. Figure 8.2 shows the declaration for the procedure *monthdays* of Section 8.1. Have a close look at it before reading the commentary below.

We begin by looking in detail at the procedure heading. This begins with the reserved word **procedure**, followed by the procedure's identifier. The source data and results parameters of the specification are collected together in a single list. Each parameter in the list is declared to be of a particular type in the same way as variables of programs are declared – that is, identifier, colon, type. Results parameters are distinguished by being preceded by the word **var**. Any parameter that corresponds to results must be declared in this way. We can therefore deduce that parameters which are not preceded by **var** must be source data. Source data parameters are called **value** parameters and results parameters are called **var** parameters.

```
procedure monthdays(month : integer; var days_in_month : integer;
                    var valid : boolean);
  begin
    valid := true;
    case month of
      2                      : days_in_month := 28;
      4, 6, 9, 11            : days_in_month := 30;
      1, 3, 5, 7, 8, 10, 12 : days_in_month := 31
    else
      valid := false
    end {end case}
  end; {end procedure}
```

Figure 8.2 An implementation of a procedure

Initially, we can choose the order in which the formal parameters are placed so that the following would also be a valid declaration for *monthdays*:

```
procedure monthdays(var days_in_month : integer; month : integer;
                    var valid : boolean);
```

However, once the procedure has been defined, the formal parameter order is fixed and cannot be altered. As we shall see in the next section, the order has to be known when the procedure is used. It is good practice to use the same parameter order as that used in the design. Parameters that are of the same type can be declared together, separated by a comma. So, for example, a procedure having parameters given by the following table:

source data parameters (type *real*)	results parameters (type *integer*)
first, second	third, fourth

would be declared as:

```
procedure example(first, second : real; var third, fourth : integer);
```

Parameters which are both source data and results are only listed once, but because they are results they must be declared as **var** parameters. So a procedure having the following parameters:

source data parameters (type *integer*)	results parameters (type *integer*)
first, second	second, third

would be declared as:

```
procedure example(first : integer; var second, third : integer);
```

Notice, in particular, that the declaration of *first* has to be a **value** declaration while that of *second* must be a **var** declaration. We have chosen to combine the declarations of *second* and *third* although it would be legal to declare them separately as:

```
procedure example(first : integer; var second : integer; var third : integer);
```

One consequence of listing only once parameters which are both source data and results is that it becomes impossible to distinguish from the procedure heading those parameters which are both source data and results from those which are results only. This is one of the inadequacies of Pascal and will be discussed further in Section 8.7.

Exercise 8.1 Write down procedure headings for each of the following parameter combinations. You should assume that all the parameters are of *integer* type and that the procedure is called *example*.

	source data parameters	results parameters
(a)	`first, second`	`first`
(b)	`first`	`second`
(c)	{none}	`first`
(d)	`first`	{none}
(e)	{none}	{none}

Exercise 8.2 Write down procedure headings for each of the following parameter combinations in which identifiers beginning *int* are of *integer* type and those beginning *str* are of *string* type. The procedure is to be called *example*.

	source data parameters	results parameters
(a)	`int1`	`str1`
(b)	`int1, str1`	`str1`
(c)	{none}	`int1, str1`
(d)	`int1, int2, str1`	`int1, str1, str2`

The syntax for a procedure heading is given in Figure 8.3.

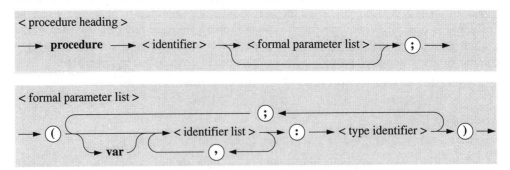

Figure 8.3 The syntax of < procedure heading > and < formal parameter list >

As you can see, this diagram is in two parts, with the formal parameter list being treated as a separate term. The diagram shows that a procedure which does not have any parameters should not include any brackets in its declaration. Examination of the formal parameter list syntax confirms that **value** and **var** parameters can be listed in any order and that parameters of the same type can be declared together, separated by commas. However, there is one additional detail, which is that the type of the parameter must be specified using a type identifier. The implication of this is that parameters of structured type have to be declared by using a type definition to create an identifier corresponding to the structured type. That type identifier is then used in the procedure declaration.

Exercise 8.3 Decide whether each of the following procedure headings is valid. For any valid ones, identify the source data parameters and the results parameters. For invalid declarations, identify the error.

(a) **procedure** *example(first; second : integer)*;
(b) **procedure** *example(first : integer;* **var** *list : listtype)*;
(c) **procedure** *example(first :* **array**[1..10] **of** *integer)*; *invalid*
(d) **procedure** *example(first : string[10])*; *string* ✓ *strings[*] ✗*

In subsequent problem sections, procedures that have parameters of structured type will be specified using type identifiers whose definitions will be given in a data table.

- Guideline (procedure heading) The form of a procedure heading is the reserved word **procedure**, followed by the procedure's identifier, the formal parameters enclosed in braces, and a semicolon.
- Guideline (procedure formal parameters) Parameters are declared in a list, the components of which are separated by semicolons. Each component has the form: identifier list (each identifier being separated by a comma) followed by a colon followed by a type identifier. Parameters of structured type must be declared using a type identifier. Results parameters must be preceded by the word **var**.

The procedure in Figure 8.2 has a particularly simple structure – it consists of a procedure heading followed by a compound statement. By analogy with a program body, we shall refer to the compound statement of a procedure as a **procedure body**. The code in Figure 8.2 only involves the parameters. More generally, procedures will need to use variables other than the parameters. The design for the specification below is a case in point.

Data table for parameters

Identifier	Description	Type
maxsize	Array upper bound	*integer* constant value 10
arraytype	Type definition	**array**[1..*maxsize*] of *string*

reverse

given	Array to be reversed	*arraytype* parameter
{Reverse the elements of *given* so that the element indexed 1 is stored at index *maxsize*, that at index 2 is stored at *maxsize* − 1 and so on. All elements of the array are assumed to be initialized.}		
given	The reversed array	*arraytype* parameter

reverse

given

```
1    loop for index := 1 to (maxsize div 2)
2        temp := given[index]
3        given[index] := given[maxsize – index + 1]
4        given[maxsize – index + 1] := temp
5    loopend
```

given

Data table for reverse

Identifier	Description	Type
index	Loop control variable	1..*maxsize* variable
temp	Temporary element value store	*string* variable

This design exploits the variables *index* and *temp*. These two variables are said to be declared **local** to the procedure *reverse*. The implementation of this design, in which *arraytype* is already assumed to be defined, is as follows:

```
procedure reverse(var given : arraytype);
  var
    index : 1..maxsize;
    temp  : string;
  begin
    for index := 1 to (maxsize div 2) do
      begin
        temp := given[index];
        given[index] := given[maxsize - index + 1];
        given[maxsize - index + 1] := temp
      end
  end;
```

The whole of this procedure has a very familiar structure – other than the heading it has the appearance of a normal program. Indeed, a program and a procedure do have a similar structure, as we can see from Figure 8.4.

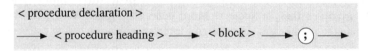

Figure 8.4 The syntax of < procedure declaration >

To convince yourself of this you may need to look back to the syntax of a program given in Figures 2.5 and 2.6. As a reminder, the term < block > consists of the declarations followed by a compound statement. So a procedure block can make **const** and **type** definitions and **var** declarations in just the same way that a program can. Indeed, as we shall see, a procedure can even declare another procedure. All of these definitions and declarations will be called local to the block. The block of **procedure** *reverse* is quite modest as it only involves **var** declarations (corresponding to the data table for the procedure design). Essentially, the only difference between a program and a procedure is in the heading and in the final punctuation character, which for a program is a full stop and for a procedure a semicolon.

One thing that was not reflected in the code for *reverse* is the fact that it assumes the parameter *given* is initialized. If it is not, then references to its elements within the procedure body are in error. A condition like this, that must be true before the procedure is called, is known as a **precondition**. A condition that must be true after the execution of the procedure is called a **postcondition**. The explicit statement of preconditions and postconditions provides valuable documentation and specifies what assumptions have been made in developing the code. The conditions can be included as comments within the code as follows:

```
procedure reverse(var given: arraytype);
   {Pre : given is an initialized array.
    Post: The elements of given are in reverse order.}
   var
      index : 1..maxsize;
      temp  : string;
   begin
      for index := 1 to (maxsize div 2) do
         begin
            temp := given[index];
            given[index] := given[maxsize - index + 1];
            given[maxsize - index + 1] := temp
         end
   end;
```

Here, the single precondition is that *given* must be an initialized array. The postcondition says that, as a result of the procedure's processing, *given* will have its elements reversed. In general, the preconditions list the conditions that must apply to the source data parameters and the postconditions list those pertaining to the results.

Exercise 8.4 Write down the pre- and postconditions for the procedure in Figure 8.2.

8.3 DESIGNS THAT USE PROCEDURES

A simple program design that exploits the procedure *monthdays* of Figure 8.2 is given in Figure 8.5. It requests a user to enter the number corresponding to a month and outputs the number of days in that month. In fact, this program is designed to test the procedure *monthdays*. Programs to test procedure implementations are sometimes called **driver** programs. Driver programs tend to be rather simple, but they must enable every part of the procedure to be thoroughly tested. Therefore, in designing a driver program thought must be given to the data values that will be used to test the procedure. For the procedure *monthdays*, test data values will have to include the integer values 1 to 12 inclusive. It will also have to be tested to see that appropriate action is taken for inputs that do not lie in the range 1 to 12. A driver program does not need to be sophisticated – the one in Figure 8.5 has to be executed for each data value tested.

```
1      write out 'Enter the number of a month'
2      read in wantedmonth
3      monthdays(wantedmonth, days, flag)
4      if flag then
5         write out 'You did not enter a number in the range 1 to 12'
6      else
7.1       write out 'There are ', days, ' days in this month'
7.2       if wantedmonth = 2 then
7.3          write out 'But leap years have 29 days'
7.4       ifend
8      ifend
```

Figure 8.5 A design which makes a procedure call

We could have introduced a loop to avoid this repeated execution, but that would have complicated the test program and given marginal benefit. In the problems section in this chapter we shall consider driver programs in more detail. Until then you should bear in mind that they have an important testing role.

Step 3 of Figure 8.5 shows the form that a procedure call takes. The variables on which the procedure is to act are called **actual parameters**. Here, they are *wantedmonth*, *days* and *flag*. As a result of the call, *days* will hold one of the values 28, 30 or 31 and *flag* will be true, or *days* will be undefined and *flag* will be false. The value of *wantedmonth* remains unaltered as a consequence of the call and thus is available for reference in step 7.2.

Actual parameters are said to be **passed** to the procedure and one can think of them as replacing the formal parameters in which the code of the procedure is expressed. A more precise description of the passing mechanism will be given later; the important point here is to distinguish between formal and actual parameters. The other crucial point is that the actual parameter list must match the formal parameter list in order, number and type: in other words, for the procedure *monthdays*, the first actual parameter must be the month number and be of *integer* type; the second actual parameter must correspond to the number of days and be of *integer* type; and the final actual parameter must be a *Boolean* variable. The data table for this program design records these declarations.

Data table

Identifier	Description	Type
wantedmonth	Month input by user	*integer* variable
days	Number of days in input month	*integer* variable
flag	Flag denoting success of call	*Boolean* variable
monthdays	(*month, days_in_month, valid*)	procedure(*integer, integer, Boolean*)

The first three declarations are straightforward – they merely define the variables that will act as actual parameters. The fourth declaration says that *monthdays* is a procedure having three formal parameters called *month*, *days_in_month* and *valid* of type *integer*, *integer* and *Boolean* respectively. Notice how the formal parameter identifiers are defined in column 2 and their corresponding types in column 3. The data table declaration of *monthdays* is the design equivalent of the Pascal statement

```
procedure monthdays(month : integer; var days_in_month : integer;
                    var valid : Boolean)
```

The problem sections will use this design method of declaring procedures and ask you to implement them in their Pascal equivalent form. Note that the data table thereby determines the order, number and type of the formal parameters. A Pascal procedure call has the same form as that used in the design, so step 3 is coded in Pascal as:

```
monthdays(wantedmonth, days, flag)
```

An actual parameter corresponding to a formal **var** parameter must be a variable. This can be contrasted with the situation for **value** parameters where literal values, rather than values stored in a variable, can be passed to the procedure. For example, it would be perfectly legal to pass the integer literal value 4 to *monthdays* in the call

```
monthdays(4, days, flag)
```

As a result, *days* would be returned with the value 30. Indeed, expressions can be used wherever a value parameter is expected, as in the call

`monthdays(2*4 - 1, days, flag)`

The only restriction on the expression is that it must evaluate to a value of the type expected by the formal parameter. So here, any expression that evaluates to an integer would be permitted. These examples illustrate the more formal description given in Figure 8.6.

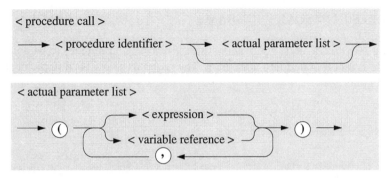

Figure 8.6 The syntax of a procedure call

Exercise 8.5 Which of the following calls to *monthdays* are valid?

(a)   `monthdays(4/3, days, flag)`
(b)   `monthdays(wantedmonth + 1, days, flag)`
(c)   `monthdays(days, days, flag)`
(d)   `monthdays(length('September'), days, flag)`
(e)   `monthdays(month, days_in_month, valid)`

Exercise 8.6 Determine the effect of the following procedure and write a sequence of calls using only *writechars* and *writeln* to produce the following output.

```
*****
AAA
 B
```

```
procedure writechars(number : integer; ch : char);
   {Pre : number is a positive integer.
    Post: None - number copies of ch are written out on a single line.}
   var
     i : integer;
   begin
     for i := 1 to number do
       write(ch)
   end;
```

Exercise 8.7 Write a fragment of Pascal that exploits the procedure *writechars* of Exercise 8.6 and that receives a string from the keyboard and writes out, as a sequence of asterisks, the number of characters in the string. Thus, if the entered string is 'computing' then the output should be '*********'.

Exercise 8.8 This example is concerned with the following declaration:

procedure *example(formal1, formal2 : integer;* **var** *formal3 : integer);*

Assuming that *actual1*, *actual2* and *actual3* are initialized integer variables, write down which variables might have been updated after each of the following calls:

(a) *example(actual1, actual2, actual3)*

(b) *example(actual2, actual2, actual1)*

8.4 PROCEDURES IN PASCAL PROGRAMS

In Section 8.2 we saw how to code a procedure in Pascal so all that remains to be done is to see how that code is incorporated into a program. The program below is an implementation of the design in Figure 8.5.

```
program calendar;
var
  wantedmonth, days : integer;
  flag              : Boolean;
procedure monthdays(month : integer; var days_in_month : integer;
                    var valid : Boolean);
    {Pre : month is an integer.
     Post: If months is in range 1 to 12 inclusive,
           days_in_month has value 28, 30 or 31 and valid is assigned true,
           otherwise valid is false and days_in_month is undefined.}
  begin
    valid := true;
    case month of
      2                      : days_in_month := 28;
      4, 6, 9, 11            : days_in_month := 30;
      1, 3, 5, 7, 8, 10, 12 : days_in_month := 31
    else
      valid := false
    end {end case}
  end;  {end procedure}
begin    {main program}
  writeln('Enter the number of a month');
  readln(wantedmonth);
  monthdays(wantedmonth, days, flag);
  if flag then
    begin
      writeln('There are ', days, ' days in this month');
      if wantedmonth = 2 then
        writeln('But leap years have 29 days')
    end
  else
    writeln('You did not enter a number in the range 1 to 12')
end.
```

The code for the whole of the procedure implementation occurs immediately after the **var** declarations and immediately before the main program body. The procedure is said to be **declared**: this explains its position in the declarations part of the program. This can be seen in the modified syntax diagram for < declarations > given in Figure 8.7 below.

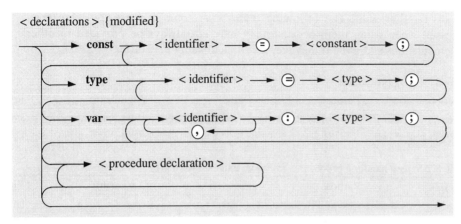

Figure 8.7 The updated syntax of < declarations >

This shows that a program can make more than one procedure declaration, and we shall see examples of this shortly. You may need to refer to Figure 8.4 and the definition of < block > if you want to convince yourself that the following guideline is correct.

- Guideline (procedure declaration) Procedures are declared immediately after the **var** declarations. A procedure declaration consists of a procedure heading which contains the procedure identifier, the parameters enclosed in braces and a semicolon. Then there are the local declarations in the usual order **const**, **type**, **var** (and potentially procedure). Finally, there is the compound statement corresponding to the procedure body. The word **end** of this compound statement is followed by a semicolon.

Exercise 8.9 Write a complete program, based on the design below, which asks a user to enter data into an array, *strarray*, and which produces as output the array elements in reverse order. The design exploits the procedure *reverse* developed above.

1   read data into the array *strarray*
2   use the procedure *reverse* to reverse the elements in the array *strarray*
3   write out the array elements

Data table

Identifier	Description	Type
maxsize	Array upper bound	*integer* constant value 10
arraytype	Type definition	array[1..*maxsize*] of *string*
strarray	The array whose elements are to be reversed	*arraytype* variable

In the solution to Exercise 8.9 you may have noticed that the constant identifier *maxsize* is used in the declaration of the local variable *index* within the procedure *reverse*. In Section 8.7 we shall be studying how an identifier like this, which is defined outside the procedure, can be referenced within the procedure itself. For now we note that an identifier defined or declared in the main program is called a **global identifier**, which means it can be referenced by any part of the program following its definition or declaration.

Turbo Pascal provides a wide variety of built-in procedures, some of which we are already familiar with. The following tables give some of these, but care needs to be exercised when using them because they may not always be provided in other Pascal implementations and, even if they are, their functionality may differ.

Table 8.1 String procedures

Function	Purpose	Arguments	Result
delete(s, place, span)	Delete *span* characters of *s* starting at *place*	*string, integer, integer*	*string*
insert(s1, s2, place)	Insert *s1* into *s2* at position *place*	*string, string, integer*	

Table 8.2 Screen handling procedures in Pascal unit *crt* (see text)

Function	Purpose	Arguments	Result
clreol	Clears all characters from current cursor position to the end of line	none	none
clrscr	Clears the screen	none	none
gotoxy(x, y)	Positions the cursor at column *x* row *y*	0..255, 0..255	none

The string procedures in Table 8.1 should not be declared in the declaration part of a program. They are built-in, and so are available to any program that wishes to make use of them. Another way of saying this is that they are global procedures within a program and so can be referenced anywhere within it. By contrast, the procedures in Table 8.2 are not immediately available but are stored in a Pascal unit called *crt*. We remind you that to use the procedures in *crt* a program must declare what is known as a **uses** statement immediately after the program heading, as illustrated below.

```
program screenplay;
uses crt; {This tells the system the screen procedures are required}
  :
begin
  clrscr;   {This will clear the screen}
```

8.5 PROBLEMS

Problems 8.1–8.4 give you the opportunity to code some procedure designs. Procedures have to be tested using specifically written driver programs. In the solutions, the part headed *Test data* will sometimes include a specific design for such a driver program and at other times will contain a description of what such a program should be capable of doing.

8.6 FUNCTIONS AND NESTED ROUTINES

A special kind of procedure is one that has only a single results parameter. Some procedures having this property can be implemented as a **function**. Programs can declare both procedures and functions, and we shall refer to them collectively as **routines**. Thus, we shall say that a program can declare routines. The same terminology will be used for their corresponding designs.

The essential difference between a function and a procedure lies in the way they are called, but there is also a small difference in the way they are declared. The single result of a function call is usually not stored in a variable but is used immediately in some expression or condition. In other words, the value's existence is very transitory. You are already familiar with the *length* function which returns the current dynamic length of a string: it has tended to appear in conditions like:

```
for i := 1 to length(name)
```

in which *name* is a string variable and *length*(*name*) is evaluated within the loop construct to generate its terminating value. By contrast, a procedure call will assign its results to actual parameters which are then manipulated like any other program variable.

8.6.1 Function declarations

There are several factors to take into account when determining whether a routine should be implemented as a procedure or a function. Certainly if a routine has more than one result it cannot be implemented as a function, but when it does have a single result there is a choice: procedure or function? This choice is constrained in standard Pascal because only routines that have a simple type can be implemented as a function. Turbo Pascal has an extension that permits string results: this leads to the following guideline:

- Guideline (function) If a routine has a single result of simple type then it should be implemented as a function.

We have adopted this guideline for simplicity. However, there may well be situations where a routine does have a single result of simple type that is better implemented as a procedure. The reason for this would be the way in which it was envisaged the routine would be called. If it is unlikely that the result would be used in an expression, then a procedure could be preferred. We have also not included routines with a string result. If you use this Turbo Pascal extension and the result is not the default string, then you must use a type identifier for the function result type. The use of functions that have string results should be avoided if there is any possibility of the code having to be compiled on another compiler.

In the specification below, *string4* is already assumed to be a type identifier representing *string*[4]. Study the details of the specification implementation and then read the commentary that follows.

allcaps

given	A string of four characters	*string4* parameter
{If all the characters of *given* are upper case then return the value true, otherwise return the value false.}		
allcaps	True for 'y' or 'Y'	*Boolean* parameter

```
function allcaps(given : string4):Boolean;
   {Pre : given has exactly four characters.
   {Post: allcaps is returned true if all 4 characters are upper case, false otherwise.}
   var
      i : 1..4;
   begin
      allcaps := true;
      for i := 1 to 4 do
        if not(given[i]) in ['A'..'Z'] then
           allcaps := false
   end;
```

The declaration as a whole is similar to that of a procedure; it has a heading followed by a block. First, there is a reserved word (here **function**), then an identifier, then a parameter enclosed in brackets. Some functions will have more than one parameter, but the result of a function is not declared using a **var** parameter in the parameter list. Instead, there is a colon after the parameter list, followed by the function result type which here is *Boolean*. One thing that should be noted is that the implementation assigns the result to *allcaps*. We shall look at this again in Section 8.6.2.

The syntax of a function heading is shown in Figure 8.8 below in which the term < formal parameter list > is as given in Figure 8.3.

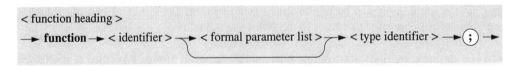

Figure 8.8 The syntax of < function heading >

This syntax does not preclude the possibility that the formal parameter list can contain a **var** parameter. This should never be exploited because a function should only return a single result. Section 8.7 will give circumstances that will explain why the syntax permits **var** parameters in a function parameter list. The following guidelines should be used when implementing a function:

- Guideline (function heading) The form of a procedure heading is the reserved word **function**, followed by the procedure's identifier, followed by the formal parameters enclosed in braces, followed by a colon, followed by a simple type.
- Guideline (formal parameters) Parameters are declared in a list, the components of which are separated by semicolons. Each component has the form: an identifier list (each identifier being separated by a comma), followed by a colon, followed by a type identifier. Parameters of structured type must be declared using a type identifier; **var** should not be used.

Exercise 8.10 Decide whether each of the following function headings is valid. For any which are invalid, identify the error.

(a) **function** example(first, second : integer) : real;
(b) **function** example(first : integer; **var** list : listtype) : integer;
(c) **function** example(first : **array**[1..10] **of** integer) : char;
(d) **function** example(first : string[10]) : string;

8.6.2 Functions in programs

The body of the function has exactly the same form as that of a procedure. However, there is one important point shared by all functions, which is that every function body must contain at least one statement that assigns a value to the function identifier. The reason for this is that it is the function identifier that holds the returned value on conclusion of the function call. For example, the first statement of the body of the function *allcaps* initializes *allcaps* to true. This value is then updated if a lower case letter is encountered.

Exercise 8.11 Write a function declaration corresponding to the following specification:
validrange

number	Value being tested	*integer* variable
lowlimit	The lower value of range	*integer* variable
highlimit	The upper value of range	*integer* variable
{Return the value true if number satisfies *lowlimit* <= *number* <= *highlimit*, otherwise return the value false. It is assumed that *lowlimit* <= *highlimit*.}		
validrange	True if number in stated range	*Boolean* function value

Functions, like procedures, are declared immediately after the **var** declarations. Figure 8.9 below updates Figure 8.7 to reflect this.

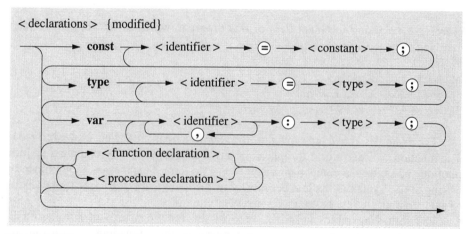

Figure 8.9 The updated syntax of < declarations >

Figure 8.9 shows that a program can declare both procedures and functions and that they can be declared in any order. As we shall see, this does not mean that they can be declared in random order. The use to which they are put may well determine the order in which they have to be declared. The following guideline on routine declarations is a generalization of the earlier one for procedures:

- Guideline (routine declaration) Routines are declared immediately after the **var** declarations. A routine declaration consists of a routine heading followed by the local declarations in the usual order, **const**, **type**, **var** (and potentially procedure). Finally, there is the compound statement corresponding to the procedure body. The word **end** of this compound statement is followed by a semicolon.

The program fragment below illustrates the use of a function in a simple program.

```
program functionex;
const
  low  = 1;
  high = 10;
var
  input : integer;
function validrange(number, lowlimit, highlimit : integer) : Boolean;
  {Pre : number, lowlimit, highlimit are all integer values and lowlimit <= highlimit.
   Post: validrange is returned true if lowlimit <= number <= highlimit,
         false otherwise.}

  begin
    validrange := (lowlimit <= number) and (number <= highlimit)
  end;

begin {main program}
  repeat
    write('Enter an integer in the range ', low, '..', high, ' ');
    readln(input)
  until validrange(input, low, high)
    :
```

Exercise 8.12 Using the identifiers of this program, which of the following statements involving calls to *validrange* are valid?
(a)   **until** validrange(input, 4, 3*8)
(b)   **until** validrange(input, 7, 5)
(c)   validrange(input, low, high)
(d)   input := validrange(input, low, high)

The examples above are typical of the way functions are called. However, the syntax of a function call permits it to appear in any expressions of any complexity. Indeed, a function call is itself a component of the syntactic term < expression >. We have avoided looking at this syntax in the text because of its difficulty. Appendix I gives the details, but we shall continue to rely on examples and your intuition here.

The following tables describe some of the functions provided in Turbo Pascal. Different implementations of Pascal may not provide these functions or their functionality may differ. Also notice that the result type of *concat* and *copy* is string. We repeat that we, as users, are not allowed to declare a function having a non-simple type result but, as Table 8.5 shows, the system can!

The function *readkey* is typically used when a single character is requested from the keyboard. The character read from the keyboard is not echoed to the screen nor is a new line generated. This enables data validation to be carried out on the input, and if it fails no action is required in terms of tidying up the screen. If it passes the validation then the character has to be explicitly written to the screen using *write* or *writeln* if that is what the program requires. This function will be used extensively in the case study that forms part of Chapter 9.

Table 8.3 Arithmetic functions

Function	Purpose	Argument	Result
abs(x)	Returns the absolute value of its argument	*real* or *integer*	same
arctan(x)	Returns the arctan of its argument	*real*	*real*
cos(x)	Returns the cosine of its argument	*real*	*real*
exp(x)	Returns the exponential of its argument	*real*	*real*
int(x)	Returns the integer part of its argument	*real*	*integer*
ln(x)	Returns the natural logarithm of its argument	*real*	*real*
odd(x)	Tests if argument is odd number	*integer*	*Boolean*
round(x)	Rounds a real to nearest integer	*real*	*integer*
sin(x)	Returns the sine of its argument	*real*	*real*
sqr(x)	Returns the square of its argument	*real* or *integer*	same
sqrt(x)	Returns the square root of its argument	*real*	*real*
trunc(x)	Truncates real to integer	*real*	*integer*

Table 8.4 Functions for ordinal types

Function	Purpose	Arguments	Result
chr(x)	Returns character with given ordinal number	*integer*	*char*
ord(x)	Returns ordinal number of ordinal type value	Any ordinal type	*integer*
pred(x)	Returns the predecessor of its argument	Any ordinal type	same
succ(x)	Returns the successor of its argument	Any ordinal type	same
upcase(x)	Converts a character to upper case	*char*	*char*

Table 8.5 String functions

Function	Purpose	Arguments	Result
concat(s1, s2, …)	Concatenates strings	*string*	*string*
copy(s, index, span)	Returns the substring consisting of *index* characters of *s* starting at position *span*	*string, integer, integer*	*string*
length(s)	Returns the length of its argument	*string*	*integer*
pos(pattern, s)	Finds position of *pattern* in *s*	*string, string*	*integer*

Table 8.6 Screen handling function in unit *crt*

Function	Purpose	Arguments	Result
readkey	Reads a character from the keyboard without echo to screen	none	*char*

8.6.3 Nested routines

We conclude this section with some examples which require one routine to be nested within another. We shall consider a simple guessing game in which one player enters a two digit number (the leading digit of which can be zero) and a second player is to guess the number. The problem will make use of routines in the Pascal Unit *crt* as well as some of the standard built-in routines. Study the program fragment that follows and then read the commentary below.

```pascal
program guessgame;
uses crt;
type
  range = 0..99;
  digit = 0..9;
var
  guess, target : range;
procedure getnumber(var x : range);
  {Pre : None.
  {Post: Returns in x an integer in the range 0..99 read in from keyboard.
        Input must be terminated with a <ret>.}
  var
    tens, units : digit;
  function getdigit : digit;
    {Pre : None.
    {Post: Reads the keyboard and returns a digit in the range 0..9.
          All non-digit inputs are ignored. Once entered, the digit cannot be altered.}
    var
      ch : char;
    begin
      repeat
        ch := readkey
      until ch in ['0'..'9'];
      getdigit := ord(ch) - ord('0')
    end;   {function getdigit}
  begin   {procedure getnumber}
    tens := getdigit;
    write(tens);
    units := getdigit;
    write(units);
    readln;
    x := 10*tens + units
  end;   {procedure getnumber}
begin   {main program}
  clrscr;
  write('First player: Enter a two digit target number (leading digit can be zero) ');
  getnumber(target);
  clrscr;
  repeat
    write('Second player: Enter a two digit guess (leading digit can be zero) ');
    getnumber(guess)
  until (guess = target)
end.
```

Since the program uses screen facilities held in the *crt* unit, a **uses** statement follows the program heading. The procedure *getnumber* makes three declarations: two local integer variables, *tens* and *units* and the function *getdigit*. The latter function has no source data and thus has no parameter list. Note there are no brackets following the function identifier when the parameter list is empty as here. The function then declares a local variable *ch* and its body exploits the built-in functions *chr* and *ord*. These built-in functions do not have to be declared explicitly – they are always available for use. The conversion of the character value to digit is done by subtracting the ordinal value of the character '0' from that of the input character.

The structure of this program illustrates the declaration of a function within that of a procedure. The declarations are structured in this way because the function is only called by the procedure and so is declared local to it. This ensures that it is only available to be called by *getnumber* – the main program cannot call *getdigit* and indeed is not aware of its existence. We shall say that the function *getdigit* is invisible to the main program.

Suppose now the game was altered so that the second player first had to guess the tens digit and then the units digit. A program to do this would wish to exploit the function *getdigit*. The code below illustrates a solution.

```pascal
program guessgame2;
uses crt;
type
  range = 0..99;
  digit = 0..9;
var
  target : range;
  tensguess, unitsguess : digit;
function getdigit : digit;
  {Pre : None.
  {Post: Reads the keyboard and returns a digit in the range 0..9.
         All non-digit inputs are ignored. Once entered, the digit cannot be altered.}
  var
    ch : char;
  begin
    repeat
      ch := readkey
    until ch in ['0'..'9'];
    getdigit := ord(ch) - ord('0')
  end;
procedure getnumber(var x : range);
  {Pre : None.
  {Post: Returns in x an integer in the range 0..99 read in from keyboard.
         Input must be terminated with a <ret>.}
  var
    tens, units : digit;
  begin {procedure getnumber}
    tens := getdigit;
    write(tens);
    units := getdigit;
    write(units);
    readln;
    x := 10*tens + units
  end;      {procedure getnumber}
begin   {main program}
  clrscr;
  write('First player: Enter a two digit target number (leading digit can be zero) ');
  getnumber(target);
  clrscr;
```

```
  repeat
    write('Second player: Enter a guess for the tens digit (can be zero) ');
    tensguess := getdigit;
    writeln(tensguess)
  until (tensguess = target div 10);
  repeat
    write('Second player: Enter a guess for the units digit (can be zero) ');
    unitsguess := getdigit
    writeln(unitsguess)
  until (unitsguess = target mod 10)
end.
```

In this program the function *getdigit* is declared as part of the main program declarations and so it is a global variable. Thus, this program declares two routines, *getdigit* and *getnumber*, whereas the program *guessgame* declared just one routine, *getnumber*.

The syntax diagram in Figure 8.9 shows that a program can declare as many routines as it likes, but it does not tell us in which order the declarations should appear. This is part of the program logic and is determined from the way the routines will be called. In program *guessgame2*, both the procedure *getnumber* and the main program make calls to *getdigit*. Since an identifier must be declared before it is referenced, we can deduce that the declaration of *getdigit* must precede that of *getnumber*. This leads to the following guideline:

- Guideline (routine declaration order) If routine *a* calls routine *b* then the declaration of routine *b* must precede that of *a*.

Exercise 8.13 The procedure *getnumber* will write out a leading zero if one is entered by the user. Modify the design of this routine so that inputs like 04 are written out as 4.

8.7 PROBLEMS

Problems 8.5 and 8.6 are concerned with the straightforward implementation of functions. Problem 8.6 illustrates how functions are declared in a data table. In the remainder of the problems there is a mixture of procedures and functions.

8.8 SCOPE AND PARAMETER PASSING

So far we have stressed that data which are required by a procedure or function must be passed through the parameter mechanism. We shall continue to emphasize this, but one question which may have occurred to you when you studied the solution to Exercise 8.9 is 'How does the procedure *reverse* "know about" the constant identifier *maxsize*?' This information is not passed via parameters, and yet *reverse* uses *maxsize* in its definition of the variable *i*. It would seem that procedures are not so self-contained as we have been suggesting. This is indeed the case, and in this section we shall answer the question just posed. We shall also look at the parameter passing mechanism in detail and see how it is that reference to local procedure variables is not possible outside the procedure itself. We begin with the latter, and a simple model that you can use as a mental image of the process. Then we will refine the model in terms of the memory of the machine. Since this will be a more complex model you may prefer to study only the introductory model. Consider the following declarations:

```
type
   arraytype = array[1..100] of integer;
var
   single, double : arraytype;
procedure copydouble(x : arraytype; var result : arraytype);
   {Pre : x is an initialized array.
    Post: elements of result are double the corresponding element of x.}
   var
    i : 1..100  {used to access array elements}
```

These declarations will be used in a program whose purpose is to read values into the array *single* from the keyboard. The procedure *copydouble* will then be used to assign to the elements of the array *double*, values that are double the corresponding elements of *single*. We shall use the word **invoke** to describe the action of a procedure being called.

As a result of the declarations of *single* and *double*, sufficient memory is allocated to hold their values. This process does not assign values to the reserved memory locations – it merely sets them aside. When *single* is initialized, its reserved memory locations are updated to reflect the input values. We will now consider what happens to the memory when the main program invokes *copydouble* with the following call:

```
copydouble(single, double)
```

At the moment of the invocation, the memory reserved for *double* is still uninitialized and the following actions take place.

(a) Space is created in memory to hold the values of the formal parameters *x* and *result* and for the local variable *i*. At this stage we can imagine the memory as having the form shown below, in which question marks denote uninitialized values and the shaded area denotes initialized locations.

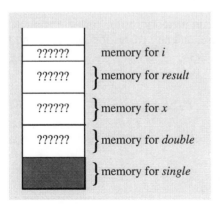

(b) The value of the actual parameter *single* is copied to *x*. Since this parameter is an array, all 100 elements must be copied. The memory state is then:

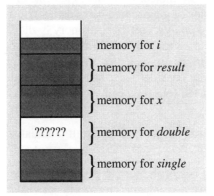

(c) The formal parameter *x* now has values. These values are then used to compute and assign values to the formal parameter *result*. This will involve the use of the variable *i*. When this task is completed, the memory can be pictured as:

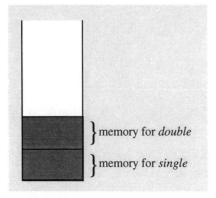

(d) The value of the formal parameter *result* is copied to the actual parameter *double*. This means copying all 100 element values. At this stage all memory locations have values assigned to them.

(e) The call having been completed, the space in memory for the formal parameters and the local variable is returned for general use, and any values it contains are no longer available. Thus, the memory can be pictured as:

The white area in this diagram shows the memory available for general use. Although data recorded in it are not physically removed they are no longer assigned to any identifier and so cannot be referenced.

Exercise 8.14 Draw a sequence of similar diagrams to show the state of the memory at the same stages for the following invocation in which the identifiers for the formal and actual parameters are identical:

copydouble(x, result)

As before, you should assume that the actual parameter *x* is initialized from the keyboard just prior to the invocation.

The solution to Exercise 8.14 should enable you to see how it is possible for formal and actual parameters to share the same identifier and yet remain distinct. It is the fact that the values are copied which enables this to be done.

The model of parameter passing presented above will suffice for most purposes, but it makes some simplifications, particularly with regard to **var** parameters, whose explanation requires a more sophisticated model. The memory set reserved when a procedure is invoked is called an **activation record**. The activation record is somewhat more complex than the diagrams above would suggest because it has associated with it a great deal of housekeeping data that record the start address of each of the parameters and local variables associated with the call. However, we can safely ignore this as it is the parameters that interest us. What is different from the model above is the way **var** parameters are handled. The difference occurs at step (a). The **value** parameters have space reserved as described in (a), but **var** parameters are reserved only enough space to hold an address. In this case, what is eventually stored is the start address of the variable *result* so that, just after the invocation, memory is set aside as follows:

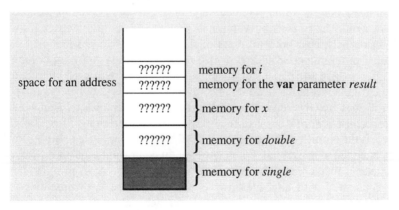

When the actual parameter *double* is passed, the memory allocated to the **var** parameter *result* is assigned the start address of the variable *double*.

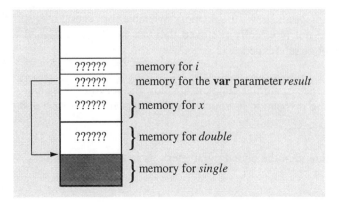

The effect of this inside the procedure is that a reference to *result* is now taken as a reference to the variable pointed to by the contents of *result*. In other words, during the call *result* and *double* are effectively synonymous; a statement updating *result* will be an update to *double*. Because the means of communication between a formal **var** parameter is by address, i.e. by reference, this method is called **passing a parameter by reference**.

The two models have illustrated the two methods of parameter communication: passing by value, where values are copied to the formal parameters, and passing by reference, where the communication is by address. In theory, programmers should not need to concern themselves with these details. What they require is a facility whereby each parameter can be described according to its role as either source data, results or both. In the programming language ADA this is achieved by specifying each parameter as either **in**, **out** or **in/out**. The use of these terms carries no implication as to whether a parameter will be passed by value or by reference. So, you may well ask, how does ADA decide which parameter passing method to adopt and why does it matter? To answer this, suppose the parameter *x* of the procedure *copydouble* had, say, 1 000 elements. This parameter is source data only, and so in Pascal is a value parameter and in ADA would be an **in** parameter. In Pascal, the array would be passed by value and that would involve copying all 1 000 elements. This has a high cost both in terms of memory space and execution time. An experienced Pascal programmer would recognize these overheads and might circumvent them by declaring *x* to be a **var** parameter, thereby getting the array passed by reference. If this was done, the routine declaration would make it look as if this parameter corresponded to results when it does not (because it is declared as a **var** parameter). But worse, the security of the procedure is at risk because any update to one of the elements of *x* within the procedure body would be reflected as a change in the actual parameter *single*. Such an update might be intended or accidental, but in any event it contravenes the specification that the source parameter is unaltered by the procedure. In contrast, the ADA programmer does not have to be concerned with how the array is passed because the compiler takes the decision. So, for this large array it would pass it by reference and for a smaller one it would pass it by value. Any attempt by the programmer to exploit the fact that the large array is passed by reference to update the contents of *single* from within the procedure would be thwarted. This is because an error condition would be generated by virtue of the fact that the parameter is specified as an **in** parameter.

This model has enabled us to see how the system distinguishes between formal and actual parameters even when the same identifiers are used for both. It also shows how local variables are used and how the values of the local variables are no longer available on conclusion of the call. What it has not done is to give precise rules governing the use of multiple copies of the same identifier, nor has it explained how identifiers like *maxsize* in Exercise 8.9, which are neither parameters nor local variables, are accessible within routines. The rules that govern these issues are called **scope rules**, and they are concerned with all identifiers, be they related to constants, types, variables, procedures, functions, parameters or whatever. The first rule is as follows:

Scope Rule 1
No identifier may be declared more than once in the same block.

The term 'block' in this definition corresponds to the combination of the syntactic terms < block > and < formal parameter list >. It is probably easier to think of block as used here, in the diagrammatic form of Figure 8.10, in which detailed coding has been removed for clarity.

```
program exercise;

    const
       maxsize = 10;
    type
       arraytype = array[1..maxsize] of string;
    var
       strarray: arraytype;
       i        : 1..maxsize;

    procedure reverse( var given: arraytype);

       var
          index: 1..maxsize;
          temp : string;
       begin
          :
       end;   {procedure reverse}

    begin   {main program}
       :
    end .
```

Figure 8.10 A program with scope blocks identified

The reason for Scope Rule 1 is obvious: if an identifier could be declared twice in the same block then each occurrence of that identifier would be ambiguous. However, the rule does not exclude the possibility of declaring the same identifier more than once, provided that the declaration is in a different block. So, in Figure 8.10 the identifier *index* could be replaced by the identifier *i* because the declarations are in different blocks. If this was to be done then the programmer needs to know which version of *i* can be referenced at any particular point in the program. An identifier that can be referenced at a particular point in a program is said to be **in scope** at that point. Scope Rule 2 defines the scope of an identifier.

Scope Rule 2

An identifier may be referenced only within the block in which it is declared or defined. Its scope extends from its declaration to the end of the block.

If we examine this rule in the context of Figure 8.10 we can see that the scope of the parameter *given* extends from its declaration to the end of its block – namely to the end of the procedure *reverse*. Similarly, *index* and *temp* extend from their declaration to the end of this block. This means that none of these identifiers can be referenced outside this block and therefore they are not accessible to the main program block. Their use is bounded to within the box of Figure 8.9 and they are said to be **local to** *reverse*.

The situation for the identifier *arraytype* is slightly more complex. Its scope extends from its definition to the end of its block – that is, to the end of the main program block. This effectively means its scope is the whole program, including the procedure *reverse*. Identifiers whose scope extends over the whole program are often described as **global** identifiers. It is because the scope of *arraytype* includes the procedure *reverse* that *given* can be declared to be of type *arraytype*. Informally, we could say that *arraytype* is visible within *reverse*.

In the same way, the identifiers *i* and *strarray* are also global and are therefore visible within *reverse*. More surprisingly, the identifier *reverse* is also in scope within this block and so could be referenced within it. This implies that the function *reverse* can reference *reverse*, that is, it can make a function call to itself! The ability of a routine to be able to call itself is called **recursion**, which we shall be studying in Chapter 15.

Suppose now we change the identifier *index* to *i*. (We shall continue to refer to it as *index* so that you can tell which identifier we are referring to.) This is legal by Scope Rule 1, but Scope Rule 2 would seem to imply that both *index* (now called *i*) and *i* can both be referenced within *reverse*. Scope Rule 3 resolves this potential ambiguity.

Scope Rule 3

If an identifier is (legally) declared more than once, then the occurrence currently in scope is the one in the smallest surrounding block.

Thus, within the procedure *reverse*, the *i* that is in scope is the one previously called *index* whereas *elsewhere* it is the other version of *i*. We say that within *reverse* the variable *i* has been **locally redeclared**.

Exercise 8.15 Determine which identifiers are in scope in each of the blocks in the following program. Distinguish between those which are local to the block and those which are not.

```
program powers;
const
   constant = 10;
type
   small = 1..constant;
var
   x : real;
procedure one(formal1 : real; var formal2 : real);
   var
     actual1 : small;
```

```
function two(value : real):real;
  var
    x : integer;
  begin   {function two}
    :
  end;      {function two}
begin {procedure one}
  :
end;   {procedure one}
function three;
  begin   {function three}
    :
  end;      {function three}
begin {main program}
  :
end.     {main program}
```

The solution to Exercise 8.15 illustrates an important point. Only identifiers declared or defined in the main program are truly global. Others are local to the routine in which they are defined. Thus, the adjective 'local' needs to be used with care and often needs qualifying to indicate to which routine it applies. Furthermore, when routines are nested one within another the innermost ones are only accessible to those in which they are contained.

One of the consequences of the scope rules is that a global variable can be referenced by any routine (except when it is redeclared locally). This can lead to problems, which we shall illustrate with the following program:

```
program side_effect;
var
  netpay, grosspay, taxdue, expenses : real;
procedure taxcalc(amount : real; var tax : real);
  {Pre : amount is a real value.
  {Post: tax is a real value.}
  begin
    tax := 0.25*amount;
    netpay := amount - tax
  end;
begin
  write('Enter the gross pay on which tax is due ');
  readln(grosspay);
  taxcalc(grosspay, taxdue);
  write('Enter any tax free expenses due ');
  readln(expenses);
  netpay := grosspay + expenses;
  writeln('Gross pay is ', grosspay:5:2);
  writeln('Net pay is ', netpay:5:2);
  writeln('Tax paid is ', taxdue:5:2)
end.
```

Exercise 8.16 Why does the reference to *netpay* in the procedure *taxcalc* not lead to an undeclared variable error?

The solution to Exercise 8.16 shows that the reference to and updating of the variable *netpay* within *taxcalc* is syntactically valid. Although the program produces the results required, it is very poorly designed. We can see why by examining the heading of the procedure *taxcalc*. It has two parameters, only one of which is a **var** parameter. We can therefore deduce that the actual parameter corresponding to *amount* will not be updated, while that corresponding to *tax* will be updated. This is what we might expect from the identifier used for the routine. What the heading fails to tell us is that the routine also updates *netpay*. Now, routines that update variables other than actual parameters corresponding to **var** parameters are very dangerous. One reason is because of the difficulty of their maintenance. A more realistic procedure for calculating tax would involve many more lines of code than in this simple illustration, and a line by line analysis would not be so obvious. When tested in isolation, the procedure would produce the correct tax due, but the fact that it also updated *netpay* might not immediately come to light.

A situation like this where a global variable (or more generally a non-local variable) is updated by a routine is called a **side-effect** and is a result of poor design. Side-effects can be avoided by ensuring that any variable which is updated by a routine is included as one of the **var** parameters. It is Scope Rule 2 that enables non-local variables to be referenced and so you may ask why Pascal introduces a rule, which would at worst encourage poor design style or at best not discourage it. This seems to contrast with, for example, Pascal's approach to types that are very restrictive and do not allow the assignment of a value to a variable of a different type. Surely it would be better to adopt a similar approach with scope rules and formulate them in such a way that a block is only allowed to reference the identifiers that it declares locally. Then side-effects would be syntactically invalid and would be detected by the compiler. There are some writers who believe that this approach should be adopted. However, one consequence of this would be that global constant and type definition identifiers could not be available for use in local routine declarations. Another difficulty arises with routines which have very long parameter lists – their clarity is lessened by such lists. We shall take the view that side-effects should be avoided and any data required by a routine should be passed into it using the parameter passing mechanism.

8.9 EXERCISES

Exercise 8.17 Determine which identifiers are in scope in each of the blocks in the program *guessgame* of Section 8.6.3. Distinguish between those which are local to the block and those which are not.

Exercise 8.18 Determine which identifiers are in scope in each of the blocks in the program *guessgame2* of Section 8.6.3. Distinguish between those which are local to the block and those which are not.

8.10 PARAMETER COMPATIBILITY

Actual parameters corresponding to **var** formal parameters must be declared using the same type identifier. In simple terms this means that if a **var** formal parameter is of type *integer* then so must be the corresponding actual parameter. However, this is rather too restricting when it comes to value parameters. Suppose we have a routine with a single *real* formal value parameter, then we would want to be able to pass to an *integer* value to it. That this is permitted means that there have to be rules governing what is permissible and what is not. The types of two value parameters are compatible if:

- The formal and actual parameters are name equivalent.
- The formal and actual parameters are both subranges of the same base type. Run-time errors will occur if values outside the subrange are encountered.
- A value formal parameter is *real* and the actual parameter value is *integer.*
- A value formal parameter is *string* and the actual parameter value is *char.*
- A value formal parameter is a string and the actual parameter value is a string of different static length. If the static length of the formal parameter is exceeded then the actual value is truncated.

The first of these rules is the one that should normally apply – namely, the parameters must be declared using the same type identifier. The second allows values of one subrange type to be passed to parameters that have the same base type but a different range. For example, given the following declarations:

```
type
   short = 5..10;
   long  = 1..100;
var
   x : long;
procedure range(a : short);
```

it would be permissible to call *range* with the actual value 6. However, if a value like 20, which lies outside the range of *short*, is passed a run-time error will occur.

The third rule allows an integer value to be passed to a *real* value parameter. The integer value could of course be an expression that evaluates to an integer. Thus, integer values are said to be assignment compatible with *real* variables. The fourth rule says that any *char* value can be passed to a string parameter and the fifth rule generalizes this to strings of any static length. Should the static length of the formal parameter be insufficient for the actual parameter value, then the actual value is truncated to fit.

8.11 PROGRAMMING HINTS

Data that are required by a routine should be specified as source data. Data that are required to be altered by a routine should be specified as source data and results. All source data and results should then be implemented using parameters. Routines should include, as a comment at the beginning of the routine declaration, the pre- and postconditions that apply to the source data and results. Routines should be specified so that they only perform a single operation. For example, the first routine in this chapter was the procedure *monthdays*, which was concerned with finding the number of days in a given month. It neither read in the value for the month on which data were sought nor wrote out the computed result. Notice that *monthdays* did not display an error message in the event that the month was an illegal value. It returned a flag to indicate that an error had occurred so that the calling program could report the error. Routines that perform a single operation are called **cohesive** routines. It is good programming style to write cohesive procedures as it keeps the code relatively simple, easy to read and write, and most important, easy to maintain. Having said that, it will not always be the case that routines in which error conditions can occur will employ an error flag. Using an extra parameter for error conditions can itself add to complexity, and so there will be situations where we choose to deal with errors as they arise within the routine itself. With this potential exception you should endeavour to write cohesive routines.

Routines should be thoroughly tested and debugged before being incorporated into the program for which they are required. This will involve writing a specific driver program to test all aspects of the procedure. Driver programs do not have to be too sophisticated, but the small investment in writing them pays off by reducing the time spent debugging a large program that contains several procedures which have not been separately tested.

(a) Guideline (function) If a routine has a single result of simple type then it should be implemented as a function.

(b) Guideline (procedure heading) The form of a procedure heading is the reserved word **procedure**, followed by the procedure's identifier, followed by the formal parameters enclosed in braces, followed by a semicolon.

(c) Guideline (procedure formal parameters) Parameters are declared in a list, the components of which are separated by semicolons. Each component has the form: an identifier list (each identifier being separated by a comma), followed by a colon, followed by a type identifier. Parameters of structured type must be declared using a type identifier. Results parameters must be preceded by the word **var**.

(d) Guideline (function heading) The form of a procedure heading is the reserved word **function**, followed by the procedure's identifier, followed by the formal parameters enclosed in braces, followed by a colon, followed by a simple type.

(e) Guideline (formal parameters) Parameters are declared in a list, the components of which are separated by semicolons. Each component has the form: an identifier list (each identifier being separated by a comma), followed by a colon, followed by a type identifier. Parameters of structured type must be declared using a type identifier; **var** should not be used.

(f) Guideline (routine declaration) Routines are declared immediately after the **var** declarations. A routine declaration consists of a routine heading, followed by the local declarations in the usual order, **const**, **type**, **var** (and potentially procedure). Finally, there is the compound statement corresponding to the procedure body. The word **end** of this compound statement is followed by a semicolon.

8.12 SUMMARY

In this chapter we have looked at the implementation of procedures and functions. A function should be used to implement a routine which has a single result of simple type. Routine declarations follow the **var** declarations, but the order in which they are made will be determined by the semantics of the program. Routines may also be nested, one within another. The structure of procedure and function declarations is very similar and differs only in the routine headings.

9

SEPARATE COMPILATION AND FILES

A desirable feature of a programming language that supports modular design is its ability to allow the individual routines to be separately compiled. The reason for this is that it enables separate parts of a complex program to be developed and tested independently of the rest of the code. Another advantage is that libraries of routines can be built up and used by other programs, thereby minimizing the development time of subsequent programs and maximizing their reliability. We have already seen an example of a library of separately compiled routines when we introduced the unit *crt* in Chapter 8. It provides many routines concerned with the manipulation of the screen. Finally, separately compiled units contribute to what is known as **data hiding**, where some implementation details are deliberately hidden from a main program. This will be explored in more detail in later chapters. As separately compiled units are stored in files we shall also be looking at file structures in Pascal. The naming conventions for files will be those of MSDOS and will therefore be presented as upper case characters only.

Separate compilation was not an available facility when the original standard for Pascal was written. A consequence of this is that there is no uniform approach across different Pascal implementations. Thus, there will be syntactic differences between implementations. However, many of them have a similar structure to the Turbo Pascal version that we describe below.

9.1 PASCAL UNITS

We have already seen how a program declares its intention to use a separately compiled unit. The following program fragment should remind you:

```
program guessgame;
uses crt;
```

The **uses** statement tells the compiler that a separately compiled unit is going to be used. Separately compiled units are very similar to programs. In particular, a unit has an identifier and the code of which it comprises is stored in a file. When we write our own units, the identifier will be both the file name under which the code is stored and the identifier of the unit itself. Although Turbo Pascal does not force this dual use of identifier on us, it does simplify matters. A drawback of using it is that the eight-character restriction on file names imposed by the MSDOS operating system means that unit identifiers have to be similarly restricted. This will lead to some rather abbreviated unit identifiers.

Throughout this chapter we shall assume that files corresponding to Pascal units and those corresponding to programs are stored in the same directory. In this way, we can avoid the problems associated with telling the compiler that unit files and program files are stored under different directories. The **uses** statement is actually part of a program's declarations and so we can update the syntax diagram for < declarations > to reflect this (Figure 9.1).

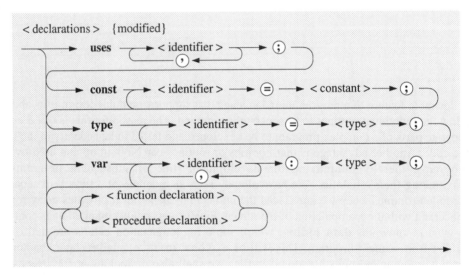

Figure 9.1 The syntax of < declarations >

We shall begin by seeing how a separately compiled unit is written and then look again at the details required by a program that uses it. The code opposite is for a Pascal unit called *uDataIni* which is stored in a file called UDATAINI.PAS. Study the details before reading the description below.

This has a structure that is somewhat different from those we have seen so far. Essentially, it consists of two major parts:

(a) An **interface** part:
This contains the definitions and declarations. In this example there are **const** and **type** definitions and a **procedure** declaration. In general, the interface can contain any of the variety of definitions and declarations we have seen so far. Note that in the interface part only the procedure heading is present – it is not accompanied by its body. It is the identifiers in this part that are available to programs which use the unit. We shall say that the unit **exports** the identifiers in the interface part and a program which uses the unit **imports** the identifiers.

(b) An **implementation** part:

This includes the bodies for each of the routines declared in the interface but, as we shall see, it can contain much more besides. Here, there is only the one routine from the interface that needs implementing, but in general there will be many. The routine body is preceded by a shortened form of routine heading that omits the formal parameter list. The local declarations and compound statement for the routine follow this shortened heading. The **end** corresponding to the end of the procedure's compound statement *is* followed by a semicolon even though the following word is also **end**.

```
unit uDataIni;

interface
  const
    maxsize = 10;
  type
    range     = 1..maxsize;
    arraytype = array[range] of string;
  procedure initialize(var given : arraytype);

implementation
  procedure initialize;
    {(var given : arraytype)
     Pre : None.
     Post: All elements of given are initialized to the null string.}
    var
      i : range;
    begin
      for i := 1 to maxsize do
        begin
          write('Enter data for element ', i, ' ');
          readln(given[i])
        end
    end; {procedure initialize. Note the semicolon here}
end. {implementation part}
```

Finally, the unit is terminated with **end.** in just the same way that a program is. That a unit exports the identifiers in the interface part can be made explicit by means of a comment as illustrated below.

```
unit uDataIni;

interface
  {Exports: maxsize, range, arraytype and initialize}
  const
    maxsize = 10;
  type
    range     = 1..maxsize;
    arraytype = array[range] of string;
  procedure initialize(var given : arraytype);

implementation
  procedure initialize;
    :
```

Unless the interface is particularly complex the comment is not likely to improve the clarity of the code. Remember that only the identifiers in the interface are exported – any identifiers appearing in the implementation part remain private to that part. The overall structure of a unit is given in Figure 9.2.

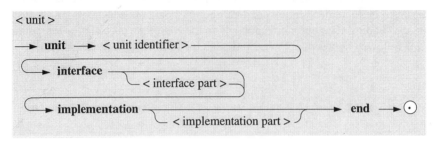

Figure 9.2 The syntax of < unit >

We can see from this that the reserved words **interface** and **implementation** are mandatory but that the code associated with each is optional. This means that a unit can have an empty interface part or an empty implementation. The < interface part > has the syntax specified in Figure 9.3.

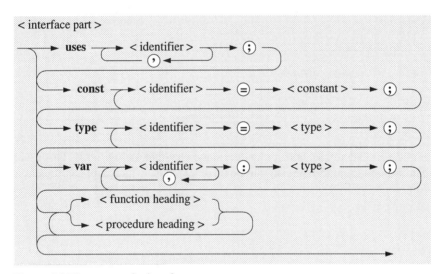

Figure 9.3 The syntax of < interface part >

This diagram is virtually the same as that of < declarations > in Figure 9.1. The only difference is that here the routines declare only their headings and not their bodies. It also tells us that the interface part of a unit is the same as the declarations part of a program. So an interface can include a **uses** statement, can make **const**, **type** and **var** declarations and can declare procedure headings. The case study in Section 9.3 includes illustrations that include most of these possibilities.

The interface part has the syntax shown in Figure 9.4.

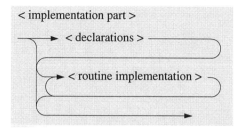

Figure 9.4 The syntax of < implementation part >

We remind you that < declarations > is as defined in Figure 9.1 so that the implementation part may also invoke a Pascal unit with a **uses** statement, may make **const**, **type** and **var** declarations and may declare local procedures (both heading and body). The latter are, of course, not the routines declared in the interface part. Following this are the routine implementations for the routines declared in the interface part. The form of these implementations is the same as for any routine declaration except that the formal parameters are not listed in the heading. Figure 9.5 states this explicitly.

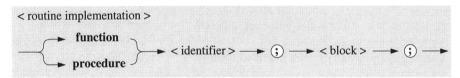

Figure 9.5 The syntax of < routine implementation >

- Guideline (unit declaration) A unit declaration consists of two parts: an interface part and an implementation part. The interface part must contain declarations for all the identifiers that are to be exported, but it should only contain routine headings (not bodies). The implementation part may declare any identifiers required in the implementation of the routines declared in the interface. A unit always terminates with **end.** which must be preceded by a semicolon.

We can now turn our attention to a program that uses a unit. We shall use the unit *uDataIni*, given above, and assume that it has been compiled to a file of the same name. Turbo Pascal appends the extension .TPU to code files corresponding to units, and so the compiled code corresponding to the unit *uDataIni* will be stored in a file UDATAINI.TPU. Consider the following program fragment:

```
program illustration;
uses crt, uDataIni;
  {Imports clrscr from unit crt
   Imports from unit uDataIni
    const
      maxsize = 10
    type
      range    = 1..maxsize
      arraytype = array[range] of string
    procedure initialize(var given : arraytype)}
```

```
var
  names, addresses : arraytype;
procedure writelabels(title, location : arraytype);
  var
    i : range;
  begin
    :
  end;   {procedure writelabels}
begin   {main program}
  clrscr;
  initialize(names);
  initialize(addresses);
  writelabels(names, addresses);
    :
end.
```

This program uses the library unit *crt* and the unit *uDataIni*. Below the **uses** statement we have included a comment which informs us of the identifiers that are imported with these units. All the identifiers listed in this comment can be accessed by the program *illustration*, and can be thought of as global program identifiers. This explains how the variables *names* and *addresses* can be declared to be of type *arraytype*. On the face of it, *arraytype* would appear to be an undeclared identifier because it does not appear explicitly as a declaration within the code. That it is imported from *uDataIni* is not obvious without looking at the interface for the unit. We shall adopt the convention of including a comment after a **uses** statement that lists the imported identifiers. When the list consists of a sequence of declarations, as in the above example, we shall suspend our usual typographical conventions of using bold for reserved words so that the comment is not confused with actual declarations. To emphasize the point further we shall not include semicolons in such a listing.

When a unit declares the use of more than one unit, the scope of the identifiers contained in their interfaces is rather more subtle than the previous paragraph has suggested. Each unit in a **uses** clause imposes a new scope which encloses the remaining units and the entire program. The first unit in the **uses** clause represents the outermost scope and the last unit represents the innermost scope. In the example above, the identifiers contained in the interface of *crt* have outermost scope and those of *uDataIni* the innermost scope. This can be represented pictorially as in Figure 9.6.

Here, we can see that *clrscr* is in the outermost block, the identifiers from *uDataIni* are in an inner block and then comes the familiar program block with its nested inner blocks. We can use this diagram to illustrate what happens if two or more units declare the same identifier. Scope Rule 3 will be used to determine which identifier is in scope at any particular place. Suppose that *crt* declares an identifier *maxsize*. The one that is in scope in the main program is the one representing the constant value 10, because the smallest surrounding block contains its definition. Now suppose the identifier *maxsize* in Figure 9.6 was changed to *clrscr*. What would a reference to *clrscr* be taken to mean in the main program? The reference would be the definition in the smallest surrounding block, that is, the block of unit *uDataIni*. Hence the reference would be to the constant value 10. A consequence of using this identifier is, of course, that there is now no procedure available for clearing the screen because we have redefined the meaning of *clrscr*.

```
Imports from crt;
  clrscr

    Imports from unit uDataIni
    const
      maxsize = 10
    type
      range = 1..maxsize
      arraytype = array[range] of string
    procedure initialize

      program exercise;

      uses crt, uDataIni;

      var
        names, addresses : arraytype;

      procedure writelabels( title, location : arraytype );

        var
          i : 1..maxsize;

        begin
          :
        end;   {procedure writelabels}

      begin   {main program}
        :
      end .
```

Figure 9.6 Scope for a program which uses units

Exercise 9.1 The unit *crt* includes a procedure called *clreol*. Suppose we had not remembered, or indeed not even known about this procedure, and had inadvertently used this identifier in place of the identifier *names*. What would be the outcome?

The solution to Exercise 9.1 shows that if an identifier appears in a main program as well as a unit that it uses, then the redefined version of the main program is the one in scope in the main program body. This is convenient for situations when you might not know or remember all the identifiers in a large unit – ignorance is bliss!

Exercise 9.2 Suppose the author of unit *uDataIni* does not know that the unit *crt* also includes a function called *delay*. What would have been the outcome if the author now uses this identifier rather than *maxsize* when writing the unit?

It is because of the potential for a unit identifier to be redefined by a program that it is a good practice to list all the imported identifiers in a comment under the **uses** statement. In this way it is clear to a reader which external identifiers the program is calling upon.

We conclude this section with some remarks on compilation. A unit must be compiled before a program that uses it. When the unit is a library unit, as is the case with *crt*, this compilation has already been done and is part of the system. Units you write yourself have to be done explicitly. If a program uses several units then all must be compiled before the program. Unless the units themselves use each other the order in which they are compiled does not matter. In Section 9.3 we shall give an example of where units use other units, and so the order of compilation will be important.

- Guideline (unit compilation) A unit must be compiled before a program which uses it is compiled.

A Pascal unit is often designed to be used in many different applications programs. Indeed, that is the purpose of library units like *crt*. This reusability is one of the most powerful features of units. Collections of routines can be tested and built up in a unit and then compiled. Exploiting an existing unit then removes the need for testing the code relating to it and simplifies the development of programs.

9.2 PASCAL FILES

Files are the means whereby data are stored permanently on disk. The Turbo Pascal environment has facilities for making permanent file copies of program source code and program compiled code. The use of an integrated environment like that of Turbo Pascal hides the details of the file manipulation from the user. Usually, to retrieve a file or write one to disk, all these systems require is a file name. One type of file that you may not have recognized as a file before is keyboard input. It is called a **standard input file**. In the same way, there are standard output files, usually the screen. However, the keyboard and the screen are not always the most useful files for the input and output of data into memory. For programs with much input data it may be more convenient to read it from a disk rather than entering it from the keyboard. Similarly, if a program produces lots of output then disk may again be more convenient. In either case, if a permanent copy of the data is required then disk storage is essential. If data produced by one program are to be used as input to another then disk storage is also required.

The facilities described in this section are only available in Turbo Pascal. Its file handling is far from standard, so unlike most of the material in this book, what we describe here is not extensible to other implementations of the language. For this reason we give only a superficial treatment to the subject.

9.2.1 Text files

A text file enables values of type *char*, *integer*, *real*, *string* or *Boolean* to be written to a file. The program below stores the integer values 1 to 10 in a file called DATAFILE on the default directory of the default drive. Study the code before reading the commentary below.

```
program testfile;
var
  intfile : text;
  intdata : integer;
begin
  assign(intfile, 'DATAFILE');
  rewrite(intfile);
  for intdata := 1 to 10 do
    writeln(intfile, intdata);
  close(intfile)
end.
```

The type *text* that appears in the **var** part declares *intfile* to be a variable of type *text*, that is, it declares it to be an **internal** text file variable. The word internal is important here because it is through this variable that the communication takes place between the internal memory and the file on disk. In the compound statement the identifier *assign* corresponds to a built-in procedure whose task is to associate the internal file variable *intfile* with the external file that here is called DATAFILE. Any program that wishes to make use of a file must have an *assign* statement. The next statement, *rewrite(intfile)*, creates and opens a file in preparation for writing to it. The procedure *rewrite* creates the external file DATAFILE. If a file with this name already exists it is deleted and a new empty file is created in its place. Data are sent to the file using the procedure *writeln* with two parameters, the first of which is the internal file variable and the second a variable of *integer* type which holds the value to be stored. Finally, the statement *close(intfile)* closes the file. All files must eventually be closed before program execution ends. It ensures that the external file is completely updated and that the operating system has completed its part of the file writing.

Exercise 9.3 Write an analogous program to store the real numbers 1.5, 2.5, ..., 10.5 in an external file called MYFILE.

The program in Exercise 9.3 and the program above are remarkably similar. The same type of file is being used to store different types of data. In fact, *text* files are able to distinguish what type of data is to be stored and the appropriate representation is used. The user is unaware of the particular storage details, the procedure *writeln* doing the conversion into the representation in which the value is stored. Either program could be modified so that it could store *char*, *string* or *Boolean* values. The program below retrieves data stored in DATAFILE back into main memory.

```
program getdata;
var
  intfile : text;
  intdata : integer;
begin
  assign(intfile, 'DATAFILE');
  reset(intfile);
  while not eof(intfile) do
    begin
      readln(intfile, intdata);
      writeln(intdata)
    end;
  close(intfile)
end.
```

As before, the internal file has to be associated with the external file DATAFILE using the *assign* procedure. This time the file has to be opened ready for reading and the statement to do this is *reset(intfile)*. In general, it is not known how many data items are stored in a file and so a special function is provided which determines the end of the file. The function is denoted by *eof*, which stands for *end of file*. So the loop executes while the end of the file has not been encountered. Data are retrieved from the disk using the *readln* procedure. Note how it too has two parameters when used in this way. The first parameter corresponds to the internal file variable identifier and the second is the variable into which the value is to be transferred. In this program the value is then written immediately to the screen, but in general other processing would take place.

Exercise 9.4 Write a program to retrieve the data stored in MYFILE from Exercise 9.3.

The procedure *write* can be used to write unstructured data values to a file and *read* can be used to retrieve them from a file. However, problems can arise in keeping distinct values apart when using these routines. For example, the sequence of integers 1, 2, 3 when stored in a text file using *read* would be stored as 123. To keep them separate, action has to be taken by the program doing the storage. For this reason it is probably easier to use *writeln*, in which case the system puts an end of line marker between the entries, which then means that a *readln* will read up as far as the end of line, thereby keeping the entries separate.

9.2.2 Data type files

The file type *text* does not allow data of structured type to be stored. Instead, Turbo provides a structured file type. Study the illustrative program below before reading the commentary.

```
program structfile;
type
   rectype = record
                name  : string;
                telno : string[10]
              end;
   filetype = file of rectype;
var
   data    : rectype;
   teldir : filetype;
begin
   assign(teldir, 'TELEPHONE');
   rewrite(teldir);
   repeat
     write('Enter a name or zzz to quit ');
     readln(data.name);
     if data.name <> 'zzz' then
       begin
         write('Enter the telephone number ');
         readln(data.telno);
         write(teldir, data)
       end
   until data.name = 'zzz';
   close(teldir)
end.
```

This program first defines *rectype* to be a record type. A file consisting of this type is defined using the reserved words **file of**, followed by an identifier corresponding to the structure. The internal file variable must be associated with an external file using the procedure *assign*, and the file must be opened for writing using the *rewrite* command. In this program data are entered into a record, *data*, which is then written to the external file using *write*. The first parameter of *write* is the internal file name and the second is the identifier of the record to be stored. Note that the procedure which writes to the external file is *write* and not *writeln*. For structured file types only *write* can be used. Once all the data have been read in, the file is closed with *close*. The program below reads the file TELEPHONE and outputs each record to the screen.

```
program readstructfile;
type
  rectype = record
              name  : string;
              telno : string[10]
            end;
  filetype = file of rectype;
var
  data   : rectype;
  teldir : filetype;
begin
  assign(teldir, 'TELEPHONE');
  reset(teldir);
  while not eof(teldir) do
    begin
      read(teldir, data);
      writeln(data.name, ' ', data.telno)
    end;
  close(teldir)
end.
```

The only new point here is that structured data are retrieved from a file using *read* in which the first parameter is the internal file name and the second is a variable of suitable structured type. The procedure *readln* cannot be used to read data from a structured file.

- Guideline (structured file) A data value of structured type must be written to a file using *write*. The first parameter of *write* must be the internal file identifier, the second must be an identifier of the variable of the type being stored. It is an error to attempt to use *writeln* for this purpose.

9.3 CASE STUDY

In this section we shall have a look at a substantial piece of code to see how separate compilation can be used to aid program development. The application is a word processor in which we have made many simplifications to reduce the complexity of the code. Essentially, the user will be restricted to the following menu of possible commands (Figure 9.7):

```
Choose an option in the range 1 - 8

    1 Enter new text

    2 Add to existing text

    3 Display text

    4 Change text

    5 Format text

    6 Save

    7 Load

    8 Quit

Choice is ?
```

Figure 9.7 Case study word processor menu

Each of the options will be developed as a procedure having a name that describes its purpose. Furthermore, related procedures will be grouped together in units as follows. There will be a unit called *udefns* which contains the data structures required to store the text. A unit called *ueditor* will be used for procedures related to text manipulation and will contain a procedure *enter* which will be used for options 1 and 2 and a procedure *change* which will cover option 4. A unit called *uscreen* will be concerned with screen activities and will have a procedure called *display* whose purpose is to write out the text on the screen and a procedure called *menu* whose purpose is to handle the menu of Figure 9.7. A unit called *ufile* will handle the file storage of options 6 and 7 using procedures called *loadall* and *saveall*. Finally, a unit called *uformat* will contain the code for a procedure *format* whose purpose will be to output the text to the screen so that it is both left and right justified. This is developed as a separate unit because of its complexity.

It is not the intention of this section to design a solution to this problem. Here, we are interested in how to assemble the code contained in the separate units. Thus, what we shall do is to present the code and follow it by a description of what it does. We begin with the unit *udefns*. Most word processors use special keys to enable the user to position the cursor anywhere on the screen and to enter text at the cursor position. This is rather complex, and so to simplify the problem we shall develop what is known as a **line-oriented editor**, which means that each line must be entered in its entirety, followed by the next line and so on. By imposing this restriction we can store the individual lines of text in an array. The definitions below give the details.

As we can see, the text will be stored in an array whose elements are strings of maximum length 75. Again, for simplicity, we shall only allow 10 lines of text to be stored. This will mean that the complete text can be output on one screen and so we shall not be concerned with screen scrolling. The type *text_array* will be used to define an array *prose* whose purpose is to store the text. Many of the procedures will have, as source data, the text to be processed, and the same identifier will be used for the formal parameter corresponding to these source data. Many of the procedures will also need to know how many lines of text have been entered. The identifier *linesinput* will be used to denote this quantity. The main program code below shows these definitions.

```
unit udefns;
interface
  const
    stringsize = 75;
    maxlines  = 10;
    null      = '';
    space     = ' ';

  type
    indexrange = 1..maxlines;
    linesrange = 0..maxlines;
    sentence   = string[stringsize];
    text_array = array[indexrange] of sentence;
implementation

end. {of implementation of udefns}




program main;
uses udefns, uscreen, ueditor, ufile, uformat;

  {Imports from udefns
      constants
       stringsize = 75, maxlines = 10, null = '', space = ' '
      types
       indexrange = 1..maxlines, linesrange = 0..maxlines, sentence = string[stringsize]
       text_array = array[indexrange] of sentence
   Imports from ueditor
     procedure enter (var prose : text_array; var linesinput : linesrange)
     procedure change(var prose : text_array;     linesinput : linesrange)
   Imports from uscreen
     procedure menu(var choice : char)
     procedure display(prose : text_array; linesinput : linesrange)
     procedure getret
   Imports from uformat
     procedure format(prose : text_array; linesinput : linesrange)
   Imports from ufile
    procedure saveall(prose:text_array; linesinput:linesrange)
    procedure loadall(var prose:text_array; var linesinput:linesrange)}

var
  choice    : char;
  prose     : text_array;
  linesinput : linesrange;
begin
  linesinput := 0;
  repeat
    menu(choice);
    writeln;
    case choice of
      '1' : begin
              linesinput := 0;
              enter(prose, linesinput);
            end;
      '2' : enter(prose, linesinput);
      '3' : begin
```

```
            display(prose, linesinput);
            write('Press <ret> to continue ');
            getret;
          end;
    '4' : change(prose, linesinput);
    '5' : format(prose, linesinput);
    '6' : saveall(prose, linesinput);
    '7' : loadall(prose, linesinput);
  end;
until  choice = '8'
end.
```

The long comment after the **uses** statement describes all the global identifiers that are inherited by this program from the unit interfaces. With the exception of *getret* the identifiers of the procedures should enable you to infer their purpose in terms of the available menu options. The purpose of the procedure *getret* is to read the keyboard until a <ret> is entered. The unit *uscreen* includes the code for this procedure as well as that of *menu* and *display*.

```
unit uscreen;
interface
  uses udefns;  {Imports constant and type definitions}
  procedure menu(var choice : char);
  procedure display(prose : text_array; linesinput : linesrange);
  procedure getret;

implementation
  uses crt;  {Imports from crt: clrscr, readkey}
  procedure menu;
    {(var choice : char)
     Pre : None.
     Post: choice has one of the values '1'..'8'.}
    begin
      repeat
        clrscr;
        writeln;
        writeln('        MAIN menu');
        writeln;
        writeln('Choose an option in the range 1 - 8');
        writeln;
        writeln('   1 Enter new text');
        writeln;
        writeln('   2 Add to existing text');
        writeln;
        writeln('   3 Display text');
        writeln;
        writeln('   4 Change text');
        writeln;
        writeln('   5 Format text');
        writeln;
        writeln('   6 Save');
        writeln;
        writeln('   7 Load');
        writeln;
        writeln('   8 Quit');
```

```
      writeln;
      write('Choice is ? ');
      choice := readkey
    until  choice in ['1'..'8','c'..'f','C'..'F','a','A','s','S','l','L','q','Q'];
    case choice of
    'e', 'E' : choice := '1';
    'a', 'A' : choice := '2';
    'd', 'D' : choice := '3';
    'c', 'C' : choice := '4';
    'f', 'F' : choice := '5';
    's', 'S' : choice := '6';
    'l', 'L' : choice := '7';
    'q', 'Q' : choice := '8'
    end;
    writeln(choice)
  end;

procedure display;
  {(prose : text_array; linesinput : linesrange)
   Pre : linesinput is an initialized value in the range 0..maxlines inclusive.
   Post: None - the array prose is written to the screen.}
  var
    i : integer;
  begin
    clrscr;
    if linesinput <> 0 then
      begin
        for i := 1 to linesinput do
          writeln(prose[i]);
        writeln;
      end
    else
      writeln('No text has been entered so there is nothing to display')
  end; {procedure display}

procedure getret;
  {no parameters
   Pre : None.
   Post: None - processing awaits press of <ret>.}
  var
    ch : char;
  begin
    repeat
      ch := readkey
    until (ord(ch) = 13)
  end;

end. {of implementation}
```

The procedure *menu* first clears the screen, then writes out the menu to it. The library procedure *clrscr* is used to clear the screen. Since this is stored in the unit *crt* the implementation part has to declare this by means of a **uses** statement. Note the positioning of this **uses** statement. It is in the implementation part because its use is private to the implementation. If it was declared in the interface then all the procedures in *crt* would then be available to all blocks of code that use *uscreen*. We will see another example of an implementation using a unit shortly. The body of *menu* permits a user to enter the first letter of the option in preference to the number. This is possible because all the options have unique initial letters. Either upper or lower case is permitted, but since the procedure must return a digit character a case statement is required to perform the conversion.

The procedure *display* writes the contents of *prose* to the screen. The parameter *linesinput* tells the procedure how many lines are currently stored so that it only outputs these lines. If no text has been entered, then a message to this effect is output instead.

The procedure *getret* uses the function *readkey*, which is a Turbo Pascal function. It reads the keyboard but does not echo the input to the screen. Here, all inputs are rejected until the <ret> is pressed (<ret> has ASCII code 13).

The next easiest unit to understand is *ufile* and we examine this now.

```pascal
unit ufile;
interface
  uses udefns; {Imports constant and type definitions}
  procedure saveall(prose:text_array; linesinput:linesrange);
  procedure loadall(var prose:text_array; var linesinput:linesrange);

implementation
  uses crt; {Imports from crt: clrscr, readkey}
  procedure saveall;
    {(prose:text_array; linesinput:linesrange)
    Pre : 0 <= linesinput <= maxsize.
    Post: linesinput elements of prose are stored in file whose name is input by user.
          No checks are carried out to see if this file name already exists.}
    var
      outfile : file of sentence;
      i       : linesrange;
      filename : string;
    begin
      write('Enter file name to store data ');
      readln(filename);
      assign(outfile, filename);
      rewrite(outfile);
      for i := 1 to linesinput do
        write(outfile, prose[i]);
      close(outfile)
    end; {of procedure saveall}

  procedure loadall;
    {(var prose:text_array; var linesinput:linesrange)
    Pre : 0 <= linesinput <= maxsize.
          The file name entered by user is assumed to exist.
          The file is assumed to hold data of the correct type.
          The file is assumed to contain no more than maxsize strings.
          A run-time error occurs if any of the above are violated.
    Post: If linesinput = 0 or user chooses to lose existing data then
            linesinput strings are read from the file into prose overwriting any
            existing data so that prose contains the linesinput strings
          otherwise no action is taken.}
    var
      infile : file of sentence;
      filename : string;
      ch : char;
```

```
begin
  ch := 'y';
  if linesinput <> 0 then
    begin
      write('Warning: existing data will be lost. Do you wish to continue y/n?');
      ch := readkey;
      writeln
    end;
  if (ch = 'y') or (ch = 'Y') then
    begin
      write('Enter file name from which to load data ');
      readln(filename);
      assign(infile, filename);
      reset(infile);
      linesinput := 0;
      while not eof(infile) do
        begin
          read(infile, prose[linesinput + 1]);
          linesinput := linesinput + 1;
        end;
      close(infile)
    end
end; {of procedure loadall}
end. {of implementation}
```

The purpose of the two procedures is self-explanatory. The procedure *saveall* does not carry out any checks to see if the file name entered by the user already exists. Furthermore, the file will be stored on the system's current drive and current directory. Only the first *linesinput* elements are copied to the file because these are the only ones that contain initialized values. The procedure *loadall* does make a rudimentary check that the user is not inadvertently overwriting existing text by loading data from a file. This is determined by the value of *linesinput*. A non-zero value means data are already stored in the array so the user is given the opportunity of aborting the loading of data from a file. No checks are carried out to see whether the file from which the data are to be retrieved exists.

Exercise 9.5 Why does the implementation part declare the use of the unit *crt*?

The unit *ueditor* contains two procedures, *enter* and *change*. The procedure *enter* enables text to be entered from the keyboard into the array elements. It is called by both options 1 and 2 of the main menu. Option 1 creates new text and so invokes *enter* in such a way that data are assigned to element 1, then to element 2 and so on. Option 2 invokes it so that data are entered into the first element after the existing text; the actual parameter *linesinput* passes the index of the last used element into the procedure. The procedure permits users to enter more than 75 characters per line but truncates them to 75 characters. Only 10 lines of text can be entered.

The procedure *change* is more complicated. It enables changes to be made to individual characters on a given line, but the amount of change is fairly limited. The user is prompted for a pattern string and then for a replacement string that will be substituted for the pattern. Should the specified pattern not be there, or the replacement result in a string of more than 75 characters, then no changes are carried out. Similarly, no changes are carried out if either the pattern string or the replacement string is null. Only the first occurrence of the pattern results in a change. Figure 9.8 illustrates a typical dialogue when the *change* option is chosen.

```
This is the first line.
This line will have some of its characters changed.
This is the third line.

Lines 1 - 3 contain text.
Enter a line number in this range or 0 to return to MAIN menu ? 2
Enter      pattern :will have
Enter replacement :has
New line  2 is     :This line has some of its characters changed.

Press <ret> to continue
```

Figure 9.8 A dialogue using the *change* option

The procedure *change* was developed by identifying some major components which were then coded as procedures. The line to be entered by the user must be obtained from the keyboard. This is achieved using a procedure called *linedata*. It validates that the user enters a line number corresponding to the existing lines of text. Next, two strings have to be entered by the user, one corresponding to the pattern, the other to the replacement. Both must contain 75 or fewer characters and neither is allowed to be null. These inputs are obtained using a procedure called *data*. Other than having an obvious parameter for the string entered by the user, it also has a string value parameter which enables this single procedure to output different prompts: one for the pattern, the other for the replacement. Following this, the substitution of the replacement string for the pattern has to be carried out. But before this is attempted it must be determined whether the pattern exists, and if it does, whether the substitution would result in an illegally long string. This is achieved by a procedure *replace*, which includes an enumeration type parameter indicating the status of the substitution. If the substitution is legal then it is carried out. Finally, a procedure *report* handles the reporting of the substitution to the screen by using the enumeration status value supplied by *replace*. If the substitution is successful then the new line is written to the screen, otherwise the cause of the failure is reported. The procedure *change* is then written as a sequence of calls to these procedures.

```
unit ueditor;
interface
  uses udefns; {Imports constant and type definitions}
  procedure enter (var prose : text_array; var linesinput : linesrange);
  procedure change(var prose : text_array;     linesinput : linesrange);
implementation
  uses crt, uscreen; {Imports clrscr from crt and getret from uscreen}
  procedure enter;
    {(var prose : text_array; var linesinput : linesrange)
     Pre : 0 <= linesinput <= maxsize.
     Post: 0 <= linesinput <= maxsize.
          linesinput elements of prose are initialized.}
    var
      temp : string[255];
    begin
```

```
      clrscr;
      if linesinput <> 0 then
        display(prose, linesinput);
      if linesinput < maxlines then
        begin
          write('Enter the text one line at a time up to a maximum of ');
          writeln(maxlines - linesinput, ' lines. ');
          writeln('Only ', stringsize, ' characters are permitted per line. ');
          writeln('No single word should exceed 20 characters.');
          writeln('Terminate input by typing <ret> twice.');
          repeat
            writeln;
            writeln('Enter line ', linesinput + 1);
            readln(temp);
            if length(temp) > stringsize then
              begin
                write('You input more than ', stringsize);
                writeln(' characters. The extra characters have been ignored');
                writeln('Your input line is taken as ');
                temp := copy(temp, 1, stringsize);
                writeln(temp)
              end;
            if (temp <> null) and (linesinput < maxlines) then
              begin
                linesinput := linesinput + 1;
                prose[linesinput] := temp
              end;
          until  (temp = null) or (linesinput = maxlines)
        end;
      if linesinput = maxlines then
        begin
          writeln('No more text can be entered. Press <ret> to continue');
          getret
        end
    end; {procedure enter}

procedure change;
  {(var prose : text_array; linesinput : linesrange)
   Pre : 0 <= linesinput <= maxsize.
   Post: 0 <= linesinput <= maxsize.
         An element of prose is potentially updated.}
  type
    possible = (ok, not_there, too_long);
  var
    line                     : linesrange;
    subject, substn, pattern : sentence;
    status                   : possible;
  procedure linedata(linesinput : indexrange; var linenumber : linesrange);
    {Pre : 1 <= linesinput <= maxsize.
     Post: 0 <= linenumber <= linesinput.}
    var
      line : integer;
    begin
      writeln('Lines 1 - ', linesinput, ' contain text.');
      write('Enter a line number in this range or 0 to return to MAIN menu ? ');
```

```
      readln(line);
    while not (line in [0..linesinput]) do
      begin
        write('Number must be in the range 0 - ', linesinput, ' Re-enter ? ');
        readln(line)
      end;
    linenumber := line
  end; {procedure linedata}
procedure data(message : string; var outstring : sentence);
  {Pre : message has value 'pattern' or 'replacement'.
   Post: outstring contains non-null replacement string of length <= 75.}
  var
    temp : string[255];
  begin
    repeat
      write('Enter ', message:11, ' :');
      readln(temp);
      if length(temp) = 0 then
        writeln('The ', message, ' string is null: Please try again');
      if length(temp) > stringsize then
        begin
          write('The ', message, ' string exceeds ');
          writeln(stringsize, ' characters, please try again')
        end
    until (length(temp) <= stringsize) and (length(temp) <> 0);
    outstring := temp
  end; {procedure data}
procedure replace(var subject : sentence; pattern, substn : sentence;
                      var status : possible);
  {Pre : subject, pattern and substn are all initialized non-null strings.
   Post: If pattern is not in subject set status to not_there and leave subject.
         If pattern is in subject but substitution would result in more than 75
           characters set status to too_long and leave subject.
         If pattern is in subject and substitution is legal then set status to ok
           and update subject by carrying out the replacement.}
  var
    position : integer;
  begin
    if length(subject) + length(substn ) - length(pattern) <= stringsize then
      begin
        position := pos(pattern, subject);
        if position = 0 then
          status := not_there
        else
          begin
            status := ok;
            delete(subject, position, length(pattern));
            insert(substn , subject, position)
          end
      end
    else
      status := too_long;
  end; {procedure replace}
```

```
procedure report(message : string);
  {Pre : message is a non-null string value.
   Post: None - message is output to screen and processing halts awaiting <ret>.}
  begin
    writeln(message);
    writeln;
    writeln('Press <ret> to continue ');
    getret
  end; {procedure report}

begin {procedure change}
  clrscr;
  if linesinput > 0 then
    begin
      display(prose, linesinput);
      linedata(linesinput, line);
      while line <> 0 do
        begin
          data('pattern', pattern);
          data('substn ', substn );
          replace(prose[line], pattern, substn  , status);
          case status of
            ok       : begin
                          write('New line ', line:2, ' is :');
                          report(prose[line])
                       end;
            too_long : report('Replacement too long so no changes made');
            not_there : report('Pattern not in line so no changes made');
          end; {end case}
          display(prose, linesinput);
          linedata(linesinput, line)
        end {end while}
    end {end of then part}
  else
    report('You must enter text before you can change it')
  end; {procedure change}
end. {of implementation}
```

Exercise 9.6 Why does the implementation part of *ueditor* declare that it uses *uscreen*?

The unit *uformat* is by far the most complex. It consists of a single procedure *format* whose purpose is to output the text stored in the array *prose* so that it is both left and right justified. The user must specify the width of the line on which the text is to be justified. So suppose the first four array elements of *prose* contained the text given below.

```
In order to justify some text which uses
a mono pitch typeface we need to know
the number of characters which are to be
printed on each line.
```

If a line width of 50 is specified this text should be output as in Figure 9.9 below:

> In order to justify some text
> which uses a mono pitch
> typeface we need to know the
> number of characters which are
> to be printed on each line.

Figure 9.9 Justified text

Here, all the characters up to the final *t* of text in array element 1 are as many as will fit on a line width of 50. An extra space has been inserted between the first two words to right justify the text. The second line could only accommodate the words *which uses a mono pitch typeface*. When justified on a line 50 characters wide two additional spaces are required between all but the final pair of words. From this we can see that justification requires a knowledge of the number of additional spaces that will justify the text. This number is then evenly distributed among existing spaces. When, as here, an even distribution is not possible, then it is the spaces at the beginning of the line that are favoured with extra space. Finally, note how the last line of text is not justified. This is standard typographical practice and is exemplified by the paragraph you are reading now.

There are three essential ingredients in the code for *format*. First, the user is asked to enter a line width on which the text will be justified. This is implemented as a local procedure to *format*. Then sufficient text has to be extracted from the array elements in preparation for justification on the input line width. This process of extracting the text from the array is implemented using a procedure *extract*. Finally, the extracted text must be justified by inserting additional space characters, and this is done by a local procedure, *justify*. The latter two procedures have to keep a record of which elements of *prose* have been processed, and this leads to a rather daunting collection of parameters. The important point here is to see how the problem is broken down into parts which are implemented as local procedures. Indeed, the procedure *extract* is sufficiently complex to warrant a local procedure of its own, *split*.

```
unit uformat;
interface
  uses udefns; {Imports constant and type definitions}
  procedure format(prose : text_array; linesinput : linesrange);

implementation
  uses crt, uscreen;
       {Imports clrscr from crt
        Imports getret from uscreen}
  procedure format;
    {(prose : text_array; linesinput : linesrange)
     Pre : 0 <= linesinput <= maxsize.
     Post: None - prose is written out as justified text.}
    const
      lowwidth = 20;
    type
      widthrange = lowwidth..stringsize;
    var
      nextline                    : integer;
      linewidth                   : widthrange;
```

```
    remains, justified, ragged : sentence;
    textend                    : Boolean;
  procedure widthdata(var linewidth : widthrange);
    {Pre : None.
     Post: linewidth is an integer in range lowwidth to stringsize inclusive. A run-
           time error occurs if user input is not integer format.}
    var
      tempwidth : integer;
    begin
      write('Enter line width for formatted text in the range ');
      write(lowwidth, ' - ', stringsize, ' ? ');
      readln(tempwidth);
      while not (tempwidth in [lowwidth..stringsize]) do
        begin
          write('Line width must be in the range ');
          write(lowwidth, ' - ', stringsize, ' Re-enter ? ');
          readln(tempwidth)
        end;
       linewidth := tempwidth;
      writeln
    end; {procedure widthdata}

procedure extract(prose : text_array; linesinput : linesrange; linewidth : widthrange;
                  var nextline : integer; var ragged, remains : sentence;
                  var textend : Boolean);
  {Pre : prose: an assigned array variable.
         0 <= linesinput <= maxsize.
         lowwidth <= linewidth <= stringsize.
         1 <= nextline <= maxsize.
         ragged is an assigned value, possibly the constant value null.
         remains is an assigned value, possibly the constant value null.
         textend is an assigned Boolean value.
   Post: nextline is the index of next element of array prose to be justified. The
         value (maxsize + 1) indicates there are no more elements to process.
         Current text to be justified is stored in ragged.
         Text of current array element not yet justified is stored in remains.
         If all linesinput elements of prose are justified then textend is true
           otherwise it is false.}
  var
    spaceleft : integer;
    full      : Boolean;
    aword     : sentence;

  procedure split(subject, pattern : sentence; var leftpart, rightpart : sentence);
    {Pre : subject and pattern are assigned values.
     Post: leftpart stores all characters of subject up to but not including pattern.
           rightpart stores all characters of subject excluding leftpart.}
    var
      leftlength, rightstart, rightlength : integer;
    begin
      if pos(pattern, subject) = 0
      then
        begin
          leftpart := subject;
          rightpart := null
        end
```

```
          else
            begin
              leftlength := pos(pattern, subject) - 1;
              rightstart := leftlength + length(pattern) + 1;
              rightlength := length(subject) - rightstart + 1;
              leftpart := copy(subject, 1, leftlength);
              rightpart := copy(subject, rightstart, rightlength)
            end
        end; {procedure split}

begin {procedure extract}
  spaceleft := linewidth;
  full := false;
  textend := false;
  ragged := '';
  while (not full) and (not textend) do
    begin
      if remains = '' then
        if nextline > linesinput then
          textend := true
        else
          begin
            remains := prose[nextline];
            nextline := nextline + 1
          end;
      split(remains, space, aword, remains);
      if length(aword) > spaceleft then
        begin
          remains := concat(aword, ' ', remains);
          full := true
        end
      else
        if length(aword) > 0 then
          begin
            if ragged = null then
              ragged := concat(ragged, aword)
            else
              ragged := concat(ragged, ' ', aword);
            spaceleft := spaceleft - length(aword) - 1
          end
    end
end; {procedure extract}

procedure justify(ragged : sentence; linewidth : integer; var justified : sentence);
  {Pre : ragged: a non-null string.
         lowwidth <= linewidth <= stringsize.
   Post: justified has value ragged, but expanded with additional spaces so that its
         dynamic length is linewidth characters.}
  var
    i, index, shortfall, nospaces, gapcount : integer;
  begin
    if ragged <> null then
      begin
```

```
      gapcount := 0;
      for i := 1 to length(ragged) do
        if ragged[i] = space then
          gapcount := gapcount + 1;
      shortfall := linewidth - length(ragged);
      if (shortfall > 0) and (gapcount > 0) then
        begin
          index := length(ragged);
          while shortfall > 0 do
            begin
              index := index - 1;
              if ragged[index] = space then
                begin
                  nospaces := shortfall div gapcount;
                  for i := 1 to nospaces do
                    insert(space, ragged, index);
                  shortfall := shortfall - nospaces;
                  gapcount := gapcount - 1
                end
            end
        end;
      justified := ragged
    end; {procedure justify}

  begin {procedure format}
    clrscr;
    if linesinput > 0 then
      begin
        widthdata(linewidth);
        nextline := 1;
        remains := null;
        ragged := '';
        textend := false;
        while not textend do
          begin
            extract(prose, linesinput, linewidth, nextline, ragged, remains, textend);
            justify(ragged, linewidth, justified);
            writeln(justified)
          end
      end
    else
      writeln('You must enter text before you can Format it');
    writeln;
    writeln('Press <ret> to continue');
    getret
  end; {procedure format}
end.
```

There remains one final consideration and that is the order in which files corresponding to all the source code in this section must be compiled. Table 9.1 below gives the unit identifiers together with their dependencies.

Table 9.1 Unit dependencies

Identifier	Interface uses	Implementation uses
udefns	none	none
main	*udefns, uscreen, ueditor, ufile, uformat*	none
uscreen	*udefns*	*crt*
ufile	*udefns*	*crt*
ueditor	*udefns*	*crt, uscreen*
uformat	*udefns*	*crt, uscreen*

From this table it can be seen that since *udefns* does not depend upon anything else it can be compiled first. Indeed, since it is referred to by all other units, it must be compiled first. Once this is done, both *uscreen* and *ufile* can be compiled because they only reference *crt*, which is a library unit. The order in which they are compiled does not matter. Once *uscreen* has been compiled, both of *ueditor* and *uformat* can be compiled. The last to be compiled is *main* because it references all the other units.

9.4 PROGRAMMING HINTS

The following guidelines were developed in this chapter:

(a) Guideline (unit declaration) A unit declaration consists of two parts: an interface part and an implementation part. The interface part must contain declarations for all the identifiers that are to be exported but it should contain only routine headings (not bodies). The implementation part may declare any identifiers required in the implementation of the routines declared in the interface. A unit always terminates with **end.** which must be preceded by a semicolon.

(b) Guideline (unit compilation) A unit must be compiled before a program which uses it is compiled.

(c) Guideline (structured file) A data value of structured type must be written to a file using *write*. The first parameter of *write* must be the internal file identifier; the second must be an identifier of the variable of the type being stored. It is an error to attempt to use *writeln* for this purpose.

9.5 SUMMARY

In this chapter we have looked at separate compilation and files. Separate compilation enables programs to be broken down and developed independently of each other. The separate parts can then be tested and formed into libraries for the use of other programs. Files enable data stored in memory to be permanently stored on disk. Turbo Pascal implementation of file handling differs from other implementations, and so applications which involve files will require all the file handling to be rewritten if the application is to be ported to some other compiler.

10

ABSTRACT DATA TYPES

Data abstraction is a very powerful programming tool. It extends the concept of separate and independent program development to the design of data. The principle behind it is that such data types can be used without the user being aware of the implementation details. We have already met data abstraction without realizing it when we have used any of the built-in types. For example, we have used the data type *real* without knowing any of the details of how real numbers are implemented by the system. All that was required to use them was a knowledge of the values together with a knowledge of the operations with which the values are manipulated. The combination of permissible data values and the **operations** by which they are manipulated is called an **abstract data type**. In this chapter we shall develop some abstract data types by specifying values, defining operators which act upon them and then implementing the whole type as a separately compiled unit.

10.1 INTRODUCTORY EXAMPLE

We begin by developing a simple abstract data type for the days in the week. In Chapter 7 we used an enumeration type definition to represent them. Although the use of the enumeration type helped the program documentation there was a major problem when it came to input and output because enumeration type values can neither be read in from the keyboard nor written out to the screen. We shall rectify that deficiency here by defining an abstract data type for weekdays that includes operations for reading in and writing out. Thus, the values for the abstract data type will be the enumeration type values defined below.

```
type
  weekdays = (sunday, monday, tuesday, wednesday, thursday, friday, saturday);
```

We will define three operations, one for reading in from the keyboard and two for writing out values. They are specified as follows:

readlnDay

{Read in a day from the keyboard and assign to *inday* its enumeration type equivalent based on the first two characters of user input. If user input does not correspond to a day *inday* is undefined and *valid* is set false. Otherwise *inday* is an enumeration type value and *valid* is true.}		
inday	an enumeration type value	*weekdays* parameter
valid	flag to denote success of process	*Boolean* parameter

writelnDay

outday	an enumeration type value	*weekdays* parameter
{Write out a string corresponding to the enumeration type *outday* and then write a new line character.}		
inday	an enumeration type value	*weekdays* parameter
valid	flag to denote success of process	*Boolean* parameter

writeDay

outday	an enumeration type value	*weekdays* parameter
{Write out a string corresponding to the enumeration type *outday*.}		
inday	an enumeration type value	*weekdays* parameter
valid	flag to denote success of process	*Boolean* parameter

These operations will be implemented as procedures, and all the details will be contained in a Pascal unit ready for separate compilation. The code is as follows:

```
unit uADTdays;

interface
  type
    weekdays = (sunday, monday, tuesday, wednesday, thursday, friday, saturday);
  procedure readlnDay(var inday : weekdays; var valid : Boolean);
  procedure writeDay(outday : weekdays);
  procedure writelnDay(outday : weekdays);

implementation
  procedure readlnDay;
    {(var inday : weekdays; var valid : Boolean)
     Pre : None.
     Post: inday is assigned a value of weekdays type if first two characters of data
           read from keyboard correspond to a day of the week otherwise it is undefined.
           valid is true if inday is defined false otherwise.}
  var
    instring : string;
  begin
    readln(instring);
    valid := true;
    if (upcase(instring[1]) = 'S') and (upcase(instring[2]) = 'U') then
      inday := sunday
    else
```

```
      if (upcase(instring[1]) = 'M') and (upcase(instring[2]) = 'O') then
        inday := monday
      else
        if (upcase(instring[1]) = 'T') and (upcase(instring[2]) = 'U') then
          inday := tuesday
        else
          if (upcase(instring[1]) = 'W') and (upcase(instring[2]) = 'E') then
            inday := wednesday
          else
            if (upcase(instring[1]) = 'T') and (upcase(instring[2]) = 'H') then
              inday := thursday
            else
              if (upcase(instring[1]) = 'F') and (upcase(instring[2]) = 'R') then
                inday := friday
              else
                if (upcase(instring[1]) = 'S') and (upcase(instring[2]) = 'A') then
                  inday := saturday
                else
                  valid := false;
    end;  {procedure readlnDay}
  procedure writeDay;
    {(outday : weekdays)
     Pre : outday is a weekdays value.
     Post: Writes out outday as a string.}
    begin
      case outday of
        sunday    : write('Sunday');
        monday    : write('Monday');
        tuesday   : write('Tuesday');
        wednesday : write('Wednesday');
        thursday  : write('Thursday');
        friday    : write('Friday');
        saturday  : write('Saturday')
      end
    end;  {procedure writeDay}
  procedure writelnDay;
    {(outday : weekdays)
     Pre : outday is a weekdays value.
     Post: Writes out outday as a string followed by a new line character.}
    begin
      writeDay(outday);
      writeln
    end;
end.
```

Note how the code for *writelnDay* consists of a call to *writeDay* and a call to *writeln*. A consequence of this method of implementation is that the declaration of *writeDay* must precede that of *writelnDay*.

Once this code has been compiled it can be made available to any program that involves days of the week. All the program needs to do is to include an appropriate **uses** statement. The enumeration type values, together with the three operations, then become available to that program, just as if the type was a built-in type. The next section gives an example of its use.

19.2 USING THE ABSTRACT DATA TYPE

To test the abstract data type developed in the previous section a special driver program has to be written for the purpose. Once tested, significant advantages accrue from the use of an abstract data type by other applications programs. Firstly, program complexity is reduced because all the code associated with the data type have been separated out. Secondly, there is an improvement in program reliability because the design associated with the data has already been separately tested. Lastly, data types can be reused, time and again, in different applications programs. This reuse of 'tested, off the shelf components' makes a significant contribution to reducing the development time of a system.

The test program we shall develop here will serve a dual purpose. It will test the implementation of the operations and will simultaneously show how the abstract data type is invoked in an applications program. The test program must enable all the operations in the unit *uADTdays* to be tested and so must make use of *readlnDay*, *writeDay* and *writelnDay*. Since there are a small number of values in this abstract data type the program should enable all values to be tested. Most abstract data types do not have a restricted set of values as is the case here, and so cannot be tested in this way.

```pascal
program testADT;
uses uADTdays;
    {Imports from unit uADTdays
    type
        weekdays = (sunday, monday, tuesday, wednesday, thursday, friday, saturday)
    procedure readlnDay(var inday : weekdays; var valid : Boolean)
    procedure writeDay(outday : weekdays)
    procedure writelnDay(outday : weekdays)}
var
    day       : weekdays;
    valid_day : Boolean;
begin
    write('Enter a day of the week ');
    repeat
        readlnDay(day, valid_day);
        if valid_day then
            begin
                writeDay(day);
                writeln(' is day ', ord(day) + 1, ' of the week');
                write('Enter the day after ');
                writelnDay(day)
            end
        else
            writeln('Invalid day - processing halted')
    until not valid_day
end.
```

The overall structure of this program is the same as for any program that uses a separately compiled unit. The **uses** statement has the effect of importing the data type values and the three operations, all of which become global identifiers of the program. The comment at the top of the program explicitly lists all the identifiers imported from *uADTdays*.

The program reads in a day using the operation *readlnDay*. The output involves the use of the operations *writeDay* and *writelnDay*. A typical dialogue resulting from this program, in which user input is underlined, would be:

```
Enter a day of the week Monday
Monday is day 2 of the week
Enter the day after Monday
Tuesday
Tuesday is day 3 of the week
Enter the day after Tuesday
January
Invalid day - processing halted
```

In a more comprehensive run of the program all the days of the week would be tested. Test data should also include inputs that are restricted to two characters. They should consist of random mixtures of upper and lower case characters to test that *readlnDay* does indeed distinguish the day based on the first two input characters only.

10.3 A MORE SUBSTANTIAL EXAMPLE

In this section we will develop a more substantial example of an abstract data type. We shall consider the example from two different viewpoints: first, the implementation of the data type and then its use. We shall use the term **implementor** for the person who creates the abstract data type and the term **applications programmer** or **user** to denote the person who makes use of it. Figure 10.1 below illustrates the data that we shall model. It contains the names of towns together with the number of churches there are within the town boundaries.

Town	Churches
Tonbridge	15
Elgin	10
Buxton	15
Chard	8
Harwich	19

Figure 10.1 Town data

The table will be manipulated using the following operations:

- An operation called *isfull*, which enables the applications programmer to determine whether or not a table is full, that is, whether there is space for additional entries.
- An operation called *insert*, to insert a new entry into a table.
- An operation called *churchnumber*, which has as source data the name of a town and which will write out the number of churches in that town, or a message saying that the town was not in the table.
- An operation called *display*, to display the table on the screen.
- An operation called *create*, to create a table.

In the operator specifications that follow, the identifier *tabletype* is used to denote the type representing the table. At this stage the details of how this is to be implemented need not be known.

isfull

table	Representation of table data	*tabletype* parameter
{Return the Boolean false if the table is not full and true if it is full.}		
isfull		*Boolean* function value

insert

table	Representation of table data	*tabletype* parameter
{Prompt for and read in the name of a town and the number of churches it contains. Insert the data into the first unused row of the table. It is the responsibility of the user to check there is room for the insertion before using this operation.}		
table	Updated table	*tabletype* parameter

churchnumber

table	Representation of table data	*tabletype* parameter
searchtown	Town for which number of churches is sought	*string* parameter
{Search the town column of the table for the *searchtown*. If it is found then write out the number of churches it contains, otherwise write out a message saying the town is not in the table.}		
intown		

display

table	Representation of table data	*tabletype* parameter
{Display the contents of the table on the screen. Difficulties, such as there being more entries in the table than will fit on the screen, should be ignored. If the table is empty this procedure does nothing.}		

create

{Return a new empty table of type *tabletype*.}		
table	A new table	*tabletype* parameter

To illustrate some of the issues which can arise with abstract data type implementations we shall first choose an implementation that uses parallel arrays to hold the columns of the table rather than the more obvious and more efficient method of using records. Consecutive parallel array elements will be used to hold the data in the rows, and a variable called *size* will indicate the index of the last element currently in use. With this in mind a first attempt at writing the interface part of the unit that implements the new type is as follows:

```
unit uTableADT;
interface
  const
    maxsize = 10;
  var
    town    : array[0..maxsize] of string;
    church  : array[0..maxsize] of integer;
    size    : 0..maxsize;
```

There are several difficulties with this approach:

1. Consider the procedure *insert*. This procedure has as source data the table into which
    the insertion is to take place. With this representation three parameters would be
    required: namely, the two arrays and the value of *size*. These implementation details
    would have to be made public so that the applications programmer could supply
    appropriate actual parameters in a call. But one of the purposes of writing abstract data
    types is to relieve the burden on applications programmers. Imagine the difficulties
    that would arise if we had to know and exploit the implementation details for the real
    data type in order to use real values. Fortunately, this is not the case for reals and we
    can use the real operators totally oblivious of the way they work. This idea of not
    needing to know implementation details is known as **data** or **information hiding** and
    is something for which we strive in the implementation of abstract data types.

2. Since the details of this representation have to be made public (for the reasons given
    in 1) there is a risk that the applications programmer will be influenced by the
    representation to the extent that individual data items could be manipulated directly.
    For example, array elements could be changed without recourse to one of the provided
    operations. This would be analogous to changing the bit pattern of a real variable
    rather than using one of the real operators to update it. Furthermore, the applications
    programmer could construct further operations on the data structure, perhaps
    introducing operations which the designer of the data type would want to prohibit. The
    result of permitting this is potentially insecure software. Of course, it may turn out that
    the design of the abstract data type does not meet the application programmer's needs.
    For example, it may be discovered that the operations are insufficient for the task. In
    this case, it has to be recognized that the original specification was poor and a new one
    has to be drawn up which does include appropriate operators.

3. If a different representation is chosen, say one that uses records, then the parameters
    for all the operations would have to be altered. This would mean changing every call to
    the operators in the applications programs. This is very undesirable.

In summary, the applications programmer should be prevented from seeing the details
of the implementation and of being able to alter it in any way. The separation of
specification from implementation has great benefits for program development,
maintenance and reusability. Thus, the applications programmer should only be allowed to
see the headings of the specifications of the routines defining the operations and not the
details that support their implementation. The use of Pascal units can help this process
because the implementation part is not visible outside the unit, so as many of the
implementation details should be hidden there as possible. Examine the interface below
before reading how well it copes with these challenges.

```
unit uTable1;
interface
  const
    maxsize = 10;
  type
    tabletype = record
                    town    : array[0..maxsize] of string;
                    church  : array[0..maxsize] of integer;
                    size    : 0..maxsize;
                end;
  function isfull(table : tabletype) : Boolean;
  procedure insert(var table : tabletype);
  procedure churchnumber(table : tabletype; searchtown : string);
  procedure display(table : tabletype);
  procedure create(var table : tabletype);
```

This goes some way to meeting the criticisms above. First, it avoids explicit mention of how the table is represented and so avoids the difficulty raised in 1. It does so by **encapsulating** the three components, *town*, *church* and *size*, which are being used to model the table into a record type. So a record parameter of this type carries with it the complete model of the table structure. Secondly, a single identifier is used to represent the table, thereby taking account of item 3 above.

Item 2 is more problematic. An applications programmer who was told that *tabletype* is the identifier corresponding to the representation of the table would not be able to deduce that the implementation involved arrays and a variable *size*. The existence of the operator *isfull* might suggest an array representation, but this would not be conclusive evidence. We shall return to this point shortly.

Finally, note that the applications programmer is free to use any identifier other than *tabletype*, *isfull*, *insert*, *churchnumber*, *display* and *create* without running the risk of using the same identifier as one used in the implementation of the data structure. In particular, the application could use identifiers *town*, *church* and *size* and there would not be an 'identifier declared twice' error.

Exercise 10.1 Why could such an error not result?

Exercise 10.2 Implement each of the routines in **unit** *uTable1* using the designs below. You will need to bear in mind the following points. The table is full when all the array elements are in use, that is, when *size = maxsize*. An entry inserted into the table must be assigned to the first unused array elements. The index of the first unused elements is given by *size* + 1. The routine *insert* does not have to test to see if the arrays are full. The search algorithm used in *churchnumber* exploits the dummy element at index zero as discussed in Chapter 6. The routine *display* writes out all *size* elements holding the data values in the form of a table. All occurrences of the variable *index* in the designs are of type 0..*maxsize*. A new table is initialized by setting *size* to 0.

10.4 DATA HIDING REVISITED

In this section we shall see how the use of a record to encapsulate the abstract data type components enables changes to be made to its implementation without having any knock-on

isfull	
table	
1	$isfull := (table.size = maxsize)$
isfull	

create	
{No source data}	
	{This initializes *table*}
1	$table.size := 0$
table	

insert	
table	
1	with *table* do
2	$size := size + 1$
3	write out 'Enter the name of the town '
4	read in *town*[*size*]
5	write out 'Enter the number of churches in the town '
6	read in *church*[*size*]
7	withend
table	

churchnumber	
table, searchtown	
1	$table.town[0] := searchtown$
2	$index := table.size$
3	with *table* do
4	loop while $town[index] <> searchtown$
5	decrement *index*
6	loopend
7	if $index <> 0$ then
8	write out *searchtown*, ' has ', *church*[*index*], ' churches'
9	else
10	write out *searchtown*, ' is not in the table'
11	ifend
12	withend

display	
table	
1	write out 'Town', 'Churches'
2	with *table* do
3	loop for $index := 1$ to *size*
4	write out *town*[*index*], *church*[*index*]
5	loopend
6	withend

effect to an application program. Here, we shall change the representation of *tabletype* so that the rows of the table are now to be modelled by records rather than parallel arrays. The code fragment below gives the details of this alternative representation.

```
unit uTable2;

interface
  const
    maxsize = 10;
  type
    entrytype = record
                    town   : string;
                    church : integer;
                end;
    tabletype = record
                    entry : array[0..maxsize] of entrytype;
                    size  : 0..maxsize;
                end;
  function isfull(table : tabletype) : Boolean;
  procedure insert(var table : tabletype);
  procedure churchnumber(table : tabletype; searchtown : string);
  procedure display(table : tabletype);
  procedure create(var table : tabletype);
```

Although the rows of the table have been modelled using a record, note how the declarations of the routines corresponding to the operators are exactly the same as those for the previous representation. Calls to these routines would have exactly the same format as before so that an applications program would not need changing if this new representation was adopted. What would have to be done is to recompile the applications program, but this is a minor price to pay.

For both models, using a record to encapsulate the components of the representation has at least guaranteed that the representation is independent of the application that uses it. But is this sufficient in terms of information hiding? Certainly the code for the routines is hidden from the applications programmer because it is all in the implementation part of the unit and hence is invisible outside the unit. However, as we know from Chapter 9, all the declarations in a unit's interface become global to any program that uses it. So for the former representation the identifiers *maxsize*, *tabletype* and its associated fields are all global to any program that uses unit *uTable1*. This means that the system cannot hide the representation of the abstract data type from the applications programmer. Ideally, we would like to place the definitions of *maxsize* and *tabletype* in the implementation part of the unit, because the system would then ensure that it is invisible outside the unit. Unfortunately, Pascal does not permit the definitions of *maxsize* and *tabletype* to be placed there because the parameters in the routine declarations in the interface reference them and, as we know, identifiers must be declared before they are used. This is a major drawback of Pascal because complete information hiding cannot be achieved.

What can be done to provide further security is to restrict access to some of the interface details. Only those parts of it that relate to the data objects and operations need be released. All the applications programmer then requires is a compiled version of the unit containing the abstract data type. This would appear to have solved the problem of information hiding, and to a large extent this is so, but it is an unfortunate fact of life that if there is a possibility of an applications programmer discovering implementation details then someone at some time will do so and will circumvent the operations provided. Once the details are discovered there is nothing the system itself can do to stop unauthorized alterations to the data type. Some languages get round this by enabling identifiers like *maxsize* and the structure of *tabletype* to be declared **private**, whereas the identifiers that are exported are declared to be **public**. This enables the system to stop direct access to private identifiers and structures while allowing access to public ones. For the problems in this chapter, and in specifications in subsequent chapters, we shall adopt a convention of classifying identifiers as public or private. To do so, the data table for an abstract data type definition is divided into public and private parts even though this cannot be implemented in Pascal. Thus, the data table corresponding to **unit** *uTable2* above would be as follows:

Data table for unit uTable2

Identifier	Description	Type
	PRIVATE	
maxsize	Maximum table size	*integer* constant value 10
entrytype	Record type definition	
	town	*string* variable
	church	*integer* variable
	recordend	
tabletype	Record type definition	
	tablearray	array[1..*maxsize*] of *entrytype* variable
	size	0..*maxsize* variable
	recordend	
	PUBLIC	
tabletype	Defined above	not publicly available
isfull	(*table*)	*Boolean* function(*tabletype*)
insert	(*table*)	procedure(*tabletype*)
churchnumber	(*table, searchtown*)	procedure(*tabletype, string*)
display	(*table*)	procedure(*tabletype*)
create	(*table*)	procedure(*tabletype*)

Here, the routines are declared in the public part. The formal parameters are listed in the second column and the corresponding types of the parameters follow the routine identifier in the third column. The identifier *tabletype* is defined in the private part, but it also appears in the public part because the identifier itself is public. This data table can be transformed into its Pascal equivalent by using comments to identify the public and private parts as shown below.

```
unit uTable2;

interface
  {PRIVATE part}
  const
    maxsize = 10;
  type
    entrytype = record
                  town   : string;
                  church : integer
                end;
    tabletype = record
                  entry : array[0..maxsize] of entrytype;
                  size  : 0..maxsize
                end;
  {PUBLIC part: the identifier tabletype from above}
```

```
function isfull(table : tabletype) : Boolean;
procedure insert(var table : tabletype);
procedure churchnumber(table : tabletype; searchtown : string);
procedure display(table : tabletype);
procedure create(var table : tabletype);
```

In a totally disciplined approach to software development one might wonder why such safeguards as information hiding and private identifiers are required. After all, provided that the implementor supplies the identifiers corresponding to the data values and operations, the system will ensure that inadvertent use of the same identifier by implementor and applications programmer will not cause a problem. Experience has shown that the more safeguards that are built into the system the more robust is the final product. We can summarize the technique of coding an abstract data type implementation using Pascal units as follows:

- Guideline (abstract data types) The components forming the representation of the data being modelled should be encapsulated in a record whose identifier will represent the type.
- Guideline (abstract data type operations) The operations should be implemented using routines whose parameters are expressed in terms of the abstract data type identifier referred to above.
- Guideline (exported identifiers) Implementation details which have to be declared in the interface part should remain private to the implementor even though Pascal has no way of enforcing this.

Exercise 10.3 Write the implementation part of **unit** *uTable2*.

10.5 PASCAL LIMITATIONS

In the previous section we saw that the reason why the definition of *tabletype* could not be hidden in the implementation part of the unit was the requirement that a type identifier must be declared before it is used. Therefore, *tabletype* had to be declared before it appeared in the parameter lists of the routines corresponding to the operations. One way round this problem is to declare the data type structure in the implementation part of the unit but to remove the parameter lists from the routine declarations. The (incomplete) code below shows how this can be achieved. The representation uses records.

```
unit uTable3;

interface
  type
    town_name = string;
    churches  = integer;
  function isfull : Boolean;
  procedure insert;
  procedure churchnumber(searchtown : string);
  procedure display;
  procedure create;
```

```
implementation
  uses
    crt;
  const
    maxsize = 10;
  type
    entrytype = record
                    town    : string;
                    church : integer
                end;
    tabletype = record
                    entry : array[0..maxsize] of entrytype;
                    size  : 0..maxsize
                end;
  var
    table : tabletype;
```

Exercise 10.4 Complete the details of the implementation part.

This code exhibits a style which so far we have regarded as poor. This is because it exploits side-effects. In other words, *table* is updated because it is a global variable of the implementation part. It is impossible to tell from the headings which routines update *table* and which do not. Comments could be added to the code to clarify this, and this would be acceptable given that the unit is solely concerned with routines corresponding to operations on *table*. One other slight oddity is the declaration of the types *town_name* and *churches*. This would appear to be just a renaming of the built-in types *string* and *integer* respectively. The reason it is required is that the applications programmer has to be told the identifier of the type that has been used to model the individual column elements of the table.

An applications program which used this abstract data type would then require declarations along the following lines:

```
program application;
uses uTable3;
  {Imports
   type
     town_name = string
     churches  = integer
   function isfull : Boolean
   procedure insert
   procedure churchnumber(searchtown : string)
   procedure display
   procedure create
   These routines manipulate a hidden representation of a table}
var
  town          : town_name;
begin
  create;
    :
end.
```

This method of implementation has another serious drawback. Suppose the program *application* above was required to declare two tables having the same structure as we have been considering. Then its current **uses** clause declares one of these tables. However, since the operations are not parameterized a second table cannot be declared by the applications programmer. The implementor of the abstract data type would have to provide another unit that would be identical to *uTable3* except that the identifier *table* would have to be replaced by a different identifier representing the second table.

Exercise 10.5 Modify the declarations of the program *application* so that it uses *uTable1* and declares two tables for processing. Also, write down the calls to *create* which will establish the empty tables.

10.6 EXERCISES AND PROBLEMS

The problems in this section concentrate on the implementation of abstract data types rather than on programs that use them. For completeness we give here the form that a design will take for a program that uses an abstract data type. As usual, it will consist of an algorithm expressed as a sequence of design steps together with a data table defining the identifiers. The data table corresponding to the solution to Exercise 10.5 is as follows:

Data table for program application

Identifier	Description	Type
first_table	Representation of a table	variable of *tabletype* imported from unit *uTable1*
second_table	Representation of a table	variable of *tabletype* imported from unit *uTable1*

The only new detail here is that the types of the two variables refer to the imported identifier from the unit *uTable1*. This carries with it the implication that all the public identifiers of *uTable1* are imported into the main program as well. The name of the unit from which the identifiers are imported will not always be given explicitly.

Exercise 10.6 This exercise is similar to the introductory example in the text in that it provides the user with operations for use with some enumeration type values. The solution also illustrates the use of what is known as the **initialization section** of a Pascal unit. The operation *convertmonth* converts from user input to internal enumeration type value and the operation *writemonth* converts from internal representation to a form which is then output. The enumeration type values are public, and are therefore common knowledge to both the implementor and the applications programmer. It is the way the conversion is done which is private and which we now describe. An array will store string equivalents of the enumeration type values and will be used in the implementation of *writemonth*. The implementation of *convertmonth* will simply involve converting an integer to an enumeration type value. The data table and specifications below give the details. The procedure *initialize* is private, and so will be coded in the implementation part of the unit. The variable *MonthName* is a global variable of the implementation part. Write the code for each of the three routines in this specification and then read the solution to see how they are assembled in the unit.

Data table for unit uADTmon

Identifier	Description	Type
	PRIVATE	
montharray	Type definition	array[*monthtype*] of *string*
MonthName	Array holding names of months. Global variable of the implementation part.	*montharray* variable
initialize	(*MonthName*)	procedure(*monthtype*)
	PUBLIC	
monthtype	Enumerated type definition	(*jan, feb, mar, apr, may, jun, jul, aug, sep, oct, nov, dec*)
monthrange	Subrange type definition	1..12
writemonth	(*month*)	procedure(*monthtype*)
convertmonth	(*MonthNumber*)	*monthtype* function(*monthrange*)

initialize

{Initialize *MonthName* by assigning 'January' to *MonthName* [*jan*], 'February' to *MonthName* [*feb*] and so on. }		
MonthName	An initialized array	*monthtype* parameter

writemonth

month	Enumeration value to be output	*monthtype* parameter
{Write out the name of the month corresponding to the enumeration value *month*. }		

convertmonth

MonthNumber	Number of month	*monthtype* parameter
{Return the month value corresponding to the integer value *MonthNumber*.}		
convertmonth		*monthtype* function value

10.7 PROGRAMMING HINTS

(a) Guideline (abstract data types) The components forming the representation of the data being modelled should be encapsulated in a record whose identifier will represent the type.

(b) Guideline (abstract data type operations) The operations should be implemented using routines whose parameters are expressed in terms of the abstract data type identifier referred to above.

(c) Guideline (exported identifiers) Implementation details which have to be declared in the interface part should remain private to the implementor even though Pascal has no way of enforcing this.

10.8 SUMMARY

In this chapter we have looked at the implementation of abstract data types. Abstract data types are used to separate the process of data modelling from that of the program design whose purpose is to manipulate the data. A good abstract data type implementation will hide its implementation details from an applications programmer. Pascal does not have the facilities whereby this can be rigorously achieved. The onus is therefore upon the applications programmer to declare variables using the type identifier representing the data together with the operations with which to manipulate them.

11

STACKS

11.1 INTRODUCTION

In this chapter we are going to introduce the concept of a sequence. A sequence is a data structure that allows the number of items being stored to vary during program execution. All sequences start off empty, and items are added to and removed from them through time.

A physical example of a sequence is a club membership that is maintained as a card index of names and addresses. As people join the club so the sequence grows, and when they leave it shrinks. An important property of a sequence is that the insertion of a new item is not random – there must be some rule by which it can be determined where in the sequence the new item must go. For the bridge club, an alphabetic ordering on name is an obvious choice.

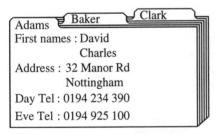

In general, an item in a sequence is retrieved by working through the sequence from the beginning until the item is found or all items in the sequence have been inspected.

The sequence is almost certainly the most common structure in data processing, and much data processing time is spent manipulating them. Many of the sequences are very long – for example, product codes for parts in the motor industry, account records in a bank, employee records in a large industry and so on. Sequences like these are often so long that they cannot be held in the working store of a computer. In this case, permanent backing store has to be used to manipulate the sequence. We shall not be considering sequences of this size, but the principles we introduce here would be applicable in such circumstances. We begin with a more rigorous definition of a sequence:

> A **sequence** is a data structure with zero or more items of data of a predefined fixed type placed one after the other in an order determined by some predefined relationship.

Note that all the items in a sequence must be of a fixed type. Typically, they are all records, but each record must have the same record structure. There are many different types of sequence, but we can identify basic operations that are associated with most of them.

- Creation of a sequence
- Retrieval of an item from a sequence
- Insertion of a new item into a sequence
- Deletion of a specified item from a sequence
- Updating the contents of an item in a sequence
- Testing whether there are any items in a sequence
- Although the definition does not constrain the number of items in a sequence, memory is finite, and so there might be a need to test whether there is room for more items in a sequence.

We shall be examining several kinds of sequences in this and later chapters and creating them as abstract data types. This will involve defining the type of the values being represented, and specifying and implementing the operations by which they are manipulated. We shall also be looking at driver programs that will test the implementation.

11.2 DEFINING A STACK

The first kind of sequence we shall look at is a **stack**. The predefined relationship that determines the order of items in a stack is the order in which they are inserted. More precisely, a new item can only be inserted at the end of a sequence. Furthermore, only the last item in the sequence can be retrieved or deleted. A physical occurrence of a stack is a column of coins on a table. Only the top coin can be retrieved from the column and a coin can only be added to the column by placing it on the top of the column (Figure 11.1).

Figure 11.1 A stack of coins

A common use for stacks is in the evaluation of arithmetic expressions. All electronic calculators and computers use a stack to perform arithmetic calculations. To see this important application, and to give you a feel for its capabilities, we shall look at how a stack can be used to evaluate expressions like:

$2 + 3, \ 5 - 2, \ (2 + 4)*5, \ (6 - 2)*(3 - 7)$

Expressions such as these, which use a combination of arithmetic operators, numbers and brackets, are said to be expressed in **infix** notation because the operators come *between* the operands. The brackets are required to avoid potential ambiguities in the expression. Expressions can of course also contain variables, but we shall concentrate on those containing only integer constants.

To evaluate an infix expression the calculator needs to rearrange it in **reverse Polish** notation, sometimes referred to as **postfix** notation. This means placing the operands before the operators. The expression $2 + 3$ would appear in reverse Polish as 2 3 +. Here, the operands 2 and 3 come first, followed by the operator +. The expression $5 - 2$ in reverse Polish is 5 2 −. Other examples are:

Standard notation	Reverse Polish notation
$(2 + 4)*5$	2 4 + 5 *
$(6 - 2)*(3 - 7)$	6 2 − 3 7 − *

Reverse Polish expressions are evaluated from left to right as follows:

- When an operand is scanned it is put onto a stack
- When an operator is scanned
  - the last two numbers are removed from the stack
  - the indicated operator is performed on the two numbers
  - the result is put back on the stack.

Figure 11.2 illustrates the evaluation of 2 3 4 * + which represents the expression $2 + (3*4)$. In the figure the stack grows from the bottom to the top. Thus, the most recently entered value is the one highest up the page.

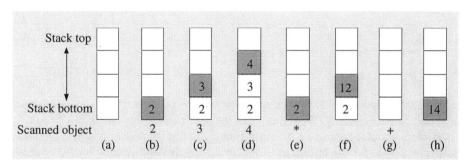

Figure 11.2 Stack evaluation of $2 + (3*4)$

Initially, the stack is empty at step (a). The first object scanned is the number 2, and so it is placed on the top of the (empty) stack to give (b). The next object is the number 3, and so it is placed on the stack at (c). Similarly, 4 is placed on the stack at (d). The next object is the operand *. The top two numbers are removed from the stack, 4 first, then 3, to give (e). They are then multiplied and the result placed back on the stack at (f). The next scanned object is +, and so 12 is removed, followed by 2, to give (g). These two numbers are added and the result is placed on the stack at (h). The scan is now complete and the result can be removed from the stack and sent to the output device.

This example shows the principles of stack operations. Rather than use this rather complex application, we shall look at a very much simpler problem which we shall solve using a stack. We shall write a program that reads in a string from the keyboard and writes out in reverse order on the screen. To solve this problem, we shall use an abstract data type that consists of a character stack together with operations with which it can be manipulated. The identifier *charstack* will be used to denote this abstract data type and it is defined by the following operations:

push

stack	Representation of character stack	*charstack* parameter
item	Character to be entered onto the stack	*char* parameter
{Place the item on top of *stack* and return the updated *stack*. If the stack is full write out 'stack overflow' and return *stack* unaltered.}		
stack	Updated stack	*charstack* parameter

pop

stack	Representation of character stack	*charstack* parameter
{Remove and return the item on top of *stack* and return the updated *stack*. If the stack is empty write out 'stack underflow'.}		
stack	Updated stack	*charstack* parameter
item	Character removed from top of stack	*char* parameter

isempty

stack	Representation of character stack	*charstack* parameter
{Return the value true if the stack is empty, false otherwise.}		
isempty	A new stack	*Boolean* function value

create

{Return a new empty stack of type *charstack*.}		
stack	A new character stack	*charstack* parameter

The implementation of this abstract data type will be contained in a separately compiled Pascal unit called *uchStack*. We remark that the user can test for potential stack underflow and therefore avoid it happening by using *isempty* to test for an empty stack. No analogous routine is supplied for the testing of a full stack. This is done to simplify the abstract data type and to minimize the number of operations we have to consider. There are many different ways of dealing with error conditions such as stack overflow or underflow. We shall content ourselves with the simple method given above.

11.3 USING A STACK

We will illustrate how these operators work and use them in an applications program without worrying how the stack is to be represented in memory. To convince you of this, we shall develop the program to reverse a string input from the keyboard. The program, called

StrReverse, will use the stack *uchStack*. We shall assume that the stack is large enough to hold all the characters of the input string and so we shall ignore the potential problem of stack overflow. The design and data table for the program *StrReverse* are as follows:

```
1    create(stack)
2    write out 'Enter the string to be reversed'
3    read in input
4    loop for i := 1 to length(input)
5        push(stack, input[i])
6    loopend
7    if isempty(stack) then
8        write out 'The input string was null'
9    else
10       loop while not isempty(stack)
11           pop(stack, ch)
12           write ch
13       loopend
14   ifend
```

Data table for program StrReverse

Identifier	Description	Type
stack	Representation of a char stack	variable of *charstack* imported from unit *uchStack*
i	Loop control variable	*integer* variable
ch	Character of string	*char* variable
input	User input	*string* variable

Exercise 11.1 Implement this design as a Pascal program. You will have to include a suitable **uses** statement.

11.4 IMPLEMENTING THE ABSTRACT DATA TYPE STACK

To implement the stack we shall use an array together with a variable whose purpose is to record the index corresponding to the top of the stack. This immediately imposes an upper limit on the number of items that may be on the stack. The size of the stack is therefore determined by the representation rather than by a constraint of the stack's specification. It also means that whenever the stack is used, memory space for the whole array must be set aside irrespective of the number of elements on the stack, and this may be very wasteful of storage space. In Section 11.5 we shall see how to overcome these restrictions, but to do so requires the use of a data type that we have not yet introduced. The index 0 will be used to denote an empty stack and so the item at the top of a stack containing one item will be referenced by index 1, the item at the top of a stack of two items will be referenced by index 2 and so on.

11.4.1 A stack of *char*

We begin by designing and implementing a stack whose elements will be of type *char*. The data table below defines the identifiers and structures which we shall use in the implementation.

Data table for unit uchStack

Identifier	Description		Type
	PRIVATE		
maxsize	Maximum stack size		*integer* constant
charstack	Record type definition		
	stackarray	{Stack array item}	array[1..*maxsize*] of *char* variable
	stacktop	{Top of stack}	*integer* variable
	recordend		
	PUBLIC		
charstack	Type definition		
push	(*stack, item*)		procedure(*charstack, char*)
pop	(*stack, item*)		procedure(*charstack, char*)
isempty	(*stack*)		procedure(*charstack*)
create	(*stack*)		procedure(*charstack*)

Exercise 11.2 Write a Pascal unit interface that defines the stack represented by the above data table in which *maxsize* has value 255. You will need to look at the specifications of the operators to determine whether parameters are **value** or **var**.

Exercise 11.3 Write the implementation part of *uchStack* based on the following designs:

push
stack, item

1	with *stack* do
2	if *stacktop* = *maxsize* then
3	write out 'stack overflow'
4	else
5	*stacktop* := *stacktop* + 1
6	*stackarray*[*stacktop*] := *item*
7	ifend
8	withend

stack

pop
stack

1	with *stack* do
2	if *isempty*(*stack*) then
3	write out 'stack underflow'
4	else
5	*item* := *stackarray*[*stacktop*]
6	*stacktop* := *stacktop* − 1
7	ifend
8	withend

stack, item

isempty
stack,

1	*isempty* := (*stack.stacktop* = 0)

isempty

create

1	*stack.stacktop* := 0

stack

11.4.2 Writing a driver program to test the stack implementation

In order to write a program to test this implementation we have to think of the kind of values with which to test it. The difficult test data to think of is that which is in some sense abnormal. We shall refer to such data as **extreme data** and use examples to illustrate what this term means. A guideline will be given to help you identify, and hence generate, extreme test data values. Although we concentrate on extreme data in this section, it does not mean that you should ignore testing with normal values. So, for example, we take it as read that the operation *push* will be tested when there are some elements on the stack but the stack is nowhere near full. The guideline will need to be interpreted in the context of the data type being developed, but examples of their use over the next few chapters should make it clear how this can be done. The guideline can be summarized by the words *empty*, *full*, *first* and *last*. To illustrate how the questions can be generated, we shall suppose that we are working with a general sequence and are considering the *insert* operation. Once the questions have been generated we shall see how they can be interpreted with the *push* operation for a stack. The questions to be framed are:

(a)　Are there problems inserting into an *empty* sequence?
(b)　Are there problems inserting into a *full* sequence?
(c)　Are there problems associated with *first* element of the sequence?
(d)　Are there problems associated with *last* element of the sequence?

These questions do not have to be remembered – you should be able to generate them by just remembering the key words *empty*, *full*, *first* and *last*.

Exercise 11.4 Interpret each of the above questions in the context of a stack where the insert operation is *push*, and hence describe the kind of test data that you would need to generate.

Exercise 11.5 Write down a collection of similar questions for the operation of deletion on a sequence and interpret them in the context of the stack operation *pop*.

By repeating this process for all the operations defined we can draw up a description of the kinds of tests we would need to perform.

- *pop* an empty stack
- *pop* a full stack
- *pop* a non-empty stack so the result is not empty
- *pop* a stack consisting of one element and test if the result is empty
- *push* onto an empty stack
- *push* onto a full stack
- *push* onto a stack to make it become full
- *push* onto a non-empty stack that has plenty of spare capacity
- test to see if the stack is empty
- *create* a stack and test if the created stack is empty

Perhaps the easiest program to write which enables all the above tests to be carried out is a menu-driven one that enables each of the operations to be selected. However, one problem remains, and that is that we cannot 'see' the state of the stack. What is needed is a routine that will display the stack on the screen. As implementors we have access to the details of the implementation method and so are able to write such a routine. Here is a program that will provide us with the necessary tools to do the testing.

```
program TestuchStack;
uses uchStack, crt;            comments
  {Imports
   const
     maxsize = 10
   type
     charstack (details are private)
```

```
      procedure push(var stack : charstack; item : char)
      procedure pop(var stack : charstack; var item : char)       Comment
      function isempty(stack : charstack) : Boolean
      procedure create(var stack : charstack)}
var
   mystack      : charstack;
   choice, data : char;
procedure display(stack : charstack);
   {Pre : stack.stacktop is initialized and is less than or equal to maxsize.
    Post: None - stack is written to the screen with the top of the stack uppermost.}
   var
      i : 1..maxsize;
   begin
      writeln('Top of stack');
      if not isempty(stack) then
        for i := (stack.stacktop) downto 1 do
          writeln(stack.stackarray[i]);
      writeln('Bottom of stack')
   end;

procedure getret;
   {Pre : None.
    Post: None - processing awaits press of <ret>.}
   var
      ch : char;
   begin
      writeln;
      write('Press <ret> to get to main menu ');
      repeat
        ch := readkey
      until (ord(ch) = 13)
   end;

begin
   clrscr;
   create(mystack);
   repeat
     clrscr;
     writeln('1 : Push data on to stack');
     writeln('2 : Pop data from stack');
     writeln('3 : Test for empty stack');
     writeln('4 : Display the stack');
     writeln('5 : Quit');
     writeln;
     write('Enter your choice ');
     repeat
       choice := readkey
     until choice in ['1'..'5'];
     writeln(choice);
     case choice of
       '1' : begin
               write('Enter character to be pushed on to stack ');
               readln(data);
               push(mystack, data);
               getret
             end;
```

```
    '2' : begin
            if isempty(mystack) then
              begin
                writeln('Attempting to pop an empty stack');
                pop(mystack,data)
              end
            else
              begin
                pop(mystack,data);
                writeln('Popped item was ', data)
              end;
            getret
          end;
    '3' : begin
            if isempty(mystack) then
              writeln('Stack is empty')
            else
              writeln('Stack is not empty');
            getret
          end;
    '4' : begin
            display(mystack);
            getret
          end
    end;
  until (choice = '5')
end.
```

We have included the imported identifiers as comments in this code although we have not specified them as public or private because, as implementors of the data type, we have privileged knowledge of them all. Despite this privilege, the unit is imported just as it would be by an applications programmer. This ensures that any additional routines we introduce for the purpose of testing do not interfere with those which constitute the stack operations. The test program actually introduces two new procedures. The procedure *getret* is virtually identical to the version introduced in Chapter 9, except that here it includes a prompt. It simplifies the flow of menu control. The other procedure displays the contents of the stack. For this, it needs the privileged information of how the stack is implemented. Care also has to be taken that it is written out in the correct order, with the top of the stack at the top of the screen. Finally, notice how *maxsize* is defined to be 10 rather than 255. This is done so that a full stack can be more quickly filled up. It requires the unit *uchStack* to be recompiled with this revised constant value.

11.4.3 Generic stacks

The abstract data type that we have just implemented represented a stack of character values. Suppose now we wanted to implement a stack of integer values to tackle the arithmetic calculation problem mentioned earlier. We would have to implement another version of the stack called, say, *integerstack*, but this time defining *stackarray* to be an array of base type *integer*. The same problem would arise if we then wanted a stack of records or indeed a stack of any other data type. Each application would require a specially written unit which would implement the stack for the particular items that were to be placed on it. What we really want to be able to do is to define a **generic** stack, that is, a stack whose operations can be applied to any data type. Furthermore, we would want the applications programmer to be able to declare the type of items to be stacked and then have these items operated upon by the unit that implements the stack. Unfortunately, Pascal does not have facilities whereby generic abstract data types can be written. What we can do is to provide a partial solution, but a rather imperfect one. Consider the following interface which is a modified version of *uchStack*.

```
unit uGenStk0;

interface
  {PRIVATE part}
  const
    maxsize = 255;
  type
    itemtype = {Type of items to be stacked to be inserted here.}
    genstack = record
                  stackarray : array[1..maxsize] of itemtype;
                  stacktop   : 0..maxsize;
               end;
  {PUBLIC part: the identifiers genstack and itemtype from above}
  procedure push(var stack : genstack; item : itemtype);
  procedure pop(var stack : genstack; var item : itemtype);
  function isempty(stack : genstack) : Boolean;
  procedure create(var stack  : genstack);
```

Basically, all we have done here is to introduce a new type, *itemtype*, to represent the type of the items that are to be put on the stack. So every reference to the previously specific *char* has been replaced by a reference to *itemtype*. The definition of *itemtype* itself is incomplete and would have to be provided for each different applications program. Essentially, we have performed some abstraction on the previous code.

One problem arising from this method relates to information hiding. Who is to supply the missing details in this code? If the applications programmer takes the responsibility, all our efforts at information hiding are gone – the implementation details are laid bare. Ideally, we would like the definition of *itemtype* to be passed into the unit by the system, but that is not possible. Another drawback is illustrated by the next example.

Exercise 11.6 Would the unit *uGenStk0* be helpful to a program that required the use of both a stack of integers and a stack of characters?

11.5 EXERCISES AND PROBLEMS

The problems in this section give you the opportunity of implementing modifications to the abstract data type stack. In Problems 11.1–11.4 we shall modify the definition of *uGenStk0* to include new operations or to modify the existing ones. We shall call the different implementations by different identifiers, as summarized in Table 11.1 below. The first column gives the name of the Pascal unit that contains the implementation, the second gives the identifier that is used to declare a variable of that particular abstract data type, and the third gives the type of the items being placed on the stack. All except the first are listed as being of base type *itemtype*. By suitably defining *itemtype* in the interface of each unit, stacks to store different base types can be created. In the problems, *itemtype* will be defined to be *integer*. The numbers in brackets refer to problems in which new or updated specifications are given for the operation. Operations that are not followed by a number may be assumed to have the specification given in the text.

Table 11.1 Names of Pascal units and their operations

Unit	ADT name	Base type	Operations
uchStack	*charstack*	*char*	*create, isempty, push, pop*
uGenStk0	*genstack*	*itemtype*	*create, isempty, push, pop*
uGenStk1	*genstack*	*itemtype*	*create, isempty, push, pop, print* (11.1)
uGenStk2	*genstack*	*itemtype*	*create, isempty, push, pop, revprint* (11.2)
uGenStk3	*genstack*	*itemtype*	*create, isempty, push, pop* (11.3), *top* (11.3), *print* (11.1)

Exercise 11.7 This exercise asks you to write a program to perform simple arithmetic calculations using an integer stack. A single reverse Polish expression is to be entered from the keyboard into a string variable. The expression is to be evaluated character by character, and its value is to be output to the screen. Expressions are assumed to be valid Polish expressions, and only digits are allowed as operands. The latter constraint will simplify the problem of converting the characters '0', '1', ..., '9' into the integers 0, 1, 2, ..., 9. The design below carries out the conversion by means of a case statement in which characters representing digits are pushed onto the stack as integers. You may assume that the unit *uGenStk0* is available for use with *itemtype* defined as *integer*.

1.1	*create*(*calculator*)
2.1	write 'Enter a reverse Polish string '
2.2	read in *polish*
3.1	loop for *index* := 1 to *length*(*polish*)
4.1	select case depending on *polish*[*index*]
4.2.1	'+' : *pop*(*calculator*, *FirstOff*)
4.2.2	*pop*(*calculator*, *SecondOff*)
4.2.3	*result* := *SecondOff* + *FirstOff*
4.2.4	*push*(*calculator*, *result*)
4.3.1	'−' : *pop*(*calculator*, *FirstOff*)
4.3.2	*pop*(*calculator*, *SecondOff*)
4.3.3	*result* := *SecondOff* − *FirstOff*
4.3.4	*push*(*calculator*, *result*)
4.4.1	'*' : *pop*(*calculator*, *FirstOff*)
4.4.2	*pop*(*calculator*, *SecondOff*)
4.4.3	*result* := *SecondOff* * *FirstOff*
4.4.4	*push*(*calculator*, *result*)
4.5.1	'0' : *push*(*calculator*, 0)
4.5.2	'1' : *push*(*calculator*, 1)
4.5.3	'2' : *push*(*calculator*, 2)
4.5.4	'3' : *push*(*calculator*, 3)
4.5.5	'4' : *push*(*calculator*, 4)
4.5.6	'5' : *push*(*calculator*, 5)
4.5.7	'6' : *push*(*calculator*, 6)
4.5.8	'7' : *push*(*calculator*, 7)
4.5.9	'8' : *push*(*calculator*, 8)
4.5.10	'9' : *push*(*calculator*, 9)

4.6 selectend
5   loopend
6.1 *pop(calculator, result)*
6.2 write out 'The value of the expression is ', *result*

Data table

Identifier	Description	Type
calculator	Representation of an integer stack	*genstack* variable
polish	A reverse Polish expression	*string* variable
index	Loop control variable	*integer* variable
FirstOff	First item popped off stack	*integer* variable
SecondOff	Second item popped off stack	*integer* variable
result	Calculation result	*integer* variable

11.6 POINTER VARIABLES

This section discusses how Pascal can be used to create dynamic variables. Dynamic data structures are data structures that expand and contract as the program executes. This requires memory to be allocated as new dynamic variables are created during execution. As dynamic variables are discarded during execution, the memory they occupied can be recovered. This can be contrasted with an array in which the amount of storage required is calculated before execution and this amount of space is reserved for the whole execution. Whether all the elements are initialized, updated and so on is not of concern here – the storage space has been allocated and will not change in size. The memory area in which dynamic variables are stored is called the **heap**. Dynamic variables are referred to as **pointer variables** and they complete the list of available types in Pascal.

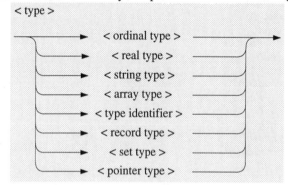

Figure 11.3 The syntax of < type >

Essentially, a pointer variable contains an address into the heap. The address denotes the start of a portion of the heap at which a value will be stored. Figure 11.4 shows how pointer variables will be represented diagrammatically.

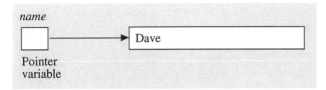

Figure 11.4 Pointer variable

Figure 11.4 contains a pointer variable *name*, which points to the string value 'Dave'. Pointer variables can be made to point to values of any simple or structured type. In order for the compiler to know how much memory to allocate for the values being stored, the declaration of a pointer variable must include details of their type. So for Figure 11.4 *name* points to a string value and could be declared as follows:

```
var
   name : ^ string[8];
```

This is read as '*name* is defined to be of type pointer to *string*[8]'. The circumflex symbol, ^, indicates that the variable is a pointer variable and *string*[8] specifies that the type of data to which it points is a string of static length 8. We say that *name* is a pointer type bound to the type *string*[8]. More usually, we would use a type definition as follows:

```
type
   StringPtr = ^ string[8];
var
   name : StringPtr;
```

The syntax for a pointer declaration is contained in Figure 11.5.

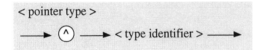

Figure 11.5 The syntax of < pointer type >

Exercise 11.8 Write down declarations for a variable that is bound to the type *integer* and for a variable that is bound to a record which has three fields: a *string* field, a *Boolean* field and an *integer* field.

- Guideline (pointer type definition) Pointer type definitions have the form: identifier, equals sign, circumflex and then the identifier of the type to which it points. Note that the circumflex precedes the type being pointed at.

To give you a mental image of a pointer variable, we ask you to picture the heap of a computer as a sequence of consecutively numbered storage locations. The locations will be numbered #1, #2, #3 .... (The symbol # will help to distinguish address locations from integers that might well be stored at a memory location.) A pointer variable stores a heap address, and so we can imagine *name* will store a value like #8. The value to which a pointer variable points is actually a variable. In Figure 11.4 *name* points to a *string*[8] variable which is referenced using the identifier *name*^. Figure 11.6, in which question marks denote uninitialized memory locations, shows how we shall represent this diagrammatically.

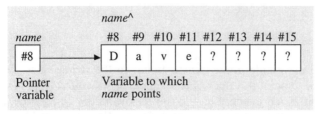

Figure 11.6 Pointer variable with hypothetical addresses

- Guideline (pointer variable) The variable pointed to by a (pointer) variable whose identifier is *ptr* is denoted by *ptr*^. Here, the circumflex follows the identifier.

More formally, the syntax of a variable reference has the following form:

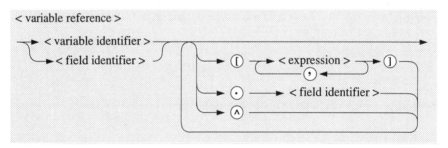

Figure 11.7 The updated syntax of < variable reference >

In Figure 11.6, we have assumed that each character requires one storage location, so the start address of the variable *name*^ is #8. Although many of the diagrams in this section will contain hypothetical addresses it should be remembered that addresses cannot be manipulated by the user. Indeed, the user has no direct access to them.

The variable *name*^ can be updated like any other string variable so, for example, we could update it as follows:

```
name^[3] := 'l'
```

after which *name*^ would have value 'Dale'.

The declaration of a pointer variable *name* tells the compiler to reserve enough space to hold an address. As with any variable, its value remains undefined until it is initialized during program execution. So how did the variable *name* get initialized with the heap address #8? A procedure called *new* performs the task. It does two things, which we can illustrate using Figure 11.6. First, it reserves enough space in the heap for the value of the type to which the pointer is bound. In Figure 11.6 this is heap storage locations #8 to #15, this being the space required to store a string of static length 8. Next, the start address of these reserved locations is assigned to the pointer variable. So here, *name* is assigned the heap address #8. We can represent the state of the memory at this stage as in Figure 11.8:

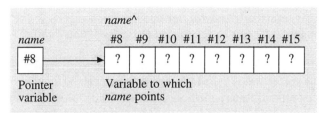

Figure 11.8 The effect of the call *new*(*name*)

The important point to realize is that as a result of the call the value of *name*^ is still undefined. Furthermore, note that the allocation of memory just described takes place during program execution.

- Guideline (*new*) This reserves enough memory in the heap for the value of the type to which the pointer variable is bound and then assigns to the pointer variable the start address of this range. (This address cannot be accessed directly by the user.)

Using the definitions in the solution to Exercise 11.6, the following program fragment would initialize the variable *RecPtr* and then assign values to the record to which it points.

```
new(RecPtr);
RecPtr^.stringfield := 'Dave';
RecPtr^.Booleanfield := true;
RecPtr^.integerfield := 20;
```

As we have already stated, an address cannot be directly assigned to a pointer variable, but the value of an existing pointer variable can be assigned to another one of the same type. Consider the following declarations and program fragment.

```
type
    IntPtrType = ^integer;
var
    WholePointer, IntPointer : IntPtrType;
    :
new(WholePointer);
WholePointer^ := 100;
IntPointer := WholePointer
```

At compilation, enough space for two addresses is reserved for the two pointer variables. At run-time the call to *new* reserves space from the heap for an integer value and assigns the start address of this space to *WholePointer*. Suppose this address is #2. The next statement assigns the integer value 100 to the memory beginning at location #2, that is, to *WholePointer*^. Next, the (address) value of *IntPointer*, which had hitherto been undefined, is assigned the value currently stored in *WholePointer*. This means *IntPointer* is assigned the value #2. Figure 11.9 summarizes the position.

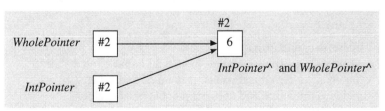

Figure 11.9 Assignment of pointer variables

The effect of this assignment is to make *WholePointer* and *IntPointer* point to the same address. Thus, the data beginning at #2 can be referenced either by *WholePointer^* or by *IntPointer^*.

There is one exception to the rule that an address cannot be directly assigned to a pointer variable, and that is the special value called *nil*. The value *nil* can be thought of as a heap address that does not correspond to any memory location. Thus, a pointer variable which is assigned this value is initialized but does not point anywhere. Given the declaration of *IntPointer* above, the statement

```
IntPointer := nil
```

would have the effect of initializing the variable with the 'address' *nil*. This situation can be represented diagrammatically as shown in Figure 11.10.

Figure 11.10 Initializing a pointer variable with *nil*

We shall see later an application of the use of a pointer with value *nil*. For now it is important to understand the difference between an uninitialized pointer variable, a pointer variable with value *nil*, an initialized pointer variable whose bound value is not initialized and an initialized pointer variable whose bound value is initialized.

Pointer variables can be tested for equality and inequality provided that they are bound to data of the same type. If two pointer variables are equal, they point to the same address and hence the same data. This is the situation depicted in Figure 11.9 after the execution of line 6. If two pointer values differ, then they do not point to the same address.

Exercise 11.9 For each of the following numbered lines of code choose from the following list the description that best describes the state of each pointer variable after the line has executed. Lines that you think are syntactically invalid should be ignored when you decide the status of subsequent lines, but you should try to explain why the syntax error occurs.

```
var
  p, q, r : ^integer;
begin
  new(p);          {line 1}
  q := nil;        {line 2}
  q^ := 50;        {line 3}
  r^ := 25;        {line 4}
  p^ := 10;        {line 5}
  p := nil;        {line 6}
```

(a)   The pointer variable is uninitialized.
(b)   The pointer variable is initialized and points to an uninitialized value.
(c)   The pointer variable is initialized and points to an initialized value.
(d)   The pointer variable is initialized and does not point to a data value.
(e)   The line contains a syntax error.

Exercise 11.10 What would be written out by each of the *writeln* statements in the following program fragment in which all the variables are pointers bound to the type *char*?

```
new(FirstPointer);                                          {line 1}
FirstPointer^ := 'a';                                       {line 2}
writeln('First output ', FirstPointer^);                    {line 3}
SecondPointer := FirstPointer;                              {line 4}
writeln('Second output ', FirstPointer^, SecondPointer^);   {line 5}
SecondPointer^ := 'b';                                      {line 6}
writeln('Third output ', SecondPointer^);                   {line 7}
new(SecondPointer);                                         {line 8}
SecondPointer^ := 'c';                                      {line 9}
writeln('Fourth output ', SecondPointer^);                  {line 10}
FirstPointer := SecondPointer;                             {line 11}
writeln('Fifth output ', FirstPointer^, SecondPointer^);    {line 12}
```

Figure 11.11 represents the state of the memory at various points during the execution of the code fragment in Exercise 11.10.

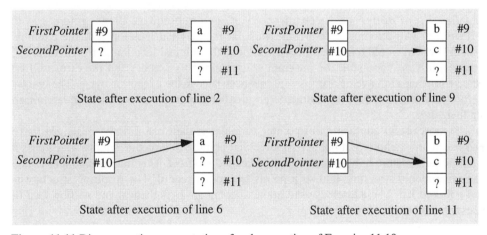

Figure 11.11 Diagrammatic representation of code execution of Exercise 11.10

A point to note here is that the data at location #9 cannot be accessed after the execution of the code fragment because nothing points to it. That memory location has become lost for the remainder of any subsequent execution. For data which occupy very little memory space such a loss would not be important, but if such lost space is allowed to build up then memory space can become exhausted because large amounts of it have become lost and therefore no longer usable. To avoid lost memory, space has to be released before it becomes detached from the pointer that points to it. Pascal provides a routine called *dispose* to do this. The code below shows the modification that would be required.

```
new(SecondPointer);                                        {line 8}
SecondPointer^ := 'c';                                      {line 9}
writeln('Fourth output ', SecondPointer^);                  {line 10}
dispose(FirstPointer);                                     {new line}
FirstPointer := SecondPointer;                             {line 11}
writeln('Fifth output ', FirstPointer^, SecondPointer^);    {line 12}
```

The call to *dispose* has to be placed after the last reference to *FirstPointer* in line 4 but before its update in line 11. We have placed it just before the update. Diagrammatically, the effect of a call to *dispose* can be pictured as shown in Figure 11.12.

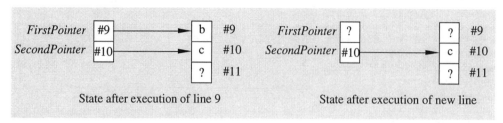

Figure 11.12 The state after a call to *dispose*

In good implementations of *dispose* any attempt to access a disposed variable should be detected by the system because references to it should be undefined. Moreover, the data to which it used to point should no longer be available. This is not the case in Turbo. It will not detect that *FirstPointer* has been disposed of, and subsequent illegal references to *FirstPointer^* will attempt to return the value at the original location. For the example above, the system would try to interpret the value at the original location as a *char* value. If, by chance, this is successful, the program will continue to execute and the error will go undetected perhaps to have disastrous consequences later in the execution cycle. The onus is therefore very much on the programmer to ensure that disposed variables are not referenced again thereafter.

The most useful application of pointer variables is their use in linked lists. We have already seen an example of a pointer variable that pointed to a record. Figure 11.13 uses a similar record structure but it has an extra field called *linkfield*. This field is a pointer bound to the same record structure, and so it points to another record. The resulting structure is called a **linked list**. The addresses used in the diagram are hypothetical and will be used in the description below.

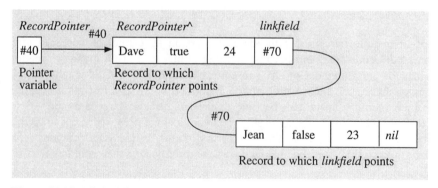

Figure 11.13 A linked list of records

The linked list in Figure 11.13 can be declared and initialized as follows. Study it before reading the commentary below.

```
type
  ptype = ^details;
  details = record
              name      : string;
              married   : Boolean;
              age       : integer;
              linkfield : ptype
           end;
var
  RecordPointer : ptype ;
begin
  new(RecordPointer);
  with RecordPointer^ do
    begin
      name := 'Dave'
      married := true;
      age := 24;
      new(linkfield)
    end;
  with RecordPointer^.linkfield^ do
    begin
      name := 'Jean';
      married := false;
      age := 23;
      linkfield := nil
    end
```

We begin by examining the record type definition. The first three fields are straightforward and need no explanation. The fourth field, *linkfield*, is declared to have type *ptype*, and so this field is a pointer to a record of type *details*. In other words, this field contains a pointer to another record of the same type. There is one rather subtle point you may not have spotted here and that is in the definition of *ptype*. Its definition references the identifier *details*, but at the time of the reference *details* has not been defined. There would appear to be an undeclared identifier error. An attempt at overcoming this would be to place the definition of *ptype* after that of the record *details*. The problem with this is that then the identifier *ptype* is referenced (in the definition of *details*) before it is defined. There would appear to be a Catch-22 situation. Pascal permits, in this instance, the referencing of an identifier before it is declared, in what is often referred to as an **implicit forward reference**. This term will become very familiar in this and later chapters. The variable *RecordPointer* is then defined to be of type *ptype*, and so is a pointer variable which points to a record of type *details*.

The first statement of the program body initializes *RecordPointer*. This means it reserves enough space on the heap for a record of type *ptype* and assigns to *RecordPointer* the start address of this reserved space. Using the hypothetical addresses of Figure 11.13 *RecordPointer* is assigned the value #40. The reference *RecordPointer^* refers to the whole of the record beginning at location #40, and so the first **with** statement gives access to its fields. The first three field initializations need no explanation. The fourth field has to be initialized to point to a second record. A call to *new* with parameter *linkfield* is what is required, and in terms of Figure 11.13 this field is given value #70. At this point the structure could be pictured as being in the following state (Figure 11.14):

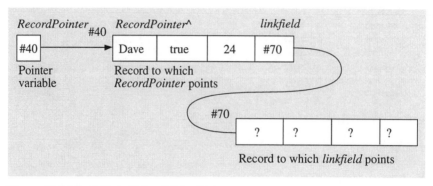

Figure 11.14 Partially initialized linked list

The record pointed to by the #70 field has an identifier which consists of the link field identifier followed by a circumflex, that is, *RecordPointer^.linkfield.^*. This identifier references the whole of the record beginning at #70 and this accounts for the form of the second **with** statement. The individual fields of this record can then be assigned values in the now familiar way.

Exercise 11.11 Rewrite the code consisting of the second **with** statement without using **with**.

Exercise 11.12 Suppose a third record was to be attached to the linked list in Figure 11.13. Write down statements which would create the record and link it in. You will need to adjust the value of the *linkfield* of the record currently shown as *nil* in Figure 11.13. The new record should have values of your own choice in the first three fields and the value *nil* in the fourth field. Do not make use of a **with** statement.

11.7 POINTER-BASED REPRESENTATION OF STACKS

In Section 11.4 we used an array to implement a stack. We remarked at the time that this imposed the restriction that the stack was thereby limited to some maximum number of elements that it could contain. A problem then arises if it becomes necessary to exceed this maximum number because the whole of the code providing the abstract data type has to be updated. In this section we shall use a linked list that will enable us to implement a stack whose size is limited only by the memory capacity of the machine. The specification of the stack will be the same as for *genstack* of Section 11.4.2. This will enable us to create stacks of any base type. However, for illustrative purposes, all the diagrams in this section will assume that this base type is *integer*. There is one difference to the previous operation specifications, namely, we shall assume the memory is large enough to accommodate any stack and so we shall ignore the possibility of stack overflow. Hence the new specification of *push* is:

push

stack	Representation of character stack	*genstack* parameter
item	Character to be entered onto the stack	*itemtype* parameter
{Place the item on top of *stack* and return the updated *stack*. The memory is assumed to be large enough to accommodate all stacks.}		
stack	Updated stack	*genstack* parameter

Figure 11.15 illustrates diagrammatically how we can use a linked list to implement a stack. The diagram shows the contents of a stack being built up and the corresponding state of the pointer representation. The identifier *stack* represents the pointer variable that points to the linked sequence.

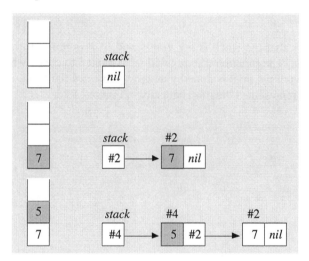

Figure 11.15 A stack and its representation as a sequence

Notice that the item on the top of the stack is the first item in the linked list of records and the item at the bottom of the stack is the last item in the list. Thus, when a new item is pushed onto the stack it goes to the front of the list so that it is the record directly referenced by the pointer variable *stack*. Reading the diagram from the bottom upwards shows what effect *pop* must have on the list. The item to be popped is the item that is first in the sequence. You should also notice that for an empty stack the variable *stack* has value *nil*. The following declarations define the generic stack of Section 11.4.2 using a pointer representation.

```
unit uGenStk0;
interface
  {PRIVATE part}
  type
    itemtype = {Type of items to be stacked is to be inserted here}
    genstack = ^stackrecord;
    stackrecord = record
                    stackitem : itemtype;
                    link      : genstack;
                  end;
```

```
{PUBLIC part
  genstack from above (but not its structure)}
procedure create(var stack : genstack);
function isempty(stack : genstack) : Boolean;
procedure pop(var stack : genstack; var item : itemtype);
procedure push(var stack : genstack; item : itemtype);
```

The public part is exactly as it was before. This is just what we would expect, because the user sees this part and it must not contain any data type design details. In the private part *genstack* is now not a record but is defined to be of type pointer to *stackrecord*.

Exercise 11.13 Write the implementation of the procedure *create* and the function *isempty*. You will need to modify the designs in Section 11.4 appropriately.

The procedure *pop* has to check that the stack is not empty and, if it is not, return then remove the first item from the list. The function *isempty* will be exploited to check whether or not the stack is empty. Removing the item is done by assigning to *stack* the value of the linkfield of the first item. This is represented diagrammatically in Figure 11.16.

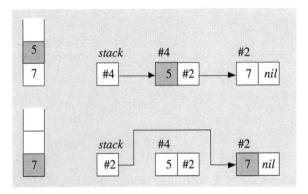

Figure 11.16 Popping an item from a stack

The code for this is:

```
procedure pop;
  {(var stack : genstack; var item : itemtype)
  Pre : stack is initialized.
  Post: If stack is not empty it is returned with top item removed, the latter value
        being placed in item; otherwise an error message is written out.}
  begin
    if isempty(stack) then
      writeln('Underflow')
    else
      begin
        item := stack^.stackitem;
        stack := stack^.link
      end
  end;
```

Exercise 11.14 Figure 11.16 suggests that the record containing the popped item is lost in memory because it is no longer pointed to. This is so. Modify the code above so that the record is disposed of and its memory space thereby returned to the heap.

Figure 11.17 shows hypothetical values of the pointer variables when a new item is pushed onto the stack. Study the figure to work out a strategy for the design of *push*.

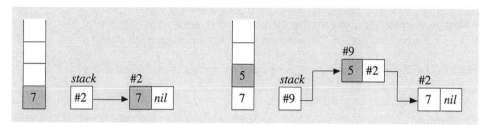

Figure 11.17 Pushing an item onto the stack

A temporary pointer variable will be required which is initialized to the new entry and which is then linked into the beginning of the list by adjusting pointer values appropriately. The code is as follows:

```
procedure push;
  {(var stack : genstack; item : itemtype)
   Pre : stack is initialized.
          item is an itemtype value.
   Post: stack is returned with item pushed on it.}
  var
    temppointer : genstack;
  begin
    new(temppointer);
    temppointer^.stackitem := item;
    temppointer^.link := stack;
    stack := temppointer
  end;
```

11.8 TESTING THE POINTER REPRESENTATION OF STACKS

The implementations corresponding to the operations of an abstract data type need to be tested so we will now develop a test driver program. We can base the program on that developed earlier for testing the array implementation. However, this implementation will require subtly different test data to ensure it works as planned. Furthermore, the routine we used earlier for displaying the stack will need updating for this new representation.

When an implementation uses pointer variables there are often particular difficulties that need to be guarded against. We know that it is an error to reference a variable which has not been initialized. The same is true of pointer variables, but with the latter we have to consider both the variable itself and the variable to which it points. This can be further complicated in sequences because the operations may involve access to their beginning or their end. Some operations may need to take particular action when the sequence is empty or full.

In this section we shall use the guideline for testing that was introduced earlier to see if we can identify some of these difficulties. We remind you that the guideline can be summarized by the words *empty, full, first* and *last*. The questions below are the ones we generated for the array implementation in Section 11.4.2.

(a) Does *push* correctly insert into an *empty* stack?
(b) Does *push* correctly insert into a *full* stack?
(c) Does *push* correctly insert the *first* element into an *empty* stack?
(d) Does *push* correctly insert the *last* element, that is, after all existing ones?
(e) Does *push* correctly insert the *last* element which results in a *full* stack?

Exercise 11.15 Which of these questions is relevant to this implementation?

We first consider the question of whether the operation *push* works correctly on an empty stack. The sequence of diagrams in Figure 11.18 traces the design of *push* as each step is executed.

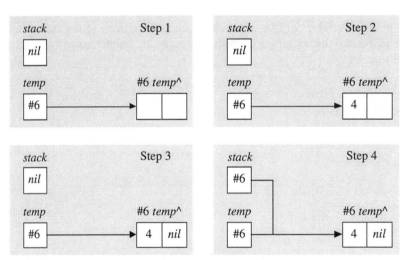

Figure 11.18 Testing *push* when stack is empty

This trace shows that the design does work when the stack is empty. We leave you to re-examine the questions raised in Exercise 11.15 to see which are relevant here. The list of situations that need to be tested is:

• *pop* an empty stack
• *pop* a non-empty stack so the result is not empty
• *pop* a stack consisting of one element and test if the result is empty
• *push* onto an empty stack
• *push* onto a non-empty stack
• test to see if the stack is empty
• *create* a stack and test if the created stack is empty.

Exercise 11.16 Write a program based on the test program *TestuchStack* in Section 11.4.2 that will enable this representation of the stack to be tested.

11.9 EXERCISES AND PROBLEMS

The problems in this section give you the opportunity of implementing stacks using pointers. In Problems 11.5–11.8 we shall write pointer-based implementations corresponding to Problems 11.1–11.4. These new implementations will have the same Pascal unit identifiers as before. The reason for this is to avoid having to make changes to an application that uses the abstract data type. All that will be required to use the new implementation will be to recompile the application with the new unit. To remind you of the names of the data types we reproduce an extended version of Table 11.1 here as Table 11.2.

Table 11.2 Names of Pascal units and their operations

Unit	ADT name	Base type	Operations
uchStack	*charstack*	*char*	*create, isempty, push, pop*
uGenStk0	*genstack*	*itemtype*	*create, isempty, push, pop*
uGenStk1	*genstack*	*itemtype*	*create, isempty, push, pop, print* (11.1)
uGenStk2	*genstack*	*itemtype*	*create, isempty, push, pop, revprint* (11.2)
uGenStk3	*genstack*	*itemtype*	*create, isempty, push, pop* (11.3), *top* (11.3), *print* (11.1)
uGenStk4	*genstack*	*itemtype*	*create, isempty, push, pop, print* (11.1), *count* (11.6)
uGenStk5	*genstack*	*itemtype*	*create, isempty, push, pop* (Ex 11.15)

Exercise 11.17 Write a pointer-based representation of the stack developed in the text that incorporates calls to *dispose* where appropriate.

11.10 PROGRAMMING HINTS

The following guidelines were developed when implementing designs involving pointers:

(a) Guideline (pointer type definition) Pointer type definitions have the form: identifier, equals sign, circumflex and then the identifier of the type to which it points. Note the circumflex precedes the type being pointed at.
(b) Guideline (pointer variable) The variable pointed to by a (pointer) variable whose identifier is *ptr* is denoted by *ptr^*. Here, the circumflex follows the identifier.
(c) Guideline (*new*) This reserves enough memory in the heap for the value of the type to which the pointer variable is bound and then assigns to the pointer variable the start address of this range. (This address cannot be accessed directly by the user.)

11.11 SUMMARY

In this chapter we have looked at two representations of a stack. The first involved using an array. Two items of data were required with this representation: the array itself and a variable that recorded which index in the array corresponded to the top of the stack. These two pieces of information were encapsulated by enclosing them in a record in the stack representation.

The second approach used pointer variables. A pointer variable is a variable that points to an area of memory called the heap. The procedure *new* gets sufficient memory from the heap to store the data item being pointed to. The procedure *dispose* returns no longer wanted data in the heap back to the heap for reuse.

In the pointer representation, the top of the stack was pointed to by a pointer variable. Subsequent items on the stack were held as a linked list of records, one of whose fields was a pointer to the next record in the list. When using pointer variables care has to be taken in testing the designs, paying particular attention to operations that may involve an empty or full list or which require the first or last item to be inspected.

The advantage of using pointers to implement stacks is that the size of the stack can be changed as items are pushed onto it or popped from it. In this way, storage space allocated to the stack expands and contracts as needed. In the array implementation, the amount of space required for the stack representation is fixed and is determined by the declared index range. Changes in the stack size with this representation are reflected by the number of elements that are effectively in use. For an empty stack, no elements are actively in use so all the memory used by the array is wasted. With respect to time, it is usually quicker to access a pointer than an array element because a computation has to be carried out to translate the index value into a memory location. However, these apparent savings of memory and time are not without cost. The pointer representation is more complex to design and code.

12
QUEUES

12.1 INTRODUCTION

In this chapter we shall look at another kind of sequence in which the pre-defined relationship governing the order of the elements is determined strictly by the order in which they are inserted. The method of insertion is that a new item can be inserted at one specified end of the sequence which we shall call its **tail**. The other end is called the **head** of the sequence and is the end from which an item can be retrieved or deleted. You may have recognized that what we have just described is a **queue**. An illustration of a queue with which we are all familiar from our everyday lives is a queue for a bus (Figure 12.1).

Figure 12.1 A bus queue

People join the queue at the end furthest away from the bus stop sign, that is, they join at the tail of the queue. When a bus arrives then people are admitted to it from the front or head of the queue.

We shall also use this data structure to illustrate some of the techniques which can be applied to the occurrence of errors. The errors we shall be interested in are those associated with the actions to be taken in the event that the operation is supplied with inappropriate data. An example is the *pop* operation defined in Section 11.2 (reproduced below).

pop

stack	Representation of character stack	*charstack* parameter
{Remove and return the item on top of *stack* and return the updated *stack*. If the stack is empty write out 'stack underflow'.}		
stack	Updated stack	*charstack* parameter
item	Integer removed from top of stack	*char* parameter

This specification includes a description of what action should be taken if an attempt is made to pop an empty stack. For simplicity, in what was already a conceptually demanding chapter, the simple approach of writing out an error message was adopted. This can create difficulties. Suppose an application does make a call to *pop* when the stack is empty – what is the outcome? The error message is output but the value of *item* is undefined. What happens if this undefined value of *item* is then referenced? Effectively, a run-time error occurs which should lead to the system aborting the program. The usefulness of the message is therefore minimal.

The applications programmer can of course avoid the potential run-time error by testing for an empty stack before calling *pop* as illustrated below:

```
if isempty(mystack) then
    writeln('Attempting to pop an empty stack');
else
  begin
    pop(mystack, item);
    writeln('Popped item was ', item)
  end;
```

By testing for an empty stack, the reference to *item* is now guaranteed to be valid. What the applications programmer has done here is to take the responsibility for testing that *pop* is not applied to an empty stack. This responsibility could have been given to the applications programmer explicitly in the specification, as follows:

pop

stack	Representation of character stack	*charstack* parameter
{Remove and return the item on top of *stack* and return the updated *stack*. It is the responsibility of the calling program to ensure *pop* is not called with an empty stack.}		
stack	Updated stack	*charstack* parameter
item	Integer removed from top of stack	*char* parameter

These two specifications illustrate the two ways in which error situations like this can be handled. In the former method, the implementor of the abstract data type takes responsibility for potential error situations whereas, in the latter, the onus is placed on the applications programmer. It may well be that leaving the applications programmer to handle the error is the most appropriate course of action. This demands that suitable action must be taken by the applications programmer before any invocation of an operation which could lead to an undefined outcome. This is not as secure a situation as one would like, for while the specification makes the position clear it does not force the applications programmer to take account of the possible malfunction. The error situation is dealt with implicitly. This can be overcome by sharing the responsibility for dealing with errors between the implementor and the applications programmer. This would be done here by introducing a third results parameter whose value would indicate the success, or otherwise, of the call. The specification would then be:

pop

stack	Representation of character stack	*charstack* parameter
{If the stack is not empty then set *success* to true. Then remove and return the item on top of *stack* and return the updated *stack*. If the stack is empty then set *success* to false and return *stack* unaltered.}		
stack	Updated stack	*charstack* parameter
item	Integer removed from top of stack	*char* parameter
success	Error status flag	*Boolean* parameter

The inclusion of the extra parameter forces the applications programmer to take account of it in a call, thus making potential error situations explicit. In this chapter, the text will use the implicit method of dealing with errors and the problem sections will use the explicit method. This will minimize the complexity of the code in the text, and once you have mastered it will enable you to develop the alternative strategy.

We shall begin by looking at a queue of *string*, in fact a queue of names. The abstract data type *stringqueue* will be defined by five operations whose specifications are given below. In these specifications *queue* is a parameter of type *stringqueue* and *item* is a string parameter, and we shall assume that they are to be implemented in a unit called *uqueue*.

create

{Return a new empty queue of type *stringqueue*.}		
queue	A new character stack	*stringqueue* parameter

front

queue	Representation of string queue	*stringqueue* parameter
{Return the item at the head of the queue leaving *queue* unaltered. It is the responsibility of the calling program to ensure that *front* is not called with an empty queue.}		
item	Item at head of queue	*string* parameter

insert

queue	Representation of string queue	*stringqueue* parameter
item	Item to be inserted at tail	*string* parameter
{Insert *item* at tail of *queue* and return the updated *queue*.}		
queue	Updated queue	*stringqueue* parameter

remove

queue	Representation of string queue	*stringqueue* parameter
{Remove the item at the head of *queue* and return updated *queue*. It is the responsibility of the calling program to ensure that *remove* is not called with an empty queue.}		
queue	Updated queue	*stringqueue* parameter

isempty

queue	Representation of string queue	*stringqueue* parameter
{Return the value true if the queue is empty, false otherwise.}		
isempty		*Boolean* function value

The operations involving the head of the queue are subtly different from the corresponding operation on stacks. Here, *front* returns the item at the head of the queue but leaves the queue unaltered. In other words, *front* allows the item at the head of the queue to be inspected without removing it. To remove an item from the head of the queue the operation *remove* has to be used. Notice that *remove* does not return the removed item. It is not a peculiarity of queues that dictates this method of removal – we have chosen this definition to contrast it with the definition of *pop* used in Chapter 11. The point is that there are many ways in which we can model a queue, or indeed any data structure. Here, we have chosen five operations. As this discussion shows, we could have chosen slightly different ones to represent the queue. Each different choice of operations leads to a different abstract data type because of the different operations involved, but each collection of operations would be a model for the queue.

12.2 WRITING A DRIVER PROGRAM FOR A QUEUE

Now that the operations defining a queue have been specified, we shall develop a program that will enable the operations to be tested. This will give you the opportunity to become familiar with the operations before working on their implementation. Because the purpose of the program is to test the operations it will consist of a simple menu that will enable each of the operations to be selected and invoked. We have also included two options concerned with displaying the queue. A top-level design for such a program is:

```
      {Queue testing program}
 1    create(queue)
 2    repeat
 3       write out menu
 4       read in choice
 5       select case depending on choice
 6          'I' :  insert data into queue
 7          'D' :  display current contents of queue
 8          'R' :  remove an item from the queue
 9          'F' :  display the item at the front of the queue
10          'E' :  display 'empty' if queue is empty, display 'not empty' otherwise
11       selectend
12       read in choice
13    until choice = 'Q'
```

The code below was developed from a refinement of this design. It assumes the abstract data type *stringqueue* is stored in a file called *uqueue*. Since the abstract data type does not provide an operation to write out the contents of a whole queue, a procedure *displayqueue* has been specially written for the test program. Since this procedure requires knowledge of the implementation details we shall omit its code here and leave it for you as an exercise in the next section.

```pascal
program TestuQueue;
uses
  crt, uqueue;
  {Imports
   type
     stringqueue   (details are private)
   procedure create(var queue : stringqueue)
   function  isempty(queue : stringqueue) : Boolean
   procedure front(queue : stringqueue; var item : string)
   procedure insert(var queue : stringqueue; item : string)
   procedure remove(var queue : stringqueue)}
var
  queue  : stringqueue;
  name   : string;
  choice : char;
procedure displayqueue(queue : stringqueue);
  var
    {See Exercise 12.3};
  begin
    {See Exercise 12.3}
  end;
procedure getret;
  {Pre : None.
   Post: None - processing awaits press of <ret>.}
  var
    ch : char;
  begin
    writeln;
    write('Press <ret> to get to main menu ');
    repeat
      ch := readkey
    until (ord(ch) = 13)
  end;

begin
  create(queue);
  choice  := ' ';
  repeat
    clrscr;
    writeln('I : Insert new data into queue');
    writeln('D : Display existing data');
    writeln('R : Remove an item from queue');
    writeln('F : Display the item at front of queue');
    writeln('E : Display status of queue as empty or not empty');
    writeln('Q : Quit');
    writeln;
    writeln('Enter your choice ');
    choice := readkey;
    case upcase(choice) of
      'I' : begin
              write('Enter a name for insertion into queue ');
              readln(name);
              insert(queue, name);
            end;
```

```
        'D' : begin
                displayqueue(queue);
                getret
              end;
        'R' : if not isempty(queue) then
                remove(queue);
        'F' : begin
                if not isempty(queue) then
                  begin
                    front(queue, name);
                    writeln('Item at front of queue is ', name)
                  end
                else
                    writeln('An empty queue has no front member');
                getret
              end;
        'E' : begin
                if isempty(queue) then
                  writeln('Queue is empty')
                else
                  writeln('Queue is not empty');
                getret
              end
      end
  until (upcase(choice) = 'Q')
end.
```

To determine the sort of test data that we will want to submit to the program, we can use the abstract data type test guideline from Chapter 11. The kinds of questions it might generate are as follows:

- Are there problems inserting into an *empty* queue?
- Are there problems associated with *first* element of the queue?
- Are there problems associated with *last* element of the queue?
- Are there problems deleting from an *empty* queue?
- Are there problems deleting the *first* element of the queue?
- Are there problems deleting the *last* element of the queue, that is, a single element queue?

We shall return to some of these points as we develop the implementations of the operations.

12.3 IMPLEMENTING THE ABSTRACT DATA TYPE QUEUE

In this section we shall develop a pointer-based implementation for the abstract data type *stringqueue*. It will be implemented in a Pascal unit called *uqueue*. The same diagrammatic representation will be used for queues as was used for stacks in Chapter 11. They will include hypothetical heap addresses, and we remind you that these are there to help your understanding and do not reflect the amount of memory that the data depicted might require in a machine. Figure 12.2 gives an example of a linked list representation.

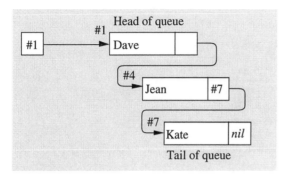

Figure 12.2 A linked list representation of a queue

Here, we have a queue of names each of which is in the first field of a record. The other field in the record is a pointer to the next record, that is, it is a link field. The queue itself is identified by a pointer variable whose value in this diagram is #1 and it points to the record at the head of the queue. Note that the record at the tail of the queue has the value *nil* in its link field. It turns out that the representation in Figure 12.2 does not lead to the simplest designs for the operations specified in Section 12.1. To see why, we shall look at some of the design issues involved.

The hardest operation to design is *insert* because insertions have to take place at the tail of the queue. This involves sequentially searching the queue to find its end. It turns out to be easier if we have two pointers to the queue: one pointing to the head of the queue and one pointing to the tail. Figure 12.3 incorporates this modification using the identifiers *head* and *tail* in the obvious way.

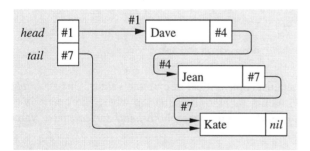

Figure 12.3 A linked list representation of a queue using head and tail pointers

We begin by investigating what has to be done to insert a new item into the example given in Figure 12.3. Insertions are made at the tail of the queue and so the new item will have to go after the record containing 'Kate'. Figure 12.4 shows the result of this insertion.

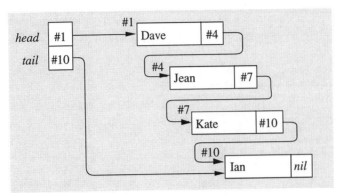

Figure 12.4 The queue after the insertion of Ian

We begin with an initial attempt at defining a representation for this linked list. Clearly, the items in the list will have to be records consisting of a data field of type *string* and a field that points to the next item in the list. Thus, this second field will have to be a pointer to the record. More precisely, a potential representation is:

```
type
    PtrToQueueRec = ^QueueRecord;
    QueueRecord   = record
                        queueitem : string;
                        link      : PtrToQueueRec;
                    end;

var
    head, tail, temp : PtrToQueueRec;
```

If we now consider the insertion described above, a new record, with identifier *temp* of type *PtrToQueueRec*, can be created using the procedure *new*. This record can then be initialized with the new entry details. Then the link field of Kate's record has to be updated to point to this new record and finally *tail* has to be updated to point to this new *tail* record.

```
new(temp);                    {temp points to new record}
temp^.queueitem := 'Ian';     {Initialize the string data field}
temp^.link := nil;            {This will signify the end of the queue}
tail^.link := temp;           {Make Kate record point to the new one}
tail := temp;                 {Make tail point to new record}
```

This now needs to be tested against some critical or extreme values. One such instance which we have already identified would include the situation where the queue is empty before insertion takes place. The queue is empty when both *head* and *tail* have value *nil*. Figure 12.5 illustrates this situation.

Figure 12.5 An empty queue

Taking this as a starting point and using 'Dave' as the item to be inserted then, after the first three statements of the code above have executed, the state of the variables can be represented as shown in Figure 12.6.

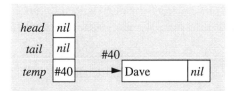

Figure 12.6 The situation after the execution of the first three statements

The fourth statement of the code updates *tail^.link*, but the value of *tail* is *nil* and so attempting to reference the record to which *tail* points is an error. There are two ways to overcome this. The first would be to redesign the code so that it treats the situation when the queue is empty as a special case. All that this would require is a conditional statement that separates the two possibilities of an empty and a non-empty queue. An alternative approach is to introduce a dummy record into the queue so that *head* and *tail* always point to this record. When we do this an empty queue then looks like that shown in Figure 12.7.

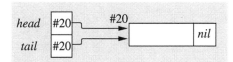

Figure 12.7 An empty queue using a dummy record

Here, *head* and *tail* both point to the record at #20 and so the problem we had above cannot arise. This time there is no difficulty referencing *tail^.link* because this value does exist and it has value *nil*. The diagram also shows that an empty sequence can be recognized by virtue of the fact that *head* and *tail* both have value *nil*, in other words, an empty queue has the property that *head* = *tail*.

Using a dummy record the queue of Figure 12.4 would be represented diagrammatically as in Figure 12.8.

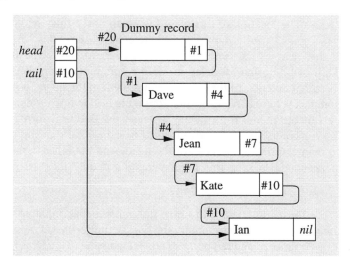

Figure 12.8 A queue with a dummy record

This model, which uses both *head* and *tail* pointers together with a dummy item, appears to solve the problems associated with insertion. We also need to see whether it works well with the other operators.

The procedure *create* will have to initialize the dummy record as well as deal with any other necessary initialization. The following code fragment gives the details.

```
new(head)
tail := head
head^.link := nil
```

Finally, we consider whether the model is suitable for the operation *remove*. This operator must remove the item at the head of the queue. In Figure 12.8 this would be the record containing the item 'Dave'. Figure 12.9 shows how this record can be deleted.

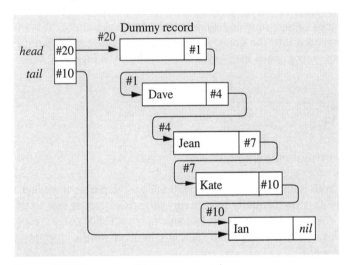

Figure 12.9 The queue with Dave removed

To carry out this deletion the link field of the dummy record has to be updated to point to the record containing 'Jean'. The location of this record is given in the link field of the record containing 'Dave'. Hence *head^.link* has to be updated to contain *head^.link^.link*, the latter being the identifier that denotes the link field of Dave's record. Thus, the model appears to lead to a straightforward design for deletion. Before committing ourselves to it we ought to satisfy ourselves that deletion of the last remaining item in the queue does not require an unnecessarily complex solution. We leave that for you to decide in Exercise 12.2.

Having established a suitable model for a queue we can now define it formally in Pascal. Exercise 12.1 asks you to do this. You will need to bear in mind that the queue essentially consists of two pointers: one to the head of the queue and the other to the tail. These will have to be encapsulated to keep this implementation detail hidden from the applications programmer.

Exercise 12.1 Write the code for the interface part of the unit *uqueue* that implements the abstract data type *stringqueue*. You will need to modify the type definitions used in the text to take account of the fact that both head and tail pointers are being used.

Exercise 12.2 Write the code for the implementation part of the unit *uqueue* using the definitions from the solution to Exercise 12.1.

The implementation of *remove* shows that removing the last item in a queue has to be treated as a special case. The reason for this is that an extra pointer to the last item in the queue is being used. Unlike *insert*, where the dummy item avoided having to deal with the empty queue as a special case, no such advantage accrues here.

Exercise 12.3 Write an implementation for the procedure *displayqueue* used in the program *TestuQueue*.

12.4 GENERIC QUEUES

The queue we have developed in the previous sections has elements that are strings. Provided we are happy for the applications programmer to insert details into the interface part of the abstract data type implementation then we can write a more general queue type. All we have to do is to abstract the code for *uqueue* so that it does not contain explicit references to *string*. Instead, we declare the type of data in the queue using the identifier *itemtype*, which will be defined in the interface. The new interface for such an approach is shown below.

```
unit uGenQue;
interface
  {Private part}
  type
    itemtype      = {To be supplied by the user}
    PtrToQueueRec = ^QueueRecord;
    genqueue    = record
                      head : PtrToQueueRec;
                      tail : PtrToQueueRec;
                  end;
    QueueRecord   = record
                      queueitem : itemtype;
                      link      : PtrToQueueRec;
                  end;
  {Public part}
  {The identifier genqueue from above but not its type}
  procedure create(var queue : genqueue);
  function  isempty(queue : genqueue) : Boolean;
  procedure front(queue : genqueue; var item : itemtype);
  procedure insert(var queue : genqueue; item : itemtype);
  procedure remove(var queue : genqueue);
```

The implementation part is exactly as it is for the unit *uqueue*. This is because the implementations of the routines do not include any local variables whose type is the element being placed on the queue. There is one minor change to the precondition comment for the procedure *insert* which would now have to say that *item* was an initialized queue element.

12.5 EXERCISES AND PROBLEMS

Exercise 12.4 Modify the implementation of remove in *uqueue* so that it disposes pointers from the heap when an element is removed.

Problem 12.1 asks you to extend the operations defined on a queue and Problem 12.6 looks at a different implementation of a queue in which error conditions are explicit in the sense described earlier. The remaining problems are concerned with developing an abstract data type that has queue-like properties.

The card game Gin Rummy uses a pack of cards in a queue-like fashion. There are two players, each of whom are dealt 10 cards; the remaining cards then form what is known as the **stock**, and this will be the concern of the remaining problems. The stock contains 32 cards, which are placed face down on the table. The top card is turned over and placed beside the stock. Players may exchange one of their own cards for either the face-up card or the face-down card on the top of the stock. They do so by picking up one of these two cards and then returning a discard, face uppermost, to the face-up pile beside the stock. Thus, discards always go on the face-up pile so that at any time only one face is visible. There is in fact no need to have a face-up pile. The single pile will do, provided that both players can see the bottom card of the stock. This can be arranged by placing the stock on a glass-topped table arranged above the eye-line. Now a player can take either the top (hidden) card of the stock or the bottom (exposed) card. Discards will be to the bottom of the stock. Note that when a player chooses to take from the bottom of the stock this exposes the card underneath it. In the remainder of this problem section, an abstract data type to represent the stock and the allowable operations on it will be developed. The operations defined on the stock are given below. The problems will ask you to make definitions for the types *cardtype* and *stocktype*.

makestock

{Return a new stock containing 32 cards.}		
stock	A stock of 32 cards	*stocktype* parameter

drawtop

stock	A stock of 32 cards	*stocktype* parameter
{Remove the top card as *draw* from the stock and return the updated stock. It is the responsibility of the user to ensure that *replace* is called prior to the next request to draw a card.}		
stock	Updated stock if 31 cards	*stocktype* parameter
draw	The top card of the stock	*cardtype* parameter

drawbottom

stock	A stock of 32 cards	*stocktype* parameter
{Remove the bottom card as *draw* from the stock. Display the new bottom card exposed by this removal. It is the responsibility of the user to ensure that *replace* is called prior to the next request to draw a card.}		
stock	Updated stock if 31 cards	*stocktype* parameter
draw	The card removed from the stock	*cardtype* parameter

replace

stock	A stock of 31 cards	*stocktype* parameter
discard	Card to be replaced in *stock*	*cardtype* parameter
{Replace *discard* at the bottom of the stock and return updated stock.}		
stock	Updated stock of 32 cards	*stocktype* parameter

showbottom

stock	The stock	*stocktype* parameter
{Display the card at the bottom of the stock.}		

12.6 SUMMARY

In this chapter we have looked at the abstract data type queue using a pointer-based representation. Two pointers were used: one pointing to the head of the queue and the other to the tail. Although it is not strictly necessary to use two pointers it makes the design of some of the operations easier. It became apparent that it would be beneficial to use a dummy as the first item in the linked list. This was so because the operation of inserting a new item required special attention if a dummy item was not used. We also looked at two ways in which errors can be handled. In the first, the onus is placed on the user to ensure all the preconditions of a call to an operation are met. If they are not, a run-time error results. In the second, an additional result status parameter was included in the operation specification so that the success or otherwise of the call could be determined.

13

GENERAL SEQUENCES

13.1 INTRODUCTION

In this chapter we are going to look at a more general type of sequence where the pre-defined relation that determines the order of the items in the sequence is to be found in the data item itself. Typically, we shall be looking at sequences of records, and the sequence will be ordered on one of the fields of the record. A field used for ordering a sequence is called a **key field** and it must have the property that it uniquely identifies each record. The other fields of the records are called **non-key fields**.

As an illustrative example we shall consider a computer system which maintains a list of flights due to arrive at an airport and which provides facilities for keeping this information up to date. This will involve adding new flights to the list, deleting flights that are cancelled and updating the estimated time of arrival of other flights. Output of the list will be to an information screen, an example of which is shown in Figure 13.1. Data on the screen are presented in chronological order of expected arrival time. The second column shows the codes by which individual flights are known. These codes are called flight numbers, even though they consist of both digits and characters. The third column gives the place from which the flight originated and the final column gives the estimated time of arrival.

```
Due        Flight    From      ETA

12.03      BA547     London    12.00
12.05      VA057     Dallas    Landed
12.10      AF600     Paris     Delayed
12.15      BA548     London    12.20
12.20      DA394     Glasgow   12.20
```

Figure 13.1 An arrivals screen

Exercise 13.1 Each row of data in Figure 13.1 can be represented as a record. Which fields of the record structure have the potential for being key fields?

Given the remarks in the solution to Exercise 13.1 we shall designate the arrivals time as the key field and hence the field on which the data will be ordered in the sequence. This choice will make the output of the arrivals board easier because the data can be displayed in the order in which they are stored.

Exercise 13.2 Given this decision, can the flight number be described as a key field?

The problem that we shall consider is a great simplification of a real system. All that we shall require is that the operator of the flight information program be presented with a menu of five choices:

1   Add new flight information
2   Delete a flight
3   Update estimated time of arrival
4   Display the arrivals board
5   Quit

To save space and reduce complexity the program will serve both as an example of the use of a sequence and as a driver program to test the abstract data type implementation. Thus, the options listed in this menu have been chosen as much for their ability to test the operations in the abstract data type as for their use in a real application.

When option 1 is chosen, the operator should be prompted for a new flight arrival time, a flight number, the place from which the flight originates and the estimated time of arrival. None of this input is to be validated, and it may be assumed that the time entered is not already in the list and so is unique. For choices 2 and 3, the operator is to be prompted for a flight number. If the entered number is not in the list then a suitable message is to be output and execution of the option is to cease. When the flight number does exist, then option 2 will delete details of that flight, while option 3 should prompt for a new ETA and update the appropriate entry. Option 4 is to output the contents of the list, but should not take account of the possibility that there may be more entries in the list than will fit on a screen.

It has been decided to represent the data of Figure 13.1 as a linked sequence of records stored on the key field, that is, stored in chronological order of the expected arrival time. The following operator specifications define the abstract data type, *ArrivalsSeq*, which will be designed as a Pascal unit called *uSeq*.

insert

arrivals	Representation of the sequence	*ArrivalsSeq* parameter
newtime	New expected arrival time	*real* parameter
newflight	Flight number	*string* parameter
newfrom	Place flight originated	*string* parameter
neweta	Estimated time of arrival	*string* parameter
{Insert new flight details, time expected, flight number, place of origin and estimated time of arrival, as given by the parameters *newtime*, *newflight*, *newfrom* and *neweta* respectively, into *arrivals*. It may be assumed that *newtime* does not already exist in the sequence.}		
arrivals	Updated sequence	*ArrivalsSeq* parameter

For simplicity, the time data have been specified as *real* parameters. The data corresponding to the estimated time of arrival are specified as *string* parameters. This is because it will not always be a time – the entry may contain the string 'Landed' or 'Delayed'.

delete

arrivals	Representation of the sequence	*ArrivalsSeq* parameter
flightgiven	Flight number to be deleted	*string* parameter
{Delete the entry whose flight number is *flightgiven*. If no such flight exists or the sequence is empty, write out an error report and take no further action.}		
arrivals	Updated sequence	*ArrivalsSeq* parameter

create

{Return a new empty sequence of type *ArrivalsSeq*.}		
arrivals	A new sequence	*ArrivalsSeq* parameter

update

arrivals	Representation of the sequence	*ArrivalsSeq* parameter
flightgiven	Flight number whose ETA is to be updated	*string* parameter
{If the flight number, *flightgiven*, is in the sequence then prompt for and read in the new estimated time of arrival and enter this in the appropriate record. If the flight number does not exist, write out an error message and take no further action.}		
arrivals	Updated sequence	*ArrivalsSeq* parameter

display

arrivals	Representation of the sequence	*ArrivalsSeq* parameter
{Clear the screen and write out the whole of the sequence. If the sequence is empty, take no further action. It may be assumed that the whole sequence will fit onto one screen.}		

13.2 DESIGNING THE ABSTRACT DATA TYPE SEQUENCE

A pointer-based linked list representation will be used for the sequence. As before, we shall begin by representing the sequence diagrammatically and use the diagrams to discover the difficulties involved in creating designs for the operations. The diagrams will include hypothetical heap memory addresses, and the values used do not take any account of the actual amount of memory the data might need.

A significant difference between the sequence we are considering here and what has gone before is that the order of the records here is determined by the key field. This means that when a record is to be inserted then the sequence must be searched to see where the new record should go. Diagrams that represent the sequence will have the same style as those in earlier chapters.

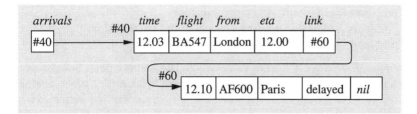

Figure 13.2 A sequence with two records

Figure 13.2 represents a sequence of two records, each of which has five fields. The first four fields correspond to the data in the columns of Figure 13.1 and the final field is a link to the next record. The last record has the value *nil* in its link field to denote the end of the sequence. The link fields are pointers whose type, *ArrivalsSeq,* is defined below. The whole sequence is identified by the pointer variable *arrivals*, also of type *ArrivalsSeq.*

```
unit uSeq;

interface
  {Private part}
  type
    ArrivalsSeq = ^SeqRec;
    SeqRec      = record
                      time   : real;
                      flight : string;
                      from   : string;
                      eta    : string;
                      link   : ArrivalsSeq
                  end;
```

The model for the sequence in Figure 13.2 turns out not to be the most simple. To see why, we need to look at some of the issues relating to the design of the routines corresponding to the operations. The operation of inserting a new record in the sequence is the most complex because it involves discovering where it should be located. This will involve searching the key field of the sequence. Suppose we were searching to see where a record with *time* field of 12.00 should go. A potential design fragment for such a search would be:

1 initialize variables
2 loop while *time* field < 12.00 and it is not the last record
3   move to next record
4 loopend

This may be expressed in more detail using the identifiers in the declarations above together with a variable *location*, of type *ArrivalsSeq*:

1 *location* := *arrivals*
2 loop while (*location^.time* < 12.00) and (it is not the last record)
3   *location* := *location^.link*
4 loopend

We should apply the test guidelines of Chapter 11 to this design. The questions that the guideline should suggest include the following:

- Are there problems inserting into an *empty* sequence?
- Are there problems associated with *first* element of the sequence?
- Are there problems associated with *last* element of the sequence?

For an empty sequence, *arrivals* will have value *nil* (and so will not point to a record). This means an error will occur at step 2 when an attempt is made to access *location^.time*. This is very similar to the problem we encountered when trying to insert the first item into a queue. Rather than treat the empty sequence as a special case, we shall employ the same trick that we used there, namely, we shall use a dummy first record. The sequence in Figure 13.2 would then be represented by that in Figure 13.3.

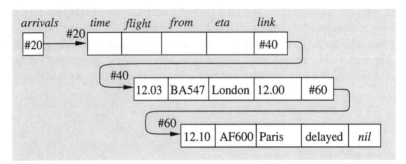

Figure 13.3 A diagrammatic representation of a sequence with dummy first record

Exercise 13.3 Flight YA057 from Dallas is due to arrive at 12.05 and its estimated time of arrival is 12.00. The details of this flight will be inserted as a record between the 12.03 and 12.10 flights. Which of the latter records do you think should be identified by the search?

It will be convenient to develop the search as a procedure, *timesearch*. Its source data will be the sequence together with *timegiven*, the time of the new flight, and its results will be a pointer variable whose value is the location of the record just prior to the insertion point.

timesearch

arrivals	Representation of the sequence	*ArrivalsSeq* parameter
timegiven	Time to be searched for	*real* parameter
{Search the *time* field of the sequence of records pointed to by *origin*. Return to *location* the pointer value that identifies the record whose time field is the last one that has a value less than *timegiven*. (All subsequent records would have a time field that is greater than *timegiven*.).}		
location	Pointer to sought record	*ArrivalsSeq* parameter

The following design is an attempt to find *location* when *timegiven* has value 12.05 and the sequence is as shown in Figure 13.3. Why is it incorrect?

```
1   location := arrivals^.link   {No need to examine the dummy item}
2   loop while (location^.time < 12.05) and (it is not the last record)
3       location := location^.link
4   loopend
```

The problem is that after this search, *location* points to the record at #60 and that is one record too far. This can be resolved using two pointers, one of which lags one record behind the other. The technique of using two pointers in this way is very common in sequence operations. In the following design the value of *location* would be correct for the data in Figure 13.3.

```
1   lag := arrivals
2   lead := arrivals^.link        {No need to examine the dummy item}
3   loop while (lead^.time < 12.05) and (it is not the last record)
4       lag := lead
5       lead := lead^.link
6   loopend
7   location := lag
```

The designs in the following exercise are attempts to generalize this design to search for *timegiven* rather than the specific value 12.05.

Exercise 13.4 Both the designs below contain errors. Identify the circumstances in which the errors occur by tracing the design when *timegiven* has value 12.20 and the sequence is in the state depicted in Figure 13.3. You may like to bear in mind the question: 'Are there problems associated with *last* element of the sequence?'

```
1   lag := arrivals
2   lead := arrivals^.link        {No need to examine the dummy item}
3   loop while (lead^.time < timegiven) and (lead^.link <> nil)
4       lag := lead
5       lead := lead^.link
6   loopend
7   location := lag
```

```
1   lag := arrivals
2   lead := arrivals^.link        {No need to examine the dummy item}
3   loop while (lead^.time < timegiven) and (lead <> nil)
4       lag := lead
5       lead := lead^.link
6   loopend
7   location := lag
```

The difficulties encountered in Exercise 13.4 only arise because the time being sought comes after all the times in the sequence. Essentially, we need to know when we have reached the end of the sequence and can go no further. Rather than trying to identify the end of the sequence we can make the last record point back to the dummy record, as shown in Figure 13.4.

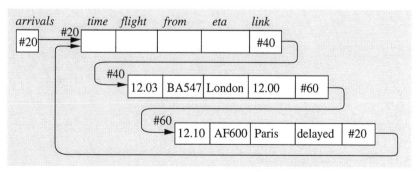

Figure 13.4 A sequence with last record pointing to the dummy record

The dummy record can then be exploited in a similar way to when a dummy element with index 0 was used when searching an array. The time being sought is entered into the time field of the dummy record, and searching begins at the first actual record. When the sought time exceeds all those in the sequence, the search progresses past the last record to the dummy, where of course a match occurs and the search ceases. The pointer *lag* then points to the last record. In this way, we do not have to worry about falling off the end of the sequence. The code for *timegiven* can then be developed as:

```
procedure timesearch(arrivals: ArrivalsSeq; timegiven : real;
                     var location : ArrivalsSeq);
  {Pre : arrivals is an initialized sequence, possibly empty.
         timegiven is an initialized real value.
   Post: location points to the record whose time field is the last one which has a
         value less than timegiven. All subsequent records have a time field which
         is greater than timegiven.}
  var
    lead, lag : ArrivalsSeq;
  begin
    arrivals^.time := timegiven;
    lag := arrivals;
    lead := arrivals^.link;
    while lead^.time < timegiven do
      begin
        lag := lead;
        lead := lead^.link
      end;
    location := lag
  end;
```

Exercise 13.5 Write a code fragment which, starting with Figure 13.4, will insert a new record at time 12.05 as shown in Figure 13.5. The highlighted part of Figure 13.5 indicates the changes that are required. Your fragment should include a call to *timesearch*.

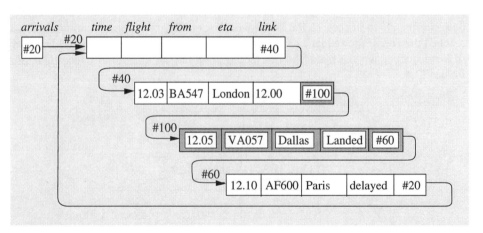

Figure 13.5 Insertion of a new record

The solution to Exercise 13.5 can be generalized into a design for the procedure *insert*. The exercises at the end of the section will ask you to complete the details.

We now turn our attention to a preliminary investigation of the design of *delete* and *update*. Both of these operations are required to search the non-key *flight* field of the records for the value *flightgiven*. This search process will be designed as a procedure, *flightsearch*, with source data *arrivals* and *flightgiven*. What should its results be? Should the result be a pointer to the record containing *flightgiven* or to its predecessor? We can see what is required by looking at Figure 13.5 and supposing *flightgiven* is 'VA057', so that the record at #100 is the one being sought. To *update* this record, the result has to be a pointer with value #100. But to *delete* it, the result would need to be a pointer with value #40 so that the 12.03 record can have its link field updated to value #60. The procedure *flightsearch* will be specified so that it returns both pointers, one to the sought item and the other to its predecessor.

flightsearch

arrivals flightgiven	Representation of the sequence Flight number to be deleted	*ArrivalsSeq* parameter *string* parameter
{Search the flight arrivals sequence for the record containing *flightgiven* in its *flight* field. Return to *lead* the pointer value that identifies this record and to *lag* the pointer to the previous record. If no such record exists then *lead* should be assigned the value *arrivals*.}		
lead lag	Sought record Predecessor of sought record	*ArrivalsSeq* parameter *ArrivalsSeq* parameter

By putting *timegiven* in the dummy item, success of the search is assured and the correct value will be assigned to *lead* if the flight number is not in the sequence. An implementation of procedure *flightsearch* is:

```
procedure flightsearch;  {arrivals : ArrivalsSeq; flightgiven : string;
                          var lead, lag : ArrivalsSeq}
  {Pre : arrivals is an initialized sequence, possibly empty.
         flightgiven is an initialized string.
  {Post: If flightgiven is in the sequence then lead points to the record containing
         it and lag points to the record preceding it.
         Otherwise lead is assigned the value arrivals.}
begin
  arrivals^.flight := flightgiven;
  lag := arrivals;
  lead := arrivals^.link;
  while lead^.flight <> flightgiven do
    begin
      lag := lead;
      lead := lead^.link
    end
end;  {end of procedure flightsearch}
```

Exercise 13.6 Given the sequence in Figure 13.5, and supposing that *lead* and *lag* have values resulting from the search for flight 'VA057', write down a statement that will remove this record from the sequence.

In the following exercise we ask you to collect together all the code developed in this section and write the Pascal unit for the whole of the abstract data type. Your code for each of the procedures *update* and *delete* should call the procedure *flightsearch*.

Exercise 13.7   Write the Pascal unit *uSeq*.

13.3 TESTING THE ABSTRACT DATA TYPE SEQUENCE (CONTINUED)

The program to test the abstract data type was introduced briefly in Section 13.2. We shall complete it here. It will consist of a loop shown by the following top-level design:

```
        {Arrivals board program}
 1    create a new sequence
 2    repeat
 3        write out menu
 4        read in choice
 5        select case depending on choice
 6          '1'  :   add new flight information
 7          '2'  :   delete flight information
 8          '3'  :   update flight information
 9          '4'  :   display flight information
10        selectend
11    until choice = '5'
```

Each of the options will have to be refined to prompt for and receive from the keyboard appropriate input data. We shall not go through the details of this refinement, but present the final code. In it we have used the procedure *getret*, which was first developed in Chapter 8.

```
program seqtest;
uses uSeq, crt;

  {Imports
    type
      ArrivalsSeq = Private
    procedure create(var arrivals : ArrivalsSeq)
    procedure insert(var arrivals : ArrivalsSeq; newtime : real;
                      newflight, newfrom, neweta : string)
    procedure delete(var arrivals : ArrivalsSeq; flightgiven : string)
    procedure update(var arrivals : ArrivalsSeq; flightgiven : string)
    procedure display(arrivals : ArrivalsSeq)}
var
  arrivalsboard                   : ArrivalsSeq;
  choice                          : char;
  newtime                         : real;
  newflight, newfrom, neweta      : string;
  flightgiven                     : string;
procedure getret;
  var
    ch : char;
  begin
    repeat
      ch := readkey
    until (ord(ch) = 13)
  end;
```

```
begin
  clrscr;
  create(arrivalsboard);
  repeat
    clrscr;
    writeln('1 : Add new flight information');
    writeln('2 : Delete a flight');
    writeln('3 : Update estimated time of arrival');
    writeln('4 : Display the arrivals board');
    writeln('5 : Quit');
    writeln;
    write('Enter your choice ');
    repeat
      choice := readkey
    until choice in ['1'..'5'];
    writeln(choice);
    case choice of
      '1' : begin
              write('Enter the due arrival time as a real ');
              readln(newtime);
              write('Enter the flight number ');
              readln(newflight);
              write('Enter where from ');
              readln(newfrom);
              write('Enter new ETA ');
              readln(neweta);
              insert(arrivalsboard, newtime, newflight, newfrom, neweta);
            end;
      '2' : begin
              write('Enter flight number of deleted flight ');
              readln(flightgiven);
              delete(arrivalsboard, flightgiven);
              writeln;
              write('Press <ret> to return to main menu');
              getret;
            end;
      '3' : begin
              write('Enter flight number to be updated ');
              readln(flightgiven);
              update(arrivalsboard, flightgiven);
              writeln;
              write('Press <ret> to return to main menu');
              getret;
            end;
      '4' : begin
              display(arrivalsboard);
              writeln;
              write('Press <ret> to return to main menu');
              getret;
            end;
    end;
  until (choice = '5')
end.
```

Data need to be generated against which the abstract data type can be tested. The guidelines for generating test data that were introduced in Chapter 11 can be used here. We have already seen the first three when we were looking at the design of *insert*.

- Are there problems inserting into an *empty* sequence?
- Are there problems associated with inserting before the *first* element of the sequence?
- Are there problems associated with inserting after the *last* element of the sequence?
- Are there problems deleting from an *empty* sequence?
- Are there problems deleting the *first* element of the sequence?
- Are there problems deleting the *last* element of the sequence?
- Are there problems deleting from a single element sequence?

These questions should enable you to generate sets of test data. The test program above was designed with these possibilities in mind and enables you to carry out consecutive tests.

13.4 PROBLEMS

There is only one problem in this section, but it is a substantial one to develop an abstract data type for a special kind of queue.

13.5 SUMMARY

In this chapter we have looked at general sequences using a pointer-based representation. The difficulty of finding the item at the end of a sequence represented in this way led to the trick of making the last link field point back to the dummy item. In this way, searches would always be successful because the search item can be placed temporarily in the dummy item. It also avoids the difficulty of 'falling off' the end of the sequence.

14

TREES

14.1 INTRODUCTION

In this chapter we shall study an abstract data type that is not a form of sequence. A tree structure is one which is capable of representing hierarchical data. Figure 14.1 shows the job titles in a business organization and their hierarchical relation.

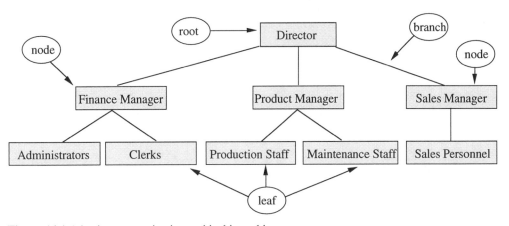

Figure 14.1 A business organization and its hierarchies

This figure introduces some terminology, as follows. The individual entries are called **nodes** and the node at the highest level is called the **root node** or, more simply, the **root**. Here, the root node contains the Director of the organization. Strictly speaking, a node and the data it contains are different things, but it becomes rather cumbersome to refer to things like 'the node containing the item Director'. We shall therefore refer to a node and the data it contains by expressions such as 'the node Director' or 'the Director node'.

In Figure 14.1 the Director node has three **children**, the Finance Manager, the Product Manager and the Sales Manager. The Sales Personnel node is an example of a **leaf** node. A leaf node has no children. The Sales Manager node is the **parent** of the Sales Personnel node. The part of the tree that contains the Finance Manager node and all the nodes below it is an example of what is known as a **subtree**. You may assume that whatever is said about a tree applies to a subtree because a subtree is itself a tree. What is not apparent from this example is that the nodes of a tree must all be of the same type. We can define a tree as follows:

A **tree** is a data structure that has zero or more nodes organized in a hierarchical manner, called **levels**, such that:

1.   Except when the tree is empty there is one node at the top of the hierarchy which is called the root node.
2.   Every node except the root node is joined by a branch to just one node at the next highest level of the hierarchy.
3.   One item of a pre-defined type is associated with each node.
4.   A pre-defined relationship exists between data on adjacent levels.

In general, the number of children that a node can have is unrestricted, but in the special case where a node can have at most two children, the tree is called a **binary tree**. We shall only be studying binary trees in this chapter. Since any node of a binary tree can have at most two children, then it can have at most two subtrees, which are called the **left** and **right subtrees** of the node. Figure 14.2 shows some examples of binary trees.

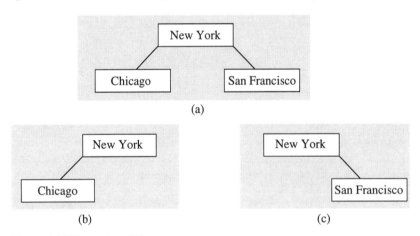

Figure 14.2 Examples of binary trees

You should note that examples (b) and (c) have different tree structures because (b) has a left subtree and no right subtree, whereas (c) has no left subtree but does have a right subtree. The pre-defined relationship that exists between data on adjacent levels is as follows:

(a)   each left subtree of a node contains only names which come alphabetically before that in the node;

(b)   each right subtree of a node contains only names of cities which come alphabetically after that in the node.

We shall call trees that satisfy this relationship **binary search trees**. In the next sub-section we shall look at the specification of the abstract data type binary search tree, but we first look at the operations by describing them using diagrams. We shall restrict the number of operations defining a binary search tree to a few only. The operations of *create* and *isempty* will be required, as will some way of building a tree, and we shall need to define an operation of *insert* for this purpose. Unlike the other abstract data types we have considered, we shall not have an operation that allows deletions to be made. This is because we are restricting our attention to search trees, and so deletion is not required. Additionally, there are difficulties associated with the removal of a non-leaf node. Since the tree is to be used for searching, an operation will be required which can search the tree for a given data item and report whether or not it is there. For many applications these operations are sufficient, but we shall include one more in our definition and that is the operation of printing out the data items in a tree. There are many ways in which this can be done, and this will be the subject of Section 14.4.

The method of how and where a new node is entered into a binary search tree can be illustrated by looking at how the city Dallas would be appended to the tree of Figure 14.2(a). There are three steps to the insertion:

(a)   find where the node is to be inserted;
(b)   create a new node containing the required data;
(c)   insert the new node into the tree.

Step (a) is essentially a loop in which Dallas is repeatedly compared with the current node. The root node is where the loop starts. Since Dallas precedes New York, it must be placed in the left subtree of the New York node, so move down to the node in this left subtree. This takes us to the Chicago node. Dallas comes after Chicago alphabetically and so it must be placed in the right subtree of this node. Since Chicago is a leaf node the new node for Dallas must be inserted as a right subtree of the Chicago node. Figure 14.3 shows the resulting tree after the creation and insertion of this new node.

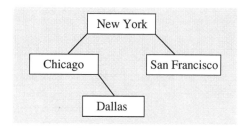

Figure 14.3 Appending a new node

Exercise 14.1 Add Atlanta, Boston and Baltimore, in that order, to the tree in Figure 14.3. Draw the tree when they are inserted in the order Baltimore, Atlanta, Boston.

If a data item to be inserted already exists in the tree then this is to be reported and no further action should be taken. Previous experience would suggest that particular care should be taken to ensure that the design for *insert* works for the insertion of the first item into an empty tree.

Searching a tree to find a particular data item is similar to inserting a new item. Starting at the root node, the data that each node contains are compared with the sought item. If the sought item precedes the node item, then the subtree to the left of the current node is examined. If it comes after the node item, then the right subtree is examined. This continues until either the item is found or a leaf node is reached, that is, a node that has neither left nor right subtrees. In this case, the item is not in the tree.

14.2 SPECIFYING A BINARY SEARCH TREE

In this section an abstract data type called *stringtree*, corresponding to the tree described in Section 14.1, will be specified and implemented. Thus, the data items to be held in the tree will be strings. We will define a minimal set of operations for manipulating the tree. These are specified below.

create

{Return a new empty binary search tree for data items of type *string*.}		
tree	A new tree of *string* items	*stringtree* parameter

isempty

tree	Representation of a tree	*stringtree* parameter
{Return the value true if the tree is empty, false otherwise.}		
isempty	The value true or false	*Boolean* function value

insert

tree	Representation of a tree	*stringtree* parameter
item	Item to be inserted into tree	*string* parameter
{If *item* is in *tree* then write out 'Duplicate entry'. Otherwise insert *item* in *tree* at a leaf in the way described above.}		
tree	Updated string tree	*stringtree* parameter

isthere

tree	Representation of a tree	*stringtree* parameter
item	Item to be sought	*string* parameter
{If *item* is in *tree* then return true otherwise return false.}		
isthere		*Boolean* function value

print

tree	Representation of a tree	*stringtree* parameter
{Write out the contents of a tree. (This will be discussed in Section 14.4 and implemented in Chapter 15.)}		

Records will be used to represent the nodes of the tree. They will have three different fields – a field containing a pointer to the left subtree, a field for the data item and a field for a pointer to the right subtree. Figure 14.4 illustrates the use of these records to represent the tree of Figure 14.2(a).

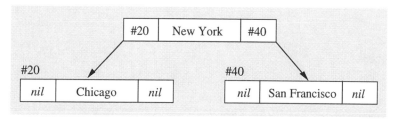

Figure 14.4 Tree representation using records

A variable *tree* will then be a pointer to this sequence of records and may be represented as in Figure 14.5.

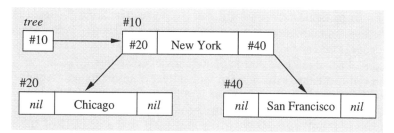

Figure 14.5 A diagram representing *tree*

An empty tree is then represented by *tree* having the value *nil*. These diagrams also enable us to see how *insert* will need to be designed. To insert Detroit, the node to which it is to be attached must first be found. This search would start at *tree* and so would inspect the data field of *tree^*. Since Detroit precedes New York, the left subtree of this node must be searched, that is, the subtree whose address is given in the left link field (#20). The data field of this node, Chicago, is compared with Detroit, from which it can be deduced that the right subtree must be searched. But the right link field of the Chicago record has value *nil*, indicating that there is no right subtree of this node. The search is therefore complete and the new record should be inserted as a right subtree of the Chicago record.

14.3 IMPLEMENTING THE ABSTRACT DATA TYPE *STRINGTREE*

The abstract data type will be modelled using the declarations in the code overleaf. It is included in a unit called *utree1*.

```
unit utree1;

interface
  {Private part}
  type
    stringtree = ^treerecord;
    treerecord = record
                   left  : stringtree;
                   data  : string;
                   right : stringtree
                 end;
  {Public part}
  {The identifier stringtree from above but not its structure.}
  procedure create(var tree : stringtree);
  function isempty(tree : stringtree) : Boolean;
  procedure insert(var tree : stringtree; item : string);
  function isthere(tree : stringtree; item : string) : Boolean;
  procedure print(tree : stringtree);
```

The design of some of these routines is not straightforward and so we shall have a brief look at some of the issues involved. We shall begin by looking at the design of *insert*. This will involve the same sorts of problems encountered in the design of the *insert* routine for general sequences. In particular, the tree will have to be searched, but for trees there is nothing analogous to the dummy item of a general sequence. In Chapter 13, the searches of the sequence were developed as separate routines. As a contrast, we shall not do so here, but the later parts of this chapter will give you an opportunity of doing this.

The same sort of difficulty arises in searching a tree as in searching a sequence. We need to determine the last node that precedes the insertion point. The example above shows that if we use a variable to hold the address of the record currently being examined, its value at the end of the search will be *nil*. What we also need is the address of the record containing this *nil* pointer. In other words, two variables will be needed during the search process, one of which lags one record behind the other. This should be a familiar technique from Chapter 13, where the two pointers were referred to as *lead* and *lag*. The following is a top-level design for *insert*:

insert
tree, item

1	create new node containing *item*
2	if *tree* is empty then
3	insert new node into *tree* as the root node
4	else
5	find where node is to be inserted
6	if *item* is not already in *tree* then
7	insert new node into *tree*
8	else
9	write out 'Duplicate entry'
10	ifend
11	ifend

tree

You may be wondering why the empty tree is treated as a special case by the statement at step 2. The reason is to be found in step 7. Using the insertion of Detroit into Figure 14.5 as an example, the search will result in *lag* having value #20. This value does not tell us whether Detroit goes in the left or right subtree of Chicago. To find out, the data field of *lag* has to be referenced and compared with Chicago. But when the tree is empty, *lag* will have the value *nil*, and attempting to reference a field of the *nil* pointer is an error.

In the following fragment from the implementation part of the unit *utree1*, the function *isempty* is assumed to be available:

```
procedure insert;
  {var tree : stringtree; item : string
  Pre : tree is initialized, possibly empty.
       item is an initialized string value.
  Post: tree is returned with the new item inserted at the appropriate leaf.}
  var
    lead, lag, temp : stringtree;
    exists : Boolean;
  begin
    new(temp);                              {1  create new node containing item }
    temp^.left := nil;
    temp^.right := nil;
    temp^.data := item;
    if isempty(tree) then                   {2  if tree is empty then          }
      tree := temp                          {3     insert new node as root node }
    else                                    {4  else                           )
      begin                                 {5     find where node to be inserted}
        exists := false;
        lead := tree;                       {       lag points to leaf after    }
        lag := tree;                        {       which new item is placed    }
        while (lead <> nil) and not exists do {     loop while not found        }
          begin
            lag := lead;
            if item < lead^.data then       {         if item precedes this node}
              lead := lead^.left            {           go left down the tree   }
            else                            {         else                      }
              if item > lead^.data then     {           if it comes after it    }
                lead := lead^.right         {             go right down the tree}
              else                          {           else                    }
                exists := true              {             item exists           }
          end;                              {5     end search of step 5         }
        if not exists then                  {6     if item not in tree then     }
          if item < lag^.data then          {7       insert node into l/r branch }
            lag^.left := temp               {         insert into left leaf      }
          else
            lag^.right := temp              {            insert into right leaf  }
        else                                {8     else                        }
          writeln('Duplicate entry')        {9       write out 'Duplicate'      }
      end;                                  {10    ifend                        }
  end;                                      {11 ifend                           }
```

Exercise 14.2 Write the whole of the implementation part of the unit *utree1* with the exception of the procedure *print*.

Testing the abstract data type will involve writing a driver program that will be able to call each of the operations. The Problems section asks you to develop such a program.

14.4 PRINTING BINARY TREES

The operation which we have, as yet, not implemented is that of printing out the data in all the nodes of a tree. To do so, we must choose a **path** through the nodes. A path that visits each node just once is called a **tree traversal**. For a given tree there are many different tree traversals, but we shall consider three different traversals called **inorder**, **preorder** and **postorder** traversals. In this section we shall explain what these terms mean and give examples of where they could be used. Designing procedures to carry out tree traversals turns out to be quite difficult, and so it will be left until Chapter 15.

A traversal can be pictured as a walk around the tree, passing each node as the walk progresses. In Figure 14.6 the curved line represents such a walk.

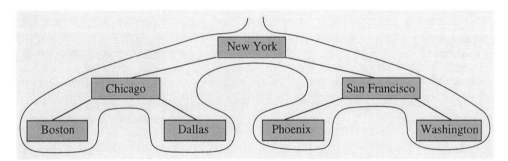

Figure 14.6 A tree traversal

We can see from this traversal that each leaf is visited once but that each non-leaf node is visited three times. An inorder traversal means that the data are written out when the walker passes *under* a node. The numbers in Figure 14.7 identify the order in which the data values are written out for an inorder traversal.

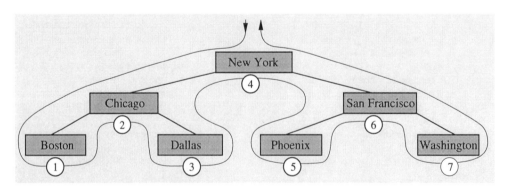

Figure 14.7 An inorder tree traversal

This shows that the cities are output in the order Boston, Chicago, Dallas, New York, Phoenix, San Francisco and Washington, that is, in alphabetical order. The reason for this is that the walk visits everything in the left subtree of a node, then the node itself and finally its right subtree. We shall return to this description in Chapter 15. We can see from this example why a binary tree is such a useful device for searching. Names can be inserted into the tree in a random order and an inorder traversal will output the data in alphabetical order.

Examples of the use of preorder and postorder traversal are found in more general binary trees. The binary tree in Figure 14.8 is a representation of the arithmetic expression

$(2 + 3) - (4*5)$

This diagram appears not to satisfy the condition that a tree must have nodes of the same pre-defined type. This is so, but in real expressions each node would be an identifier representing, in this case, either an arithmetic operator or an integer. It is easier to see what is going on if this complication is avoided, so we shall allow the nodes in the figure. Examine it before reading the commentary below.

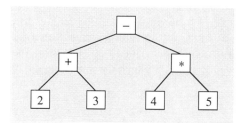

Figure 14.8 A tree representation of $(2 + 3) - (4*5)$

This tree, called an **expression tree**, enables the expression to be evaluated. We see that every non-leaf node has exactly two branches. To evaluate the expression, leaf nodes having a common parent are combined and replaced by the value represented by the subtree. Figure 14.9 shows how the expression in Figure 14.8 would be evaluated.

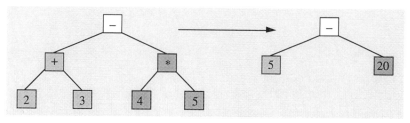

Figure 14.9 The evaluation of $(2 + 3) - (4*5)$

Here, we can see that each of the lower subtrees has been evaluated and the result has replaced the item in the appropriate node. To complete the evaluation, the calculation $5 - 20$ would be performed. In addition to their use for evaluation, expression trees can also be used to convert algebraic expressions into reverse Polish form. We have already seen in Chapter 11 that expressions like that above are usually translated into reverse Polish form for evaluation. Figure 14.10 shows the traversal that generates the reverse Polish form for the expression represented by the tree in Figure 14.8.

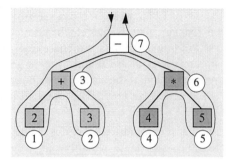

Figure 14.10 A postorder traversal

This traversal is called a postorder traversal, which means that the data are written out when the walker passes a node for the last time. Since non-leaf nodes are passed three times and leaf nodes just once, this is a fairly simple way of viewing a postorder traversal. An alternative description is to say: for a non-leaf node all its subtrees must be written out before the data it contains are output, but leaf nodes are written out as soon as they are encountered. The numbers on the diagram give the order in which the node data are output. It is:

2 3 + 4 5 * −

which you may recognize as the reverse Polish expression equivalent to

$(2 + 3) − (4*5)$

You will recall that reverse Polish notation is also known as postfix notation, from which this traversal gets its name.

The final traversal we shall consider is the preorder traversal. This enables the prefix form of an expression to be generated. Figure 14.11 shows the order in which the nodes are processed for the preorder traversal.

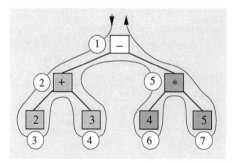

Figure 14.11 The preorder traversal

In this traversal the data in the node are written out on the first time past a node. For the tree in Figure 14.11 this would yield the **prefix expression**

− + 2 3 * 4 5

in which the operators precede the operands.

In the specification of the abstract data type given in Section 14.2 the *print* procedure was not specified in detail. The three traversals we have looked at in this section could be used as print operation specifications. We shall be considering the design of *print* procedures in Chapter 15.

Exercise 14.3 The expression tree of Figure 14.8 can be traversed to recover the infix version of the expression that it represents. The infix version will have to bracket items together. Which traversal can be modified to do this and what modifications would be required?

14.5 GENERALIZING THE ABSTRACT DATA TYPE

In this section we shall develop a more general tree abstract data type called *GenTree*. In particular, the items to be stored on the tree will be records whose type will be denoted by the identifier *itemtype*. The records will have a key field whose type is denoted by *keytype* and the implementation will not refer to the other fields. A more comprehensive set of operations will be defined as given below. In this implementation, errors arising from the operations will be reported by means of an error parameter flag.

create

{Return a new empty binary search tree for data items of type *itemtype*.}		
tree	A new tree of *itemtype* items	*GenTree* parameter

isempty

tree	Representation of a tree	*GenTree* parameter
{Return the value true if the tree is empty, false otherwise.}		
isempty	The value true or false	*Boolean* function value

insert

tree	Representation of a tree	*GenTree* parameter
item	Item to be inserted into tree	*itemtype* parameter
{If *item* is in *tree* then set *success* to false. Otherwise set *success* to true and insert *item* in *tree*.}		
tree	Updated tree	*GenTree* parameter
success	Flag denoting outcome of insert	*Boolean* parameter

getnode

tree	Representation of a tree	*GenTree* parameter
key	Key value whose record is sought	*keytype* parameter
{If *key* value is in *tree* then return *success* with value true and assign to *item* the record whose key is *key*. Otherwise return *success* with value false.}		
item	Record whose key is *key*	*itemtype* parameter
success	Flag denoting outcome of search	*Boolean* parameter

countnodes

tree	Representation of a tree	*GenTree* parameter
{Return the number of nodes in the tree. (This will be discussed in Section 14.4 and implemented in Chapter 15.)}		
countnodes	The count of the number of nodes	*integer* parameter

printkeys

tree	Representation of a tree	*GenTree* parameter
{Write out the contents of all the keys in tree. (This will be implemented in Chapter 15.)}		

These specifications do not include an operation for writing out the contents of the tree. This is because we are allowing the user to determine the structure of the records it will contain. To output the values of a user-defined structured type on the screen requires knowledge of the structure. The only detailed knowledge we have is that of the key field, and so only its values may be written out. (We are assuming here that the key is of built-in type as defined in the definition of *keytype*.) This is a severe restriction on the generality of this abstract data type. This structure is implemented in a unit called *uGenTree* whose interface is given below.

```
unit uGenTree;
interface
  {Private part}
  type
    keytype  = {to be filled in for the particular application}
    itemtype = record
                   key    : keytype;
                   field2 : {to be filled in for the particular application}
                       :   {to be filled in for the particular application}
               end;
    GenTree = ^treerecord;
    treerecord = record
                     left  : GenTree;
                     data  : itemtype;
                     right : GenTree
                 end;
  {Public part}
  {The identifier GenTree from above but not its structure.}
  procedure create(var tree : GenTree);
  function isempty(tree : GenTree) : Boolean;
  function isthere(tree : GenTree; key : keytype) : Boolean;
  procedure insert(var tree : GenTree; item : itemtype; var success : Boolean);
  procedure getnode(tree : GenTree; key : keytype; var item : itemtype;
                    var success : Boolean);
  function countnodes(tree : GenTree) : integer;
  procedure printkeys(tree : GenTree);
```

Exercise 14.4 Write the implementation part for the routines *insert*, *isthere* and *getnode*. You should base your code for *insert* on the design given in the text.

Exercise 14.5 Write a driver program for this abstract data type. You should base your design on a modification of that for Exercise 14.3.

14.6 PROBLEMS

The problems in this section are concerned with the concordance of a piece of text. A **concordance** is a list of all the separate words in the text, together with the frequency with which they occur. An abstract data type will be implemented as a Pascal unit *uconcord*. There are only three operations that are defined and they are given below. The problems will ask you to make definitions for the type *concordtype*.

create

{Return a new empty concordance.}		
concordance	A new representation of a concordance	*concordtype* parameter

insert

concordance	Representation of a concordance	*concordtype* parameter
inword	Word to be added to concordance	*string* parameter
{If *inword* is in the concordance then increase its frequency count by 1 otherwise insert it into the concordance and give it a frequency of 1.}		
concordance	Updated concordance	*concordtype* parameter

howmany

concordance	Representation of a concordance	*concordtype* parameter
inword	Word whose frequency is required	*string* parameter
{Return the frequency of *inword* in the concordance. If it is not in the concordance return the value zero.}		
howmany	Frequency of *inword*	*integer* function value

14.7 SUMMARY

In this chapter we have looked at the definition and implementation of an abstract data type corresponding to a binary search tree. It was defined in terms of the operations *create*, *isempty*, *insert*, *isthere* and *print*. To insert a new item in a binary search tree it is necessary to compare the item to be inserted with the data item at each node. If the new item precedes the node data item, then the left subtree is searched in a similar manner, otherwise the right subtree is searched. The design of this operation required the use of two pointer variables, one that lagged one node behind the other.

We looked at three ways in which the operation of *print* could be specified. They all relied on the notion of a tree traversal that can be thought of as a walk round the nodes of the tree. Three traversals were considered: the inorder, preorder and postorder traversals. Designs corresponding to these traversals will be considered in Chapter 15.

15

RECURSION

15.1 INTRODUCTION

In this chapter we shall look at a design technique called **recursion**. Broadly speaking, a recursive routine is one whose design includes a call to itself. This can be a difficult concept to grasp, as it would appear that if a routine calls itself, then that call includes a further call and so on. The process would appear not to stop. In order to see how this does not happen, we shall begin by using recursion to design some routines with which we are already familiar and for which we have seen non-recursive designs. There is then the problem of deciding which of the designs, the non-recursive or the recursive, is the better. We shall discuss this briefly in Section 15.4, but to give a gentle introduction to the subject this section will contain designs which are better done without recursion. However, in Section 15.4, we shall look at some problems that are very difficult to solve without recursion. By that stage we hope you will have mastered the techniques required and so be in a better position to appreciate the power of recursive methods.

In the problems section of Chapter 11 we implemented a procedure to print out a stack. This is reproduced below. We shall assume for simplicity that *stackitem* is of type *integer*. (This implies that *itemtype* has been defined to be *integer*.)

```
procedure print;
  {(stack : genstack)
   Pre : stack is initialized, possibly empty.
   Post: None - stack is written to the screen with the top of the stack uppermost.}
  var
    current : genstack;
  begin
    writeln('Top of stack');
    current := stack;
    while current <> nil do
      begin
        writeln(current^.stackitem);
        current := current^.link
      end;
    writeln('Bottom of stack')
  end;
```

This code processes all the items in the same way. It starts at the top of the stack and works its way down through the stack until it reaches the bottom. An alternative way of looking at the printing of a stack is to think of the stack in a special way, as a top item together with the remaining items of the stack. We shall call the 'remaining items' of the stack a **substack**, in order to emphasize that the items which comprise it themselves form a stack. Viewed in this way, a stack of n items can be printed by first printing out the item at the top of the stack, followed by the printing of the substack consisting of the remaining $n - 1$ items. Printing the substack can again be carried out by printing the item at the top of the stack and then printing out the substack of $n - 2$ items. At every stage the top item is printed out and a shorter substack remains to be processed. Eventually this substack will be empty – printing it out requires no action and the task is complete. In this description, printing out the substack is exactly the same process as printing out the stack! In other words, we have described a method of printing which refers to itself within the description. This is called **recursion**. The design below expresses the method more succinctly. Read it and see if you can identify the substack and the handling of the final empty stack. The comments correspond to the design from which the code was implemented, and they will be referred to extensively in the commentary below.

```
procedure recprint;
  {(stack : genstack)
   Pre : stack is initialized, possibly empty.
   Post: None – stack is written to the screen with the top of the stack uppermost.}
  begin
    if stack = nil then                    {1  if stack = nil then              }
      {do nothing}                         {2     do nothing                    }
    else                                   {3  else                             }
      begin
        writeln(stack^.stackitem);         {4     write out stack^.stackitem    }
        recprint(stack^.link)              {5     recprint(stack^.link)         }
      end                                  {6  ifend                            }
  end;
```

We shall now trace through the execution. A stack is passed to the procedure. If the stack is not empty then the **else** clause is executed and the item at the top of the stack is written out. This is immediately followed by a call to *recprint* to print out the substack given by *stack^.link*, that is, the remainder of the stack. Thus, *recprint* is called as part of the design of the procedure *recprint* itself, but with a stack that has one item fewer than on the original call. So eventually, *recprint* will be called with an empty stack. This means *stack* will have value *nil* and step 2 will be executed and the process will terminate.

In Chapter 8 we saw a model of how the invocation of a routine causes an activation record for the variables and parameters to be placed on the run-time stack. In general, when a routine is invoked any existing variable values remain on the stack below this activation record for use after the invocation is complete. Here, we are going to present a slightly different diagrammatic model of this process. Figure 15.1 shows a linked list representation of a stack of integers, the integer data being in the first field and the links being in the second field.

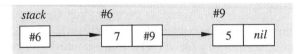

Figure 15.1 An example stack

As usual, this diagram uses hypothetical addresses for the pointer variables. When *recprint* is called, an address is passed to it, in this instance #6. The notation *recprint*(#6) will be used to denote that *recprint* has been invoked with actual parameter #6. The series of diagrams below traces the calls to *recprint*.

recprint (#6)

1	if #6 = *nil* then
4	write out 7
5	*recprint* (#9)

The heading in the diagram above shows that *recprint* is called with *stack* having value #6. This value results in the **if** statement of step 1 being false, and so execution continues at design step 4. This writes out the value of *stack^.stackitem*, that is, the data field of the record at #6. Step 5 then calls *recprint* with actual parameter *stack^.link*, that is, with actual parameter #9. Another invocation of *recprint* now follows. Note that the first invocation is not yet finished because step 6 has not yet been executed. The diagram below shows how we shall deal with the second invocation:

recprint (#6)

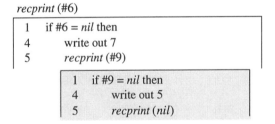

Each invocation is surrounded by a box to emphasize its separate identity. At this stage of the processing the boxes are incomplete because none of the invocations have terminated. In this second invocation step 4 writes out the data of the record at #9 and calls *recprint*, using the link field as actual parameter. There is now a third invocation of *recprint,* this time with actual parameter *nil*:

recprint (#6)

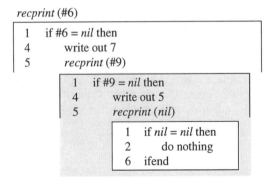

For this invocation the stack passed to the procedure is the empty stack and so execution is completed. This is emphasized by the box surrounding this invocation being complete. This being the case, the second invocation in which the passed parameter had value #9 can now continue its execution. What remains to be done is trivial, namely the execution of step 6. However, as we shall see, this will not always be the case. The situation at this stage is:

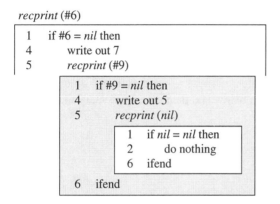

The intact box around the second invocation shows that it is now completed. All that remains is the completion of the first invocation:

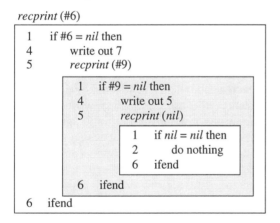

We can now stand back and see that the numbers 7 and 5, in that order, have been written out by this procedure. In other words, it has printed out the stack items. This example illustrates three fundamental properties of recursive routines:

1. First, there must be some stopping condition – that is, there must be some value(s) of the input for which the routine does not call itself. In the example above the value corresponded to an empty stack.
2. For values of the input not covered by the stopping condition, the routine calls itself.
3. For all input values, the stopping condition must be reached after a finite number of recursive calls.

This last feature is perhaps the most difficult to appreciate. We shall therefore look at it in more detail by examining a template that can be adapted to the design of most recursive routines. Of necessity it is rather vague and imprecise, and the terms in which we express it are not technical ones. However, we hope that with suitable interpretation it will enable you to design recursive routines.

If we examine the design of *recprint*, we can see that it works by taking an item from the stack and processing it together with the substack that remains. The substack gets smaller on each invocation (requirement 3 above). For any routine that you want to design recursively there is an analogy to the stack item and its substack. For convenience we shall refer generally to an **article** and a **subarticle**. We can think of a subarticle as being the article with one or more items removed from it. We shall refer to the item that is removed from the article as an **entity**. This enables us to write a template for a general recursive routine. Read through the template design below and then the commentary that follows.

recurse

---

article

1	if the *article* is trivial then
2	process it
3	else
4	identify the *article* and *subarticle*
5	*recurse(subarticle)*
6	process *entity*
7	ifend

---

results   {detail depends upon purpose of routine}

In step 1 the word *trivial* is used to convey the meaning that the stopping condition has been reached and the article can be directly processed. That this is reached after a finite number of steps is conveyed by the notion of article and subarticle. Step 4 may not appear explicitly as a separate step, but it must be there implicitly. It was not evident in *recprint*, but it did appear implicitly in step 2 where the stack item was written out. Again, identifying the subarticle was not a separate step in *recprint*, but it did appear within the recursive call statement itself. A further difficulty with this general design template is that processing the *entity* at step 6 may have to precede the recursive call with the subarticle. When you come to design your own recursive routines it will be apparent what order is required.

We shall now demonstrate the use of this template to write a recursive procedure that reverses the characters in a string. The procedure specification is:

reverse

given	A non-empty string	*string* parameter
{Write out the characters of *given* in reverse order, that is, starting with the last and finishing with the first. The string *given* may be assumed to have at least one character.}		

The first task is to identify the roles of *entity, article* and *subarticle* in the template design. Clearly, the source data *given* will be the *article*, but what are *entity* and *subarticle* here? The subarticle will in some sense have to 'get smaller' because it will eventually provide the stopping condition. If we think of how to write out a reversed string, one way is to write out the last letter, which then leaves all characters but the last to be reversed. So the *entity* would appear to be the last letter and the *subarticle* all the characters preceding it.

Exercise 15.1 What condition is equivalent to the template condition *the article is trivial*?

A top level design for *reverse* is then given by:

reverse	
given	
1	if *length(given)* = 1 then
2	write out *given*[*i*]
3	else
4	write last character of *given*
5	reverse all but last character of *given*
6	ifend

This can be implemented as follows:

```
procedure reverse(given : string);
  {Pre : given is an initialized non-empty string.
   Post: None - given is written out in reverse order.}
  var
    i : integer;
  begin
    if length(given) = 1 then
      write(given[1])
    else
      begin
        write(given[length(given)]);
        reverse(copy(given, 1, length(given) - 1))
      end
  end;
```

Figure 15.2 illustrates calls to *reverse* assuming that *given* has value 'bat':

reverse ('bat')

1	if 3 = 1 then
4	write 't'
5.1	*given* = 'ba'
5.2	*reverse* ('ba')

1	if 2 = 1 then
4	write 'b'
5.1	*given* = 'a'
5.2	*reverse* ('a')

1	if 1 = 1 then
2	write 'a'
6	ifend

6	ifend

6	ifend

Figure 15.2 Invocations of *reverse* with actual parameter 'bat'

Exercise 15.2 An alternative design for *reverse* is to remove the first character, reverse the remaining characters and then write out the removed character. Implement this design.

---

reverse

given

1	if *length(given)* = 1 then
2	write *given*[1]
3	else
4	remove first character from *given*
5	reverse what is left of *given*
6	write first character
7	ifend

A more complicated example arises if we try to write a recursive function to test whether a given string is palindromic. You will recall that a string is palindromic if it reads the same backwards as forwards: for example, the word madam is palindromic. The specification below gives the details of what is required.

palindrome

given	A non-empty string	*string* parameter
{If *given* is palindromic then write out 'palindrome' else write out 'not a palindrome'. The source data are assumed to be a non-empty string.}		

The first task is to identify the roles for *entity*, *article* and *subarticle*. The *article* will be the given input string. To determine whether a string is palindromic its first and last characters must be compared, then the second and penultimate characters, and so on. So *entity* would need to be the first and last characters and the *subarticle* is the string with these characters removed.

Exercise 15.3 Describe the condition that the *article* is *trivial* for this procedure.

One point which ought to be remembered is that as soon as two end characters are found to differ there is no point examining the others because the word cannot be palindromic. The design below caters for this:

palindrome

given

1	if (*length(given)* = 0) or (*length(given)* = 1) then
2	write out 'palindrome'
3	else
4	if *given*[1] = *given*[*length(given)*] then
5	*delete(given, 1, 1)*
6	*delete(given, length(given), 1)*
7	*palindrome(given)*
8	else
9	write out 'not a palindrome'
10	ifend
11	ifend

This may be coded as follows:

```
procedure palindrome(given : string);
  {Pre : given is an initialized non-empty string.
   Post: None - a message is written out saying whether or not given is a palindrome.}
  begin
    if (length(given) = 0) or (length(given) = 1) then
      writeln('palindrome')
    else
      if given[1] = given[length(given)] then
        begin
          delete(given, 1, 1);
          delete(given, length(given), 1);
          palindrome(given)
        end
      else
        writeln('not a palindrome')
  end;
```

Exercise 15.4 Draw a diagram similar to Figure 15.2 showing the invocations of *palindrome* with actual parameter 'madam' and then with actual parameter 'reader'.

Although it would not be too difficult to write a non-recursive design for this procedure, the recursive design is very clear. It can even be described quite clearly: if the first and last characters are the same, then call *palindrome* with the string obtained by removing the first and last characters.

We shall now consider a problem where a non-recursive design is considerably more difficult than a recursive one. In Problem 11.7 we considered the task of designing a procedure, *revprint*, which writes out the items on a stack in reverse order, that is, starting at the bottom item and finishing at the top. The non-recursive solution was based on the following design:

```
1   count the number of items in the stack
2   loop for i := count downto 1
3     move down to ith entry
4     write out data
5   loopend
```

An alternative approach is to use two pointers in a lead and lag role so that when the bottom item is found, *lag* points to its predecessor. The value of *lag* would then determine the stopping position for *lead* on the next pass through the stack and so on. Neither approach is particularly obvious. Let us compare a recursive design. In terms of the recursive template, the stack is the *article*. What takes the role of the *entity*? Printing the stack in reverse means that the top of the stack is printed last. Hence the rest of the stack is printed in reverse, followed by the item at the top of the stack. Thus, the top of the stack takes the role of *entity*. This implies that the *subarticle* is just the stack with the first item removed. A strategy for the design is then to *revprint* (the stack with top item removed) and then write out the first item. This leads to the design and code shown below. The identifiers used in both are the same as those used in Chapter 11 so that the code is part of the implementation of the unit *uGenStk2*.

revprint

stack
1   if *stack = nil* then
2   do nothing
3   else
4   *revprint(stack^.link)*
5   write out *stack^.stackitem*
6   ifend

```
procedure revprint
  {(stack : genstack);
   Pre : stack is initialized.
   Post: None but stack items are written out in reverse order.}
  begin
    if stack = nil then
      {do nothing}
    else
      begin
        revprint(stack^.link);
        writeln(stack^.stackitem)
      end;
  end;
```

Exercise 15.5 Draw a diagram similar to Figure 15.2 showing the invocations of *revprint* with the stack of Figure 15.1. Use the hypothetical addresses in that figure as actual parameters for each call.

15.2 RECURSIVE DESIGNS FOR TREE OPERATIONS

In this section we shall produce recursive implementations for some of the operations defined on trees. In particular, we shall look at the procedures for printing out a tree using tree traversals introduced in Chapter 14. We begin by completing the design of the abstract data type *stringtree*, for which we have not yet designed the operation *print*. An inorder traversal will be used to print out the data in the nodes of a tree, as described in the following specification:

print

tree	Representation of a tree	*stringtree* parameter
{Write out the data field of the nodes of *tree* using an inorder traversal.}		

In Chapter 14 the inorder traversal was described as a walk which visits everything in the left subtree of a node, then the node itself and finally its right subtree. We have reproduced Figure 14.6 to illustrate the operation of *print* (Figure 15.3).

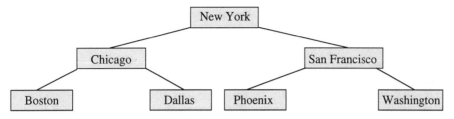

Figure 15.3 A city name search tree

To print the data in Figure 15.3 using an inorder traversal:

- print the data in the left subtree of New York
- print the data in the root node itself, i.e. New York
- print the data in the right subtree of New York.

To accomplish the first of these tasks we note that the left subtree of New York is the tree whose root node is Chicago. The same technique is therefore applied to this tree:

- print the tree in the left subtree of Chicago
- print the data in the root node itself, i.e. Chicago
- print the data in the right subtree of Chicago.

What we are using here is a recursive description of the task. It gives us a clue as to what should be the roles of *article*, *entity* and *subarticle* in a recursive design and what condition corresponds to the *article* being trivial. The current node takes the *entity* role, but what plays the role of the *subarticle*? In this instance there are two subarticles – the left and right subtrees pointed to by the parameter *tree*. The *subarticle* being trivial corresponds to the tree being empty, that is, to *tree* having value *nil*. This leads to the following implementation for *print*:

```
procedure print;
  {(tree : stringtree)
  {Pre : tree is initialized, possibly empty.
   Post: None - the tree is printed out. See Section 14.4.}
  begin
    if tree = nil then
      {do nothing}
    else
      begin
        print(tree^.left);
        writeln(tree^.data);
        print(tree^.right)
      end
  end;
```

Exercise 15.6 Draw a diagram similar to Figure 15.2 showing the invocations of *print* with the tree of Figure 14.5. Use the hypothetical addresses in that figure as actual parameters for each call.

This design shows the power of recursive techniques. Designing an inorder print routine without using recursion is very complex. This is because the design would start off by going down the leftmost subtree until it reached a leaf. The data in the leaf would then be written out. The next step would be to move up to the leaf's parent node and look at its right subtree. The leftmost leaf of this subtree would then be found, after which its parent's right subtree would be traversed. We can see from this that after each data item is printed the design has to go to the leaf's parent node. The location of the parent node must therefore be stored on the way down through the tree. But every node, except the leaf nodes, is a parent of some other subtree! Compare this description with the recursive design above. The recursive design is simple by comparison.

The tree operation *insert* can also be designed recursively. We must first decide the roles for each of *article*, *entity* and *subarticle*, and what corresponds to the notion of the *article* being trivial. The general process will be to compare the new data with the data in the current node. If the new data precede the data in the current node then they are inserted in the left subtree and if they come after it then they are inserted in the right subtree. If neither holds, then the new data form a duplicate entry. This suggests that *entity* should be the current node and that *subarticle* should be the appropriate subtree (left or right) of the current node. The *article* being trivial corresponds to the tree being empty, that is, *tree* having value *nil*. When this is the case the new data are attached at this subtree. This leads to the following implementation:

```
procedure insert;
   {(var tree : stringtree; item : string)
    Pre : tree is initialized, possibly empty.
          item is an initialized string value.
    Post: tree is returned with the new item inserted at the appropriate leaf.}
   var
      temp : stringtree;
   begin
      if isempty(tree) then            {1  if tree is empty then                         }
         new(temp);                    {2     insert item into empty tree               }
         temp^.left := nil;
         temp^.right := nil;
         temp^.data := item;
         tree := temp
      else                             {3  else                                         }
         begin
            if item < lead^.data then  {4     if item precedes this node                }
               insert(tree^.left, item) {        call insert with left subtree          }
            else                       {        else                                    }
               if item > lead^.data then {      if it comes after it                     }
                  insert(tree^.right, item) {      call insert with right subtree        }
               else                    {        else                                    }
                  writeln('Duplicate entry') {9     write out 'Duplicate'               }
         end;                          {10    ifend                                      }
   end;                                {11 ifend                                         }
```

15.3 PROBLEMS

Problems 15.1 and 15.2 are general routines which can be implemented recursively. All the other problems are concerned with writing recursive routines for tree operations.

15.4 EFFICIENCY OF RECURSION

In this chapter we have seen examples of designs that are much easier to write using recursion and some for which the recursive design had little or no advantage over its non-recursive counterpart. How can we judge whether a recursive approach should be adopted? We shall not attempt to give firm guidelines, but the usual general design principles apply. The method adopted should be the natural and logical way of solving the problem. So, for the first example we looked at, the problem of printing the contents of a stack, the natural design is to start at the top of the stack and work down it to the bottom, writing out the data on the way. Hence a non-recursive approach is the most natural. By contrast, printing out the contents of a tree proved to be very difficult using a non-recursive approach. The recursive design is very transparent and has nowhere near the same number of complications.

Another factor which might have to be taken into account is the overheads associated with recursive designs. Diagrams like Figure 15.2 give some idea of what overheads are involved. Each time a recursive routine is called, the system has to save the current values of all the variables and parameters. This occupies space and takes time. When the recursion eventually completes with the trivial stage, then all the previous invocations are completed in turn. This involves re-establishing the appropriate data values and then releasing the space they occupied when the invocation is completed. In general, a non-recursive version of a routine will execute more efficiently in terms of space and time than its recursive counterpart. This is essentially because of all these housekeeping tasks undertaken by the system.

15.5 SUMMARY

In this chapter the concept of recursion has been introduced. For some designs recursion can be used but it is not necessarily the best approach. However, for others recursion is a natural and clear method. This is particularly so for tree operations which involve the tree being searched or traversed in some way.

16

OBJECT-ORIENTED PROGRAMMING

16.1 INTRODUCTION

In this chapter we look at a different approach to software development – object-oriented programming. In many ways this can be viewed as an extension of what we have been doing in the last few chapters when developing abstract data types. An abstract data type is an object, but we shall be more interested in what are known as classes of objects. Although we shall draw on some of the similarities, we hope also to show the underlying fundamental difference of the approach. In such a small space we can only hope to give you a flavour of object programming, but one that will enable you to embark on a more detailed study. We begin with an overview which introduces some of the language used in object-oriented programming. This can be read superficially as the details of the new terms will be studied in subsequent sections.

One of the major problems with software development is that the user requirements change, either during development or at a later stage when a system is running. This means that the users want the system to do different things or perform additional tasks from those that were originally specified. The challenge is to try to respond to such changes. Analysis of changes to existing software systems has shown that although the functionality of the programs may change, the data upon which they operate tend to be more stable. For example, in a system controlling current accounts within a bank, the underlying data on which processes are to be carried out will probably be quite stable. The software will probably always be concerned with processing customer details and the state of the account. Thus, the data structure of the account details will be quite stable in its structure, but the way it is processed will change through time to allow for changes in customer services or the way the bank operates as a business. Object-oriented programming exploits this relative stability of the data structure. Essentially, an object is a data structure together with the operations by which the data values are manipulated.

The requirement for larger and more complex computer systems also requires new development methods. There are now well established software engineering principles for the creation of large systems. One of the major strengths and challenges of an engineering approach is the emphasis it places on software reuse. The ability to reuse a tried and tested piece of software makes an immediate impact on reducing development costs but, more importantly, it improves reliability.

The first facility that enabled software reuse was the introduction of the named procedure in the 1940s. The fact that procedures had names meant that they could be assembled in libraries for reuse as and when required. So, for example, a user could go to a library of sort routines, choose an appropriate one and incorporate it into a new development without having to worry about how the sorting algorithm worked. The use of library routines enabled languages to be extended to provide facilities that were not available in its original form.

Other developments which have contributed to reuse are separate compilation and abstract data types. Advantages of the former include the ability to break down problems into smaller portions and to hide implementation details from the user. The latter established yet more abstraction by providing the user with complex data structures and the routines with which they were manipulated. These new data types could be used just as if they were built-in types such as integer.

Object-oriented languages have enabled even higher levels of abstraction to be achieved. In Chapter 11 we discussed the problem of attempting to define a generic stack, that is, to define a stack capable of storing any data type. Our solution was far from perfect, because of the constraints of the implementation language. Object-based languages overcome the problems. In object terminology a stack would be an instance of an object class onto which would be pushed objects and from which would be popped objects. What is pushed and popped would not have to be objects of the same type (that is, class). Object-based languages define a large number of such classes. These classes have a hierarchical tree structure. To illustrate this, we can think of a stack as being a special kind of sequence where, for example, the operation push is a modified version of sequence insertion. So if we have a sequence class at our disposal, a stack can then be defined as a subclass of it. In other words a stack is a sequence but with some operations modified. (This is an oversimplified view, but we hope it gives you a flavour of class hierarchies.) The stack would be said to inherit behaviour from the sequence.

A different example is illustrated by the way help screens often function. They enable a user to get help on aspects of the system he or she is using. Usually, the help screen consists of a window in which the help is given in the form of some text. Often, help screens allow the user to point to a word within the text using a mouse and have a definition of that word presented on the screen. In an object approach to developing a system like this, the window, the text and the words on which the user can obtain definitions would all be instances of different object classes. So, for example, the window object would provide the window frame together with any special facilities such as the menus in the menu bar, the means by which the window can be resized or moved, and so on. If the help facility is to be applied to a different system then all that has to be done is to tell the window object that it is to function with new text and word objects. All the code relating to creating the window, resizing it and moving it can all be reused.

In the object world, an object is made to do something by 'passing it a message'. The event of pressing the mouse to activate a word definition described above would result in the word object being sent a message to show itself on the screen. The notion of message passing is fundamental to the object approach. To get things to happen, objects have to be sent messages. What is very powerful is the fact that different objects can respond to the same message in different ways. Thus, in a windowing environment, clicking the mouse button on an icon will have a different effect from clicking it on a word in the help facility just described. The act of clicking the mouse button is always the same, but different objects will respond in different ways to receiving it. This idea of the same message generating different responses in different objects is called **polymorphism**.

Existing languages like Pascal have incorporated objects by means of extensions to their syntax. Thus, recent versions of Turbo Pascal all support Turbo's implementation of objects. The language is therefore a mixture of the traditional procedural approach and the object method. It is convenient to refer to this mixture as a hybrid approach because it does not force the programmer to think exclusively in object terms. In a pure object language, for example Smalltalk, everything, including the system itself, is an object. Thus, programming in a pure object language is mainly concerned with the definition of classes to which messages will be sent. In general, defining a new class requires a considerable knowledge of the existing classes. When everything is an object as in a pure object language there is therefore a very steep learning curve to be overcome before even the most trivial object can be implemented. Using a hybrid object language has the disadvantage that it does not enforce an object discipline but it has the advantage that a more gentle learning approach can be adopted and that existing knowledge can be exploited.

We shall therefore begin our exploration by referring back to abstract data types where we had the notion of data values and operations to act on them. Object-oriented programming in Turbo Pascal extends these ideas by enabling us to define classes of objects. An **object class** consists of data and operations. Conventionally in an object approach the operations are called **methods**, and so an object class will consist of data and methods wrapped up as a single structure. The data and methods of an object class should be thought of as inseparable. Throughout this chapter we shall consider several classes of objects without giving any justification as to why the data values or the methods were chosen. The rationale behind the choice is to make the comprehension of what is involved as simple as possible. The object classes do not attempt to solve any particular problem nor necessarily are the methods a comprehensive list of what would be required in any system. The idea is to give you as small a collection of data values and methods as possible consistent with the objective of introducing the new concepts. In this way we hope you can keep the model that we developed in your head all in one go throughout the whole chapter. The exercises and problems will give you a chance to consider different object class models.

Throughout this chapter we shall suppress the comments that contain pre- and postconditions to routines. The reason for this is that we shall not be particularly interested in the detailed code of the routines and wish to make their declarations as short as possible.

16.2 A SIMPLE EXAMPLE

We begin by looking at a very simple object class. The data to be stored represent a map reference on the earth's surface as given by its longitude and latitude. For simplicity we shall represent latitude and longitude by real numbers, where longitude can take values between 0 and 360 (including 0 but excluding 360) and latitude can take values between − 90 and + 90. Initially, the object class will have two methods associated with it: one to read values in called *readin* and the other to write them out called *print*. A Pascal definition for such an object is given below. For this initial introduction we shall develop the object as part of a complete program. Later in the section we shall look at its implementation as a Pascal unit.

```
program objectprog;
type
  MapRef = object
             latitude  : real;
             longitude : real;
             procedure readin;
             procedure print;
           end;
```

The form of this definition is very similar to that used for a record. However, a major distinction between a record and an object is that the data fields are only there to support the methods; they are never accessed directly by the applications programmer. Turbo Pascal cannot enforce this, but we shall adhere to it as a principle of good practice. Another difference between this definition and code that you have seen before is that neither of the procedures has any parameters. We might have expected them to have two formal parameters, corresponding to the two real values that they process. To see the significance of this difference the following exercise asks you to take an abstract data type approach to this definition.

Exercise 16.1 The abstract data type approach to model these data would define *MapRef* to be a type and declare the procedures with which variables of this type would be manipulated. Write down the declarations.

The data values in an object class definition are available to all the methods because they are part of the same structure. In the approach of Exercise 16.1 the data values are separate from the operations, and so the parameter mechanism has to be used to provide communication between values and operations. By contrast, the object approach carries all the information in the single structure.

Variables of the object class can be declared within a **var** declaration. Such variables are referred to as **instances** of the object class. Thus, we can have:

```
var
  myplace, greenwich : MapRef;
  capitalcities : array[1..100] of MapRef;
```

The implementation of the methods follows the very similar syntax rules of the implementation of any routine. The only difference is that an object method identifier consists of the object identifier followed by a dot followed by the method identifier. In other words, a method is referenced using exactly the same notation that is used to reference a field of a record. The code overleaf contains the complete declarations for the object *MapRef* and its instances.

An object instance is manipulated by invoking one of the methods and its internal state can only be altered by such means. As for any Pascal program an object variable must be initialized before it is referenced. As we shall see, even more care has to be taken to ensure that objects are properly initialized because the system has to keep track of both the data values and the associated methods. We can see this more clearly if we consider a model of

```
program objectprog;
type
  MapRef = object
              latitude  : real;
              longitude : real;
              procedure readin;
              procedure print;
            end;
var
  myplace, greenwich : MapRef;
  capitalcities : array[1..100] of MapRef;
procedure MapRef.readin;
  begin
    write('Enter a latitude value ');
    readln(latitude);
    write('Enter a longitude value ');
    readln(longitude)
  end;
procedure MapRef.print;
  begin
    write(latitude:6:2, longitude:6:2);
  end;
begin   {main program}
```

how the compiler deals with objects. When any program is compiled the result is a file which, when executed, occupies space in memory that we shall refer to as the **codefile segment**. The contents of the codefile segment do not alter during program execution. Values that are manipulated by the program do not reside in this area of memory but in a memory area called the **data segment** area of memory. When dealing with an object the compiler only sets aside enough memory in the data segment area for the data part of the object. None is set aside for the methods. The reason for this is that any instance of a given object has exactly the same methods as any other instance. It would be wasteful of storage if every instance carried around with it a copy of the methods. Thus, the code corresponding to the methods resides in the code segment and is shared by all instances of a given object. We shall represent this situation as shown in Figure 16.1.

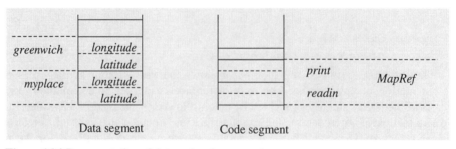

Figure 16.1 Representation of data and code segments

In this figure we have assumed that each data field requires only one unit of memory and to save space we have represented the code for each of the methods as requiring only two units of memory. Values in the data segment will change as execution proceeds, but those in the code segment will not.

Object instances can only be initialized by calling an appropriate method. For objects of class *MapRef* the appropriate method is *readin*. The code below illustrates how it is used.

```
myplace.readin;
for i := 1 to 100 do
  capitalcity[i].readin;
capitalcity[50].print;
```

We can see from this example that the way a method is invoked is by using the dot notation. It has the form: object instance identifier, dot, method identifier. The terminology associated with this notation is often known as **message passing** and is referred to as sending a message to an object. So *myplace.readin* sends the message *readin* to the object *myplace*. In other words, *myplace* is told to go and *readin*. This idea of an instance knowing how to do something like *readin* is very important in object programming. It is the object itself which knows how to perform a *readin*. If we had another object class which also had a method called *readin* then there would be no ambiguity between the two methods because each instance knows which *readin* method applies to itself. We shall see later why this terminology is so useful in object programming.

Exercise 16.2 Identify the message associated with the statement *capitalcity*[50].*print*?

The choice of methods and their specification involves important design decisions which are beyond the scope of this text. However, to illustrate the difficulties we shall write a new implementation of the object *MapRef* that has different method specifications. This time, the implementation will use a Pascal unit called *uMapRef*. We shall continue with the idea that the implementor of an object class is different from the applications programmer who is using it.

The method *readin* above contains all the prompts for reading in the values to the instance. Since this is the only method provided for initializing instances of *MapRef*, all initializations will involve these prompts. This may not suit the applications programmer. Greater flexibility can be provided by using a slightly different form of initialization method. Furthermore, the methods above do not give the implementor much scope for manipulating map references, and so we have included additional methods in the version below. The two methods which recover the values of latitude and longitude from an object instance have been specified as procedures rather than functions to illustrate the use of **var** parameters in object methods.

```
unit uMapRef;
interface
type
  MapRef = object
             latitude  : real;
             longitude : real;
             procedure init(inlat, inlong : real);
             procedure print;
             procedure GetLat(var outlat : real);
             procedure GetLong(var outlong : real);
           end;
```

```
implementation
  procedure MapRef.init;
    begin
      latitude := inlat;
      longitude := inlong
    end;
  procedure MapRef.print;
    begin
      write(latitude:6:2, longitude:6:2);
    end;
  procedure MapRef.GetLat;
    begin
      outlat := latitude
    end;
  procedure MapRef.GetLong;
    begin
      outlong := longitude
    end;
end.
```

The first question that might be worrying you is why do three of these methods have parameters when we have already said that methods have automatic access to the data defined within the object? The reason is that they have to communicate values between the inside world of the object and the outside world as it is viewed by an applications programmer. The applications programmer should not know the internal structure of an object. To illustrate this, try the following exercise in which you play the part of an applications programmer who is using an object whose internal workings are private and unknown to you. You *must* read the solution to this exercise as it contains important teaching information.

Exercise 16.3 The object *MapRef* is redefined in this exercise so that it can store a latitude, longitude and time as represented by a 24-hour clock. The time is used to record the time at which, say, a vehicle was at a particular location. A method called *init* is provided that requires four actual parameters. The first two correspond to latitude and longitude respectively and are of type *real*, and the second two correspond to hours and minutes on a 24-hour clock and are of type *integer*. How are the data represented in this object?

The method *init* has two parameters corresponding to the longitude and latitude. This enables an applications programmer to enter values into the object's internal structure. Notice how the formal input parameter values are assigned to the internal object field data values in this implementation. In a similar way, *GetLat* and *GetLong* enable the individual latitude and longitude values to be recovered from the internal structure. Here, the internal data object field values are assigned to the output parameters. The following program illustrates the use of these methods.

```
program testMapRef;
uses
  uMapRef;
var
  lat, long          : real;
  position, greenwich : MapRef;
```

```
begin
  greenwich.init(0, 51.5);
  write('Enter your latitude as a real ');
  readln(lat);
  write('Enter your longitude as a real ');
  readln(long);
  position.init(lat, long);
  greenwich.GetLong(long);
  writeln('Greenwich is at longitude ', long:6:2);
  write('Your position is ');
  position.print
end.
```

This program initializes the instance *greenwich* by means of real literal parameter values and initializes *position* by reading in values from the keyboard and then using them in a call to *init*. The longitude of Greenwich is retrieved from the instance *greenwich* by the method *GetLong* and this value is then output to the screen. Finally, both the latitude and longitude of the instance *position* are written to the screen using the method *print*.

Exercise 16.4 Write an implementation of the object *MapRef* in which the methods *GetLat* and *GetLong* are implemented as functions rather than procedures. Rewrite the program *testMapRef* using this alternative implementation.

Exercise 16.5 Write an implementation for the procedure *init* for the object *MapRef* as defined in the solution to Exercise 16.3.

We conclude this subsection with the definition of a new object class that uses the same methods identifiers as those we have used already in *MapRef*. Here, the method *init* is responsible for all the input of data values and so does not have any parameters.

```
unit ucountry;
interface
type
  country = object
              name       : string;
              population : integer;
              procedure init;
              procedure print;
            end;
```

A program that uses instances of objects of type *MapRef* and *country* contains the following declarations:

```
program TwoObjects;
uses
  uMapRef, ucountry;
var
  myplace   : MapRef;
  mycountry : country;
```

Both these object instances have identically named methods whose functionality clearly differs. For example, the method *print* outputs two real values when referring to *myplace*, but outputs a string and an integer when applied to *mycountry*. These two outputs would be generated by the calls

```
myplace.print;
mycountry.print
```

You may be wondering how the system knows which version of *print* to use. For the former, it uses the method declared in the class of which *myplace* is an instance, that is, the method declared in *MapRef*. In other words, the class tells it which is the appropriate *print*. We can think of *myplace.print* in message terms as 'go and write yourself out'. The fact that *myplace* knows about its own structure, including its methods, means it knows how to write itself out. There is no confusion between the two methods called *print*. Compare this with the situation we met in Chapters 11 and 12 when we implemented *print* operations for the abstract data types *stack* and *queue*. In both cases, the identifier *print* was used for this operation. This was fine at the time because none of the applications programs used both a stack and a queue. However, if both are required then the implementations would have to be altered to avoid the clash of print operation identifiers. Presumably something like *printqueue* and *printstack* would do. The applications programmer who is using the implementation would then have to be careful to ensure that the correct print routine was used to print each structure. The object approach removes both the need for using different identifiers and remembering which structure is being printed. The object knows how to print itself!

An action like that of *print* is often called a **polymorphic** action (from the Greek meaning 'many shaped') so that *print* would be described as a polymorphism. A polymorphic action is informally described as the ability of an action to have a different interpretation over more than one class. So here, *print* performs different actions depending upon which class is involved. Polymorphism is one of the characteristic features of object-oriented systems.

Exercise 16.6 What would happen if an attempt to initialize *mycountry* was made that included parameters?

16.3 INHERITANCE

We begin by defining an object which will be used extensively throughout this section. The object class is called *employee* and has data fields for storing a name and address. The methods for manipulating these data are an initialization routine that has two parameters, one for each piece of data. There are also two routines called *GetName* and *GetAddress* which return to the user the values stored in the name and address fields.

```
unit uemploy;
interface
type
  employee = object
            name    : string;
            address : string;
            procedure init(newname, newaddress : string);
            function GetName : string;
            function GetAddress : string;
        end;
```

```
implementation
  procedure employee.init;
    begin
      name := newname;
      address := newaddress
    end;
  function employee.GetName;
    begin
      GetName := name;
    end;
  function employee.GetAddress;
    begin
      GetAddress := address;
    end;
end.
```

16.3.1 Extending an object

The definitions below define a new object class, *PartTime*. It is an extension of the class *employee* and has all the features of *employee* plus a few additions. The class *PartTime* is said to be a **subclass** of *employee*, or equivalently, *employee* is a **superclass** of *PartTime*.

```
unit uemploy2;
interface
type
  employee = object
                name    : string;
                address : string;
                procedure init(newname, newaddress : string);
                function GetName : string;
                function GetAddress : string;
              end;
  PartTime = object(employee)
                hoursworked : real;
                hourlyrate  : real;
                procedure init(newname, newaddress : string; hourslogged : real);
                function CalcPay : real
              end;
```

A subclass may itself declare a subclass, thereby enabling a hierarchy of object classes to be defined. We shall look at one such hierarchy in Section 16.4. For now we shall restrict ourselves to this simple hierarchy of *employee* with its single subclass.

Instances of the object *PartTime* will have the features contained in its definition together with those of *employee*. So its data fields will consist of *name*, *address*, *hoursworked* and *hourlyrate* and the new method *init* and *CalcPay*. The object class *PartTime* is said to **inherit** the data fields *name* and *address* from *employee*. In a similar way, it inherits the methods *GetName* and *GetAddress* from *employee*. (The method *init* is also inherited, but as *PartTime* also declares a method with this name further explanation will be required shortly.) Inheritance is a very powerful tool in object programming because it allows existing objects to be extended and enhanced.

The new initialization method enables new values for the name, address and hours worked to be entered into an object instance. It will also be responsible for setting the value of the hourly rate, which will represent a fixed value of £4.50 per hour. Before we look at how this new class is implemented we shall see how an applications programmer could use the two classes *employee* and *PartTime*. Consider the following program fragment:

```
var
  worker1, worker2  : employee;
  retired, gardener : PartTime;
begin
  worker1.init('Smith', '10 Downing St');
  retired.init('Adsworth', 'The Orchards', 10.5);
  gardener.init('Birch', '23 Sloane Sq', 5.0);
  worker2 := retired;
  writeln(retired.GetName, ' has earned ', retired.CalcPay:4:2);
```

Notice how three parameters are required for initializing the *PartTime* instances but only two are required for the *employee* instance *worker1*. The initialization of *worker2* is a little different. We would have expected from our earlier work that the value of *worker1* could be assigned to that of *worker2* because they are of identical type. However, *worker2* and *retired* are not of the same type and yet the assignment is legal. This demonstrates an extension to the type compatibility rules as they apply to objects. The value of a subclass instance can be assigned to the value of a superclass. You can think of the reason why this is allowed in the following terms: the subclass object has at least the same data fields as its superclass (potentially it has more), so it can fill all the data fields of the superclass object. Here, the subclass object, *retired*, has data fields *name*, *address*, *hoursworked* and *hourlyrate*, and so can easily fill the data fields of its superclass, *employee*, which has only the two data fields, *name* and *address*. Similar reasoning shows that an assignment of this type cannot be carried out the other way round. *worker1* could not be assigned to *retired* because there is nothing to go in the *hoursworked* and *hourlyrate* fields. The same sort of reasoning can be applied to the methods. The method *CalcPay* associated with *retired* cannot be applied to *worker2* because this method does not exist in *employee*.

We have already explained that the reason why the calls to *init* here are unambiguous is because the object class determines which is appropriate. However, the call *retired.GetName* needs some explanation. When the compiler encounters this call it searches the class of which *retired* is an instance for a method called *GetName*, that is, it searches the definition of *PartTime* for *GetName*. If you examine this definition this method is not listed. What happens is that the compiler looks to see if *FullTime* has a superclass. It does, and so the methods of the superclass *employee* are searched. This illustrates a general principle. If a method cannot be found in the current class, then search the immediate superclass in the class hierarchy. Continue up the hierarchy until the method is found. (If the search fails, then a compilation error occurs because an attempt has been made to reference a class that is not in the class hierarchy.) This shows that only one copy of the code for a method exists even though that method may be inherited by any number of subclasses. Figure 16.2 represents this diagrammatically and, moreover, shows the form of the data segment for the declarations above.

We shall now look at the implementation part of *PartTime*. The heading for its initialization method would be:

```
implementation
  procedure PartTime.init;
```

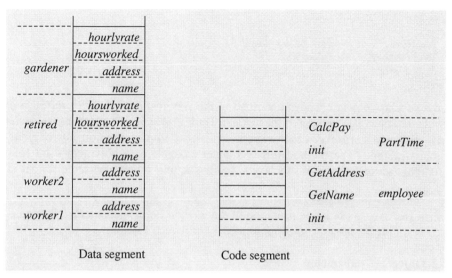

Figure 16.2 Memory and inheritance

This procedure has three source data parameters corresponding to the data fields: *name*, *address*, and *hoursworked*. The data field *hourlyrate* will be assigned the constant value 4.50 because this rate is common to all part-time workers. (In a more realistic scenario a **const** definition could be used for this value.) One way of coding the initialization would be:

```
procedure PartTime.init;
  begin
    name := newname;
    address := newaddress;
    hoursworked := hourslogged;
    hourlyrate := 4.50
  end;
```

This method illustrates very well that a subclass has all the attributes of a superclass and so, in particular, can directly access the fields *name* and *address* that do not appear explicitly as part of the definition of *PartTime*. However, this approach is considered to be poor style. Effectively, what we ought to be doing here is to extend the earlier definition to cater for the new data fields. We should therefore exploit *employee*'s *init* method. This is not only a matter of good style; it is entirely possible that *employee*'s *init* performs some important hidden initialization or stores the values in a different format (as, for example, in Exercise 16.5 where the input data had to be stored in a record). By exploiting the inherited method we can ensure that the subclass object includes its superclass functionality. However, the first two lines in the above code cannot simply be replaced by *init(newname, newaddress)* because this would be taken as a reference to the *init* being defined. In other words, it would result in a recursive call. The syntax for calling an inherited method is for the method identifier to be preceded by that of the object in which it is defined. This leads to the following implementation:

```
procedure PartTime.init;
  begin
    employee.init(newname, newaddress);
    hoursworked := hourslogged;
    hourlyrate := 4.50
  end;
```

When a subclass object changes a method in the way just described for *init*, it is said to **override** the superclass version of the method. Thus, *PartTime.init* overrides the declaration of *init* given in *employee*. However, note that its implementation has exploited the superclass method. The method *init* is another example of a polymorphism. Here, the polymorphic action is through subclasses, and the actions it performs are different in each class.

Exercise 16.7 Write the implementation of the method *PartTime.CalcPay*. The amount to be paid is simply the hours worked multiplied by the hourly rate.

16.3.2 Objects as parameters

A procedure or a function can have formal parameters that correspond to objects as well as the more conventional parameters we have discussed so far. They can be **var** or **value** parameters and are used in the way with which we are now very familiar. However, there is one extension, and that is that a formal parameter can take as an actual parameter an object of its own, or any subclass type. We shall illustrate this with a simple example.

A function *equalname* will be declared which has two parameters of type *employee* and returns the value true if they have the same name. The fragment below gives its declaration.

```
function equalname(firstemp, secondemp : employee) : Boolean;
  begin
    equalname := (firstemp.GetName = secondemp.GetName)
  end;
```

Using the following identifiers and initializations:

```
var
  worker1, worker2  : employee;
  retired, gardener : PartTime;
begin
  worker1.init('Smith', '10 Downing St');
  worker2.init('Birch', '5 Acacia Avenue');
  retired.init('Adsworth', 'The Orchards', 10.5);
  gardener.init('Birch', '23 Sloane Sq', 5.0);
```

the following call can be made to *equalname*:

```
if equalname(worker1, worker2) then
```

This would evaluate to false because *worker1* and *worker2* do have the same name. Now the function can also be called with parameters that are in a subclass of *employee*, and so in particular it can be called with *retired* and *gardener*. The following examples are therefore all valid calls of *equalname*:

```
if equalname(worker2, gardener) then
  :
if equalname(retired, gardener) then
```

The first of these calls would evaluate to true and the second to false. Some care has to be taken with **var** parameters. Consider the following procedure in which the **var** parameter returns the object whose name comes the alphabetically earlier of the two source parameters.

```
procedure earliername(var firstemp : employee; secondemp : employee);
  begin
    if firstemp.GetName > secondemp.GetName then
      firstemp := secondemp
  end;
```

Given the initializations above, the call

```
earliername(worker1, worker2)
```

would result in *worker1* holding the instance of the object with name Birch. The subsequent call

```
earliername(worker1, retired)
```

is valid because the class of *retired* is a subclass of *employee*. Furthermore, the result of the call is to assign to *worker1* the object instance *retired*. Note that this is a valid assignment because a subclass instance is assignment compatible with a superclass instance. As a result of the call, *worker1* will of course only hold the two *employee* data fields and not the four data fields that *retired* holds.

Finally, we remark that if a formal parameter is a pointer to an object type, the actual parameter can be a pointer to that object type or a pointer to any of the object's subclasses. We shall see an example of this in Section 16.5.

16.4 VIRTUAL METHODS

It is possible to define subclasses of subclasses and so obtain a hierarchical tree structure of objects. In this section we shall define the hierarchy defined by Figure 16.3.

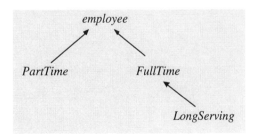

Figure 16.3 A tree of classes

Each class will inherit the functionality of its superclass, but we will add to each subclass some special feature relating solely to itself. The subclasses will be developed as separately compiled units. We shall suppose that the unit *uemploy* is only available to us in compiled form. Nevertheless, as we shall see, we shall be able to extend its definition to include new data fields and new methods. The ability to add features to an existing class or change the functionality of a method without access to the source code of that class is a novel facility. Hitherto, once an implementation was compiled it remained unalterable until such time as it was recompiled.

The object class *FullTime* has two additional data fields, *salary* and *years*. The *years* field records the number of years the employee has been with the company. The method *CalcLeave* calculates the leave entitlement based upon a formula. Examine the declarations and hence determine the purpose of each method.

```
unit uFull;
interface
  uses
    uemploy;
    {Imports object employee
     type
        employee = object
                     name
                     address
                     procedure init(newname, newaddress : string)
                     function GetName : string
                     function GetAddress : string
                   end}
  type
    FullTime = object(employee)
                 salary : real;
                 years  : integer;
                 procedure init(newname, newaddress : string; newsalary : real);
                 procedure UpdateYears;
                 function CalcLeave : integer;
                 procedure report;
                 function GetSalary : real;
                 function GetYears : integer
               end;

implementation
  procedure FullTime.init;
    begin
      employee.init(newname, newaddress);
      salary := newsalary;
      years := 0
    end;
  procedure FullTime.UpdateYears;
    begin
      years := years + 1;
    end;
  function FullTime.CalcLeave;
    begin
      if years < 10 then
        CalcLeave := 15 + years
      else
        CalcLeave := 25
    end;
  procedure FullTime.report;
    begin
```

```
      writeln(GetName);
      writeln(GetAddress);
      writeln('You are entitled to ', CalcLeave, ' days of annual leave')
    end;
  function FullTime.GetSalary;
    begin
      GetSalary := salary
    end;
  function FullTime.GetYears;
    begin
      GetYears := years
    end;
end.
```

For clarity we have included a comment that informs us what is imported from *uemploy*. We have not included the field type identifiers in the object definition because these fields ought to be accessed only by means of the methods. By excluding the type we are discouraging access other than through the methods. The other point to note is how the implementation of the method *report* references the method *CalcLeave*.

At this point we should pause to take stock of what we have achieved. Using only the code file of the unit *uemploy* we have been able to extend the definition of the object *employee* to obtain a new object class, *FullTime*. The new object class has all the functionality of *employee* so that it can *GetName* and *GetAddress* but it also has additional functionality provided by its own methods and data fields. At this point we could write a program which contained instances of both *employee* and *FullTime* and use the appropriate methods on them. All this has been done without having to alter or recompile the unit *uemploy*.

We shall now extend the class *FullTime* to a new subclass called *LongServing*. Instances of the latter type correspond to employees who have been employed in the company for at least 15 years. In recognition of their long service they become entitled to additional annual leave amounting to one day plus an extra day for every two years of service over 15 years. An initial attempt at defining this new object is given below:

```
unit uLong;
interface
  uses
    uFull;
    LongServing = object(FullTime)
                    procedure init(newname, newaddress : string; newsalary : real);
                    function CalcLeave : integer;
                  end;
```

This object class will have to have a method for initializing instances of the object. This version of the initialization will differ from that of *FullTime* because it will set the value of *years* to 15. This is straightforward, and simply requires the *init* of *FullTime* to be overridden as follows:

```
procedure LongServing.init;
  begin
    FullTime.init(newname, newaddress, newsalary);
    years := 15
  end;
```

We can see why an *init* procedure is required for this object class if we consider what happens when an employee has just completed 15 years' service. Suppose the employee details are stored in the instance *existing*, which is of class *FullTime*. These details have to be transferred to an instance, which we shall call *old*, of class *LongServing*. This cannot be done by assignment of *existing* to *old* because a subclass instance cannot be assigned to a superclass instance. We have to call *LongServing.init* with parameters whose values are obtained from *old*. Thus, we would have:

```
old.init(existing.GetName, existing.GetAddress, existing.GetSalary)
```

A similar approach of overriding the definition of *CalcLeave* might seem to be appropriate with the *LongServing* version along the following lines:

```
function LongServing.CalcLeave;
  begin
    CalcLeave := 25 + (years - 13) div 2
  end;
```

Suppose we have implemented these changes and they are available to the following declarations and program fragment:

```
var
  novice  : FullTime;
  oldtimer : LongServing;
begin
  novice.init('Green', 'New estate', 12000);
  oldtimer.init('Old', 'The Vicarage', 25000);
  novice.report;
  oldtimer.report
```

The output from this fragment should be that Green has a leave entitlement of 15 days and Old has a leave entitlement of 26 days, this being 25 days plus one day for long service. To understand what happens when this code is executed we need to consider what happens when the main program is compiled. By the time the compiler reaches the main program it has already compiled the methods associated with each object, and so their address within the code segment is known. The first initialization call would result in the message *init* being passed to *novice*. The compiler looks for a method called *init* within the object class of *novice*. Since this is a valid method for this object, the compiler replaces the call *novice.init* by the code segment address of the method *init*. When this statement is executed, control passes to this address. Upon completion, control returns to the next statement of the fragment. This is illustrated in Figure 16.4.

At the bottom of this figure are the compiled methods for each class of object. The call *novice.init* , contains the address of its *init* procedure and the figure shows execution jumps to this code. Once complete, execution continues with the next statement, namely, the call to *oldtimer.init*.

Because the address of the method *init* is known at compile time, the method is said to be **static**. In other words, the compiler already knows where the appropriate code for *init* is, and so it has the simple task of replacing the call by the appropriate address. This process is often described in object programming terms as **early binding** or **static binding**. This means that the method call is bound by the compiler to a certain address within the code segment.

For the call *oldtimer.init* the compiler searches the methods of the object class *LongServing* for a method called *init*. Since a method of that name is found in this object

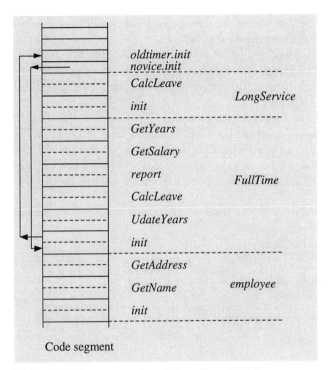

Figure 16.4 A representation of the call *novice.init*

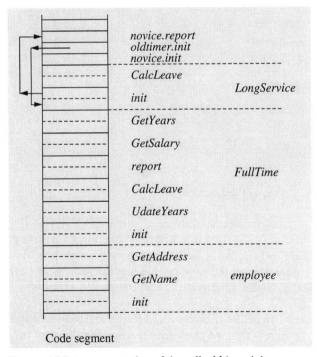

Figure 16.5 A representation of the call *oldtimer.init*

class, the compiler replaces the call by the address in the codefile segment at which this version of *init* is stored. This can be represented as follows.

Note here how the overridden version of *init* is referenced. Figures 16.4 and 16.5 illustrate how the two different versions of *init* are incorporated into the compiled version of the fragment. Essentially, the calls result in different addresses, each corresponding to the location of the different code fragments.

For the third statement, the message *report* is passed to *novice* which responds by looking for a method called *report* in its methods list. Since novice is of type *FullTime* this results in the methods of this class being searched. Again, the compiler finds the method and replaces the call *novice.report* by the address in the codefile segment at which *report* is stored. The representation of this is more complex because *report* calls *CalcLeave* (Figure 16.6).

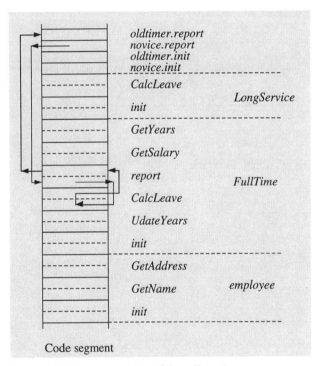

Figure 16.6 A representation of the call *novice.report*

Figure 16.6 A representation of the call *novice.report*

The call *novice.report* is replaced by the address of the method *report*. However, within this call there is a call to *CalcLeave*. This is indicated by the flow of control going to the code segment corresponding to *CalcLeave* before returning to complete the call to *report*. This flow of control is achieved by the compiler binding the address of *CalcLeave* within the code for *report*. Finally, control returns to the next statement's execution, namely, *oldtimer.report*.

A similar process happens when the message *report* is passed to *oldtimer*. The compiler looks for a method called *report* in the class *LongServing*. But this time it does not find one and so the immediate superclass, *FullTime*, is searched. The address of its *report* method then replaces the call *oldtimer.report*. This is shown in Figure 16.7 below.

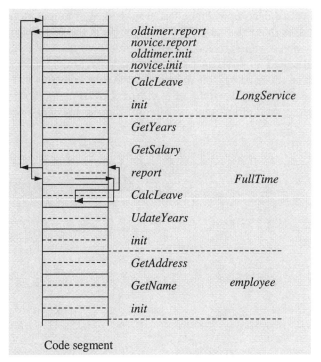

Figure 16.7 A representation of the call *oldtimer.report*

But this is not what we want because the code for *FullTime.report* includes a call to the wrong version of *CalcLeave*. It's the *LongServing* version of *CalcLeave* that should be used here. Remember that references to *CalcLeave* are already bound to the fixed address of *FullTime*'s *CalcLeave*, and this cannot be altered. The difficulty is that different versions of *CalcLeave* must be used by *report* depending upon the class of the object that calls *report*.

How can this be overcome? A new facility known as **late binding** (or sometimes as **dynamic binding**) is required, in which the compiler does not replace a method call by a bound address within the code segment. Instead, the code to be executed is determined at run-time by the class of the object making the call. Methods that are to be late bound have to be specified as **virtual**. Here, we want the different versions of *CalcLeave* to be used depending upon which object class calls them. Instances of *FullTime* class should use one version whereas instances of the inherited class *LongServing* should use another. Routines can be declared to be virtual by appending the word 'virtual' to their heading, thus:

```
type
  FullTime = object(employee)
           :
           function CalcLeave : integer; virtual;
           procedure report;
           :
         end;
  LongServing = object(FullTime)
             :
             function CalcLeave : integer; virtual
           end;
```

A peculiarity of Turbo Pascal is that once a procedure has been marked as virtual, it must be marked as virtual in all subclasses that redefine it. You can see this in the fragment above. Another peculiarity is that any object which includes a virtual procedure must be initialized by invoking a special method called a **constructor**. A constructor is simply an ordinary method with the word 'procedure' replaced by 'constructor'. Because the constructor must be invoked before any other method it is usual to turn the initialization method into a constructor method. The revised definitions which we require in the unit *employee* are therefore:

```
employee = object
              name    : string;
              address : string;
              constructor init(newname, newaddress : string);
              function GetName : string;
              function GetAddress : string;
            end;
```

and in the unit *uFull* are:

```
FullTime = object(employee)
              salary : real;
              years  : integer;
              constructor init(newname, newaddress : string; newsalary : real);
              procedure UpdateYears;
              function CalcLeave : integer; virtual;
              procedure report;
              function GetSalary : real;
              function GetYears : integer
            end;
```

and in the unit *uLong* are:

```
LongServing = object(FullTime)
                 constructor init(newname, newaddress : string; newsalary : real);
                 function CalcLeave : integer; virtual;
               end;
```

The implementation details remain as before with the exception that the headings for all the *init* routines need to be changed from **procedure** to **constructor**. The reason a constructor is required is because every class that contains a virtual method has associated with it a **Virtual Method Table** or VMT. VMTs are stored in the data segment area and so only exist at run-time. Only one copy of the VMT is generated per class, but every instance of a class must have access to its corresponding VMT. This is done by recording the address of the VMT within the instance, and it is one of the tasks of the constructor to do this.

We will now look at what happens when these methods are compiled. Each of the static routines is compiled as before and will be called exactly as described above. When a virtual method is encountered the compiler sets up the VMT in the data segment area. Figure 16.8 shows the state of both the data segment area and the code segment for the program fragment above.

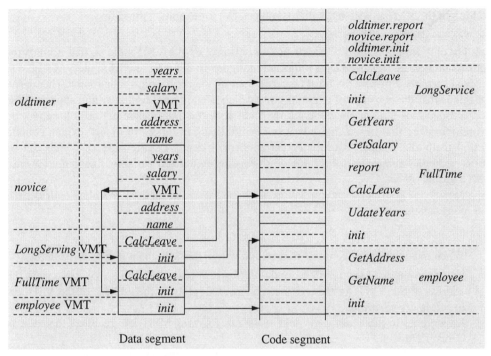

Figure 16.8 Memory when virtual methods are used

Compilation begins with the object classes. Since *employee* contains a virtual method (remember constructors are virtual methods) it sets up a VMT for this class in the data segment area. Other than housekeeping data (not shown in Figure 16.8) the VMT consists of a list of addresses. Each address represents the start address within the code segment of the associated method. So for the class *employee* the VMT holds the code segment address of *employee.init*. The object class *FullTime* has two virtual methods so its VMT has two entries that record the code segment addresses of these methods. Similarly, the VMT for *LongServing* also has two entries. In Figure 16.8 these addresses are indicated by the lines joining the data and the code segments.

When the declarations of instances of the object classes are compiled sufficient space for the data fields of the objects is created, but the compiler also allocates an extra field called the **virtual method field**. This field is used to record the address of the VMT associated with that object class. So when the declaration of *novice* is encountered, space for the fields *name*, *address*, *salary* and *years* data fields is reserved together with the space for the VMT field. (The order in which they are allocated is of no concern to us here but of course is important if you study the implementation in greater detail.) Similarly, the declaration of *oldtimer* reserves space for its data fields together with space for its VMT field.

Just after the declarations have been compiled the entries in all the data fields will be undefined. An object's constructor performs the task of inserting into the VMT field the address of the VMT associated with that object. So, for example, the call

novice.init('Green', 'New estate', 12000)

will not only initialize the data fields but will also set up the VMT field so that it holds the address of the *FullTime* VMT (as indicated in Figure 16.8 by the line from the VMT field to the VMT itself). This process must be carried out by the appropriate constructor. The reason for this is that the constructor contains code which is additional to that which appears in its declaration. This hidden code sets up the field with the appropriate address. It cannot be overemphasized that this is the only way of initializing instances of objects which contain virtual methods. Unlike an ordinary variable (or, indeed, a static object), which can be initialized by assigning to it the value of an existing initialized variable, this is not the case with a virtual object.

Now let us consider the compilation of a call to a virtual method. We shall consider the following statement:

writeln(*oldtimer.CalcLeave*)

When the compiler encounters the method within this statement it does three things:

1. It goes to the data segment and finds *oldtimer*. Within this data space it recovers the address of the VMT for this class. So here it will recover the address of the VMT for the class *LongServing*.
2. It then goes to the *CalcLeave* field of the *LongServing* VMT and recovers the address in that field.
3. It is the code at this address that the compiler then knows is to be executed.

Following this process through using Figure 16.8 we can see that the code which is executed is the *CalcLeave* of the object class *LongServing* – precisely what we wanted.

Exercise 16.8 Trace through in a similar way the following call:

writeln(*novice.CalcLeave*)

Understanding how the method *report* is compiled is a little more tricky. It is a static method and it calls a virtual method. For convenience, the code is reproduced below.

```
procedure FullTime.report;
  begin
    writeln(GetName);
    writeln(GetAddress);
    writeln('You are entitled to ', CalcLeave, ' days of annual leave')
  end;
```

The first two statements of the body are straightforward. It is the third statement that involves the virtual method. Associated with any given method is an invisible parameter called *Self*. This parameter carries with it details of the object instance making the call. Hence we can think of the call *CalcLeave* here as being equivalent to the call *Self.CalcLeave*. What this says is go and apply *CalcLeave* on yourself, whatever type of object you are. So the compiler creates code that examines *Self* to determine what kind of object class is involved and creates the code corresponding to steps 1 – 3 above. So although the code for *report* appears in the code segment, within it there are instructions to go to the VMT determined by the class of *Self*. This in turn will then call whichever version of *CalcLeave* is required before returning control to *report*.

If we now take stock of progress we shall see that we have done something rather remarkable. The unit *uFull* contains the code for the method *report*. Let us assume that someone else wrote *uFull* and only gave us access to the compiled version of it. What we have done is to alter the functionality of *report* as it relates to our object class *LongServing*. All this has been done without having access to the code for *report*! This is indeed a very powerful programming tool and is made possible by late binding.

16.5 VIRTUAL METHODS OR OVERRIDING?

As we have just seen, the introduction of late binding allows systems to evolve without the need for recompilation. If systems are statically bound, then it will be necessary to generate new code for the whole system to ensure that all method invocations use the correct implementation. With late binding this is not necessary. It ensures that the correct method implementation is used for a particular object instance because the VMT of the class is inspected in order to get the address of the appropriate code.

This would appear to suggest that all methods should be specified as virtual. That certainly is one view, but there are drawbacks in using virtual methods. Each time a virtual method is called, the appropriate VMT has to be found and then it has to be searched for the address of the required method. Searching is perhaps a partial overstatement as the locations are found by using offsets which are stored in the housekeeping area that was briefly referred to in the previous section. However, all this takes time. Another disadvantage is if the method does not exist. If failed dynamic bindings are not anticipated by the programmer, their failure cannot be detected until run-time. Avoiding run-time errors of this type adds to program complexity.

This has been but a brief discussion of the issues, but one clear case where virtual methods are a necessity can be derived by generalizing the situation that we encountered in the previous section. If a method makes a call to another method within its body, and it is anticipated that this inner method may need to be changed by a subclass object, while leaving the calling method the same, then the inner method must be specified as virtual. Unfortunately, this simple guideline is insufficient, and we conclude the text with a more significant example in which the choice of the use of static or virtual methods is more difficult. The example makes use of dynamic objects, that is, objects that are allocated on the heap. In other words, we shall be using pointers to objects. The purpose of the example is to illustrate how a stack can be implemented that is capable of storing items of different types can be implemented. Each item on the stack will point to one of two object classes. The object classes will be based on the *MapRef* object class of Section 16.2, and will have two fields, called *latitude* and *longitude*. A subclass of *MapRef* will be defined, called *Position*, which will have an additional data field, *height*. Each class will have a print method, where the *MapRef* version outputs a latitude and longitude and the *position* version outputs latitude, longitude and height. *MapRef* and *Position* will be implemented in a single unit called *uMapRef*. The stack will be represented as a linked list of nodes where each node will consist of a record of two fields. The first field will be a pointer to an instance of one of the object classes and the second field will point to the next item on the stack. Figure 16.9 illustrates this model in which there are four items on the stack, and it shows some of the identifiers we shall use. The stack itself will also be implemented as an object in a unit called *uStckObj*.

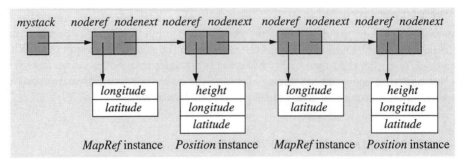

Figure 16.9 A stack of object instances

For brevity we shall not define the methods for the stack in depth as we have already discussed them in some detail in Chapter 11. The items that will be stored on the stack will be pointers to objects of type *MapRef* (and its subclass *Position*). Therefore, it is pointers to objects that will be popped and pushed, and this is reflected in the incomplete definitions below.

```
unit uStckObj; {Unit for the stack object class}
interface
  uses
    uMapRef;
  type
    refptr = ^MapRef;
    posptr = ^Position ;
    nodeptr = ^node;
    node = record
              noderef  : refptr;
              nodenext : nodeptr
            end;
    stacktype = object
                    stack : nodeptr;
                    procedure push(item : refptr);
                    procedure pop(var item : refptr; var success : Boolean);
                    :
                  end;
```

Note how *push* has a single parameter of type *refptr*. From our work on parameters we know that this method can also be used to push pointers that point to instances of the subclass *Position*. This means that *push* can be called with an actual parameter of type *posptr*.

What happens when an item is popped? A pointer *item* is returned. Again, due to the extension of parameter compatibilities to objects, *item* could point to either an instance of *MapRef* or its subclass *Position*. We actually do not know which of these it will be. Suppose it is a pointer to *MapRef*. To recover the data, *item* needs to be dereferenced and passed the message to print itself. This can be achieved with *item^.print*. The version of print that is used is determined by the class to which *item* points, namely *MapRef*, and so a latitude and longitude will be output – just what we expect. Now suppose that *item* points to a *Position* type object. What will *item^.print* do this time? Unfortunately, it will only output the latitude and longitude and not the height. The reason for this is that *pop* declares *item* to be of type *refptr* and so *item^* is assumed to be an object of type *MapRef* (the object class to which *refptr* points) rather than one of its subclasses. We want to force *print* to determine the object class of *item^* by examining its class. In other words, we want *print* to look at the *Self* of *item^* in order to determine the class to which it belongs. You have probably guessed by now that to do this we shall need to specify *print* as a virtual method. The code below gives the complete interface for the unit *uMapRef*.

```
unit uMapRef;   {Unit for map reference object classes}
interface
  type
    refptr = ^MapRef;
    MapRef = object
                 latitude  : real;
                 longitude : real;
                 constructor init(inlat, inlong : real);
                 function GetLat  : real;
                 function GetLong : real;
                 procedure print; virtual;
               end;
    posptr = ^Position  ;
    Position  = object(MapRef)
                 height : real;
                 constructor init(inlat, inlong, inheight : real);
                 function GetHeight : real;
                 procedure print; virtual;
               end;
```

Exercise 16.9 Write the implementation part of *uMapRef*.

Exercise 16.10 The missing definitions of *stacktype* are as follows:

```
stacktype = object
                 stack : nodeptr;
                  :
                 procedure create;
                 function isempty : Boolean;
                 procedure print;
               end;
```

Using these additional definitions write the implementation part of the unit *uStckObj*.

We conclude with a brief look at a driver program to test the two units above. It will have the following declarations and will include the code fragment shown:

```
program stackuse;
uses uMapRef, uStckObj, crt;
var
  teststack          : stacktype;
  choice             : char;
  data               : refptr;
  flag               : Boolean;
  lat, long, height  : real;
```

```
procedure getret;
  {As in earlier examples}
begin
  clrscr;
  teststack.create;
  choice := '9';
  while choice <> '6' do
    begin
      clrscr;
      writeln('1 : Push a map reference on the stack');
      writeln('2 : Push a position on the stack');
      writeln('3 : Pop an item from the stack');
      writeln('4 : List all items on the stack');
      writeln('5 : Test for an empty stack');
      writeln('6 : Stop');
      write('Enter choice ');
      readln(choice);
      case choice of
```

First, notice that the stack is created by sending the message *create* to *teststack*. Two different options for entering data onto the stack are required because the user will have to enter two data items for a map reference but three for a position. The code corresponding to option 1 will read values into the variables *lat* and *long*. A temporary variable, called *data*, will then be initialized and pushed onto the stack. This involves three tasks. Firstly, space has to be allocated for *data* on the heap using the procedure *new*. Secondly, the object instance *data^* has to be initialized. You will recall that for objects involving virtual, methods every instance must be initialized using its constructor. Finally, data has to be pushed onto the stack. The code required is:

```
new(data);
data^.init(lat, long);
teststack.push(data);
```

Turbo Pascal provides an extension to the syntax of *new* to allow a more compact and convenient means of allocating space on the heap for an object. It can be invoked as a function that has two parameters. The first parameter is the type of the pointer to the object and the second is the constructor invocation. This removes the need for the temporary variable *data* so that all three of the above statements can be replaced by:

```
teststack.push(new(refptr, init(lat, long)));
```

Exercise 16.11 Assuming that *lat*, *long* and *height* have all been initialized, write down a single statement that will push a pointer to the object having these values onto the stack.

Exercise 16.12 Write the code corresponding to options 3 and 4.

16.6 SUMMARY

In this chapter we have seen how abstract data types can be extended so that the data and the operations which act on the data are encapsulated in an object. Object operations are referred to as methods so that an object consists of a collection of data and methods. The data should only be manipulated via the methods although Turbo Pascal cannot enforce this. An object class can be extended to a subclass that inherits all the attributes of the original class. This enables class hierarchies to be built up. A method at one level of the hierarchy can be overridden by redefining the method within the subclass. Procedures and functions can have object class parameters. Actual parameters used in calls can correspond to subclasses of the formal parameters.

When it is not possible to determine at compile time the method that should be applied to an object then that method must be specified as virtual. Any object instance whose class contains a virtual method must be initialized with a constructor in order that the instance is given the address of the Virtual Method Table in the data segment. It is through the VMT that virtual method calls are executed.

SOLUTIONS TO EXERCISES

Exercise 1.1

In order to produce a blank line a call to *writeln* is required. The call should not have any parameters and so it might seem reasonable to code this as *writeln( )*. This is not so. The brackets must be omitted when there are no parameters.

```
program lines;
begin
  writeln('The next line is completely blank');
  writeln;
  writeln('This is the third line');
  writeln('This is the last line');
end.
```

Exercise 1.2

The third output is the most complex. Note how the comma and its following space character have to be output as a string enclosed in quotes.

```
writeln(sum, ' is the sum of the inputs');
writeln('The number ', sum, ' is the sum of the inputs')
writeln('Inputs were ', FirstNumber, ', ', SecondNumber, ' and their sum is ', sum)
```

Exercise 1.3

```
program difftwo;
{A program to input two integers from the keyboard and write out their difference}
var
  FirstNumber, TakeAway, difference : integer;
begin
  write('Enter the first integer ');
  readln(FirstNumber);
  write('Enter the integer which is to be subtracted ');
  readln(TakeAway);
  difference := FirstNumber - TakeAway;
  writeln('The difference is ', difference)
end.
```

Exercise 1.4
Because it is immediately followed by the word **end**.

Exercise 1.5
The *writeln* statements are not followed by a semicolon because they are immediately followed by the word **end**. The first **end** is not followed by a semicolon because it essentially represents the end of the single compound statement of the **then** clause.

Exercise 1.6
```
var
    one, two, three : integer;
    first, second   : real;
```

Notice that even though this is a fragment the final statement is followed by a semicolon. That is because all declarations are always followed by a semicolon. Alternatively, the real declarations could precede those of the integer variables as follows:

```
var
    first, second   : real;
    one, two, three : integer;
```

Exercise 1.7
We have chosen the name 'Dave' in the solution.
```
program myname;
begin
    writeln('Dave')
end.
```

Exercise 2.1
(a) This is valid.
(b) This is valid.
(c) This is not valid because an identifier cannot begin with a digit.
(d) This is not valid because an identifier cannot begin with an underscore.
(e) This is valid; an identifier can contain many underscore characters.

Exercise 2.2
(a) This is valid – there does not have to be a title; there is a single firstname and 'David' is a valid value; there is a surname and its value, 'Sargent', is valid.
(b) This is invalid – 'Prof.' is neither a valid title value nor a valid firstname.
(c) This is valid – there is a title and 'Dr' is a valid title value; there does not have to be a firstname; there is a surname and 'Polson' is a valid value.
(d) This is invalid – the title is valid but then the name 'Kate' must correspond to a surname because all names must have a surname. 'Kate' is not a valid surname value.
(e) This is invalid – a title is optional so its absence here is valid; the names 'Ian' and 'Robert' must correspond to the term < firstname > because we can identify 'Sargent' as being a valid surname. Both 'Ian' and 'Robert' are in turn valid values of < name >. However, the syntax of < firstname > indicates that if a person has more than one name then they must have at least three such firstnames. (They could of course have five, seven or any positive odd number of first names.)
(f) This is syntactically valid, despite being a strange combination of names.

Exercise 2.3

Yes. If a program has declarations then they are part of the program block. Do not confuse a program block with what we refer to as the program body, which is that part of the code which corresponds to the program design.

Exercise 2.4

It is valid because the declaration of the first two variables corresponds to traversing the syntax diagram via the short loop under < identifier >. After the first semicolon the long loop back can be traversed, which shows that the declaration of *sum* can be made separately.

Exercise 2.5

The identifier *integer* used in this declaration is actually valid – it conforms to the syntax required of an identifier. Having said that, you would never try to redefine one of the built-in type identifiers in this way despite it being syntactically permissible. What is syntactically wrong is the identifier *first*. This is not a valid < type >, which in this chapter must be either *real* or *integer*.

Exercise 2.6

Since there are two constructs (steps 3.5 and 3.6) within the *else* clause a compound statement is required. This explains its **begin/end** pair. The reason that this latter **end** is followed by a semicolon is because the **if** statement as a whole is not the last statement of the compound statement of which it is a part.

Exercise 2.7

Here, the *then* clause consists of two constructs: an assignment and a write out, and so it must be implemented using a compound statement. Note in particular the punctuation associated with its implementation. The **end** which terminates the **then** clause is followed by a semicolon because it is one of the statements of the main program body compound statement.

```
program leapyear4;
var
  year, days : integer;
begin
  write('Enter a year in the range 1990 to 1993 inclusive ');
  readln(year);
  days := 365;
  if year = 1992 then
    begin
      days := 366;
      writeln('This year is a leap year')
    end;
  writeln('There are ', days, ' days in this year')
end.
```

Exercise 2.8

In this solution we have introduced two new terms corresponding to the second and third components of a registration plate.

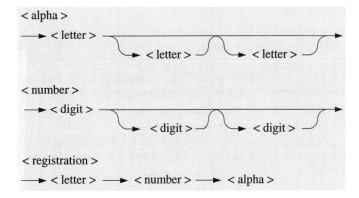

Exercise 2.9

In order to accommodate this change it is necessary to define the digits 1 ... 9 separately.

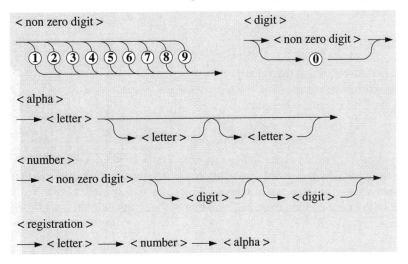

Exercise 2.10

It must start and end with a letter and have an odd number of characters (letters or digits).

Exercise 2.11

```pascal
program calcint;
var
  balance : real;
  year    : integer;
begin
  balance := 100.0;
  year := 1993;
  while balance < 1000.0 do
    begin
      balance := balance*1.08;
      year := year + 1
    end;
  writeln('The investment reaches £1000 in the year ', year)
end.
```

Exercise 2.12

The code is not correct. The easy way to see why is to suppose the problem required the largest power of 4 which is less than, say, 6, because the number 6 is easier to deal with than 200. When we have convinced ourselves with this value it will be easier to see what goes wrong when the value is 200. If we do this, then of course the largest power of 4 which is less than 6 is 1. So the answer we expect is 1. The code does not produce this as we can see by tracing it through line by line. Initially, *power* has value 1 and the loop executes because *number* < 6 is true. Within the loop *number* is reassigned the value 16 and *power* is incremented to 2. The next test of the loop condition returns false and so the output stage is reached with *power* having a value which is one too many. The fault lies in the initial value assigned to *power*. It should be 0, not 1.

Exercise 3.1

(i)   2
(ii)   − 2
(iii)   − 2
(iv)   2
(v)   1
(vi)   Undefined, but Turbo returns the value 1.
(vii)   2, but Turbo returns the value − 1.
(viii)   Undefined, but Turbo returns the value − 1.

Exercise 3.2

The first column contains only single digits and so can have a field width of 1. The 16 in the second column, together with the minimum separation of the columns, dictates that the field width must be 5. This allows for three initial spaces followed by two spaces for two digits. Similarly, the width of the third column must be 5 and that of the fourth column must be 6.

```
writeln(2:1, 4:5, 8:5, 16:6);
writeln(3:1, 9:5, 27:5, 51:6);
writeln(4:1, 16:5, 64:5, 256:6)
```

Exercise 3.3

```
writeln(two:1, two*two:5, two*two*two:5, two*two*two*two:6);
writeln(three:1, three*three:5, three*three*three:5, three*three*three*three:6);
writeln(four:1, four*four:5, four*four*four:5, four*four*four*four:6)
```

Exercise 3.4

(i)   43940.0
(ii)   0.0023
(iii)   9000.0 (This example shows that a mantissa does not have to include a decimal point.)

Exercise 3.5

(i)   5.826E2
(ii)   6.28E–3
(iii)   1.023E1

Exercise 3.6
(i)   Valid
(ii) Invalid – the decimal point must be preceded by a digit, here 0
(iii) Valid
(iv) Valid
(v)   Invalid – if the E notation is used it must be followed by at least one digit
(vi) Valid. This number is actually converted to the real number 34.0 for storage. If this value is assigned to a real variable a similar conversion takes place.

Exercise 3.7
The first column is right justified on the second character position. The second column is right justified 8 positions from the first column.

```
writeln(1:2, 20.56:8:2);
writeln(2:2, 3.67:8:2);
writeln(20:2, 127.56:8:2);
```

Exercise 3.8
The character A will be assigned to *first*, B will be assigned to *second* and the input buffer will then be flushed ready for the next input so the extra data will be lost.

Exercise 3.9
Data corresponding to two characters have been entered and that is sufficient for this statement. However, the input buffer will not be processed until a <ret> is received. Thus, processing will halt. When an additional <ret> is entered then A is assigned to *first* and <ret>, that is, the character with ASCII code 13, is assigned to *second*.

Exercise 3.10
The asterisk will be written out followed by the output of *second*. But this has value 'carriage return' which repositions the cursor at the leftmost column. The variable *first* is then written out to give A and this is followed by the exclamation mark. So the output is:

```
A!
```

Note how the asterisk gets overwritten as a result of the carriage return.

Exercise 3.11
The two asterisks will be written out, at which point the cursor will be at column 3. This is followed by the output of *second*, that is, a linefeed. This moves the cursor to the next line at column 3. The two % signs are then output at positions 3 and 4. The variable *first* is then written out and, this being a carriage return, it sends the cursor back to the leftmost position of its current line. The exclamation mark is then output which leaves the cursor at column 2. Hence we get:

```
**
! %%
```

Exercise 3.12
(a)   Valid. The expression evaluates to a real value which can be compared with an integer value.

(b) Invalid. The types are incompatible – string values cannot be compared with integer values.

(c) Invalid. The expression in brackets evaluates to a string value which cannot be compared with an integer value.

(d) Valid. The expression in brackets evaluates to a string value which is then compared with the string '20'.

Exercise 3.13

str1 has dynamic length 14. *str2* has dynamic length 28. *shortstr* has static length 10 and so is assigned only the first 10 characters of *str2*. Hence it has dynamic length 10.

Exercise 4.1

The definition of *pi* is syntactically correct and is a real constant.

The definition of *minsize* is an error because it references *maxsize* which is an undeclared identifier at this point of the compilation. This can be rectified by placing it after the definition of *maxsize*, in which case it would be an integer constant.

The definition of *maxsize* is syntactically correct and is an integer constant.

The definition of *message* is syntactically incorrect because it uses an assignment symbol rather than an equals sign. When corrected this would give a string constant.

This definition is incorrect because '0' is of type *char* and *maxsize* is of (implied) type *integer*, and these two types are not expression compatible.

This definition is syntactically correct. The literal 2 is of type *integer* and *pi* is of (implied) type *real*. These two types are expression compatible and evaluate to a real value. So, *twopi* is a real constant.

Exercise 5.1

(a)
```
for i := 1 to 8 do
    writeln(i*i)
```
(b)
```
for i := 25 downto 9 do
    writeln(4*i)
```

or equivalently

```
for i := 1 to 16 do
    writeln(100 - 4*i)
```

Exercise 5.2

It would fail to execute at all if the value of *number* input at step 1 was positive. Therefore, it would only execute if the input was zero or negative. The purpose of this fragment is to obtain a positive input from the keyboard.

Exercise 5.3

The only difficulty here is getting the punctuation correct. Note that the statement which increments *number* is not followed by a semicolon because it immediately precedes **until**.

```
program smallestsquare;
var
  number : integer;
begin
  number := 0;
  repeat
```

```
    number := number + 1
  until (number*number) > 150;
  writeln('The smallest positive integer which exceeds 150 is ', number)
end.
```

Exercise 5.4

The reserved word **while** must be followed by a Boolean expression, here it is *count* <= 20.
This is followed by the reserved word **do**. This must be followed by a < statement >, but
from Figure 5.4 we know that an occurrence of < statement > is < compound statement >.
From Figure 2.9 we know that a compound statement begins with the reserved word **begin,**
which accounts for the **begin** of the inner loop. This is followed by as many occurrences of
< statement > as we like, each separated by a semicolon. Here we have four of them, two
procedure calls (a *writeln* and a *readln*) followed by two assignments. There then follows
the **end** of the compound inner loop statement.

Exercise 5.5

The code would be syntactically correct and should be indented as follows to best illustrate
the semantics to which it corresponds:

```
if compass = 'N' then
  writeln('Compass points North')
else
  writeln('Compass is not pointing North');
if compass = 'S' then
  writeln('Compass points South')
else
  if compass = 'W' then
    writeln('Compass points West')
  else
    writeln('Compass points East');
writeln('End of fragment')
```

In this form it is perhaps easier to see that if *compass* has value 'N' the output will be:

```
Compass points North
Compass points East
End of fragment
```

Exercise 5.6

(a)   The number will either be zero or positive so the best description is non-negative.
(b)   The best description is positive.
(c)   These numbers are not all negative but they are definitely not positive and so the best
        description is non-positive.
(d)   Since the temperature never reaches zero or higher the best description is negative.

Exercise 5.7

When *number* = 10 the output is simply the message 'End of fragment'. When *number* = – 4
the **else** clause is executed and so the message that the number is positive is output!

Exercise 5.8

```
program survey;
const
  surveysize = 250;
var
  regcount, firstcount, number : integer;
  answer1, answer2           : char;
begin
  regcount := 0;
  firstcount := 0;
  number := 0;
  while number < surveysize do
    begin
      writeln('Do you fly with us regularly?');
      write('Enter Y (for yes) or N (for no). ');
      readln(answer1);
      number := number + 1;
      if answer1= 'Y' then
        begin
          regcount := regcount + 1;
          writeln('Do you fly first class?');
          write('Enter Y (for yes) or N (for no). ');
          readln(answer2);
          if answer2 = 'Y' then
            firstcount := firstcount + 1
        end
    end;
  writeln(regcount, ' passengers were regular users.');
  writeln(firstcount, ' of these fly first class.')
end.
```

Exercise 6.1

Variables *one*, *two* and *four* are valid although *two* is of little use having a single index value. Variable *three* is not valid because its lower bound exceeds its upper bound.

Exercise 6.2

```
const
  maxsize = 22;
var
  team                    : array[1..maxsize] of string;
  firstindex, secondindex : integer;
  :
for firstindex := 1 to maxsize −1 do
  for secondindex := firstindex + 1 to maxsize do
    begin
      writeln(team[firstindex], ' v ', team[secondindex]);
      writeln(team[secondindex], ' v ', team[firstindex])
    end
```

Exercise 6.3

```
for i := 0 to 10 do
  writeln(team[2*i + 1])
```

Exercise 6.4

On the first execution of the first loop i has value 2 and so *power*[2 – 1] is referenced. This is multiplied by 2 and assigned to *power*[2]. On the next execution i has value 3 and so it is *power*[3 – 1] which is referenced and multiplied by 2 so that 8 is assigned to *power*[3]. Hence the numbers 2, 4, 8, 16, 32, 64, 128, 256 are assigned to the eight elements.

The second loop executes three times. When i has value 1, *power*[1] is referenced and used as the index for *power*. This effectively references *power*[2] and so 4 is output. When i has value 2, the reference to *power*[2] results in the value 4 which is in turn used as the index to *power*. The value of *power*[4], namely 16, is then output. For the final execution i has value 3, the reference to *power*[3] results in value 8 which is then used to reference *power*[8]. The value of this element, 256, is then output.

Exercise 6.5

(a) Valid.
(b) Valid – despite the fact that 3∗8 evaluates to 24 which is greater than the upper index bound, the overall expression has value 4 which is within bounds.
(c) Invalid because *power*[4] has value 16 and this value is then used as an index.
(d) Valid – *power*[1] has value 2 and this is used as an index, the result of which is 4. This in turn is used as an index to reference *power*[4] which has value 16.

Exercise 6.6

```
const
  lowbound  = 1;
  midbound  = 10;
  highbound = 100;
type
  realarray = array[lowbound..midbound] of integer;
  strarray  = array[midbound..highbound] of string[20];
var
  numbers : realarray;
  names   : strarray;
```

Exercise 6.7

```
var
  i : integer;
for i := 1 to 5 do
  writeln(team[4*i - 1])
```

or equivalently:

```
for i := 0 to 4 do
  writeln(team[4*i + 3])
```

Exercise 6.8

```
var
  i : integer;
for i := 5 downto 0 do
  writeln(team[4*i + 1])
```

or equivalently:

```
for i := 6 downto 1 do
  writeln(team[4*i - 3])
```

Exercise 6.9

(a)   This refers to the 11th character of the name at index 10, so has value K.

(b)   This refers to the 10th character of the name at index 11, so has value W.

Exercise 6.10

```
program linsearch;
const
  maxsize = 3;   {altered from 22 for test purposes}
var
  team       : array[0..maxsize] of string;
  searchitem : string;
  index      : integer;
begin
  team[1] := 'First';   {code for initializing the array}
  team[2] := 'Second';
  team[3] := 'Last';
  write('Enter the team whose position is sought ');
  readln(searchitem);
  team[0] := searchitem;
  index := maxsize;
  while team[index] <> searchitem do
    index := index - 1;
  if index = 0 then
    writeln('Item is not in the array')
  else
    writeln('Position of ', searchitem, ' is ', index)
end.
```

Exercise 6.11

```
const
  firstmonth = 1;
  lastmonth  = 12;
  firstyear  = 1987;
  lastyear   = 1990;
type
  arraytype = array[firstmonth..lastmonth, firstyear..lastyear] of integer;
var
  births : arraytype;
```

Exercise 6.12

```
writeln('    1987  1988  1989  1990');
for month := 1 to 12 do
  begin
    write(month:2);
    for year := 1987 to 1990 do
        write(births[month, year]:6);
    writeln
  end
```

Exercise 6.13

The indexes are not in the correct order. The first index corresponds to the month and the second to the year. The error would not be reported until run-time. Since *year* would have one of the values 1987 – 1990 and a value in the range 1 – 12 inclusive is expected for the first index, an index value out-of-range error will occur.

Exercise 6.14

Using the full referencing method gives:

```
table[2].name := 'Edward Hodge';
table[2].address := '243 Lunsford Lane';
table[2].dob[1] := 13;
table[2].dob[2] := 4;
table[2].dob[3] := 1993;
```

Exploiting a **with** statement gives:

```
with table[2] do
  begin
    name := 'Edward Hodge';
    address := '243 Lunsford Lane';
    dob[1] := 13;
    dob[2] := 4;
    dob[3] := 1993
  end
```

Exercise 6.15

```
table[3] := person
```

Exercise 6.16

```
type
  dobtype = record
              day   : integer;
              month : integer;
              year  : integer
            end
  persontype = record
                 name    : string;
                 address : string;
                 dob     : dobtype
               end;
  tabletype = array[1..25] of persontype;
var
  table : tabletype;
  :
```

Using the full referencing method gives:

```
table[2].name := 'Edward Hodge';
table[2].address := '243 Lunsford Lane';
table[2].dob.day := 13;
table[2].dob.month := 4;
table[2].dob.year := 1993;
```

Exploiting a **with** statement gives:

```
with table[2] do
  begin
    name := 'Edward Hodge';
    address := '243 Lunsford Lane';
    dob.day := 13;
    dob.month := 4;
    dob.year := 1993
  end
```

Exercise 6.17

We present the solution as a complete program.

```
program enterdata;
type
  booktype = record
                author : string;
                title  : string;
                cost   : real;
                copies : integer
             end;

var
  tome : array[1..100] of booktype;
  i    : integer;
begin
  for i := 1 to 100 do
    with tome[i] do
      begin
        write('Enter the author ');
        readln(tome[i].author);
        write('Enter the title ');
        readln(tome[i].title);
        write('Enter the cost ');
        readln(tome[i].cost);
        write('Enter the number of copies ');
        readln(tome[i].copies)
      end
end.
```

Exercise 6.18

They are not name equivalent because they are of (different) anonymous type. Use of a type identifier would overcome the problem.

```
type
  arraytype = array[1..12, 1987..1990] of integer;
var
  strange, births : arraytype;
```

Exercise 6.19

The variables *rec1*, *rec3* and *rec4* are all of name equivalent type. The variable *rec2* has identical structure but is not name equivalent to the other variables.

Exercise 6.20
No – they would not be name equivalent.

Exercise 7.1
The case involving the subrange 6..8 is implemented as a single statement and is not followed by a semicolon.

```
program wordlength;
var
   word: string;
begin
   write('Enter a word ');
   readln(word);
   case length(word) of
      0    : writeln('A word has not been entered');
      1..5 : writeln('This is a short word');
      6..8 : writeln('This is a medium length word')
   else
      writeln('This is a long word')
   end
end.
```

Exercise 7.2
In this solution *response* is a *char* variable. Note that this implies that the numbered menu options are being interpreted as character values, not integers. The third case is a single construct and so is not implemented with a compound statement. It is followed by a semicolon.

```
readln(response);
case response of
   '1','A','a' : result := x + y;
   '2','S','s' : result := x - y;
   '3','D','d' : if y <> 0 then
                   result := x/y
                else
                   writeln('You cannot divide by zero');
   '4','M','m' : result := x*y
end
```

Exercise 7.3
The first case distinguishes the alphabetic characters. Since both upper and lower case have to be dealt with, the case label consists of two subranges separated by a comma.

```
case ch of
   'a'..'z','A'..'Z' : writeln('This is a letter');
   '0'..'9'          : writeln('This is a digit character')
else
   writeln('This is a punctuation character')
end
```

Exercise 7.4
The second and third cases both involve more than one construct and so have to be implemented with a compound statement. Since the third case is the last one its compound

statement is not followed by a semicolon. The default clause is a single construct and so is not implemented with a compound statement.

```
case number of
   0        : writeln('The units digit is zero');
   1..9     : writeln('The units digit is ', number);
   10..99   : begin
                writeln('The tens digit is ', number div 10);
                writeln('The units digit is ', number mod 10)
              end;
   100..999 : begin
                writeln('The hundreds digit is ', number div 100);
                writeln('The tens digit is ', (number mod 100) div 10);
                writeln('The units digit is ', (number mod 100) mod 10)
              end
else
   if number < 0 then
      writeln('Negative numbers not catered for')
   else
      writeln('Number is too large')
end
```

Exercise 7.5

number > 5 evaluates to false and *total* < 5 evaluates to true. Hence the first expression is evaluated as illustrated by the following sequence of values:

```
not (false)    or   (true)
     true       or   (true)
                     true
```

Note that in the first line here **not** has highest priority and so is evaluated first. The second expression evaluates as follows:

```
not  ((false) or (true)   )
not  (       true         )
      false
```

Here, the outermost bracket forces the evaluation of the inner expression to be done first so this time the overall expression evaluates to false.

Exercise 7.6

```
if (i = 1) xor (j = 2)
```

Exercise 7.7

In the event that both buttons are pressed simultaneously Player 1 is credited with a point rather than both players being given one. The following fragment overcomes this:

```
if button1 xor button2 then
   if button1 then
      player1total := player1total + 1
   else
      player2total := player2total + 1
else
   begin
      player1total := player1total + 1;
      player2total := player2total + 1
   end
```

Exercise 7.8

The declaration of the arrays *first*, *second* and *fifth* is syntactically correct. The index type of an array can be *char*. For *second* the index range and base types are the same type, but that is allowable. The index range of *fifth* is an enumeration type which is listed with the brackets which delimit the index range. This is syntactically valid, but it would be better to define the enumeration type using a type identifier. The declaration of *third* is in error because an index range must be ordinal and here two real values are used. The declaration of *fourth* is in error because the first index, *friday*, does not precede the second index, *wednesday*. The base type of this array is syntactically valid.

Exercise 7.9

```
for month := jan to dec do
  writeln('The 1st of ', monthstr[month], ' fell on a ', daystr[startday[month]]
```

Exercise 7.10

(a) *pred(mar)* is *feb* and *startday[feb]* is *saturday* and so the expression is valid and true.
(b) The left-hand side is of type *weekdays* and so cannot be compared with a string.
(c) *sunday* has no predecessor and so the expression is invalid.
(d) The base type of *startday* is *months* not *weekdays*.

Exercise 7.11

(a) Valid and true.
(b) Invalid because 'g' is not in the subrange 'a'..'f' and so is not in the set.
(c) Invalid – the **not** must be applied to an expression which evaluates to Boolean and **in** *dayset* is not a valid Boolean expression.
(d) Invalid – although the order of the operators is correct the Boolean expression 5 **in** *dayset* must be enclosed in brackets, otherwise the compiler interprets the 5 as a Boolean value and an error results.

Exercise 7.12

(a) ['a'..'z'].
(b) There are no common elements so the intersection is the empty set [].
(c) ['a','b'].

Exercise 7.13

(a) True.
(b) True – they are in fact identical, but the subset operator includes the possibility of equality.
(c) True – the value 'o' is not in the set to the right of the inequality.

Exercise 7.14

```
var
  response : char;

repeat
  write('Enter y/n ');
  readln(response)
until response in ['y', 'Y', 'n' ,'N']
```

Exercise 7.15

The field *number* is best defined to be 0..6 as these are the only values that should be assigned to that field. Similarly, *count* should be declared to be of type 0..6 for the same reason. The index range of *client* should use the subrange *indexrange* in its definition. Finally, *i* should be declared to be of type *indexrange* as these are the only valid index values.

```
const
  maxclients = 100;
type
  indexrange   = 1..maxclients;
  musicaltastes = (pop, funk, country, jazz, classical, folk);
  clientrecord = record
                   tastes : set of musicaltastes;
                   number : 0..6
                 end;
var
  client : array[indexrange] of clientrecord;
  taste  : musicaltastes;
  count  : 0..6;
  i      : indexrange;
begin
  for i := 1 to maxclients do
    begin
      count := 0;
      for taste := pop to folk do
        if taste in client[i].tastes then
          count := count + 1;
      client[i].number := count
    end
end.
```

Exercise 7.16

The types *first*, *second* and *third* are expression compatible because they are all subranges of the same host type, namely *integer*. The types *lower* and *upper* are expression compatible because they are subranges of the same host type, *char*. The types *weekdays*, *midweek* and *lateshop* are all expression compatible because the last two are subranges of *weekdays*. The types *lowset* and *bigset* are expression compatible because their base types are themselves expression compatible. The type *dayset* is not compatible with any of the other types.

Exercise 7.17

We have not listed all the obvious assignment compatibilities illustrated by:

- *lower* variable := *lower* value

upper and *lower* are expression compatible, but do not give rise to assignment compatibility. A variable of type *lower* cannot be assigned a value of type *upper*. Similarly, a variable of type *upper* cannot be assigned a value of type *lower*.

weekdays, *midweek* and *lateshop* are expression compatible. They give rise to the following:

- *weekdays* variable := *midweek* value
- *weekdays* variable := *lateshop* value
- *midweek* variable := *weekdays* value

- *midweek* variable := *lateshop* value
- *lateshop* variable := *weekdays* value
- *lateshop* variable := *midweek* value

lowset and *bigset* are expression compatible. However, there are no common values in their base types and so a variable of type *lowset* cannot be assigned a set whose values are from *bigset*. Similarly, a variable of type *bigset* cannot be assigned a set whose values are from *lowset*. Unfortunately, Turbo Pascal does not do any range checking on the values of set elements, and so it does not report an error if, for example, the value [20, 21] is assigned to a variable of type *lowset*.

Exercise 8.1

(a) **procedure** *example(second : integer;* **var** *first : integer)*;
(b) **procedure** *example(first : integer;* **var** *second : integer)*;
(c) **procedure** *example(***var** *first : integer)*;
(d) **procedure** *example(first : integer)*;
(e) **procedure** *example*;

The final example shows that some procedures do not have parameters. In this case, the brackets that would normally contain the parameter list are omitted.

Exercise 8.2

(a) **procedure** *example(int1 : integer;* **var** *str1 : string)*;
(b) **procedure** *example(int1 : integer;* **var** *str1 : string)*;
(c) **procedure** *example(***var** *int1 : integer;* **var** *str1 : string)*;
(d) **procedure** *example(int2 : integer;* **var** *int1 : integer;* **var** *str1, str2 : string)*;

Exercise 8.3

(a) Invalid. The variable *first* does not have a declared type. If the semicolon was replaced by a comma then the declaration would be valid. Both parameters would then correspond to source data.
(b) Valid. The parameter *first* corresponds to source data and *second* to results. We cannot tell whether *second* is also source data.
(c) Invalid. The structure, **array**[1..10] **of** *integer,* cannot appear in a declaration. To make a valid declaration, a type definition would be required that defines an identifier to represent this structure.
(d) Invalid. Again, *string*[10] is a structure and so needs to be represented by a type identifier. Note that *string* is a valid parameter type, but a string with specified static length is not.

Exercise 8.4
```
{Pre : month is an integer.
 Post: If months is in range 1 to 12 inclusive,
       days_in_month has value 28, 30 or 31 and valid is assigned true,
       otherwise valid is false and days_in_month is undefined.}
```

Exercise 8.5

(a) This is invalid. This is because the expression 4/3 does not evaluate to an integer and this parameter must be of *integer* type.

(b) Valid, provided *wantedmonth* has been initialized.

(c) This is actually syntactically valid if *days* is initialized before the call even though it is a semantic error. The actual parameters agree in number, order and type, and so the call will be executed. If *days* happened to have a value in the range 1 – 12 before the call, the effect would be to update its value to one of the integers 28, 30 or 31.

(d) Valid. Here, the expression for the first parameter is itself a procedure call with which we are already familiar. It returns the number of characters in the string literal, that is, 9. Therefore, *days* will be returned with value 30. By chance that is the number of days in September but the call

```
monthdays(length('February'), days, flag)
```

would return the value 31.

(e) This is valid, provided *month* is initialized before the call. Here, the same identifiers have been used for the formal and actual parameters. However, this can lead to the misunderstanding that they are the same variables, and this is not the case. As we shall see, the formal parameters only exist while the call is being executed and the values they receive or generate as results can only be communicated by the parameter passing method. Using identical identifiers can deceive you into thinking that formal parameters have an existence outside the procedure in which they are declared, and this is not so. Using different identifiers for formal and actual parameters avoids this potential error.

Exercise 8.6

```
writechars(5, '*');
writeln;
writechars(1, ' ');
writechars(3, 'A');
writeln;
writechars(2, ' ');
writechars(1, 'B');
writeln;
```

Exercise 8.7

In this fragment *instr* is a string variable.

```
write('Enter a string ');
readln(instr);
writechars(length(instr), '*');
```

Exercise 8.8

(a) *actual3* could potentially be updated as it is the actual variable corresponding to the **var** formal parameter.

(b) *actual1* could potentially be updated as it is the actual variable corresponding to the **var** formal parameter.

Exercise 8.9

```
program exercise;
const
  maxsize = 10;
```

```
type
  arraytype = array[1..maxsize] of string;
var
  strarray : arraytype;
  i         : 1..maxsize;
procedure reverse(var given : arraytype);
  {Pre : given is an initialized array.
   Post: given has its elements in reverse order.}
  var
    index : 1..maxsize;
    temp  : string;
  begin
    for index := 1 to (maxsize div 2) do
      begin
        temp := given[index];
        given[index] := given[maxsize - index + 1];
        given[maxsize - index + 1] := temp
      end
  end; {procedure reverse}
begin   {main program}
  for i := 1 to maxsize do
    begin
      write('Enter data for element ', i, ' ');
      readln(strarray[i])
    end;
  reverse(strarray);
  for i := 1 to maxsize do
    writeln('Data for element ', i, ' is now ', strarray[i])
end.
```

Exercise 8.10

(a) Valid.
(b) This is syntactically valid, but it is poor practice for a function to have a **var** parameter and should not be done.
(c) Invalid. The structure, **array**[1..10] **of** *integer,* cannot appear in a declaration. To make this declaration a type definition would be required which defined an identifier to represent this structure.
(d) Invalid. The result type of a function cannot be *string*. (Another error is that *string*[10] is a structure and so cannot appear as a type in a parameter list.)

Exercise 8.11

```
function validrange(number, lowlimit, highlimit : integer) : Boolean;
  {Pre : number, lowlimit, highlimit are all integer values and lowlimit <= highlimit.
   Post: Return true if lowlimit <= number <= highlimit, false otherwise.}
  begin
    validrange := (lowlimit <=number) and (number <= highlimit)
  end;
```

Exercise 8.12

(a) Valid. Actual parameters supplied to functions can be expressions provided they evaluate to a value of the correct type.

(b) This is syntactically valid but semantically invalid. Calls to *validrange* must ensure that the actual parameters corresponding to *lowlimit* and *highlimit* satisfy the inequality *lowlimit <= highlimit*. Here, that constraint is violated. The code would execute as an infinite loop. Pascal does not check that pre- and postconditions are satisfied.

(c) Not valid. The error here is that an attempt has been made to call the function as if it was a procedure. Function calls result in the value being used immediately. Part (d) illustrates one way of storing a function value for late use.

(d) Valid – the function value is assigned to *input*.

Exercise 8.13

All that needs to be done is to suppress the writing out of the tens digit in the event that it is zero. The code below gives the details.

```
begin {procedure getnumber}
  tens := getdigit;
  if tens <> 0 then
    write(tens);
  units := getdigit;
  write(units);
  x := 10*tens + units
end;  {procedure getdata}
```

Exercise 8.14

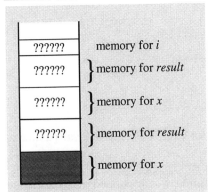

State just prior to call

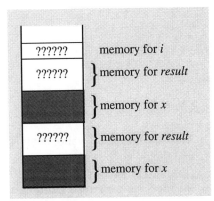

State just after call

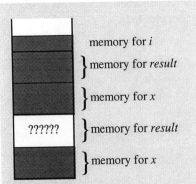

State just prior to conclusion of call

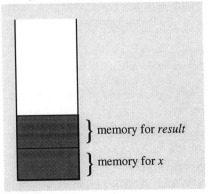

State after call complete

Exercise 8.15

procedure *one*

The identifiers local to the procedure are the formal parameters together with the identifiers contained in its declarations part. Hence the local identifiers are: *formal1*, *formal2*, *actual1*, *two*.

The non-local identifiers are: *constant*, *small*, *x*, *one*.

function *two*

The identifiers local to the function are: *value* and *x* (the integer variable). So here, the variable *x* is redeclared locally as an *integer* variable and serves a different purpose from that of the *real* variable *x*.

The non-local identifiers are: *constant*, *small*, *one*, *formal1*, *formal2*, *actual1* and *two*.

function *three*

There are no local identifiers.

The non-local identifiers are: *constant*, *small*, *x* (the real variable) and *one*. Notice that function *two* cannot be called by function *three*, it is hidden from it.

The main program

The global identifiers are: *constant*, *small*, *x*, *two* and *three*.

Exercise 8.16

This is because *netpay* is a global variable and it is in the scope of the procedure *taxcalc*.

Exercise 8.17

procedure *getnumber*

The identifiers local to the procedure are the formal parameters together with the identifiers contained in its declarations part. Hence the local identifiers are: *x*, *tens*, *units*, *getdigit*.

The non-local identifiers are: *range*, *digit*, *guess*, *target* and *getnumber*.

function *getdigit*

The identifier local to the function is: *ch*.

The non-local identifiers are: *range*, *digit*, *guess*, *target*, *getnumber*, *x*, *tens*, *units* and *getdigit*.

The main program

The global identifiers are: *range*, *digit*, *guess*, *target* and *getnumber*.

Exercise 8.18

function *getdigit*

The identifier local to the function is: *ch*.

The non-local identifiers are: *range*, *digit*, *target*, *tensguess*, *unitsguess* and *getdigit*.

procedure *getnumber*

The identifiers local to the procedure are the formal parameters together with the identifiers contained in its declarations part. Hence the local identifiers are: *x*, *tens* and *units*.

The non-local identifiers are: *range*, *digit*, *target*, *tensguess*, *unitsguess*, *getdigit* and *getnumber*.

The main program

The global identifiers are:

   range, *digit*, *target*, *tensguess*, *unitsguess*, *getdigit* and *getnumber*.

Exercise 9.1

Any reference to *clreol* would be taken as a reference to the array variable rather than the procedure because this definition is in the smallest enclosing block. (The definition of the function *clreol* is in the outermost block.) Hence the program will function in the same way as it did when *names* was the identifier for the array.

Exercise 9.2

Any reference to *delay* would be taken as a reference to the constant value 10 rather than the function because the definition of the function is in an outer enclosing block. Hence the program would function as before.

Exercise 9.3

```
program storereal;
var
  realfile : text;
  realdata : real;
  i        : integer;
begin
  assign(realfile, 'MYFILE');
  rewrite(realfile);
  for i := 1 to 10 do
    writeln(realfile, i + 0.5);
  close(realfile)
end.
```

Exercise 9.4

```
program getreal;
var
  realfile : text;
  realdata : real;
begin
  assign(realfile, 'MYFILE');
  reset(realfile);
  while not eof(realfile) do
    begin
      readln(realfile, realdata);
      writeln(realdata:4:2)
    end;
  close(realfile)
end.
```

Exercise 9.5

This is because the procedure *loadall* makes a call to the procedure *readkey* which is stored in the unit *crt*. The **uses** statement is in the implementation part and not the interface because this is a local use of *readkey* and is not to be communicated as a global identifier outside this unit.

Exercise 9.6

Because the procedures *enter* and *report* both reference *getret*.

Exercise 10.1
That error could not arise because field identifiers only have to differ within the record in which they are defined. To reference a field the record identifier is needed as a qualifier as, for example, in the identifier *table.town*.

Exercise 10.2
The code below is the implementation part of **unit** *uTable1*.

```
implementation
uses crt;   {Imports clrscr}
  function isfull;
    {(table : tabletype) : Boolean
     Pre : table.size is initialized.
     Post: isfull is true if table.size = maxsize, false otherwise.}
    begin
      isfull := (table.size = maxsize)
    end;
  procedure insert;
    {(var table : tabletype)
     Pre : table.size is initialized and is less than maxsize.
     Post: table.size is incremented to location for new entry.
           New entry inserted at index size.}
    begin
      with table do
        begin
          size := size + 1;
          write('Enter town ');
          readln(town[size]);
          write('Enter number of churches ');
          readln(church[size])
        end
    end;
  procedure churchnumber;
    {(table : tabletype; searchtown : string)
     Pre : table.size is initialized.
     Post: None. Message written out dependent on success of search.}
    var
      index : 0..maxsize;
    begin
      table.town[0] := searchtown;
      index := table.size;
      with table do
        begin
          while town[index] <> searchtown do
            index := index - 1;
          if index <> 0 then
            writeln(searchtown, ' has ', church[index], ' churches')
          else
            writeln(searchtown, ' is not in table')
        end
    end;
  procedure display;
    {(table : tabletype)
     Pre : table.size is initialized.
```

```
      Post: None. The whole table is written out under a heading.}
    var
      index : 0..maxsize;
    begin
      clrscr;
      write('Town':6, 'Churches':8);
      writeln;
      with table do
        for index := 1 to size do
          writeln(town[index]:6, church[index]:6);
    end;
  procedure create;
    {(var table : tabletype)
     Pre : None.
     Post: table.size is initialized to zero.}
    begin
      table.size := 0
    end;
end.
```

Exercise 10.3

The code below is the implementation part of **unit** *uTable2*.

```
implementation
uses crt;   {Imports clrscr}
  function isfull;
    {(table : tabletype) : Boolean)
     Pre : table.size is initialized.
     Post: isfull is true if table.size = maxsize, false otherwise.}
    begin
      isfull := (table.size = maxsize)
    end;
  procedure insert;
    {(var table : tabletype)
     Pre : table.size is initialized and is less than maxsize.
     Post: table.size is incremented to location for new entry.
           New entry inserted at index size.}
    begin
      with table do
        begin
          size := size + 1;
          write('Enter town ');
          readln(entry[size].town);
          write('Enter number of churches ');
          readln(entry[size].church)
        end
    end;
  procedure churchnumber;
    {(table : tabletype; searchtown : string)
     Pre : table.size is initialized.
     Post: None. Message written out dependent on success of search.}
    var
      index : 0..maxsize;
```

```
  begin
    table.entry[0].town := searchtown;
    index := table.size;
    with table do
      begin
        while entry[index].town <> searchtown do
          index := index - 1;
        if index <> 0 then
          writeln(searchtown, ' has ', entry[index].church, ' churches')
        else
          writeln(searchtown, ' is not in table')
      end
  end;
procedure display;
  {(table : tabletype)
   Pre : table.size is initialized.
   Post: None. The whole table is written out under a heading.}
  var
    index : 0..maxsize;
  begin
    clrscr;
    write('Town':6, 'Churches':8);
    writeln;
    with table do
      for index := 1 to size do
        writeln(entry[index].town:6, entry[index].church:6);
  end;
procedure create;
  {(var table : tabletype)
   Pre : None.
   Post: table.size is initialized to zero.}
  begin
    table.size := 0
  end;
end.
```

Exercise 10.4

We only give details for the routines and not the **implementation** part as a whole.

```
function isfull;
  {Pre : table.size is initialized.
   Post: isfull is true if table.size = i, false otherwise.}
  begin
    isfull := (table.size = maxsize)
  end;
procedure insert;
  {Pre : table.size is initialized and is less than maxsize.
   Post: table.size is incremented to location for new entry.
         New entry inserted at index size.}
  begin
    with table do
      begin
        size := size + 1;
        write('Enter town ');
        readln(entry[size].town);
```

```pascal
          write('Enter number of churches ');
          readln(entry[size].church)
        end
    end;
procedure churchnumber;
   {(searchtown : string)
    Pre : table.size is initialized.
    Post: None. Message written out dependent on success of search.}
    var
      index : 0..maxsize;
    begin
      table.entry[0].town := searchtown;
      index := table.size;
      with table do
        begin
          while entry[index].town <> searchtown do
            index := index - 1;
          if index <> 0 then
            writeln(searchtown, ' has ', entry[index].church, ' churches')
          else
            writeln(searchtown, ' is not in table')
        end
    end;
procedure display;
   {Pre : table.size is initialized.
    Post: None. The whole table is written out under a heading.}
    var
      index : 0..maxsize;
    begin
      clrscr;
      write('Town':6, 'Churches':8);
      writeln;
      with table do
        for index := 1 to size do
          writeln(entry[index].town:6, entry[index].church:6);
    end;
procedure create;
   {Pre : None.
    Post: table.size is initialized to zero.}
    begin
      table.size := 0
    end;
```

Exercise 10.5

```pascal
program application;
uses uTable1;

   {Imports
    type
      tabletype (details are private)
    function isfull(table : tabletype) : Boolean
    procedure insert(var table : tabletype)
    procedure churchnumber(table : tabletype; searchtown : string)
    procedure display(table : tabletype)
    procedure create(var table : tabletype)}
```

```
var
  first_table, second_table : tabletype;
  town                      : town_name;
begin
  create(first_table);
  create(second_table)
```

Exercise 10.6

```
unit uADTmon;
interface
  {Public part - this interface has no private part}
  type
    monthrange = 1..12;
    monthtype  = (jan, feb, mar, apr, may, jun, jul, aug, sep, oct, nov, dec);
    procedure writemonth(month : monthtype);
    function convertmonth(MonthNumber : monthrange) : monthtype;
implementation
  type
    montharray = array[monthtype] of string; {MonthName is global to implementation}
  var
    MonthName : montharray;
  procedure initialize(var MonthName : montharray); {This is a private procedure}
    {Pre : None.
     Post: Initializes the implementation variable MonthName.}
    begin
      MonthName[jan] := 'January';
      MonthName[feb] := 'February';
      MonthName[mar] := 'March';
      MonthName[apr] := 'April';
      MonthName[may] := 'May';
      MonthName[jun] := 'June';
      MonthName[jul] := 'July';
      MonthName[aug] := 'August';
      MonthName[sep] := 'September';
      MonthName[oct] := 'October';
      MonthName[nov] := 'November';
      MonthName[dec] := 'December'
    end;
  procedure writemonth;
    {Pre : Implementation variable MonthName is initialized. This is accessed as a
           global variable by this procedure.
           month is initialized.
     Post: None - a string is output corresponding to MonthName.}
    begin
      write(MonthName[month])
    end;
  function convertmonth;
    {Pre : MonthNumber has a value in the range 1..12 inclusive.
     Post: Returns enumeration type value corresponding to MonthNumber.}
    var
      month : monthtype;
      i     : integer;
    begin
      month := jan;
```

```
        for i := 1 to (MonthNumber - 1) do
          month := succ(month);
        convertmonth := month
      end;
begin  {initialization section}
  initialize(MonthName)
end.   {of unit}
```

The first thing to notice about this solution is that the implementation part declares an array of base type *string* which is used to hold the names of the months. This variable is therefore private. The code of the procedure which initializes the array is straightforward. The implementation of *writemonth*, although simple, is more subtle. It needs to access *MonthName* and so there ought to be a parameter corresponding to this source data. But *writemonth* is a public procedure, and so it cannot be allowed to have a parameter which is private. The array is accessed by virtue of it being global within the interface part. The final implementation is a straightforward coding of the function *convertmonth*.

One final point of explanation remains. The procedure *writemonth* has as a precondition the fact that *MonthName* must be initialized prior to being called. Although the implementation part provides a routine for this, it must be explicitly invoked to carry out the initialization. This is where the **initialization section** fits in. The word **begin**, just before the final **end** of the unit, is optional and has not been used in the examples so far. Its inclusion results in a compound statement that makes the implementation part as a whole look like a complete program. It is in this initialization section that data structures which the unit uses in its own code can be initialized.

Exercise 11.1

In the comment in the **uses** statement below we have anticipated the implementation of the operations as far as determining their parameters. This was done by referring to the specifications of the operations.

```
program StrReverse;
uses uchStack;
  {Imports from uchStack
   type
     charstack (details are private)
   procedure push(var stack : charstack; item : char)
   procedure pop(var stack : charstack; var item : char)
   function isempty(stack : charstack) : Boolean
   procedure create(var stack  : charstack)}
var
  stack : charstack;
  i     : integer;
  ch    : char;
  input : string;
begin
  create(stack);
  writeln('Enter the string to be reversed');
  readln(input);
  for i := 1 to length(input) do
    push(stack, input[i]);
  if isempty(stack) then
    writeln('The input string was null')
```

```
else
  while not isempty(stack) do
    begin
      pop(stack, ch);
      write(ch)
    end
end.
```

Exercise 11.2

```
unit uchStack;

interface
  {PRIVATE part}
  const
    maxsize = 255;
  type
    charstack = record
                  stackarray : array[1..maxsize] of char;
                  stacktop   : 0..maxsize;
                end;
  {PUBLIC part: the identifier charstack from above (but not its structure)}
  procedure push(var stack : charstack; item : char);
  function isempty(stack : charstack) : Boolean;
  procedure pop(var stack : charstack; var item : char);
  procedure create(var stack : charstack);
```

Exercise 11.3

The implementation part is as follows:

```
implementation

  procedure push;
    {(var stack : charstack; item : char)
    Pre : stack.stacktop is initialized and is less than or equal to maxsize
          item is a char value.
    Post: If stack is full an error message is written out
          otherwise stack is returned with item pushed on it.}
    begin
      with stack do
        if stacktop = maxsize then
          writeln('stack overflow')
        else
          begin
            stacktop := stacktop + 1;
            stackarray[stacktop] := item
          end
    end;

  function isempty;
    {(stack : charstack) : Boolean
    Pre : stack.stacktop is initialized and is less than or equal to maxsize.
    Post: isempty is true if stack.stacktop = 0, false otherwise.}
    begin
      isempty := (stack.stacktop = 0)
    end;
```

```
procedure pop;
  {(var stack : charstack; var item : char)
   Pre : stack.stacktop is initialized and is less than or equal to maxsize.
   Post: If stack is not empty it is returned with top item removed, the latter value
         being placed in item; otherwise an error message is written out.}
  begin
    with stack do
      if isempty(stack) then
        writeln('Underflow')
      else
        begin
          item := stackarray[stacktop];
          stacktop := stacktop - 1
        end
  end;
 procedure create;
  {(var stack : charstack)
   Pre : None.
   Post: A new empty stack is created.}
  begin
    stack.stacktop := 0
  end;
end.
```

Exercise 11.4
Here questions (a) and (c) are saying the same thing: that the insertion has to work correctly on an empty sequence. This may sound obvious but, as we shall see, insertion of the first element in a sequence can be troublesome. Question (b) reminds us to test that the overflow condition is correctly implemented. Since insertions take place at the top of the stack, question (d) might be thought of as redundant. However, it could be interpreted as inserting an element which will make the stack full. So we would need to test that insertion of an element which fills up the stack works correctly.

Exercise 11.5
(a) Are there problems deleting from an *empty* sequence?
(b) Are there problems deleting from a *full* sequence?
(c) Are there problems deleting the *first* element of the sequence?
(d) Are there problems deleting the *last* element of the sequence?

Question (a) reminds us to check that stack underflow is implemented as specified. If deletion works for 'ordinary' data then it ought to work for the question described in (b). Question (c) describes the way *pop* is supposed to work. Since deletions cannot take place at the bottom of a stack we can interpret question (d) as a reminder that when the last remaining element on the stack has been deleted we should get an empty stack.

Exercise 11.6
The short answer is no. Once the *itemtype* is defined, the name *genstack* represents a type corresponding to a stack of this type. So if *itemtype* was specified as *integer*, a program that used *uGenStk0* could declare as many integer stacks as memory would permit. But the character stacks would remain a problem. To overcome this, a second copy of the unit

would have to be created. This second copy would require a different unit identifier and the identifier *genstack* would have to be replaced by some other type identifier throughout. The applications program would then have to declare its use of both units.

Exercise 11.7

```
program arithstack;

uses uGenStk0;
  {Imports from uGenStk0
   type
     itemtype = integer
     genstack  {structure is private}
   procedure push(var stack : genstack; item : itemtype)
   procedure pop(var stack : genstack; var item : itemtype)
   function isempty(stack : genstack) : Boolean
   procedure create(var stack  : genstack)}
  var
    calculator                        : genstack;
    polish                            : string;
    index, FirstOff, SecondOff, result : integer;
begin
  create(calculator );
  write('Enter Polish string ');
  readln(polish );
  for index := 1 to length(polish ) do
    case polish [index] of
      '+' : begin
              pop(calculator, FirstOff);
              pop(calculator, SecondOff);
              result := FirstOff + SecondOff;
              push(calculator, result)
            end;
      '-' : begin
              pop(calculator, FirstOff);
              pop(calculator, SecondOff);
              result := SecondOff - FirstOff;
              push(calculator, result)
            end;

      '*' : begin
              pop(calculator, FirstOff);
              pop(calculator, SecondOff);
              result := SecondOff * FirstOff;
              push(calculator, result)
            end;
      '0' : push(calculator, 0);
      '1' : push(calculator, 1);
      '2' : push(calculator, 2);
      '3' : push(calculator, 3);
      '4' : push(calculator, 4);
      '5' : push(calculator, 5);
      '6' : push(calculator, 6);
      '7' : push(calculator, 7);
      '8' : push(calculator, 8);
```

```
        '9' : push(calculator, 9)
    end;
  pop(calculator, result);
  writeln(result)
end.
```

Exercise 11.8

```
type
  IntPtrType = ^integer;
  rectype    = record
                   stringfield  : string;
                   Booleanfield : Boolean;
                   integerfield : integer
               end;
  RecPtrType = ^rectype;
var
  IntegerPtr : IntPtrType;
  RecPtr     : RecPtrType;
```

Exercise 11.9

Line 1: *p* – statement B applies, namely *p* is initialized and points to an uninitialized value.

      q, r – statement A applies to both.

Line 2: *p* – statement B applies.

      q – statement D applies. *q* does not point to an actual address in memory so does not point to a value, initialized or otherwise.

      r – statement A applies.

Line 3: Statement E applies because *q*^ refers to the variable pointed to by *q* but *q* does not point anywhere (its value is *nil*) so the variable *q*^ does not exist.

Line 4: Statement E applies because *r* has not been initialized (to an address value using *new*) and so attempting to reference *r*^ is an error – it does not exist.

Line 5: Ignoring lines 3 and 4 (and assuming line 2 has just executed):

      p – statement C applies, namely *p* is initialized and points to an initialized value.

      q – statement D applies.

      r – statement A applies.

Line 6: *q* – statement D applies. Note the assignment means that the data to which *p* pointed to in line 5 are now lost.

      q – statement D applies.

      r – statement A applies.

Exercise 11.10

```
First output a
Second output aa
Third output b
Fourth output c
Fifth output cc
```

Exercise 11.11

The difficulty is getting the identifier references correct. Remember *RecordPointer*^ points to the whole of the first record so its fields are accessed by appending a dot then the required field identifier. So the link field of this first record has identifier *RecordPointer^.linkfield* – no circumflex or dot follows this. This being a pointer appending a circumflex will yield the identifier of the record to which it points. So *RecordPointer^.linkfield^* points to the whole of the second record. It is this record whose fields we want to access. Therefore, just append a dot followed by the required field identifier. Simple, isn't it!

```
RecordPointer^.linkfield^.name := 'Jean';
RecordPointer^.linkfield^.married := false;
RecordPointer^.linkfield^.age := 23;
RecordPointer^.linkfield^.linkfield := nil
```

Exercise 11.12

```
new(RecordPointer^.linkfield^.linkfield);
RecordPointer^.linkfield^.linkfield^.name := 'James';
RecordPointer^.linkfield^.linkfield^.married := false;
RecordPointer^.linkfield^.linkfield^.age := 45;
```

Exercise 11.13

A new empty stack is a pointer whose value is *nil*. Thus, *create* has to initialize a variable in this way and *isempty* has to test for the value *nil*.

```
procedure create;
  {(var stack : genstack)
  Pre : None.
  Post: A new empty stack is created, that is, stack has value nil.}
  begin
    stack := nil
  end;
function isempty;
  {(stack : genstack) : Boolean
  Pre : stack is initialized.
  Post: isempty is true if stack = nil, false otherwise.}
  begin
    isempty := (stack = nil)
  end;
```

Exercise 11.14

The difficulty here is to call *dispose* at the correct time. The value of *stack* has to be updated as in the code above, yet its current value has to be used as the parameter in the call to *dispose*. This implies that a temporary variable is required to hold the current value of *stack* so that *stack* can be updated. The temporary variable is then used in the call to *dispose*:

```
procedure pop;
  {(var stack : genstack; var item : itemtype)
  Pre : stack is initialized.
  Post: If stack is not empty it is returned with top item removed, the latter value
        being placed in item; otherwise an error message is written out. Space released
        by popping an item is returned to the heap.}
  var
    deletedItem : genstack;
  begin
    if isempty(stack) then
```

```
      writeln('Underflow')
    else
      begin
        item := stack^.stackitem;
        deletedItem := stack;
        stack := stack^.link;
        dispose(deletedItem)
      end
  end;
```

Exercise 11.15

Questions (b) and (e) can be disregarded because we are assuming the memory is sufficiently large to accommodate all stack sizes. Questions (a) and (c) are equivalent for this stack.

Exercise 11.16

Most of the code is much the same as it was before. However, a major change is the implementation of the procedure to write the stack to the screen. It must traverse the linked list, writing out data values as it goes, until the end is reached which is signified by the value *nil* in the link field.

```
program TestuGenStk0;
uses uGenStk0, crt;
  {Imports
   type
     genstack = ^stackrecord
     stackrecord = record
                      stackitem : itemtype
                      link      : genstack
                   end
   procedure push(var stack : genstack; item : itemtype)
   procedure pop(var stack : genstack; var item : itemtype)
   function isempty(stack : genstack) : Boolean
   procedure create(var stack : genstack)}
var
  mystack : genstack;
  choice  : char;
  data    : itemtype;
  procedure display(stack : genstack);
  {Pre : stack.stacktop is initialized and is less than or equal to maxsize.
   Post: None - the stack is written to the screen with the top of the stack uppermost.}
  var
    current : genstack;
  begin
    writeln('Top of stack');
    current := stack;
    while current <> nil do
      begin
        writeln(current^.stackitem);
        current := current^.link
      end;
    writeln('Bottom of stack')
  end;
```

```pascal
  procedure getret;
  {Pre : None.
   Post: None - processing awaits press of <ret>.}
    var
      ch : char;
    begin
      writeln;
      write('Press <ret> to get to main menu ');
      repeat
        ch := readkey
      until (ord(ch) = 13)
    end;
begin
  clrscr;
  create(mystack);
  repeat
    clrscr;
    writeln('1 : Push data on to stack');
    writeln('2 : Pop data from stack');
    writeln('3 : Test for empty stack');
    writeln('4 : Display the stack');
    writeln('5 : Quit');
    writeln;
    write('Enter your choice ');
    repeat
      choice := readkey
    until choice in ['1'..'5'];
    writeln(choice);
    case choice of
      '1' : begin
              write('Enter item to be pushed on to stack ');
              readln(data);
              push(mystack, data);
              getret
            end;
      '2' : begin
              if isempty(mystack) then
                begin
                  writeln('Attempting to pop an empty stack');
                  pop(mystack,data)
                end
              else
                begin
                  pop(mystack,data);
                  writeln('Popped item was ', data)
                end;
              getret
            end;
      '3' : begin
              if isempty(mystack) then
                writeln('Stack is empty')
              else
                writeln('Stack is not empty');
              getret
            end;
```

```
        '4' : begin
                 display(mystack);
                 getret
               end
      end
   until (choice = '5')
end.
```

Exercise 11.17

```
unit uGenStk5;

interface
  {PRIVATE part}
  type
    itemtype = {Insert declaration of items to be stacked here}
    genstack = ^stackrecord;
    stackrecord = record
                    stackitem : itemtype;
                    link      : genstack;
                  end;

  {PUBLIC part: the identifiers genstack and itemtype from above}
  procedure create(var stack  : genstack);
  function isempty(stack : genstack) : Boolean;
  procedure push(var stack : genstack; item : itemtype);
  procedure pop(var stack : genstack; var item : itemtype);

implementation
  procedure create;
    {(var stack  : genstack)
     Pre : None.
     Post: A new empty stack is created, that is, stack has value nil.}
    begin
      stack := nil
    end;

  function isempty;
    {(stack : genstack) : Boolean
     Pre : stack is initialized.
     Post: isempty is true if stack = nil, false otherwise.}
    begin
      isempty := (stack = nil)
    end;

  procedure push;
    {(var stack : genstack; item : itemtype)
     Pre : stack is initialized.
           item is an itemtype value.
     Post: stack is returned with item pushed on it.}
    var
      temppointer : genstack;
    begin
      new(temppointer);
      temppointer^.stackitem := item;
      temppointer^.link := stack;
      stack := temppointer
    end;
```

```
procedure pop;
  {(var stack : genstack; var item : itemtype)
   Pre : stack is initialized.
   Post: If stack is not empty it is returned with top item removed, the latter value
         being placed in item; otherwise an error message is written out. Space
         released by popping an item is returned to the heap.}
  var
    deletedItem : genstack;
  begin
    if isempty(stack) then
      writeln('Underflow')
    else
      begin
        item := stack^.stackitem;
        deletedItem := stack;
        stack := stack^.link;
        dispose(deletedItem)
      end
  end
end.
```

Exercise 12.1

To enhance the information hiding of the code, the pointers to the front and rear of the queue are encapsulated in a record.

```
unit uqueue;

interface
  {Private part}
  type
    PtrToQueueRec = ^QueueRecord;
    stringqueue  = record
                       head : PtrToQueueRec;
                       tail : PtrToQueueRec;
                     end;
    QueueRecord  = record
                       queueitem : string;
                       link : PtrToQueueRec;
                     end;
  {Public part}
  {The identifier stringqueue from above but not its type}
  procedure create(var queue : stringqueue);
  function  isempty(queue : stringqueue) : Boolean;
  procedure front(queue : stringqueue; var item : string);
  procedure insert(var queue : stringqueue; item : string);
  procedure remove(var queue : stringqueue);
```

Exercise 12.2

The description of what is required for *remove* given in the text is fine for all but the removal of the last item in the queue. When the last item is removed *head* has to be updated as described in the text. This update has the effect of putting *nil* into the link field of the dummy record. However, in this situation *tail* still points to the last element in the queue (that is, the one we are trying to remove) and needs to be made to point to the dummy item, thereby indicating that the queue is now empty.

```
implementation
  procedure create;
    {(var queue : stringqueue)
     Pre : None.
     Post: A new empty queue is created, that is, head and tail both point to a dummy
           item whose link field is set to nil.}
    begin
      new(queue.head);
      queue.tail := queue.head;
      queue.head^.link := nil
    end;

  function isempty;
    {(queue : stringqueue) : Boolean
     Pre : queue is initialized.
     Post: isempty is true if head = tail (= nil), false otherwise.}
    begin
      isempty := (queue.head = queue.tail)
    end;

  procedure front;
    {(queue : stringqueue; var item : string)
     Pre : queue is initialized and non-empty.
     Post: queue is returned with first item removed, the latter value being placed
           in item.}
    begin
      item := queue.head^.link^.queueitem;
    end;

  procedure insert;
    {(var queue : stringqueue; item : string)
     Pre : queue is initialized.
           item is an string value.
     Post: queue is returned with item at the end of the queue.}
    var
      temp : PtrToQueueRec;
    begin
      with queue do
        begin
          new(temp);
          temp^.queueitem := item;
          temp^.link := nil;
          tail^.link := temp;
          tail := temp;
        end
    end;

  procedure remove;
    {(var queue : stringqueue)
     Pre : queue is initialized and non-empty.
     Post: queue is returned with the item at the front of the queue removed, the
           latter value being placed in item.}
    begin
      with queue do
        begin
          head^.link := head^.link^.link;
          if (head^.link = nil) then
```

```
              tail := head
          end
        end;
  end.
```

Exercise 12.3

```
procedure displayqueue(queue : stringqueue);
  {Pre : queue is an initialized variable.
  {Post: None - the contents of the queue are written to the screen.}
  var
    current : PtrToQueueRec;
  begin
    current := queue.head^.link;
    writeln('Head of queue');
    while current <> nil do
      begin
        writeln(current^.queueitem);
        current := current^.link
      end;
    writeln('Tail of queue')
  end;
```

Exercise 12.4

```
procedure remove;
  {(var queue : stringqueue)
   Pre : queue is initialized and non-empty.
   Post: queue is returned with the item at the front of the queue removed, the
         latter value being placed in item. Space is returned to the heap when
         item is removed.}
  var
    deletedItem : PtrToQueueRec;
  begin
      with queue do
        begin
          deletedItem := head^.link;
          head^.link := head^.link^.link;
          if (head^.link = nil) then
            tail := head;
          dispose(deletedItem)
        end;
  end;
```

Exercise 13.1

From the data in the figure it is clear that neither the airport of departure nor the estimated time of arrival can be key fields because they contain repeat data. The time and flight number are potential candidates for a key field. In a real system the arrival would not be a key because flights will be timetabled to arrive at the same time even though this is a physical impossibility. Flight numbers are also not a key because on regular daily services a specific flight will have the same number from one day to the next. A key would therefore have to consist of a date together with flight number. We shall ignore this complication and suppose that both the arrival time and flight numbers are unique and so are potential key fields.

Exercise 13.2

No. Although the flight number uniquely identifies each record it is not used as the basis for determining the ordering of the sequence and so the field cannot be described as a key field. This illustrates that a non-key field may contain data items which uniquely identify each record. However, non-key fields do not usually have this property.

Exercise 13.3

Since the link field of the 12.03 record will have to be updated to point to the new record, the search routine should identify the 12.03 record. Note that this record is immediately before the insertion point.

Exercise 13.4

At the end of the execution of the first design *lag* has value #40 instead of #60 as it should have. The reason for this is that the condition *lead^.link <> nil*, which is there to avoid going beyond the end of the sequence, becomes false, and so the loop is not executed and *lag* is not updated.

The error arises in the second design because an attempt is made to reference *lead^.time*, when *lead* has value *nil*. This would lead to a run-time error.

Exercise 13.5

```
timesearch(arrivals, 12.05, location);    {location now has value #40)
new(temp);                                {value #100 in Figure 13.5}
temp^.time := 12.05;
temp^.flight := 'VA057';
temp^.from := 'Dallas';
temp^.eta := 'Landed';
temp^.link := location^.link;             {assign #60 to link of temp}
location^.link := temp;                   {updates #40 link field to #100}
```

Exercise 13.6

```
lag^.link := lead^.link
```

Exercise 13.7

```
unit uSeq;

interface
  {Private part}
  type
    ArrivalsSeq = ^SeqRec;
    SeqRec      = record
                    time   : real;
                    flight : string;
                    from   : string;
                    eta    : string;
                    link   : ArrivalsSeq
                  end;
  {Public part}
  {The identifier ArrivalsSeq from above but not its structure}
  procedure create(var arrivals : ArrivalsSeq);
  procedure insert(var arrivals : ArrivalsSeq; newtime : real;
                   newflight, newfrom, neweta : string);
```

```
procedure delete(var arrivals : ArrivalsSeq; flightgiven : string);
procedure update(var arrivals : ArrivalsSeq; flightgiven : string);
procedure display(arrivals : ArrivalsSeq);
implementation
  uses crt;
  procedure flightsearch(arrivals : ArrivalsSeq; flightgiven : string;
                            var lead, lag : ArrivalsSeq);
    {Pre : arrivals is an initialized sequence, possibly empty.
         flightgiven is an initialized string.
    {Post: If flightgiven is in the sequence then lead points to the record containing
         it and lag points to the record preceding it.
         Otherwise lead is assigned the value arrivals.}
  begin
    arrivals^.flight := flightgiven;
    lag := arrivals;
    lead := arrivals^.link;
    while lead^.flight <> flightgiven do
      begin
        lag := lead;
        lead := lead^.link
      end
  end;   {end of procedure flightsearch}

{Implementation of the operations}

  procedure create; {var arrivals : ArrivalsSeq}
    {Pre : None.
    {Post: A new empty sequence arrivals is created. It points to a dummy first record
         whose link field points to itself.}
  begin
    new(arrivals);
    arrivals^.link := arrivals;
  end;

  procedure insert;   {var arrivals : ArrivalsSeq; newtime : real;
                            newflight, newfrom, neweta : string}
    {Pre : arrivals is an initialized sequence, possibly empty.
         newtime is an initialized real value.
         newflight, newfrom, neweta are all initialized string values.
    {Post: arrivals is returned with the new data entered into the sequence.}
  var
    temp, location : ArrivalsSeq;

    procedure timesearch(arrivals: ArrivalsSeq; timegiven : real;
                            var location : ArrivalsSeq);
      {Pre : arrivals is an initialized sequence, possibly empty.
           timegiven is an initialized real value.
        Post: location points to the record whose time field is the last one which has a
             value less than timegiven. All subsequent records have a time field which
             is greater than timegiven.}
    var
      lead, lag : ArrivalsSeq;
    begin
      arrivals^.time := timegiven;
      lag := arrivals;
      lead := arrivals^.link;
      while lead^.time < timegiven do
```

```
        begin
          lag := lead;
          lead := lead^.link
        end;
      location := lag
    end; {procedure timesearch}
  begin {procedure insert}
    timesearch(arrivals, newtime, location);
    new(temp);
    temp^.time := newtime;
    temp^.flight := newflight;
    temp^.from := newfrom;
    temp^.eta := neweta;
    temp^.link := location^.link;
    location^.link := temp
  end; {end procedure insert}

procedure delete; {var arrivals : ArrivalsSeq; flightgiven : string}
  {Pre : arrivals is an initialized sequence, possibly empty.
         flightgiven is an initialized string value.
   Post: If flightgiven is in arrivals then it is deleted.
         If it is not there or sequence is empty write out error message.}
  var
    lead, lag : ArrivalsSeq;
  begin
    flightsearch(arrivals, flightgiven, lead, lag);
    if lead = arrivals then
      writeln('This flight is not on the list')
    else
      lag^.link := lead^.link
  end;

procedure update; {var arrivals : ArrivalsSeq; flightgiven : string}
  {Pre : arrivals is an initialized sequence, possibly empty.
         flightgiven is an initialized string value.
   Post: If flightgiven exists then read in from keyboard a new ETA and update
         the record containing flightgiven otherwise write out an error message.}
  var
    lead, lag : ArrivalsSeq;
  begin
    flightsearch(arrivals, flightgiven, lead, lag);
    if lead = arrivals then
      writeln('This flight is not on the list')
    else
      begin
        write('Enter new ETA ');
        readln(lead^.eta)
      end
  end;

procedure display; {arrivals : ArrivalsSeq}
  {Pre : arrivals is an initialized sequence, possibly empty.
   Post: None. Writes out a heading followed by all entries in the sequence.}
  var
    current : ArrivalsSeq;
```

```
begin
  clrscr;
  current := arrivals^.link;
  writeln('  Due     Flight           From      ETA');
  while current <> arrivals do
    begin
      with current^ do
        writeln(time:6:2, flight:10, from:15, eta:10);
        current := current^.link
    end
  end;  {procedure display}
end.
```

Exercise 14.1

Atlanta precedes Chicago and so goes in its left subtree. Boston also precedes Chicago and so goes in its left subtree. However, it comes after Atlanta, and so goes in the right subtree of Atlanta. Similarly, Baltimore goes to the left of Chicago, to the right of Atlanta and to the left of Boston. This gives the figure below:

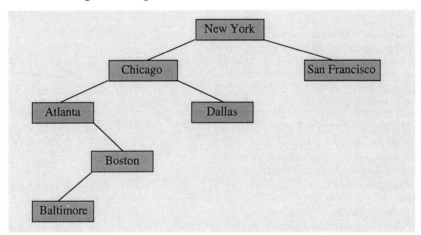

When the names are inserted in the order Baltimore, Atlanta, Boston, a different tree is obtained. Baltimore goes to the left of Chicago. Atlanta goes to the left of Chicago and to the left of Baltimore. Boston goes to the left of Chicago but to the right of Baltimore.

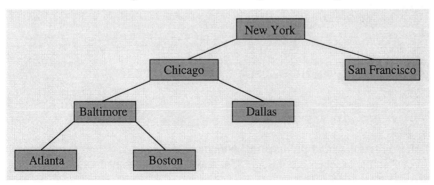

Exercise 14.2
```
implementation
  procedure create;
    {Pre : None.
     Post : A new empty tree is returned which points to the first node.}
    begin
      tree := nil
    end;

  function isempty;
    {(tree : stringtree) : Boolean
     Pre : tree is initialized.
     Post: isempty is true if tree is nil, false otherwise.}
    begin
      isempty := (tree = nil)
    end;

  procedure insert;
    {var tree : stringtree; item : string
     As given in the text}

  function isthere;
    {(tree : stringtree; item : string) : Boolean
     Pre : tree is initialized, possibly empty.
           item is an initialized string value.
     Post: isthere is true if item is in tree, false otherwise.}
    var
      current : stringtree;
      found : Boolean;
    begin
      current := tree;
      found := false;
      while (current <> nil) and not found do
        if item = current^.data then
          found := true
        else
          if item < current^.data then
            current := current^.left
          else
            current := current^.right;
      isthere := found
    end;

  procedure print;
    {tree : stringtree
     Pre : tree is initialized, possibly empty.
     Post: None - the tree is printed out. See Section 14.4 and Chapter 15.}
    begin
      {See Section 14.4 and Chapter 15.}
    end;
end.
```

Exercise 14.3

The inorder traversal would produce the symbols $2 + 3 - 4 * 5$. These symbols are in the correct order but the brackets are missing. The traversal needs to be modified so that when a non-leaf node is encountered:

- for the first time, then an opening bracket is printed
- for the second time, then a closing bracket is printed.

Exercise 14.4

All these routines are required to search the tree and so we shall develop a general key search routine called *keysearch*. This searches for a key value in the tree. If it finds that the key value already exists, then it returns a flag parameter, *exists*, which records this. The location of the match is returned by a pointer variable *lead*. If the key is not in the tree then *exists* is set to false and the parameter *lag* points to the node after which the key should appear in the tree. This routine is private to the implementation part of the unit.

implementation

```
  procedure keysearch(tree : GenTree; key : keytype; var lead, lag : GenTree;
                           var exists : Boolean);
    {Pre : tree is initialized, possibly empty, key is initialized.
     Post: If the key is in tree, lead points to the record containing key and exists is
           set true. If the key is not in tree then lag points to the node after which
           the record containing key should be inserted and exists is set false.}
  begin
    exists := false;
    lead := tree;
    lag := tree;
    while (lead <> nil) and not exists do
      begin
        lag := lead;
        if key < lead^.data.key then
          lead := lead^.left
        else
          if key > lead^.data.key then
            lead := lead^.right
          else
            exists := true
      end
  end;

  procedure insert;
    {var tree : GenTree; item : itemtype; var success : Boolean
     Pre : tree is initialized, possibly empty.
           item is an initialized itemtype value.
     Post: If the item is not a duplicate tree is returned with new item inserted at the
           appropriate leaf and success is set true. Otherwise success is set false.}
  var
    lead, lag, temp : GenTree;
    exists          : Boolean;
  begin
    new(temp);
    temp^.left := nil;
    temp^.right := nil;
    temp^.data := item;
    success := true;
    if isempty(tree) then
      tree := temp
    else
```

```
      begin
        keysearch(tree, item.key, lead, lag, exists);
        if not exists then
          if item.key < lag^.data.key then
            lag^.left := temp
          else
            lag^.right := temp
        else
          success := false
      end;
  end;

function isthere;
  {(tree : GenTree; key : keytype) : Boolean
   Pre : tree is initialized, possibly empty.
         key is an initialized keytype value.
   Post: If key is in tree, isthere is true. Otherwise isthere is false.}
  var
    lead, lag : GenTree;
    exists    : Boolean;
  begin
    keysearch(tree, key, lead, lag, exists);
    isthere := exists
  end;

procedure getnode;
  {(tree : GenTree; key : keytype; var item : itemtype; var success : Boolean)
   Pre : tree is initialized, possibly empty.
         key is an initialized keytype value.
   Post: If the key is not in the tree success is false.
         Otherwise set item to the record with key value key and set success true.}
  var
    lead, lag : GenTree;
  begin
    keysearch(tree, key, lead, lag, success);
    if success then
    item := lead^.data
  end;
```

Exercise 14.5

```
program TestuGenTree;
uses uGenTree, crt;
var
  btree   : GenTree;
  choice  : char;
  item    : itemtype;
  success : Boolean;
procedure getret;
  {Pre : None.
   Post: None - processing awaits press of <ret>.}
  var
    ch : char;
  begin
    writeln;
    write('Press <ret> to get to main menu ');
```

```
    repeat
        ch := readkey
    until (ord(ch) = 13)
  end;
begin
  clrscr;
  create(btree);
  choice := '1';
  while choice <> '6' do
  begin
    clrscr;
    writeln('1 : Insert a new item into tree');
    writeln('2 : Test to see if a key is in the tree');
    writeln('3 : Print all keys');
    writeln('4 : Test for an empty tree');
    writeln('5 : Get record for a given key');
    writeln('6 : Stop');
    write('Enter choice ');
    readln(choice);
    case choice of
      '1' : begin
              write('New key is ?');
              readln(item.key);
              write('New non-key is ?');
              readln(item.field2);
              insert(btree, item, success);
              if success then
                writeln('Data entered')
              else
                writeln('Duplicate entry');
              getret
            end;
      '2' : begin
              write('Key requested is ?');
              readln(item.key);
              if isthere(btree, item.key) b
                writeln(item.key, ' is in the tree')
              else
                writeln(item.key, ' is not in the tree');
              getret
            end;
      '3' : begin
              if isempty(btree) then
                writeln('Tree is empty so cannot be printed')
              else
                printkeys(btree);
              getret
            end;
      '4' : begin
              if isempty(btree) then
                writeln('Tree is empty')
              else
                writeln('Tree is not empty');
              getret
            end;
```

```
'5' : begin
        write('Key requested is ?');
        readln(item.key);
        getnode(btree, item.key, item, success);
        if success then
          writeln(item.key, item.field2)
        else
          writeln(item.key, ' is not in the tree');
        getret
      end
  end
 end
end.
```

Exercise 15.1

It is trivial when it has length 1 because to write out a string of length 1 in reverse simply requires the single character to be output.

Exercise 15.2

```
procedure reverse(given : string);
  {Pre : given is an initialized non-empty string.
   Post: None - given is written out in reverse order.}
  var
    first : char;
  begin
    if length(given) = 1 then
      write(given[i])
    else
      begin
        first := given[1];
        delete(given, 1, 1);
        reverse(given);
        write(first)
      end
  end;
```

Exercise 15.3

The *article* is *trivial* corresponds to the article having length zero or 1 because in either case it is palindromic.

Exercise 15.4

palindrome('madam')

```
1   if (5 = 0) or (5 = 1) then
4     if 'm' = 'm' then
5       given = 'adam'
6       given = 'ada'
7       palindrome('ada')

        1   if (3 = 0) or (3 = 1) then
        4     if 'a' = 'a' then
        5       given = 'da'
        6       given = 'd'
        7       palindrome('d')

                1   if (1 = 0) or (1 = 1) then
                2     'palindrome'
                11 ifend

        10    ifend
        11  ifend

10    ifend
11  ifend
```

palindrome('reader')

```
1   if (6 = 0) or (6 = 1) then
4     if 'r' = 'r' then
5       given = 'eader'
6       given = 'eade'
7       palindrome('eade')

        1   if (4 = 0) or (4 = 1) then
        4     if 'e' = 'e' then
        5       given = 'ade'
        6       given = 'ad'
        7       palindrome('ad')

                1   if (2 = 0) or (2 = 1) then
                4     if 'a' = 'd' then
                9         'not a palindrome'
                10    ifend
                11  ifend

        10    ifend
        11  ifend

10    ifend
11  ifend
```

Exercise 15.5

revprint(#6)

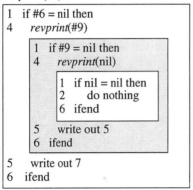

```
1   if #6 = nil then
4      revprint(#9)

       1   if #9 = nil then
       4      revprint(nil)

              1   if nil = nil then
              2      do nothing
              6   ifend

       5      write out 5
       6   ifend

5      write out 7
6   ifend
```

Exercise 15.6

print(#10)

```
1   if #10 = nil then
4      print(#20)  {the left subtree of New York record}

       1   if #20 = nil then
       4      print(nil)  {the left subtree of Chicago record}

              1   if nil = nil then
              2      do nothing
              7   ifend

       5      write out Chicago
       6      print(nil)  {the right subtree of Chicago record}

              1   if nil = nil then
              2      do nothing
              7   ifend

       7   ifend

5      write out New York
6      print(#40)  {the right subtree of New York record}

       1   if #40 = nil then
       4      print(nil)  {the left subtree of San Francisco record}

              1   if nil = nil then
              2      do nothing
              7   ifend

       5      write out San Francisco
       6      print(nil)  {the right subtree of San Francisco record}

              1   if nil = nil then
              2      do nothing
              7   ifend

       7   ifend

7   ifend
```

Exercise 16.1

To keep the two items of data together the abstract data type approach demands that they are encapsulated in a record. Records of this type then have to be parameters of the two routines.

```
program adtprog;
type
   MapRef = record
                latitude  : real;
                longitude : real
            end;
   procedure readin(var indata : MapRef);
   procedure print(outdata : MapRef);
```

Exercise 16.2

The message is *print* and it tells *capitalcity*[50] to write out its contents.

Exercise 16.3

The answer is that you cannot possibly know! The code below gives one possible representation.

```
interface
type
   timerec = record   {Private for use by the object}
                hour   : integer;
                minute : integer
            end;
   MapRef = object
                latitude  : real;
                longitude : real;
                time      : timerec;
                procedure init(inlat, inlong : real; hour, minute : integer);
```

Here, the method *init* would have to assign the actual parameters hour and minute to the appropriate field values. A more complex scenario would be if times were entered on a 12-hour basis together with an additional parameter which indicated a.m. or p.m. The same internal representation could be used, but the p.m. hours would have to be processed into their 24-hour equivalent form before being assigned to the hour field. Indeed, this record representation may not be appropriate at all because it makes time-elapsed calculations rather difficult. A single data item representing the number of seconds since midnight might be a better representation if elapsed times are required. Nevertheless, the method whereby a time is read in might still take the form of *init* shown above. The point is that the user is ignorant of the way data are represented within the object but needs methods whereby values can be input and retrieved from this internal representation.

Exercise 16.4

In the implementation we only give the code which differs from that in the text. In the program the call to *greenwich.GetLong* has to be removed and replaced in the *writeln* statement.

```
punit uMapRef;
interface
type
  MapRef = object
              latitude  : real;
              longitude : real;
              procedure init(inlat, inlong : real);
              procedure print;
              function GetLat : real;
              function GetLong : real;
           end;
implementation
    :
  function MapRef.GetLat;
    begin
      GetLat := latitude
    end;
  function MapRef.GetLong;
    begin
      GetLong := longitude
    end;
end.
program testMapRef;
    :
  writeln('Greenwich is at longitude ', greenwich.GetLong);
```

Exercise 16.5

```
procedure MapRef.init;
  begin
    latitude := inlat;
    longitude := inlong;
    time.hour := hour;
    time.minute := minute
  end;
```

Exercise 16.6

The instance *mycountry* object 'knows' that its *init* routine does not have parameters and so the call would result in a compilation error.

Exercise 16.7

```
function PartTime.CalcPay;
  begin
    CalcPay := hoursworked*hourlyrate
  end;
```

Exercise 16.8

The VMT field of the instance *novice* is recovered. This contains the address of the VMT for the object class *FullTime*. The *CalcLeave* field of this VMT contains the address of the *FullTime CalcLeave* method. So it is this version which is executed.

Exercise 16.9

```
implementation
  constructor MapRef.init;
    begin
      latitude := inlat;
      longitude := inlong
    end;
  function MapRef.GetLat  ;
    begin
      GetLat   := latitude;
    end;
  function MapRef.GetLong  ;
    begin
      GetLong := longitude
    end;
  procedure MapRef.print;
    begin
      write(latitude:6:2, longitude:6:2)
    end;
  constructor Position.init;
    begin
      MapRef.init(inlat, inlong);
      height := inheight
    end;
  function Position.GetHeight;
    begin
      GetHeight := height;
    end;
  procedure Position.print;
    begin
      MapRef.print;
      write(height:6:2)
    end;
end.
```

Exercise 16.10

```
implementation
  procedure stacktype.create;
    begin
      stack := nil
    end;
  procedure stacktype.push;
    var
      temppointer : nodeptr;
    begin
      new(temppointer);
      temppointer^.noderef := item;
      temppointer^.nodenext := stack;
      stack := temppointer;
    end;
  function stacktype.isempty;
    begin
      isempty := (stack = nil)
    end;
```

```
procedure stacktype.pop;
  begin
    if stacktype.isempty then
      begin
        success := false;
        item := nil
      end
    else
      begin
        item := stack^.noderef;
        stack := stack^.nodenext;
        success := true
      end
  end;
procedure stacktype.print;
  var
    temp : nodeptr;
  begin
    temp := stack;
    writeln('Top of stack');
    while temp <> nil do
      begin
        temp^.noderef^.print;
        writeln;
        temp := temp^.nodenext
      end
  end;
end.
```

Exercise 16.11

```
teststack.push(new(posptr, init(lat, long)));
```

Note that the identifier *posptr* in this statement is the type identifier of the pointer to a *Position* object.

Exercise 16.12

```
'3' : begin
        teststack.pop(data, flag);
        if flag then
          begin
            data^.print;
            writeln
          end
        else
          writeln('Cannot pop an empty stack');
        getret
      end;
'4' : begin
        teststack.print;
        getret
      end;
```

PROBLEMS

We remind you that problems marked with an asterisk are not derived from the author's book *An Introduction to Program Design*. Those which are derived from it contain a development of the designs used here and so can be used for reference purposes.

Problem 1.1*

Problem statement

Write a complete program for the following design in which a user enters an amount of money expressed as a real number and a message is output depending on the size of the input.

Design

```
1.1      write out 'Enter the value of the cheque'
1.2      read in cheque
2.1      if cheque <= 50 then
2.2          write out 'A bankers card is sufficient'
2.3      else
2.4          write out 'A bankers card plus other identification is required'
2.5      ifend
3        write out 'Program done'
```

Data table

Identifier	Description	Type
cheque	value of a cheque	*real* variable

Test data

At least three values should be used, one less than 50, one exactly 50 and one greater than 50.

Problem 1.2*

Problem statement

Write a program fragment for the following design. The Pascal symbol for division is a backslash as used in the design.

Design

1.1	write out 'Enter a non-zero integer value'
1.2	read in *number*
2.1	if *number* = 0 then
2.2	write out 'Zero does not have a reciprocal'
2.3	else
2.4	*reciprocal* := 1/*number*
2.5	write out 'The reciprocal is ', *reciprocal*
2.6	ifend
3	write out 'Program done'

Data table

Identifier	Description	Type
number	Input integer	*integer* variable
reciprocal	The reciprocal of *number*	*real* variable

Test data

A minimum set of test data would be zero and an integer for which you can easily calculate the reciprocal.

Problem 3.1

Problem statement

A quarterly gas bill consists of two parts: a standing charge and a charge for the amount of gas used. The amount of gas used, in cubic feet, is given by the difference between the current meter reading and its previous quarterly value. From these readings the number of British thermal units (BTUs) used is calculated using the fact that one cubic foot of gas has an energy equivalent of 1.016 BTUs. Assuming the standing charge is £8.70 write a program that will enable a user to input the cost of a BTU, as a decimal number of pence, and the current and previous quarter's meter readings. It should output the total amount due, expressed in pounds. You may assume that meter readings can be represented by integers.

Design

	{Gas bill calculation}
1.1	write out 'Enter the price per BTU in pence '
1.2	read in *priceBTU*
1.3	write out 'Enter previous meter reading '
1.4	read in *previous*
1.5	write out 'Enter current meter reading '
1.6	read in *current*
2.1	*GasCost* := (*current* − *previous*)*priceBTU*1.016/100
2.2	*TotalCost* := *GasCost* + 8.70
3.1	write out 'Total gas bill is ', *TotalCost*

Data table

Identifier	Description	Type
priceBTU	Price of one BTU	*real* variable
previous	Previous meter reading	*integer* variable
current	Current meter reading	*integer* variable
GasCost	Cost of gas used	*real* variable
TotalCost	Overall bill	*real* variable

Test data
This will require doing some calculations by hand or with the help of a calculator. The value of *current* should not be less than the value of *previous*, but it is conceivable that the two have the same value. An explicit test for equal values should be carried out to ensure that the output is indeed £8.70. Looking for 'extreme' data test values like this, which match the specifications but are not quite obvious, is a skill to be developed.

Problem 3.2

Problem statement
There is no data type corresponding to fractions. If a problem involves them it is usual to convert them to a decimal approximation and thereby represent them as real numbers. However, we can model a fraction by using two integer variables: one to represent the numerator and the other to represent the denominator of the fraction. This problem is concerned with such a representation. Write a program that will enable a user to input two fractions and will output their product. The output should consist of two integers: one for the numerator of the product, the other for its denominator. You may assume that the user does not enter zero for either of the input denominators.

Design
```
          {Multiplication of fractions}
1.1       write out 'Enter the numerator of the first fraction '
1.2       read in numerator1
1.3       write out 'Enter the denominator of the first fraction '
1.4       read in denominator1
1.5       write out 'Enter the numerator of the second fraction '
1.6       read in numerator2
1.7       write out 'Enter the denominator of the second fraction '
1.8       read in denominator2
2.1       numprod := numerator1*numerator2
2.2       denomprod := denominator1*denominator2
3.1       write out 'The numerator of the product is ', numprod
3.2       write out 'The denominator of the product is ', denomprod
```

Data table

Identifier	Description	Type
numerator1	First fraction numerator	*integer* variable
denominator1	First denominator	*integer* variable
numerator2	Second numerator	*integer* variable
denominator2	Second denominator	*integer* variable
numprod	Product numerator	*integer* variable
denomprod	Product denominator	*integer* variable

Test data
You will need to do the calculations by hand, and so simple values are best. All possible combinations of positive and negative numerators and denominators should be tried. You should also allow one (or both) of the numerators to be zero.

Problem 3.3

Problem statement
Boxes of floppy disks are on sale for £5 per box or £45 for 10 boxes. All prices are subject

to tax at 15 per cent. Write a program that will enable a user to input a number of boxes and will produce as output the total cost of the boxes including tax.

Design

1.1	write out 'Enter the number of boxes bought '
1.2	read in *boxes*
2.1	*cheap* := *boxes* div 10
3.1	*expensive* := *boxes* mod 10
4.1	*cost* := 1.15*(45**cheap* + 5**expensive*)
5.1	write out 'Total cost inclusive of tax is ', *cost*

Data table

Identifier	Description	Type
boxes	Number of boxes bought	*integer* variable
cheap	Number of sets of 10 boxes	*integer* variable
expensive	Number of single boxes	*integer* variable
cost	Overall cost	*real* variable

Test data

The number of boxes entered should include numbers such as 1, 10 (the exact number for which a discount is first available), 11 (to test 10 get the discount rate and 1 does not) and 21 (to test that 20 boxes attract the required discount and 1 does not).

Problem 3.4

Problem statement

Telephone calls are charged by the number of units used where a unit is a period of time that depends on the distance of the call and the time of day when the call is made. All calls result in a charge which is an integer number of units. As soon as a call has been answered a unit is charged, and as soon as the time period of that unit has expired another unit is charged, and so on until the call is terminated. For a local cheap rate call, a unit is 360 seconds. Write a program that will enable a user to input the duration of a call and will output its cost. You should assume the duration of a call is a whole number and that a unit costs 4.4p subject to tax at 15 per cent.

Design

	{Cost of a telephone call version 1}
1.1	write out 'Enter duration of call '
1.2	read in *duration*
2.1	*wholeunits* := *duration* div 360
2.2	*timeleft* := *duration* mod 360
2.3	if *timeleft* > 0 then
2.4	increment *wholeunits*
2.5	ifend
2.6	*cost* := 1.15*4.4**wholeunits*
3.1	write out 'The cost of the call is ', *cost*

Data table

Identifier	Description	Type
duration	Length of call	*integer* variable
wholeunits	Number of units used	*integer* variable
timeleft	Time elapsed of current charged unit	*integer* variable
cost	Cost of call	*real* variable

Test data
You should try testing durations having values like 1 (zero duration is not a possibility so this is the smallest practical value), 360 (to ensure this is only charged 1 unit), 361 (to ensure this is charged 2 units) and larger values close to exact multiples of 360.

Problem 3.5

Problem statement
Write a program that will enable a user to input an integer and will produce as output a message saying whether or not the input was exactly divisible by three.

Design

```
        {Test for divisibility}
1.1     write out 'Enter an integer '
1.2     read in number
2.1     remainder := number mod 3
3.1     if remainder = 0 then
3.2        write out 'The number is exactly divisible by 3'
3.3     else
3.4        write out 'The number is not exactly divisible by 3'
3.5     ifend
```

Data table

Identifier	Description	Type
number	Input integer	*integer* variable
remainder	Remainder on division by 3	*integer* variable

Test data
Try positive and negative values, but do test three consecutive integer values.

Problem 3.6

Problem statement
This problem is concerned with working out the day of the week on which a given date falls. The rather strange formula below, attributed to Zeller, calculates the day of the week on which any date after 1 January 1583 will fall or has fallen. The date for which the corresponding day of the week is required must be coded in the following way. The day of the month is the usual day number, and so is an integer between 1 and 31 inclusive. The year must be represented by an integer, for example, the integer 1989 represents the year 1989. The month must be coded as an integer where March is coded 1, April as 2 and so on until December, which is coded as 10. January and February are coded as 11 and 12 respectively of the *previous* year. So, for example, 3 January 1992 would be represented as day 3, month 11 of year 1991. We shall think of a year as consisting of two parts: a century represented by the first two digits of its integer representation, and a decade represented by the last two digits. (Note that neither decade nor century have their usual meaning here.) Thus, in 1991, century would have value 19 and decade the value 91. With this method of coding the formula for the day of the week is given by:

$$daycode = ((13*month - 1) \text{ div } 5 + decade \text{ div } 4 + century \text{ div } 4 + decade + day - 2*century) \text{ mod } 7$$

The result of this formula is an integer in the range 0 – 6 inclusive. The integer 0 represents

Sunday, 1 represents Monday and so on. Write a program that will enable a user to enter a date in three stages: the day, the coded month and the year. (None of these inputs are to be validated to check that they correspond to actual dates.) The output produced by the program should be the code corresponding to the day of the week on which that date falls.

Design

        {Find day of the week}
1.1   write out 'Enter the number of the day as an integer between 1 and 31 inclusive '
1.2   read in *day*
1.3   write out 'Enter the coded month '
1.4   write out 'March = 1, April = 2 .. Dec = 10, Jan = 11, Feb = 12'
1.5   read in *month*
1.6   write out 'Enter 4 digit year, but subtract 1 from it if month is Jan or Feb'
1.7   read in *year*
2.1   *century := year* div 100
2.2   *decade := year* mod 100
3.1   *daycode := ((13*month − 1)* div 5 + *decade* div 4 + *century* div 4 + *decade* + *day*
           − 2*century) mod 7
4.1   write out 'Your date falls on day ', *daycode*

Data table

Identifier	Description	Type
day	See the text in the statement of the problem	*integer* variable
month	for a description of all these variables	*integer* variable
year		*integer* variable
century		*integer* variable
decade		*integer* variable
daycode		*integer* variable

Test data
You will need a diary to test this program! Certainly all 12 possible month numbers should be tested.

Problem 3.7

Problem statement
Amend the specification of Problem 3.6 so that the user inputs the number of the month in conventional format, that is, January is represented by 1, February by 2 and so on. Write a program to match this new specification.

Design

        {Find day of the week}
1.1   write out 'Enter the number of the day as an integer between 1 and 31 inclusive '
1.2   read in *day*
1.3   write out 'Enter the month as an integer in the range 1 − 12 inclusive '
1.4   read in *month*
1.5   write out 'Enter year as a 4 digit integer '
1.6   read in *year*
2.1   if *month* <= 2 then
2.2   *month := month* + 10
2.3   *year := year* − 1
2.3   else
2.4   *month := month* − 2

2.5   ifend
3.1   *century* := *year* div 100
3.2   *decade* := *year* mod 100
4.1   *daycode* := ((13*month* − 1) div 5 + *decade* div 4 + *century* div 4 + *decade* + *day*
          − 2**century*) mod 7
5.1   write out 'Your date falls on day ', *daycode*

The data table is as given in Problem 3.6.

Test data
The same test data as for Problem 3.6 can be used here.

Problem 4.1

Problem statement
The value of a microcomputer depreciates by 15 per cent compound per year. Write a program that will enable a user to input an initial value for the computer and will produce as output the value of the computer over the next five years. If the user inputs a non-positive number for the initial value of the micro, then a message is to be output saying that the value must be positive, and the user is to be prompted to try again. All subsequent input attempts must be validated in the same way. The output generated from an input value of 200 should be:

```
After year 1 depreciated value is 170.00
After year 2 depreciated value is 144.50
After year 3 depreciated value is 122.83
After year 4 depreciated value is 104.40
After year 5 depreciated value is 88.74
```

Design
      {Calculate depreciation for each of five years}
1.1   write 'Enter initial value of micro'
1.2   read in *value*
1.3   loop while *value* <= 0
1.4   write out 'The initial value must be positive, please try again'
1.5   read in *value*
1.6   loopend
1.7   *year* := 1
2.1   loop while *year* <= 5
3.1   *value* := (1 − *rate*)**value*
3.2   write out 'After year ' *year*, ' depreciated value is ', *value*
3.3   increment *year*
4   loopend

Data table

Identifier	Description	Type
rate	Depreciation rate	*real* constant value 0.15
value	Current value of micro	*real* variable
year	Number of years passed	*integer* variable

Test data
The required output is described in the specification.

Problem 4.2

Problem statement

Write a program that will enable a user to input a string and will output each character of the string on a separate line. You may assume that the user inputs at least one character.

Design

```
        {write out input string one character per line}
1.1     write out 'Input your string '
1.2     read in line
1.3     index := 1
2.1     loop while index <= length(line)
3.1         write out line[index]
3.2         increment index
4       loopend
```

Data table

Identifier	Description	Type
line	The input string	*string* variable
index	Loop control variable	*integer* variable

Test data

You will need to try input strings of varying lengths, starting with a string of just one character.

Problem 4.3

Problem statement

In Problem 4.2 the assumption that the user inputs at least one character is now removed from the specification. Write a program for this new specification.

Design

```
        {write out input string one character per line}
1.1     write out 'Input your string '
1.2     read in line
2.1     if length(line) = 0 then
2.2         write out 'No text was entered'
2.3     else
2.4       index := 1
2.5       loop while index <= length(line)
2.6           write out line[index]
2.7           increment index
2.8       loopend
2.9     ifend
```

The data table remains as in Problem 4.2.

Test data

Clearly, the new requirement has to be tested, but the test data of Problem 4.2 should be used here just to ensure that this design has not introduced errors to that part of the functionality.

Problem 4.4

Problem statement

Modify the design of the depreciation rate problem in the text so that, if the user enters a rate of zero, a message that no depreciation takes place is output.

Design

```
        {Depreciation with zero rate as a possibility}
1.1     write out 'Enter the depreciation rate as a number in range 0–100'
1.2     read in rate
2.1     if rate = 0 then
3           write out 'No depreciation ever takes place'
4       else
5.1         year := 0
5.2         NewValue := OriginalValue
5.3         loop while NewValue > OriginalValue/2
5.4            NewValue := (100 – rate)*NewValue/100
5.5            increment year
5.6         loopend
5.7         write out 'Original value will have halved by the year ', year
6       ifend
```

Data table

Identifier	Description	Type
OriginalValue	Original value of micro	*real* constant value 1000.0
NewValue	Current value after depreciation	*real* variable
rate	Depreciation rate (0 < rate < 100)	*real* variable
year	Number of years passed	*integer* variable

Test data

Zero and non-zero values are required test values here. The non-zero values can be the same as those used to test the original program.

Problem 4.5

Problem statement

A fast-food outlet requires its staff to enter the details of a customer order on a till that will produce the customer's bill. For each menu item on the order the unit price is entered, followed by the number of such items required by the customer. The bill produced by the till gives the total cost and the number of items that make up the order. The latter quantity is used as a check by the sales assistant to ensure that each customer gets the correct number of packages of food. Input of an order is terminated by zero being entered as the unit price. Write a program that will enable an order to be entered into the till and will produce as output a bill having the form given above. We give two designs for you to code.

Data table

Identifier	Description	Type
bill	Total bill of the order	*real* variable
UnitPrice	Cost of a food item	*real* variable
quantity	Quantity required of given menu item	*integer* variable
totalno	Total number of items ordered	*integer* variable

Design

{Produce a bill for fast-food outlet}

1.1 *bill* := 0
1.2 *totalno* := 0
1.3 write out 'Enter unit price or 0 to quit '
1.4 read in *UnitPrice*
2.1 loop while *UnitPrice* > 0
3.1   write out 'Enter quantity for this price '
3.2   read in *quantity*
3.3   *bill* := *bill* + *quantity*UnitPrice*
3.4   *totalno* := *totalno* + *quantity*
3.5   write out 'Enter unit price or 0 to quit '
3.6   read in *UnitPrice*
4   loopend
5.1 write out *totalno*, ' items ordered'
5.2 write out 'Total cost ', *bill*

{Produce a bill for fast-food outlet}

1.1 *bill* := 0
1.2 *totalno* := 0
1.3 *UnitPrice* := 1
2.1 loop while *UnitPrice* > 0
3.1   write out 'Enter unit price or 0 to quit '
3.2   read in *UnitPrice*
3.3   if *UnitPrice* > 0 then
3.4   write out 'Enter quantity for this price '
3.5   read in *quantity*
3.6   *bill* := *bill* + *quantity*UnitPrice*
3.7   *totalno* := *totalno* + *quantity*
3.8   ifend
4   loopend
5.1 write out *totalno*, ' items ordered'
5.2 write out 'Total cost ', *bill*

Test data

Once the user has decided to quit (by responding with 0 to the prompt for a unit price) no more requests for input should be issued by the program. In particular, the request for the number of items should not be issued. Users should be allowed to quit the program immediately (by responding with 0 to the very first prompt for a unit price) and no further user interaction should be required. The program also needs to be tested to ensure that the values it outputs are correct. This will involve some calculations by hand. A value of 0 should be tried in response to the number of items at a given unit price. (This effectively gives the operator a way to correct a unit price input typing error.)

Problem 4.6

Problem statement

Situations can arise where it is necessary to assign a real number which has a zero decimal part, for example, a real number like 3.0, to an integer variable so that it can be processed using integer operators. This problem asks you to write a program to achieve this for positive real numbers which have zero decimal parts. The output from the program should be the equivalent integer.

Design

{reals with no fractional part}

1.1 write 'Enter a real number with zero decimal part '
1.2 read in *realnumber*
1.3 *wholenumber* := 0
2.1 loop while *realnumber* > 0
2.2   increment *wholenumber*
2.3   decrement *realnumber*
3   loopend
4   write out 'The integer part of the input is ', *wholenumber*

Data table

Identifier	Description	Type
realnumber	A real number	*real* variable
wholenumber	Integer equivalent of *realnumber*	*integer* variable

Test data
A single value like 3.0 is sufficient here. (Note 0.0 is not an allowable input because it is not positive.)

Problem 4.7

Problem statement
The integer part of a real number is defined to be the largest integer that does not exceed the number. For example, the integer part of 7.91 is 7. What amendments would be required to the design in Problem 4.6 in order to assign to *wholenumber* the integer part of a positive real number input from the keyboard? (The definition of integer part applies to negative real numbers as well, but we are considering only positive real numbers here.)

Other than a minor amendment to the input prompt, the condition at step 2.1 of Problem 4.6 would need to be changed to:

2.1   loop while *realnumber* >= 1

Test data
This should include real numbers with zero decimal parts as well as those with non-zero decimal parts. Good decimal parts would include, for example, .9999 and .1, .01, .001, etc.

Problem 4.8

Problem statement
Word processors often have a utility which counts the number of words in a given document. Some provide more sophisticated utilities which can supply the average word length in a document. Here, we consider a simplified version of the latter. A line of text is to be processed to find the average length of the words it contains. The text, which is to be entered from the keyboard, must begin with a non-space character and must terminate with a single-space character. For the purposes of this problem a word is defined to be any sequence of non-space characters. Words must be separated from each other by exactly one space and no two-space characters may be placed side by side. You may assume that the user enters data as instructed. The constraints on the input format will be relaxed in Problem 5.22.

Design

```
        {word count program}
1.1     write out 'Enter your line of text with single spaces between words'
1.2     write out 'Terminate input with a single space '
1.3     read in line
2.1     index := 1
2.2     wordcount := 0
2.3     lettercount := 0
3.1     loop while index <= length(line)
4.1        if line[index] = space then
4.2           increment wordcount
4.3        else
4.4           increment lettercount
4.5        ifend
4.6        increment index
5       loopend
6.1     average := lettercount/wordcount
7.1     write out 'Average word length is ', average
```

Data table

Identifier	Description	Type
space	Space character	*char* constant value '□'
line	A line of text	*string* variable
index	Loop control variable	*integer* variable
wordcount	Number of words in *line*	*integer* variable
lettercount	Number of letters in *line*	*integer* variable
average	Average word length	*real* variable

Test data

You should try inputs of one, two and more words and check that the average is correctly calculated.

Problem 4.9

Problem statement

Most word processors give the user the option of right-justifying the text, that is, aligning the last character of each line at the right-hand side. One way of doing this is to put extra space characters between the words. In Chapter 9 we shall look at this problem in detail, but for now we shall look at a much simpler version. Write a program that will insert one extra space every time a space character is encountered in a string. Your program should enable a user to input a string, which should then be copied character by character to a new string containing the extra space characters where appropriate. Finally, the new string should be written out. You should assume that the input string does not contain adjacent space characters.

Design

```
        {Insert extra space characters in a string}
1.1     write out 'Enter the string with no adjacent space characters '
1.2     read in oldstring
1.3     newstring := ' '
1.4     position := 1
2.1     loop while position <= length(oldstring)
3.1         newstring := newstring + oldstring[position]
4.1         if oldstring[position] = space then
4.2             newstring := newstring + space
4.3         ifend
4.4         increment position
5       loopend
6.1     write out 'The new string is '
6.2     write out newstring
```

Data table

Identifier	Description	Type
space	The space character	*char* constant value '□'
oldstring	User input string	*string* variable
position	Loop control variable	*integer* variable
newstring	String with extra spaces	*string* variable

Test data

Some simple strings like 'a□b', 'a□b□c' will suffice here.

Problem 5.1

Problem statement

The design below uses a *for* loop to solve Problem 4.2. Write a complete program for this design using the data table from Problem 4.2.

Design

```
        {write out input string one character per line}
1.1     write out 'Input your string '
1.2     read in line
2.1     loop for index := 1 to length(line)
3.1         write out line[index]
4       loopend
```

Test data

The same test data as for Problem 4.2 can be used here.

Problem 5.2

Problem statement

Many problems involving strings require them to be manipulated and split into other strings. Consider the problem of holding a person's address on computer. One way would be to declare a string variable to hold the street name, another for the town, a third for the county and a fourth for the post code. However, not all addresses have this format: some houses have names, others may be situated in villages whose address includes the name of the nearest town, and so on. One way of overcoming the different address formats is to hold the whole address in a single string variable and to separate the components by a special symbol. For example, the string: 'High Bank*Lucks Farm*Greenwood Lane*Tonbridge* Kent' would represent the address that is more familiarly written:

High Bank
Lucks Farm
Greenwood Lane
Tonbridge
Kent

This method of representing addresses is sometimes called **free format**. To recover the individual components, the single string has to be split at each asterisk. This problem is a simplified version of the process. Write a program that will enable a user to input a string similar to that above but consisting of just two words separated by a single asterisk. The program should assign to *FirstWord* and *SecondWord* the two words of the input string and neither should contain the asterisk itself. The output should be the two words written out on different lines, together with appropriate prompts. You may assume that the user inputs at least an asterisk, and your solution should use a *while* loop and a *for* loop.

Design

```
1.1     write out 'Enter two words separated by a single asterisk'
1.2     read in TwoWords
2.1     FirstWord := "
2.2     SecondWord := "
2.3     index := 1
3.1     loop while TwoWords[index] <> '*'
4.1         FirstWord := FirstWord + TwoWords[index]
```

4.2   increment *index*
5   loopend
6.1   increment *index*
7.1   loop for j := *index* to *length*(*TwoWords*)
7.2   *SecondWord* := *SecondWord* + *TwoWords*[*j*]
7.3   loopend
8.1   write out 'First word is ' *FirstWord*
8.2   write out 'Second word is ' *SecondWord*

Data table

Identifier	Description	Type
TwoWords	User input string	*string* variable
FirstWord	Characters preceding * in input string	*string* variable
SecondWord	Characters after * in input string	*string* variable
index	Index into string variable	*integer* variable
j	Loop control variable	*integer* variable

Test data
Two words separated by an asterisk are standard test data. However, an asterisk on its own is a permitted input and so should be tested.

Problem 5.3
Problem statement
A competition for ice skaters has eight judges who award marks for the performance of each skater. The mark awarded by a judge to an individual skater is a real number, expressed to one decimal place in the range 0 to 6 inclusive. All eight judges present a mark for a skater and the eight marks are collected together. The highest and lowest marks are discarded, and the average of the six remaining marks is then the score obtained by that skater. This marking process is supposed to remove any bias an individual judge may have for a particular competitor. Write a program that will allow all eight marks to be entered and will produce as output the score obtained by this procedure. The eight marks entered should not be assigned to variables and then manipulated; instead, appropriate running values should be stored. We give two equivalent designs below.

Data table

Identifier	Description	Type
lowest	Lowest of eight scores	*real* variable
highest	Highest of eight scores	*real* variable
total	Sum of all eight scores	*real* variable
score	An individual judge's score	*real* variable
average	Skater's overall score	*real* variable
i	Loop control variable	*integer* variable

Test data
Values should be chosen so that they can easily be calculated by hand. Some values of zero should be included in the test data. You should try some data sets for which all eight values are the same and others for which all eight values are different.

Design

	{Ice skating judging version 1}		{Ice skating judging version 2}
1.1	*lowest* := 6	1.1	write out 'Enter score for judge 1'
1.2	*highest* := 0	1.2	read in *score*
1.3	*total* := 0	1.3	*total* := *score*
2.1	loop for *i* := 1 to 8	1.4	*lowest* := *score*
3.1	write 'Enter score for judge ', *i*, ' '	1.5	*highest* := *score*
3.2	read in *score*	2.1	loop for *i* := 2 to 8
3.3	*total* := *total* + *score*	3.1	write 'Enter score for judge ', *i*, ' '
3.4	if *score* > *highest* then	3.2	read in *score*
3.5	*highest* := *score*	3.3	*total* := *total* + *score*
3.6	ifend	3.4	if *score* > *highest* then
3.7	if *score* < *lowest* then	3.5	*highest* := *score*
3.8	*lowest* := *score*	3.6	ifend
3.9	ifend	3.7	if *score* < *lowest* then
4	loopend	3.8	*lowest* := *score*
5.1	*total* := *total* − *highest* − *lowest*	3.9	ifend
5.2	*average* := *total*/6	4	loopend
6.1	write out 'Skater has scored ', *average*	5.1	*total* := *total* − *highest* − *lowest*
		5.2	*average* := *total*/6
		6.1	write out 'Skater has scored ', *average*

Problem 5.4

Problem statement

Write a program that will enable a user to input some text into a string variable and will produce as output the text with each sentence on a new line. For this problem, a sentence is defined to be any sequence of characters terminating with a full stop. You may assume that the user does not enter a null string.

Design

	{Output sentences on a new line}
1.1	write 'Enter the text '
1.2	read in *paragraph*
2.1	loop for *i* := 1 to *length*(*paragraph*)
3.1	if *paragraph*[*i*] = *fullstop* then
3.2	write out *paragraph*[*i*]
3.3	else
3.4	write *paragraph*[*i*]
3.5	ifend
4	loopend

Data table

Identifier	Description	Type
fullstop	Constant definition	*char* constant value '.'
paragraph	Input text	*string* variable
i	Loop control variable	*integer* variable

Test data

An extreme data set would consist of a string consisting only of full stops.

Problem 5.5

Problem statement

Write a program that will enable a user to input the day of the week on which a month begins and the number of days in the month and will produce as output a calendar for the month in the format shown below.

Sun	Mon	Tues	Wed	Thurs	Fri	Sat
		1	2	3	4	5
6	7	8	9	10	11	12
13	14	15	16	17	18	19
20	21	22	23	24	25	26
27	28	29	30	31		

The day on which the month begins should be entered as an integer where 1 corresponds to Sunday, 2 to Monday and so on. We give two possible designs.

Design

{Write out a calendar version 1}
1.1 write 'Enter day on which the 1st falls
      1 = Sunday, 2 = Monday etc '
1.2 read in *firstday*
1.3 write 'How many days in the month? '
1.4 read in *monthdays*
1.5 *column* := 1
2.1 write out 'Sun ', 'Mon ', 'Tues ', 'Wed ',
      'Thurs ', 'Fri ', 'Sat '
3.1 loop for *i* := 1 to *firstday* −1
3.2   write ' '
3.3   increment *column*
3.4 loopend
4.1 loop for *i* := 1 to *monthdays*
4.2   if *column* := 7 then
4.3   write out *i*
4.4   *column* := 1
4.5   else
4.6   write *i*
4.7   increment *column*
4.8   ifend
4.9 loopend

{Write out a calendar version 2}
1.1 write 'Enter day on which the 1st falls
      1 = Sunday, 2 = Monday etc '
1.2 read in *firstday*
1.3 write 'How many days in the month? '
1.4 read in *monthdays*
2.1 write out 'Sun ', 'Mon ', 'Tues ', 'Wed ',
      'Thurs ', 'Fri ', 'Sat '
3.1 loop for *i* := 1 to *firstday* −1
3.2   write ' '
3.3 loopend
4.1 loop for *i* := 1 to *monthdays*
4.2   write *i*
4.3   if (*i* + *firstday*) mod 7 = 1 then
4.4   write out
4.5   ifend
4.6 loopend

Data table

Identifier	Description	Type
firstday	Day on which 1st falls	*integer* variable
monthdays	Days in the month	*integer* variable
i	Loop control variable	*integer* variable
column	Column in which next day is output	*integer* variable

Test data

The major problem here is getting the output aligned in columns, and so data to test all possibilities are required. Thus, each day of the week will need to be a tested start day and each should be tested with the three possible numbers of days in a month.

Problem 5.6

Problem statement

Write two programs, one of which uses a preconditioned loop, the other a postconditioned loop, that will enable a user to enter characters from the keyboard and will produce as output the number of occurrences of the lower case letter 'a'. The characters should not be stored in a string and termination of input should be by using the sentinel value '*'.

Design

<table>
<tr><td colspan="2">{Occurrences of 'a' version 1}</td><td colspan="2">{Occurrences of 'a' version 2}</td></tr>
<tr><td>1.1</td><td>write out 'Enter characters terminating
with a * and then <ret> '</td><td>1.1
1.2</td><td>*count* := 0
write out 'Enter characters terminating
with a * and then <ret> '</td></tr>
<tr><td>1.2</td><td>read in *letter*</td><td></td><td></td></tr>
<tr><td>1.3</td><td>*count* := 0</td><td>2.1</td><td>repeat</td></tr>
<tr><td>2.1</td><td>loop while *letter* <> '*'</td><td>3.1</td><td>read in *letter*</td></tr>
<tr><td>3.1</td><td>if *letter* = 'a' then</td><td>3.2</td><td>if *letter* = 'a' then</td></tr>
<tr><td>3.2</td><td>increment *count*</td><td>3.3</td><td>increment *count*</td></tr>
<tr><td>3.3</td><td>ifend</td><td>3.4</td><td>ifend</td></tr>
<tr><td>3.4</td><td>read in *letter*</td><td>4</td><td>until *letter* = '*'</td></tr>
<tr><td>4</td><td>loopend</td><td>5.1</td><td>write out 'Number of occurrences of the
letter a is ' *count*</td></tr>
<tr><td>5.1</td><td>write out 'Number of occurrences of
the letter a is ' *count*</td><td></td><td></td></tr>
</table>

Data table

Identifier	Description	Type
letter	Character input by user	*char* variable
count	Count of occurrences of 'a'	*integer* variable

Test data

This should include instances where there are no letters 'a' in the input, inputs consisting entirely of letters 'a', and inputs of a mixture of letters including 'a'. You may also like to test whether your user input can be edited before pressing <ret>.

Problem 5.7

Problem statement

When economists are discussing inflation they often quote the *rule of 72*. This says that the period in which a fixed sum of money will decline to half its value is 72 div *rate* years, where *rate* is the annual rate of inflation. Test the accuracy of this rule by writing a program that will produce a table of the values of the precise number of years for the decline and 72 div *rate* for values of *rate* from 1 to 36 per cent.

Design

<table>
<tr><td colspan="2">{The rule of 72}</td><td colspan="2">{The rule of 72}</td></tr>
<tr><td>1.1</td><td>write out 'Rate ', 'Actual ', 'Estimate '</td><td>1.1</td><td>write out 'Rate ', 'Actual ', 'Estimate '</td></tr>
<tr><td>2.1</td><td>loop for *rate* := 1 to 36</td><td>2.1</td><td>loop for *rate* := 1 to 36</td></tr>
<tr><td>3.1</td><td>*value* := 100</td><td>3.1</td><td>*value* := 100</td></tr>
<tr><td>3.2</td><td>*ActualYrs* := 0</td><td>3.2</td><td>*ActualYrs* := 0</td></tr>
<tr><td>3.3</td><td>loop while *value* > 50</td><td>3.3</td><td>repeat</td></tr>
<tr><td>3.4</td><td>*value* := *value**(100 − *rate*)/100</td><td>3.4</td><td>*value* := *value**(100 − *rate*)/100</td></tr>
<tr><td>3.5</td><td>increment *ActualYrs*</td><td>3.5</td><td>increment *ActualYrs*</td></tr>
<tr><td>3.6</td><td>loopend</td><td>3.6</td><td>until *value* <= 50</td></tr>
<tr><td>4.1</td><td>write out *rate* , *ActualYrs*, 72 div *rate*</td><td>4.1</td><td>write out *rate* , *ActualYrs*, 72 div *rate*</td></tr>
<tr><td>5</td><td>loopend</td><td>5</td><td>loopend</td></tr>
</table>

Data table

Identifier	Description	Type
rate	Annual inflation rate	*integer* variable
value	Current value of fixed sum	*real* variable
ActualYrs	Actual years to depreciate to half value	*integer* variable

Test data

Aligning the output will be one challenge here. The values that ought to be produced will have to be calculated by hand and compared with those produced by the programs. The following is a partial list:

```
Rate  Actual  Estimate
  1     69       72
  2     35       36
  3     23       24
```

Problem 5.8

Problem statement

A modified version of the 'rule of 72' described in Problem 5.7 uses an estimation technique in which real division is used in preference to integer division. The real values are rounded to the nearest whole number, with a fractional part of 0.5 being rounded up. All other values are rounded down. Using this modified rule write a program that will output a table of all the rates from 1 to 36 per cent inclusive for which the actual number of years and the estimate differ. The table should include the rate of inflation, the actual number of years for the decline and the estimate of this number of years.

Design

	{The modified rule of 72}
1.1	write out 'The differences are:'
1.2	write out 'Rate ', 'Actual ', 'Estimate '
2.1	loop for *rate* := 1 to 36
3.1	*value* := 100
3.2	*ActualYrs* := 0
3.3	loop while *value* > 50
3.4	*value* := *value**(100 − *rate*)/100
3.5	increment *ActualYrs*
3.6	loopend
4.1	if 72/*rate* − 72 div *rate* >= 0.5 then
4.2	*estimate* := (72 div *rate*) + 1
4.3	else
4.4	*estimate* := 72 div *rate*
4.5	ifend
5.1	if *ActualYrs* <> *estimate* then
5.2	write out *rate*, *ActualYrs*, 72 div *rate*
5.3	ifend
6	loopend

	{The modified rule of 72}
1.1	write out 'The differences are:'
1.2	write out 'Rate ', 'Actual ', 'Estimate '
2.1	loop for *rate* := 1 to 36
3.1	*value* := 100
3.2	*ActualYrs* := 0
3.3	repeat
3.4	*value* := *value**(100 − *rate*)/100
3.5	increment *ActualYrs*
3.6	until *value* <= 50
4.1	if 72/*rate* − 72 div *rate* >= 0.5 then
4.2	*estimate* := (72 div *rate*) + 1
4.3	else
4.4	*estimate* := 72 div *rate*
4.5	ifend
5.1	if *ActualYrs* <> *estimate* then
5.2	write out *rate*, *ActualYrs*, 72 div *rate*
5.3	ifend
6	loopend

Test data

Some calculations by hand using specific rates will be required here. Rates of 1, 2, 3, 4, 11, 13, 16 and 29 produce different estimates from actual values.

Data table

Identifier	Description	Type
rate	Annual inflation rate	*integer* variable
value	Current value of fixed sum	*real* variable
ActualYrs	Actual years to depreciate to half value	*integer* variable
estimate	Estimated period to halve value	*integer* variable

Problem 5.9

Problem statement

Problems 3.6 and 3.7 were concerned with working out on which day of the week a given date falls. The output from the solutions was a code representing the day of the week: 0 for Sunday, 1 for Monday and so on. Modify the program of Problem 3.7 so that it outputs the name of the day of the week. The numbering we have used in the following design represents a refinement of step 5 of Problem 3.7. The same identifiers are used as before.

Design

```
5.1     if daycode = 0 then
5.2         write out 'Sunday'
5.3     else
5.4         if daycode = 1 then
5.5             write out 'Monday'
5.6         else
5.7             if daycode = 2 then
5.8                 write out 'Tuesday'
5.9             else
5.10                if daycode = 3 then
5.11                    write out 'Wednesday'
5.12                else
5.13                    if daycode = 4 then
5.14                        write out 'Thursday'
5.15                    else
5.16                        if daycode 5 then
5.17                            write out 'Friday'
5.18                        else
5.19                            write out 'Saturday'
5.20                        ifend
5.21                    ifend
5.22                ifend
5.23            ifend
5.24        ifend
5.25    ifend
```

Test data

The same test data as for Problem 3.7 is appropriate here.

Problem 5.10

Problem statement

Write a program that will prompt for and read in a string, which may contain multiple space characters between its words but which must terminate with a non-space character. The output from the design should be the input text with all multiple spaces replaced by single spaces.

Design

	{Remove multiple spaces: intermediate}
1.1	read in the text
1.2	initialize loop control variable
2	loop while *i* <= *length(paragraph)*
3.1	if *paragraph*[*i*] = *space* then
3.2	write *paragraph*[*i*]
3.3	skip space characters
3.4	else
3.5	write *paragraph*[*i*]
3.6	move to next character
3.7	ifend
4	loopend

	{Remove multiple spaces: final}
1.1	write out 'Enter text with multiple spaces'
1.2	write out 'Text must end with non-space'
1.3	read in *paragraph*
1.4	*i* := 1
2	loop while *i* <= *length(paragraph)*
3.1	if *paragraph*[*i*] = *space* then
3.2	write *paragraph*[*i*]
3.3.1	loop while *paragraph*[*i*] = *space*
3.3.2	increment *i*
3.3.3	loopend
3.4	else
3.5	write *paragraph*[*i*]
3.6	increment *i*
3.7	ifend
4	loopend

Data table

Identifier	Description	Type
space	The space character	*char* constant value '□'
paragraph	Input text	*string* variable
i	Loop control variable	*integer* variable

Test data

Strings containing single spaces between their words should not be altered by this program. Clearly, test data containing multiple spaces will be required. An input consisting of spaces followed by a single non-space is allowed and should be tested.

Problem 5.11

Problem statement

We have already seen a problem related to the word-processing facility of finding the average word length in a document. Here, we shall look at a simplified version of the problem of counting how many occurrences of a particular word there are in a piece of text. Write a program that will enable the user to enter a string from the keyboard and will output the number of occurrences of the pattern 'an'. You may assume that the user enters at least one character as input. You should not use the Boolean operator *and* in your solution.

Design

	{Occurrences of 'an' version 1}
1.1	*count* := 0
1.2	write 'Enter the string '
1.3	read in *sentence*
1.4	*previous* := *sentence*[1]
2.1	loop for *current* := 2 to *length(sentence)*
3.1	if *previous* = 'a' then
3.2	if *sentence*[*current*] = 'n' then
3.3	increment *count*
3.4	ifend
3.5	ifend
3.6	*previous* := *sentence*[*current*]
4	loopend
5.1	write out 'Number of occurrences is ' *count*

	{Occurrences of 'an' version 2}
1.1	*count* := 0
1.2	write 'Enter the string '
1.3	read in *sentence*
2.1	loop for *current* := 1 to *length(sentence)* −1
3.1	if *sentence*[*current*] = 'a' then
3.2	if *sentence*[*current* + 1] = 'n' then
3.3	increment *count*
3.4	ifend
3.5	ifend
4	loopend
5.1	write out 'Number of occurrences is ' *count*

Data table

Identifier	Description	Type
count	Occurrences of pattern 'an'	*integer* variable
sentence	Input string	*string* variable
previous	Character before one being currently examined	*char* variable
current	Index of character being currently examined	*integer* variable

Test data

Words having 0, 1 and more occurrences should be supplied as test data. Words do not have to be meaningful, so a test data value of 'ananan' can be used. The latter has the advantage of terminating with the pattern.

Problem 5.12

Problem statement

The Roman numerals corresponding to the numbers 1 to 9 are I, II, III, IV, V, VI, VII, VIII and IX. Decimal numbers between 5 and 8 have a Roman numeral form of 'V' followed by an appropriate number of 'I's and those between 1 and 3 consist only of 'I's. Write a program, based on the following design, that exploits this division to convert a decimal *number* in the range 1 to 9 to a string representing the roman numeral equivalent.

Design

```
        {convert a number in range 1 to 9 to Roman numeral}
1.1     write 'Enter an integer between 1 and 9'
1.2     read in number
1.3     roman := "
2       if number >= 5 then
3.1        if number = 9 then
3.2           roman := 'IX'
3.3        else
3.4           roman := 'V'
3.5           number := number − 5
3.6           loop while number > 0
3.7              roman := roman + 'I'
3.8              decrement number
3.9           loopend
3.10       ifend
4       else
5.1        if number = 4 then
5.2           roman := 'IV'
5.3        else
5.4           loop while number > 0
5.5              roman := roman + 'I'
5.6              decrement number
5.7           loopend
5.8        ifend
6       ifend
7       write out roman
```

Data table

Identifier	Description	Type
number	An integer in the range 1 to 9	*integer* variable
roman	Roman equivalent of *number*	*string* variable

Test data

Since there are only a small number of possible inputs, all of them should be tested here.

Problem 5.13

Problem statement

Problem 4.9 introduced a first step towards solving the problem of right-justifying a piece of text by looking at the simpler problem of inserting extra space characters into a string whenever a space character was encountered. The specification is now slightly changed so that the input string is permitted to have adjacent space characters. However, when this occurs only one extra space character is to be inserted into the string that forms the result. You may assume that the input string does not terminate in a space character, nor is it null.

Design

	{Insert extra space characters in a string with potential multiple spaces version 1}		{Insert extra space characters in a string with potential multiple spaces version 2}
1.1	write out 'Enter a string '	1.1	write out 'Enter a string '
1.2	read in *oldstring*	1.2	read in *oldstring*
1.3	*newstr* := ''	1.3	*newstr* := ''
1.4	*position* := 1	1.4	*openingspace* := (*oldstring*[1] = *space*)
2.1	loop while *position* <= *length*(*oldstring*)	2.1	loop for *position* := 1 to *length*(*oldstring*)
3.1	if *oldstring*[*position*] = *space* then	3.1	if *oldstring*[*position*] = *space* then
4.1	*newstr* := *newstr* + *space*	4.1	if *openingspace* then
5.1	loop while *oldstring*[*position*] = *space*	5.1	*newstr* := *newstr* + *space* + *space*
5.2	*newstr* := *newstr* + *space*	5.2	*openingspace* := false
5.3	increment *position*	6	else
5.4	loopend	7.1	*newstr* := *newstr* + *space*
6	else	8	ifend
7.1	*newstr* := *newstr* + *oldstring*[*position*]	9	else
8.1	increment *position*	10.1	*newstr* := *newstr* + *oldstring*[*position*]
9	ifend	10.2	*openingspace* := true
10	loopend	11	ifend
11	write out 'The new string is ', *newstr*	12	loopend
		13	write out 'The new string is ', *newstr*

Data table

Identifier	Description	Type
space	The space character	*char* constant value '□'
oldstring	User input string	*string* variable
position	Loop control variable	*integer* variable
newstr	String with extra spaces	*string* variable
openingspace	Flag denoting an opening space	*Boolean* variable

Test data

Values like 'a', 'a□b', 'a□b□□c', 'a□b□□c□□□d' should be included here. Since the string can start with spaces, strings like '□a', '□□a' are valid test data.

Problem 5.14

Problem statement

Write a program that will act as a ready reckoner to convert millimetres to feet and inches. The output should be a table in which the first column contains measurements of 100 millimetres up to 1 000 millimetres in increments of 100. The second and third columns should contain the equivalent measure in feet and inches. So, for example, 600 millimetres should appear in the table with the integer 1 in the foot column and a real number (approximately 11.6) in the inches column. (There are 12 inches in a foot, 1 inch = 25.4 millimetres.)

Design

	{Ready reckoner, millimetres to feet and inches}
1.1	write out 'Millimetres', 'Feet', 'Inches'
2.1	loop for $i := 1$ to 10
3.1	$millimetres := 100*i$
3.1	$inches := millimetres/25.4$
4.1	$wholefeet := 0$
4.2	loop while $inches >= 12$
4.3	increment $wholefeet$
4.4	$inches := inches - 12$
4.5	loopend
5.1	if $wholefeet > 0$ then
5.2	write out $millimetres, wholefeet, inches$
5.3	else
5.4	write out $millimetres,$ ' ', $inches$
5.5	ifend
6	loopend

Data table

Identifier	Description	Type
i	Loop control variable	*integer* variable
millimetres	Number of millimetres	*integer* variable
wholefeet	Number of feet	*integer* variable
inches	Number of inches	*real* variable

Test data
The program generates its own test data by virtue of the table it creates. A sample of values it produces should be tested for accuracy just to ensure that the conversion formula has been correctly implemented.

Problem 5.15

Problem statement
The process of counting occurrences of 'an' explained in Problem 5.11 could be performed dynamically, that is, as characters are entered from the keyboard. Write a program that performs this dynamic analysis where the user indicates termination of input with an asterisk.

Data table

Identifier	Description	Type
count	Occurrences of pattern 'an'	*integer* variable
previous	Character before one being currently examined	*char* variable
current	Character being examined	*char* variable

Test data
Similar data to that used in Problem 5.11 are appropriate here.

Design

We give two alternative designs:

	{Occurrences of 'an' from keyboard}			{Occurrences of 'an' from keyboard}
1.1	write 'Enter at least two characters. Terminated with * then <ret>'	1.1	write 'Enter at least two characters. Terminated with * then <ret>'
1.2	read in *previous*	1.2	read in *previous*
2.1	*count* := 0	2.1	*count* := 0
3.1	loop while *previous* <> '*'	3.1	repeat
4.1	read in *current*	4.1	read in *current*
4.2	if *previous* = 'a' then	4.2	if *previous* = 'a' then
5.1	if *current* = 'n' then	5.1	if *current* = 'n' then
5.2	increment *count*	5.2	increment *count*
5.3	ifend	5.3	ifend
5.4	ifend	5.4	ifend
5.5	*previous* := *current*	5.5	*previous* := *current*
6	loopend	6	until *previous* = '*'
7.1	write out 'Number of occurrences of an is ', *count*	7.1	write out 'Number of occurrences of an is ', *count*

Problem 5.16

Problem statement

A program is to be written that will provide a summary of a cricketer's batting performance over a season. As with many problems, you do not have to understand the game of cricket to reach a solution. If you are unfamiliar with the game, treat the problem as a challenge in which the specification tells you all you need to know to reach the solution. The output of the program will be of the form:

Innings	Not out	Runs	Average
24	4	1000	50.00

A cricketer who goes in to bat is called a batsman and is said to have started an innings. The objective for the batsman is to score *runs* during his innings. The innings may terminate in one of two ways: the batsman may be *out*, or his innings may close with him being *not out* (for example, if the weather intervenes and it is impossible to continue with the game). As with all sports, averages are important to the players. A cricketer's batting average is the total number of runs scored divided by the number of completed innings, where the number of completed innings is the number of innings minus the number of times the batsman was *not out*. It is possible for a cricketer to have batted several times and always to have been *not out*. In this case there are no completed innings, the average does not exist and so the abbreviation 'N/A' for Not Applicable should be output in the average column. It is also possible for a cricketer not to have batted at all, in which case the batting average is inappropriate and the message 'Did not bat' should be output instead of the data given in the example above. Data are to be entered into the machine as follows. The user is first to be prompted for the number of times the cricketer batted, that is, for the total number of innings. Then the score obtained for each of these innings should be entered. If the cricketer is 'not out' in an innings then the score for that innings should first be coded by having 1 000 added to it. The coded value should then be entered as the score for that *not out* innings.

Design

```
        {Prepare cricket batting averages}
1.1     notout := 0
1.2     runs := 0
1.3     write 'Enter number of innings '
1.4     read in innings
2.1     loop for i := 1 to innings
3.1        write 'Enter score for innings ', i, '. Enter score + 1000 for not out innings'
3.2        read in score
3.3        if score >= 1000 then
3.4           increment notout
3.5           runs := runs + score – 1000
3.6        else
3.7           runs := runs + score
3.8        ifend
4       loopend
5.1     if innings > 0 then
5.2        completed := innings – notout
5.3        if completed > 0 then
5.4           average := runs/completed
5.5           write out 'Innings   Not out   Runs    Average '
5.6           write out innings, notout, runs, average
5.7        else
5.8           write out 'Batsman scored ', runs, ' in ', innings, ' innings and was never out '
5.9        ifend
5.10    else
5.11       write out 'Cricketer did not bat'
5.12    ifend
```

Data table

Identifier	Description	Type
notout	Number of times 'not out'	*integer* variable
runs	Total runs scored	*integer* variable
innings	Total times batted	*integer* variable
i	Loop control variable	*integer* variable
score	Score for a single innings	*integer* variable
completed	Number of completed innings	*integer* variable
average	Average score over season	*real* variable

Test data

Data should be chosen for which a calculation by hand is not too difficult. In particular, all the different clauses of step 5 will need to be tested, and so data sets will need to be created that will ensure these are all tested. Some potential sets are:

Number of innings	Scores obtained (n.o. means not out)
0	No further inputs should be requested
1	0 n.o.
1	10 n.o.
1	10
2	20, 10 n.o.
2	20, 10
2	120, 20
2	100, 200

Problem 5.17

Problem statement

Easter in the Christian church falls on the first Sunday following the first full moon that occurs on or after 21 March. The algorithm below, attributed to Gauss, will calculate for a given *year* (>= 1583) a number, which we shall call *day*, representing the day on which Easter falls. We shall not give a derivation of this algorithm; you are asked to take it on trust. Indeed, there is no need for you to understand the details to attempt the problem.

If *day* <= 31 then Easter is on March *day*, otherwise it is on April (*day* − 31). The algorithm uses the following intermediate values to calculate *day*:

(a) *Century*: this is given by:

> (*year* div 100) + 1;

(b) *Golden*: this is the 'golden number', the number of the year in the 'Metonic cycle', and is used to determine the position of the calendar moon. Its formula is:

> (*year* mod 19) + 1;

(c) *Gregorian*: this is the 'Gregorian correction', and marks the years in which a leap year did not occur, for example, 1700, 1800, 1900, etc. The formula for this quantity is:

> (3*Century*) div 4 − 12;

(d) *Clavian*: this is the 'Clavian correction' for the Metonic cycle, and amounts to about eight days every 2 500 years. Its formula is:

> (8*Century* + 5) div 25 − 5 − *Gregorian*;

(e) *factor*: this is a variable used to store an intermediate value. It has no astronomical significance. Its formula is:

> (5*year*) div 4 − *Gregorian* − 10

(f) *Epact*: the **epact** is the age of the moon on 1 January, and is used to calculate when the full moon occurs. Its value is not given by a simple formula. First, evaluate the formula

> (11*Golden* + 20 + *Clavian*) mod 30

and assign the result to *Epact*. Then the revised value of *Epact* can be calculated from the following table:

Initial value of *temp*	Revised value of *Epact*
24	*Epact* + 1
25	*Epact* + 1 provided that *Gregorian* > 11
all other values	*Epact*

Write a program that writes out the dates of Easter for all the years from 1900 to 1999.

Design

```
        {Easter day for years 1900 to 1999}
1.1     loop for year := 1900 to 1999
2.1        Century := (year div 100) + 1
2.2        Golden := (year mod 19) + 1
2.3        Gregorian := (3*Century) div 4 − 12
2.4        Clavian := (8*Century + 5) div 25 − 5 − Gregorian
2.5        factor := (5*year) div 4 − Gregorian − 10
2.6        Epact := (11*Golden + 20 + Clavian) mod 30
2.7        if Epact = 24 then
2.8           Epact := Epact + 1
2.9        else
2.10          if Epact = 25 then
2.11             if Golden > 11 then
```

2.12	$Epact := Epact + 1$
2.13	ifend
2.16	ifend
2.17	ifend
2.18	$day := 44 - Epact$
2.19	if $day < 21$ then
2.20	$day := day + 30$
2.21	ifend
2.22	$day := day + 7 - (day + factor) \bmod 7$
3.1	if $day <= 31$ then
3.2	write out 'In ', *year*, 'Easter is on ', *day*, 'March'
3.3	else
3.4	write out 'In ', *year*, 'Easter is on ', *day*, 'April'
3.5	ifend
4	loopend

Data table

Identifier	Description	Type
year	Loop control variable	*integer* variable
Century	See above	*integer* variable
Golden	See above	*integer* variable
Gregorian	See above	*integer* variable
Clavian	See above	*integer* variable
factor	See above	*integer* variable
Epact	See above	*integer* variable
day	See above	*integer* variable

Test data

For testing purposes, the years for which Easter is calculated can be adjusted to recent ones. This involves altering the loop condition at step 1.1 to loop from, say, 1990 to 1999. The following table gives the value of *Epact* and the date on which Easter fell for four of the years in question.

Year	*Epact*	Easter
1990	3	15 April
1991	14	31 March
1992	26	19 April
1993	6	11 April

Problem 5.18

Problem statement

A test to help decide whether or not a certain author was responsible for writing a book that has lain undiscovered in an archive is to compare the frequency of occurrence of words of a given length in the book with the frequency of occurrence of words of the same length in an authenticated text. The test requires the book to be analysed to see how many words of various lengths it contains. In this problem we want you to count how many words of length 6 or more occur in a piece of text. For this problem a word is defined to be any sequence of non-space characters. The text is to be input from the keyboard into a string variable and the output is to be the count.

Design

```
        {How many words of 6 or more characters}
1.1     write 'Enter the text to be analysed '
1.2     read in paragraph
1.3     lettercount := 0
1.4     longcount := 0
2.1     loop for position := 1 to length(paragraph)
3.1       if paragraph[position] = space then
4.1         if lettercount >= 6 then
4.2           increment longcount
4.3         ifend
4.4         lettercount := 0
5         else
6.1         increment lettercount
7         ifend
8       loopend
9.1     if lettercount >= 6 then {check last word}
9.2       increment longcount
9.3     ifend
9.4     write out 'The text had ', longcount, ' words with 6 or more letters'
```

Data table

Identifier	Description	Type
space	Constant definition	*char* constant value '□'
paragraph	Input text	*string* variable
lettercount	Number of letters in current word	*integer* variable
longcount	Number of words with 6 or more characters	*integer* variable
position	Loop control variable	*integer* variable

Test data

This will need to include data sets which have no words of exactly six characters; a set which has one word of exactly six characters; a set which has one word of more than six characters; a set with two words of exactly six characters; a set with one word of exactly six characters and one word of more than six characters, and so on.

Problem 5.19

Problem statement

Problem 5.4 was concerned with writing out a piece of text, each sentence beginning on a new line. In this problem, the specification is modified as follows. Each line of output must begin with a non-space character and words must be separated by single-space characters. This means that any leading space characters are not output and multiple spaces between words are to be output as a single-space character. You may assume that the input string terminates with a full stop. Thus, if the input line is:

'□□New□sentences□□go□on□new□lines.□□Leading□and□□multiple□spaces□are□output□□as□
single□spaces.□□□Input□must□□terminate□with□□a□full□stop.'

then the output should be:

New□sentences□go□on□new□lines.   •
Leading□and□multiple□spaces□are□output□as□single□spaces.
Input□must□terminate□with□a□full□stop.

Design

```
        {Output sentences on a new line}
1.1.1   write 'Enter the text '
1.1.2   read in paragraph
1.1.3   i := 1
1.2.1   loop while paragraph[i] = space
1.2.2      increment i
1.2.3   loopend
2.1.1   loop while i <= length(paragraph)
3.1.1      if paragraph[i] = fullstop then
3.2.1         write out fullstop
3.2.2         increment i
3.3.1         if i < length(paragraph) then
3.4.1            loop while paragraph[i] = space
3.4.2               increment i
3.4.3            loopend
3.5           ifend
3.6        else
3.7.1         if paragraph[i] = space then
3.8.1            write space
3.9.1            repeat
3.9.2               increment i
3.9.3            until paragraph[i] <> space
3.10          else
3.11.1           write paragraph[i]
3.12.1           increment i
3.13          ifend
3.14       ifend
4       loopend
```

Data table

Identifier	Description	Type
fullstop	The full stop character	*char* constant value '.'
space	The space character	*char* constant value '□'
paragraph	Input text	*string* variable
i	Loop control variable	*integer* variable

Test data

This will have to take account of the new specification, and so the test data of Problem 5.4 will have to be enhanced with data which test these new features. In particular, inputs which have leading space characters and multiple spaces between words will have to be included.

Problem 5.20

Problem statement

Generalize Problem 5.11 to the situation where the pattern being searched for is 'the'. You may assume that the user inputs at least two characters.

Design

    {Count occurrences of 'the' in input string}

1.1   *count* := 0
1.2   write 'Enter the string '
1.3   read in *sentence*
1.4   *first* := *sentence*[1]
1.5   *second* := *sentence*[2]
2.1   loop for *current* := 3 to *length*(*sentence*)
3.1   if *first* = 't' then
3.2   if *second* = 'h' then
3.3   if *sentence*[*current*] = 'e' then
3.4   increment *count*
3.5   ifend
3.6   ifend
3.7   ifend
3.8   *first* := *second*
3.9   *second* := *sentence*[*current*]
4   loopend
5.1   write out 'Number of occurrences is ', *count*

Data table

Identifier	Description	Type
count	Occurrences of pattern 'the'	*integer* variable
sentence	Input string	*string* variable
first	First character of the 3 currently being examined	*char* variable
second	Second character of 3 currently being examined	*char* variable
current	Index of the third character being examined	*integer* variable

Test data

This should include words like theatre, which contains an occurrence, and words like thyme, which does not.

Problem 5.21

Problem statement

The input in Problem 5.13 could well have started with a sequence of space characters. Typically, this would happen on the first line of a new paragraph. When this occurs the initial spaces are not normally adjusted when the text is justified. Modify the design from Problem 5.13 so that any initial space characters are left unaltered, whereas subsequent ones are dealt with as before. You may assume that the input contains at least one non-space character.

    The same designs as those used in Problem 5.13 will work here except for a modification to their initialization step 1. Each of the alternatives would need to be refined as follows. (*start* is an integer variable.)

Data table

Identifier	Description	Type
start	value of a cheque	*integer* variable

Test data

The same test data can be used as in Problem 5.13, but the output for values that have leading space characters will be different.

Design

{Insert extra space characters in a string with potential multiple spaces}

1.1	write out 'Enter the string '
1.2	read in *oldstring*
1.3	*newstr* := ''
1.4	*position* := 1
1.5	loop while *oldstring*[*position*] = *space*
1.6	*newstr* := *newstr* + *space*
1.7	increment *position*
1.8	loopend
2.1	{As in Problem 5.13}

{Insert extra space characters in a string with potential multiple spaces}

1.1	write out 'Enter the string '
1.2	read in *oldstring*
1.3	*newstr* := ''
1.4	*start* := 1
1.5	loop while *oldstring*[*start*] = *space*
1.6	*newstr* := *newstr* + *space*
1.7	increment *start*
1.8	loopend
1.9	*openingspace* := (*oldstring*[*start*] = *space*)
2.1	loop for *position* := *start* to *length*[*oldstring*]
2.2	{As in Problem 5.13}

Problem 5.22

Problem statement

The specification of Problem 4.8 is now changed so that a more general input string is permitted. Here, the input may have adjacent space characters and may begin with spaces. However, it should terminate with a non-space character. The output is to be as before, namely, the average length of the words in the input.

Design

1.1	write out 'Enter your line of text terminating in a non-space character'
1.2	read in *line*
2.1	*index* := 1
2.2	*wordcount* := 0
2.3	*lettercount* := 0
3.1	loop while *line*[*index*] = *space* {skip initial spaces}
3.2	increment *index*
3.3	loopend
4.1	loop while *index* <= *length*(*line*)
5.1	if *line*[*index*] = *space* then
6.1	increment *wordcount* {because word has just ended}
7.1	loop while *line*[*index*] = *space* {skip any multiple spaces}
7.2	increment *index*
7.3	loopend
8	else
9.1	increment *lettercount*
10.1	increment *index*
11	ifend
12	loopend
13.1	increment *wordcount* {count the last word of input}
13.2	*average* := *lettercount*/*wordcount*
13.3	write out 'Average word length is ', *average*

Data table

Identifier	Description	Type
space	Space character	*char* constant value '□'
line	A line of text	*string* variable
index	Loop control variable	*integer* variable
wordcount	Number of words in line	*integer* variable
lettercount	Number of letters in line	*integer* variable
average	Average word length	*real* variable

Test data
The average should not include the space characters. Test data should contain inputs each of which consist of a single word but which have zero, one or many preceding spaces. Similar data should be created with two words, where the number of preceding and interword spaces is changed in a similar way.

Problem 5.23

Problem statement
It is hypothesized that in the English language the letter *c* precedes the letter *k* more often than any other letter. Write a program that will enable a user to test this hypothesis against a particular piece of text input as a string. The output of the program should be a message saying whether there were more, an equal number, or fewer occurrences of *ck* than of *k* preceded by any other letter.

Design

1.1	write out 'Enter text'		1.1	write out 'Enter text'
1.2	read in *sample*		1.2	read in *sample*
1.3	*index* := 1		1.3	*index* := 1
1.4	*ckcount* := 0		1.4	*ckcount* := 0
1.5	*anykcount* := 0		1.5	*anykcount* := 0
2.1	loop while *index* < *length*(*sample*)		2.1	loop while *index* < *length*(*sample*)
3.1	if *sample*[*index*] = 'c' then		3.1	if *sample*[*index* + 1] = 'k' then
4.1	if *sample*[*index* + 1] = 'k' then		4.1	if *sample*[*index*] = 'c' then
4.2	increment *ckcount*		4.2	increment *ckcount*
4.3	ifend		4.3	else
5	else		4.4	increment *anykcount*
6.1	if *sample*[*index* + 1] = 'k' then		4.5	ifend
6.2	increment *anykcount*		5	ifend
6.3	ifend		6	increment *index*
7	ifend		7	loopend
8.1	increment *index*		8.1	if *ckcount* < *anykcount* then
9	loopend		8.2	write out 'ck is less frequent than *k'
10.1	if *ckcount* < *anykcount* then		8.3	else
10.2	write out 'ck is less frequent than *k'		8.4	if *ckcount* > *anykcount* then
10.3	else		8.5	write out 'ck is more frequent than *k'
10.4	if *ckcount* > *anykcount* then		8.6	else
10.5	write out 'ck is more frequent than *k'		8.7	write out 'There is no difference'
10.6	else		8.8	ifend
10.7	write out 'There is no difference'		8.9	ifend
10.8	ifend			
10.9	ifend			

Data table

Identifier	Description	Type
space	The space character	*char* constant value '□'
sample	The input string	*string* variable
index	Index of first of character pair	*integer* variable
ckcount	Count of occurrences of *ck*	*integer* variable
anykcount	Count of any letter then *k*	*integer* variable

Test data
This does not have to consist of real words. Essentially, what need to be tested are

combinations of letters involving k, some preceded by c and others not. Input values could include the following: 'ak', 'ck', 'ckk', 'kkc', 'akk', 'ack' and so on.

Problem 6.1

Problem statement

In this problem we shall simulate the memory of a computer by an array called *memory,* indexed 1..*maxsize* of base type *integer*, where *maxsize* is the integer constant value 400. A common memory management task is to fill parts of memory with a certain fixed value. The task here is to write a program corresponding to the design below to do this, subject to the following constraints. The user is to be prompted for the initial and final addresses (in our simulation, index numbers) of the portion of memory to be filled. You may assume that both user inputs are integers and do lie in the range 1 to *maxsize*, but you should not assume that the final address exceeds the initial address. If it does not, an error message should be generated and the program should terminate, otherwise a request for the fixed value with which the locations should be filled should be made. This value should then be assigned to the appropriate locations. If the final address equals the initial address, the input is valid.

Design

```
        {Fill a memory address range with a value}
1.1     write 'Enter initial address of range to be filled '
1.2     read in initial
1.3     write 'Enter final address of range to be filled '
1.4     read in final
2.1     if initial <= final then
3.1        write 'Value to fill memory is? '
3.2        read in FillValue
4.1        loop for i := initial to final
4.2           memory[i] := FillValue
4.3        loopend
5       else
6          write out 'Initial address is larger than final address'
7       ifend
```

Data table

Identifier	Description	Type
maxsize	Array index upper bound	*integer* constant value 400
memorytype	Array type definition	array[1..*maxsize*] of *integer*
memory	Array simulating machine memory	*memorytype* variable
initial	First address of range to be filled	*integer* variable
final	Last address of memory to be filled	*integer* variable
FillValue	Value to fill range	*integer* variable
i	Loop control variable	*integer* variable

Test data

For testing the constant value, *maxsize* can be altered to something more manageable, say, 10. An additional piece of code will be needed to ascertain the values in the array after the user input. Note that elements other than those in the input range will remain uninitialized.

Problem 6.2

Problem statement

This problem is based on the same memory model as that in Problem 6.1. Another memory management task is to move a range of memory contents to another location. Write a program fragment to the design below to do this, subject to the following constraints. The user is to be prompted for the initial and final addresses, which are subject to the same validation as described in Problem 6.1, with program termination for invalid inputs. For a valid input range the user should be prompted for the start address of the destination. If there is room for the values between the destination and *maxsize*, then the contents should be moved accordingly. Otherwise, a suitable message should be output.

Design

	{Move a range of memory}
1.1	write 'Enter initial address of range to be filled '
1.2	read in *initial*
1.3	write 'Enter final address of range to be filled '
1.4	read in *final*
2.1	if *initial* <= *final* then
3.1	write 'Enter the destination start address '
3.2	read in *destination*
4.1.1	if (*destination* + *final* − *initial*) <= *maxsize* then {move is possible}
5.1.1	if *destination* < *initial* then {move in normal order}
5.2.1	loop for $i := 0$ to (*final* − *initial*)
5.2.2	memory[*destination* + i] := memory[*initial* + i]
5.2.3	loopend
5.3	else {move in reverse order}
5.4.1	loop for $i :=$ (*final* − *initial*) downto 0
5.4.2	memory[*destination* + i] := memory[*initial* + i]
5.4.3	loopend
5.5	ifend
6	else {move is not possible}
7.1	write out 'Out of memory with that destination'
8	ifend
9	else
10.1	write out 'Initial value cannot be larger than final value of range'
11	ifend

Data table

Identifier	Description	Type
maxsize	Array index upper bound	*integer* constant value 400
memorytype	Array type definition	array[1..*maxsize*] of *integer*
memory	Array simulating machine memory	*memorytype* variable
initial	First address of range to be moved	*integer* variable
final	Last address of memory to be moved	*integer* variable
destination	Address to which range to be moved	*integer* variable
i	Loop control variable	*integer* variable

Test data

In the following description the source range refers to the elements being moved. The following situations will need to be tested:

(a) The destination value precedes the initial value of the source range, and none of the source range elements will be overwritten as a result of the move.

(b) The destination value precedes the initial value of the source range, but some of the source range elements will be overwritten as a result of the move.

(c) The destination value comes after the final value of the source range, and there is room at that destination.

(d) The destination value is the initial value of the source range (results in nothing moved).

(e) The destination value comes in the middle of the source range, and there is room at that destination.

(f) The destination value is the final value of the source range, and there is room for the move at that destination.

(g) The destination value results in there being insufficient room for the move.

Problem 6.3

Problem statement

Assuming that the array *authors*, indexed 1..*maxsize* of type *string* has been initialized, write a program fragment for the design below which will output the element that precedes all the others in alphanumeric ordering.

Design

```
      {Find least element of array}
1.1   least := authors[1]
2.1   loop for i := 2 to maxsize
3.1      if authors[i] < least then
4.1         least := authors[i]
4.2      ifend
5     loopend
6.1   write out 'Least element is ' least
```

Data table

Identifier	Description	Type
maxsize	Size of the array *authors*	*integer* constant value 100
authortype	Array type definition	array[1..*maxsize*] of *string*
authors	Array of names of authors	*authortype* variable
least	Least element of *authors*	*string* variable
i	Loop control variable	*integer* variable

Test data

The array *authors* needs to be initialized in order to test the program. For testing purposes, the value of *maxsize* can be set to a value smaller than 100. Again, for simplicity the values stored do not have to be real names. In the test data lists below we have used two character strings. Possible test values for the array when *maxsize* is set to 5 are:

(a) AA AB AC AD AE {The least value occurs at index 1}
(b) AF AB AA AD AE {The least value occurs in the middle of the array}
(c) AE AB AC AD AA {The least value occurs at the highest index}
(d) AA AB AA AD AE {The least value occurs at index 1 but is not unique}
(e) AB AB AA AD AB {There are repeats of non-least values}

Problem 6.4

Problem statement

A common operation in computing is the **sorting** of data into a significant order such as numerical or alphabetical. Searching for a particular item of data is quicker when the data are sorted than when they are unsorted, because there are very efficient methods for searching sorted data. However, the drawback of using these methods is that the data have to be sorted first. One step in a sort might be to merge two data sets which are themselves in order. Write a program fragment to the design below that will merge two sorted arrays into a sorted array. You may assume that the sorted arrays are indexed 1..*maxsize*, are initialized with integer elements, and that they are to be merged into an array indexed 1..2*maxsize*.

Design

```
          {Merge two sorted arrays}
1.1       index1 := 1
1.2       index2 := 1
1.3       MergedIndex := 1
1.4       exhaustedflag := false
2         repeat
3.1         if sorted1[index1] < sorted2[index2] then
3.2           merged[MergedIndex] := sorted1[index1]
3.3           increment index1
3.4           exhaustedflag := (index1 > maxsize)
3.5         else
3.6           merged[MergedIndex] := sorted2[index2]
3.7           increment index2
3.8           exhaustedflag := (index2 > maxsize)
3.9         ifend
3.10        increment MergedIndex
4         until exhaustedflag
5.1       if index1 > maxsize then
5.2         loop for i := index2 to maxsize    {copy remaining elements of sorted2}
5.3           merged[MergedIndex] := sorted2[i]
5.4           increment MergedIndex
5.5         loopend
5.6       else
5.7         loop for i := index1 to maxsize    {copy remaining elements of sorted1}
5.8           merged[MergedIndex] := sorted1[i]
5.9           increment MergedIndex
5.10        loopend
5.11      ifend
```

Data table

Identifier	Description	Type
maxsize	Constant definition	*integer* constant
smalltype	Array type definition	array[1..*maxsize*] of *integer*
largetype	Array type definition	array[1..2*maxsize*] of *integer*
sorted1	First sorted array	*smalltype* variable
sorted2	Second sorted array	*smalltype* variable
index1	Current position in *sorted1*	*integer* variable
index2	Current position in *sorted2*	*integer* variable
merged	The merged array	*largetype* variable
MergedIndex	Current position in *merged*	*integer* variable
exhaustedflag	Flags one of the sorted arrays as exhausted	*Boolean* variable
i	Loop control variable	*integer* variable

Test data

For the purposes of testing, *maxsize* can be chosen to be a small value. In the example test data sets below, the value chosen is 6. In each case the first list refers to *sorted1* and the second to *sorted2*.

(a)   3   5   7   12   23   35
       2   4   8   11   15   16
     The sort starts by taking a value from *sorted2* and finishes with a value from *sorted1*.

(b)   2   5   7   12   23   25
       3   4   8   11   15   26
     The sort starts by taking a value from *sorted1* and finishes with a value from *sorted2*.

(c)   1   2   3   4   5   6
     10   11   12   13   14   15
     All the values of *sorted1* precede those in *sorted2*.

(d)   10   11   12   13   14   15
       1   2   3   4   5   6
     All the values of *sorted2* precede those in *sorted1*.

(e)   1   2   3   4   5   6
       1   2   3   4   5   6
     The values in the two arrays are the same.

Problem 6.5

Problem statement

Word processors often have a spelling check option so that a document can be scanned and incorrectly spelled words identified. A difficulty with spelling checkers is that many documents contain technical terms which we cannot expect to be included in the word processor's general-purpose dictionary. One way of overcoming this is to allow the user to generate what is often called a user dictionary, into which technical and specialized words can be inserted. The user dictionary is created in a file and so contains a permanent record of specialist words. However, the user may not always want to insert a specialist word into the user dictionary because some words, like proper names, may only arise in the current document. To cater for this, on the first encounter with a word that is neither in the main nor the user dictionary, the word processor will ask the user to confirm that it is spelled correctly. If so, the word is stored dynamically, in main memory. It then becomes part of the dictionary available to the word processor for checking the remainder of the document. The dynamically stored data can then be used as a temporary dictionary throughout the remainder of the document. In this problem we are going to model this dynamic part of a spelling checker by assuming that the dynamic dictionary is held in main memory as an array. Your task is to check this array to see if it contains a specified word. To make the problem more self-contained we shall make the assumption that the word whose spelling is to be checked is input from the keyboard. The result of the search will be a message output to the screen that reports whether or not the word is in the dictionary. You may assume that the array in which the words are stored is called *dictionary*, that it is indexed from 0, and that the elements 1 to *size* contain words (so that index zero represents a dummy element).

Design

       {Check spelling of a word from an array dictionary}
1.1   write out 'Enter required word'
1.2   read in *word*
1.3   *dictionary*[0] := *word*
1.4   *index* := *size*

2.1	loop while *dictionary[index]* <> *word*	
3.1	decrement *index*	
4	loopend	
5.1	if *index* = 0 then	
5.2	write out 'The word is not in the dictionary'	
5.3	else	
5.4	write out 'The word is correctly spelled'	
5.5	ifend	

Data table

Identifier	Description	Type
dictionary	Dictionary array	array[0..100] of *string* variable
size	Number of entries in the dictionary	*integer* variable (set before this extract)
word	Word whose spelling is to be checked	*string* variable
index	Loop control variable	*integer* variable

Test data

The array dictionary will have to be initialized to test this program. A small number of words only are required. For the following test data the first four values of the dictionary have been initialized and their values are: 'AA', 'AB', 'AC', 'AD'. (Note that it is not necessary to use real words!)

(a)   AA   {Tests that the first in the list can be found}
(b)   AD   {Tests that the last in the list can be found}
(c)   AC   {Tests that a non-end value can be found}
(d)   ZZ   {Tests that a value which does not exist results in correct output}.

Problem 6.6

Problem statement

A business has a small telephone exchange that requires some of its users to share an extension. A telephone directory is printed as a list, part of which is shown below.

Name	Extension
Bradford	13
Farmer	10
Fisher	13

The list is to be represented by two parallel arrays, both indexed 1..*maxsize*, where *maxsize* is an integer constant with value 100. The array *name* is to hold the names, and *ext* is to hold the telephone extension data in parallel. So, for example, *name*[2] will hold the name Farmer and *ext*[2] the extension 10. Write a program that will enable a user to enter a telephone extension and will output the names of all people who use that extension. If no such extension exists, then a suitable message should be output instead.

Design

	{Write out names which have given number of ext}	
1.1	write 'Enter the extension '	
1.2	read in *searchitem*	
1.3	*flag* := false	
2.1	loop for *i* := 1 to *maxsize*	
3.1	if *ext*[*i*] = *searchitem* then	
3.2	write out *name*[*i*]	
3.3	*flag* := true	

```
3.4      ifend
4        loopend
5.1      if flag = false then
5.2          write out 'There were no names having that extension'
5.3      ifend
```

Data table

Identifier	Description	Type
maxsize	Array index upper bound	*integer* constant value 100
searchitem	The extension for which the names are sought	*integer* variable
name	Array of names	array[0..*maxsize*] of *string* variable
ext	Parallel array of extensions	array[0..*maxsize*] of *integer* variable
i	Loop control variable	*integer* variable
flag	Set true if match found	*Boolean* variable

Test data

Both arrays will need to be initialized for testing, but *maxsize* can be set to a value smaller than 100 for this purpose. Initial values should be chosen so that there are repetitions in the array *ext*. Test values should include numbers that are not in the list as well as those that are.

Problem 6.7

Problem statement

This problem is based upon Problem 6.5. A more advanced facility offered by some spelling checkers is to suggest some words when it believes the original word is incorrectly spelled. Spelling checkers can never be sure a word *is* incorrect because the dictionaries they contain are relatively small. But when a word is encountered that is not in the dictionary the spelling checker can try to offer alternative suggestions. In this problem we shall consider a very simplistic model of this suggestion process. The specification is as in Problem 6.5 except that if a word is not in the dictionary then the output should consist of all words whose initial two letters are the same as the first two letters of the searched-for word. If there are no words in the dictionary satisfying this constraint then a message should be output saying that no suggestions are possible. This matching process implies that both the input word and all the words in the dictionary consist of at least two characters, you may assume that this is the case. Write a program based on the design of Problem 6.5 but with the following amended step 5:

Design

```
5.1      if index = 0 then
5.2.1        CantSuggest := true
5.2.2        loop for index := 1 to size
5.2.3            if word[1] = dictionary[index][1] then
5.2.4                if word[2] = dictionary[index][2] then
5.2.5                    write out dictionary[index]
5.2.6                    CantSuggest := false
5.2.7                ifend
5.2.8            ifend
5.2.9        loopend
5.2.10       if CantSuggest then
5.2.11           write out 'Sorry – cannot suggest an alternative '
5.2.12   ifend
```

5.3   else
5.4   write out 'The word is correctly spelled'
5.5   ifend

Data table

Identifier	Description	Type
CantSuggest	Flag set false when suggestion has been made	*Boolean* variable

Test data
We shall use a slightly different set of values in the dictionary to test this code. The values will be 'AAA', 'ABC', 'ACD', 'ABE'. They are chosen so that there are two words with the same two initial letters. Test data should include the following:

(a)   AAA   {Tests that an existing word can be found}
(b)   AA   {Tests that the word AAA is suggested}
(c)   AB   {Tests that both words ABC and ABE are suggested}
(d)   ZZ   {Tests that a value which does not exist results in correct output}.

Problem 6.8

Problem statement
When printing a book, a typesetter has to keep an eye open for the appearance of 'rivers' – apparent streaks of white appearing on the page. These are formed by the spaces between the words of the text. If two or three lines of text all have a space character in roughly the same position then the reader appears to see a white river within the page. The text below has several rivers:

```
We have\ printed this very
narrow in\order to
demonstrate\that rivers are
very prone to\occur when
using a narrow\ page.
However\ rivers| can occur
on\ wider| pages/ but they
are\ more/likely/ to occur
on/ narrow margins like
this.
```

In this problem we are going to develop a program to the design below for identifying rivers, but on a much simplified scale. A **river** will be defined as any sequence of two or more spaces aligned vertically. The page of text will be represented as a two-dimensional array of *char*, in which the first index will be used to denote the number of the line and the second the position of the character within that line. The program is to output the coordinates, that is, the line number and character position, of the start and finish of all the rivers on the page. The design below assumes the array is already initialized.

Design
        {Find rivers in text}
1.1   loop for *col* := 1 to *maxcols*
2.1.1   *riverlength* := 0
2.2.1   loop for *row* := 1 to *maxrows*
2.3.1   if page[*row*, *col*] = '□' then
2.4.1   increment *riverlength*

2.5	else	{a river may have just ended so test for this}
2.6.1	if *riverlength* > 1 then	{current value of row is 1 beyond the end of river}
2.7.1	write out 'There is a river from ', *row − riverlength*, *col* , ' to ', *row* − 1, *col*	
2.8.1	*riverlength* := 0	
2.9	ifend	
2.10	ifend	
2.11	loopend	
2.12	if *riverlength* > 1 then	{river may terminate in last row so test for this}
2.13	write out 'There is a river from ', *maxrows − riverlength* + 1, *col*, ' to ', *maxrows*, *col*	
2.14	ifend	
3	loopend	

Data table

Identifier	Description	Type
maxrows	Number of lines on the *page*	*integer* constant
maxcols	Number of characters per line	*integer* constant
page	Page of text	array[1..*maxrows*, 1..*maxcols*] of *string* variable
col	Loop control variable	*integer* variable
row	Loop control variable	*integer* variable
riverlength	Length of a river	*integer* variable

Test data

The values of *maxrows* and *maxcols* should be chosen to be small to ease the difficulties of testing. Data need to be generated for text which has rivers and that which does not. Rivers which terminate in the last row should be included as test data. You should also create data with adjacent rivers. The coordinates output will need to be checked for accuracy.

Problem 6.9

Problem statement

Dot matrix printers use pins in the print-head mechanism that are fired at the printer ribbon, thereby making the imprint of a dot on the page. By arranging these dots in a pattern, letters can be formed. The number of dots used to form each letter varies, but as the number increases there is generally an improvement in the quality of letter produced. Typically, each letter is formed on a nine row by seven column matrix. We have drawn some examples below:

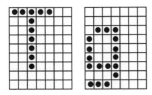

In this representation the last two columns have been reserved and left blank for the space between letters. In this problem we shall simulate the process of producing a single character by representing it using a two-dimensional array of *Boolean*. The value true will represent the presence of a dot, and the value false its absence. The output should be a single letter occupying seven columns and nine rows of the screen, and so will be a magnified version of the character being represented. The output should be similar to the examples above but without the grid lines. The design below assumes the array has already been initialized.

Design
```
        {Array representation of dot matrix letters}
1.1     initialize array elements
2.1     loop for row := 1 to 9
3.1        loop for column := 1 to 7
4.1           if dots[row, column] then
4.2              write dot
4.3           else
4.4              write space
4.5           ifend
5          loopend
6.1        write out          {Move to a new line}
7       loopend
```

Data table

Identifier	Description	Type
dot	The character representing a dot	*char* constant value '*'
space	The space character	*char* constant value '□'
dots	Array holding letter representation	array[1..9, 1..7] of *Boolean* variable
row	Row loop control variable	*integer* variable
column	Column loop control variable	*integer* variable

Test data
This simply requires the array to be initialized in a way that represents a letter.

Problem 6.10

Problem statement
Computer printout from a data-processing department often has the title of the document printed out using 'big' letters similar to the illustration below. The reason for this is that line printers only output characters of one size. Therefore, to create document headings at a large size, large letters are used.

	A	A	
A			A
A	A	A	A
A			A
A			A

This particular diagram represents a large capital 'A'. It has five rows and four columns, but usually more would be used. The symbol that makes up the shape is itself a capital 'A'. In this problem you are to represent this letter using a two-dimensional array. You are to write a program to initialize the array and then write out the contents so that a 'big' letter will be formed.

Design
```
        {Write out A}
1.1   letter[1,1] := '□'   1.2   letter[1,2] := 'A'   1.3   letter[1,3] := 'A'   1.4   letter[1,4] := '□'
1.5   letter[2,1] := 'A'   1.6   letter[2,2] := '□'   1.7   letter[2,3] := '□'   1.8   letter[2,4] := 'A'
1.9   letter[3,1] := 'A'   1.10  letter[3,2] := 'A'   1.11  letter[3,3] := 'A'   1.12  letter[3,4] := 'A'
```

1.13	*letter*[4,1] := 'A'	1.14	*letter*[4,2] := '□'	1.15	*letter*[4,3] := '□'	1.16	*letter*[4,4] := 'A'
1.17	*letter*[5,1] := 'A'	1.18	*letter*[5,2] := '□'	1.19	*letter*[5,3] := '□'	1.20	*letter*[5,4] := 'A'

```
2.1   loop for row := 1 to 5
3.1      loop for col := 1 to 4
4.1         write letter[row, col]
5        loopend
6.1      write out
7        loopend
```

Data table

Identifier	Description	Type
letter	Array representation of big character	array[1..5, 1..4] of *char* variable
row	Loop control variable	*integer* variable
col	Loop control variable	*integer* variable

Test data
The data for this program are fixed by the way the array is initialized.

Problem 6.11

Problem statement
Define an array that will enable the information in the table, part of which is shown below, to be represented. You should use a constant definition for the upper bound of the index range whose value should be set to 100. A type definition should be used for the records representing the rows.

Holiday area	Number of people	Type of car	Number of doors	Cost per week
Costa Blanca	1 to 4	VW Polo	3	£73
Costa Blanca	5	Seat Ronda	5	£105
Portugal	1 to 5	Renault 5	3	£73
Portugal	6 to 8	Two Metros	3	£135

Problem 6.12

Problem statement
The diagram below shows part of a table of computer systems and their prices. The model number is a unique identifier and the complete table has 100 entries.

Model number	Memory (K)	Floppy disk size (K)	Colour monitor option	Price
PC88C	640	360/720	yes	£775
PC1512D	512	360	no	£495
PC88S	640	360/720	yes	£825
PC1640	640	360	yes	£550

The table is to be represented as an array of records in no particular order. Write a program that will enable a user to enter a model number and will produce as output either all the details of that model listed in the table, or a message saying that the model number does not exist. You may assume that the structure holding the data has been initialized appropriately.

Design

```
          {Search for model number}
1.1       write out 'Enter model number '
1.2       read in searchmodel
1.3       table[0].model := searchmodel
1.4       index := size
2.1       loop while searchmodel <> table[index].model
3.1          decrement index
4         loopend
5.1       if index = 0 then
5.2          write out 'No data for that model'
5.3       else
5.4          with table[index] do
5.5             write model, memory, disk
5.6             if colour then
5.7                write ' colour option available '
5.8             else
5.9                write ' colour option not available '
5.10            ifend
5.11            write out price
5.12         withend
5.13      ifend
```

Data table

Identifier	Description		Type
size	Constant definition		integer constant value 100
rowtype	Record type definition		
	model	{Model number}	string variable
	memory	{Size of memory}	integer variable
	disk	{Disk capacity}	string variable
	colour	{Colour option}	Boolean variable
	price	{Price of model}	real variable
	recordend		
table	Array of records		array[0..size] of rowtype variable
searchmodel	Item to be found		string variable
index	Loop control variable		integer variable

Test data

This will involve entering data to test the search. This is probably best done by adding initialization code to the program. To minimize the effort involved, *size* can be chosen to be relatively small. Searches should be carried out to find the first entry in the array, the last entry and a middle entry. This implies that *size* should not have a value lower than 3.

Problem 6.13

Problem statement

Write a program that will enable the table in Problem 6.12 to be searched on the memory field. The user is to input a memory size, and the output of the program should be a list of all models having a memory size greater than or equal to that specified by the user. If no machine has this property then a suitable message should be written out.

Design

1.1	write out 'Enter size of memory required '
1.2	read in *memorysize*
1.3	*found* := false
2.1	loop for *index* := 1 to *size*
3.1	if *table*[*index*].*memory* >= *memorysize* then
3.2	write out *table*[*index*].*model*, ' has a memory of at least ', *memorysize*
3.3	*found* := true
3.4	ifend
4	loopend
5.1	if *found* = false then
5.2	write out 'No model has that size of memory'
5.3	ifend

Data table (Addition to Problem 6.12)

Identifier	Description	Type
memorysize	Memory size to be searched	*integer* variable
found	Flag indicating match	*Boolean* variable
index	Loop control variable	*integer* variable

Test data

The values of memory should be initialized so that they include repeats. The test data should then include searches that seek these repeat values as well as data that search for unique and non-existent values.

Problem 6.14

Problem statement

Libraries which have computerized record systems often keep a key word index of the book titles. Indeed, articles in journals are also kept in a key word index. The purpose of such an index is to enable users to find books or articles related to some key word. So, for example, if a user is interested in ornithology, a key word search of the index would list all works which included the word ornithology in their titles. We shall illustrate a key word index on the following titles:

> Introduction to Programming and Computer Science
> Software Engineering
> A Science Primer

Words such as *to, and, the* and so on are not included in the index, and so these three titles would result in the key words Introduction, Programming, Computer, Science, Software, Engineering, Primer. A query on the word Programming should produce the first title, whereas one on the word Science should output both the first and third titles. (The case of the characters in the key words would be ignored, but we shall not take account of this.) The method whereby the title can be obtained is to produce a table of key words and remainders. Essentially, a remainder contains all the words of a title other than the key word. The table for the titles above is shown below. The entries are ordered on the key word field and the remainders use the symbol □ to denote a space character.

    The titles are reconstructed by joining together, that is, concatenating, the key word and the remainder in a special way. We shall show how the first title can be reconstructed from the key word *Computer*. To this are concatenated the characters of the remainder, up

Key word	Remainder
Computer	□Science/Introduction□to□Programming□and□
Engineering	/Software□
Introduction	□to□Programming□and□Computer□Science
Primer	/A□Science□
Programming	□and□Computer□Science/Introduction□to□
Science	/Introduction□to□Programming□and□Computer□
Science	□Primer/A□
Software	□Engineering

to but not including the slash. This gives 'Computer□Science'. All characters after the slash are now placed before this string (together with a space character to separate the two parts) to give the required title. Sometimes the remainder does not contain a slash character, as in the entry Software. This is simply because the title is just the concatenation of the key word and the remainder (together with a space). Finally, if the remainder begins with a slash character this indicates that the key word is the last word of the title. The title can therefore be reconstructed by taking the remainder and concatenating the key word to it.

In this problem we want you to write a program for searching the table for a key word and, if found, reconstructing all the titles containing that key word. You may assume that the table above is represented as an array of records given in the data table below, that the table has been initialized, and that *keysearch* holds the key word for which titles are required. For simplicity you should search every item in the table.

Design

1.1	*foundmatch* := false
1.2	write out 'Enter a key word '
1.3	read in *keysearch*
2.1	loop for *item* := 1 to *size*
3.1	if *keysearch* = *keyindex*[*item*].*keyword* then
4.1.1	*foundmatch* := true
4.1.2	*prefix* := "
4.1.3	*suffix* := "
4.1.4	*slashfound* := false
4.2.1	loop for *i* := 1 to *length*(*keyindex*[*item*].*remainder*) {all the remainder}
4.3.1	*current* := *keyindex*[*item*].*remainder*[*i*] {current character}
4.3.2	if *current* = slash then
4.4.1	*slashfound* := true
4.5	else
4.6.1	if *slashfound* then
4.6.2	*prefix* := *prefix* + *current* {concatenate to *prefix*}
4.6.3	else
4.6.4	*suffix* := *suffix* + *current* {concatenate to *suffix*}
4.6.5	ifend
4.7	ifend
4.8	loopend
4.9.1	if *prefix* <> " then
4.9.2	*title* := *prefix* + *keysearch* + *suffix*
4.9.3	else
4.9.4	*title* := *keysearch* + *suffix*
4.9.5	ifend
4.9.6	write out *title*

```
5          ifend
6          loopend
7.1        if foundmatch = false then
7.2            write out 'No matches for this keyword'
7.3        ifend
```

Data table

Identifier	Description	Type
size	Constant definition	*integer* constant
slash	Constant definition	*char* constant value '/'
indextype	Record type definition	
	keyword {The key word}	*string* variable
	remainder {Rest of title}	*string* variable
	recordend	
keyindex	Key word index	array[0..*size*] of *indextype* variable
keysearch	Search item	*string* variable
foundmatch	Flag, denotes search success	*Boolean* variable
item	Index to current record	*integer* variable
prefix	Phrase preceding *keysearch*	*string* variable
suffix	Phrase after *keysearch*	*string* variable
i	Loop control variable	*integer* variable
current	Current character	*char* variable
slashfound	Flag, denotes slash found	*Boolean* variable
title	Reconstructed title	*string* variable

Test data

The description of the problem gives suitable test data for the key words and remainders. Searches which result in a single match, a repeated match and no matches at all should be carried out.

Problem 6.15

Problem statement

The MSDOS operating system records file names on the disk in a special location called a **directory**. The data stored in the directory can be modelled by the following data table:

Data table

Identifier	Description	Type
entry	Record type definition	
	filename {File name}	*string*[8] variable
	extension {File extension}	*string*[3] variable
	attribute {File attribute}	*char* variable
	time {Time file was saved}	*string* variable
	date {Date file was saved}	*string* variable
	cluster {File cluster number}	*integer* variable
	filesize {File size}	*integer* variable
	recordend	
directory	Array of *directory*	array[0..112] of *entry* variable

When a file is deleted from a disk its directory entry is not erased, but the first character of its file name is changed to a special character to denote that the file is erased. We shall use a space character for this purpose. An entry in the directory that has never been used will have this special character in its file name field. A **directory listing** outputs details of the file name, the extension, the file size, and the date and time the file was saved for all the non-erased files on the disk. It has the following form:

```
LETTER1   TXT   1024 23/04/94  12:56
MEMOCOPY  TXT   2560 04/02/93  18:30
MEMO      TXT   1145 04/02/94  01:45
```

Assuming that the directory has been represented by the variable *directory*, defined above, and that it is already initialized, a design to produce such a directory listing is as follows. The variable i is an integer variable.

Design

```
        {A directory listing}
1.1     loop for i := 1 to 112
2.2         if directory[i].filename[1] <> '□' then
3.1             with directory[i]
3.1                 write out filename, extension, size, date, time
3.3             withend
4           ifend
5       loopend
```

Test data
The array will need initializing. It should include file names that are marked as erased. These will begin with a space character but be followed by non-space characters.

Problem 7.1

Problem statement
Implement Problem 5.9 using a case statement.

Design
Step 5 needs to be refined as follows:

```
5.1.1   select case depending on daycode
5.1.2       0  :  write out 'Sunday'
5.1.3       1  :  write out 'Monday'
5.1.4       2  :  write out 'Tuesday'
5.1.5       3  :  write out 'Wednesday'
5.1.6       4  :  write out 'Thursday'
5.1.7       5  :  write out 'Friday'
5.1.8       6  :  write out 'Saturday'
5.1.9   selectend
```

Data table
See Problem 5.9.

Problem 7.2

Problem statement
This problem is concerned with validating a date input by a user. The data are to be input as two integers representing the day and the month respectively (in that order). Your task is to verify that the numbers input are consistent with each other in the sense that the date 30 2 is invalid because 30 February does not exist. You may assume that the user inputs positive integer values and that the year is not a leap year. The output from your program should be a message saying whether or not the input represents a valid date.

Design

```
          {Test for valid date}
1.1       write 'Enter day as an integer '
1.2       read in day
1.3       write 'Enter month as an integer '
1.4       read in month
1.5       dateok := true
2         select case depending on month
3.1           1, 3, 5, 7, 8, 10, 12   :   if day > 31 then
3.2                                           dateok := false
3.3                                       ifend
3.4           2                        :   if day > 28 then
3.5                                           dateok := false
3.6                                       ifend
3.7           4, 6, 9, 11              :   if day > 30 then
3.8                                           dateok := false
3.9                                       ifend
3.10          default                  :   dateok := false
4         selectend
5.1       if dateok then
5.2           write out 'Date may be valid'
5.3       else
5.4           write out 'Date is not valid'
5.5       ifend
```

Data table

Identifier	Description	Type
day	Day of the month	*integer* variable
month	Month expressed as an integer	*integer* variable
dateok	Flag set true if date is OK	*Boolean* variable

Test data

Test data for case statements must be generated so that all case labels are executed. Here, there are three case labels each of which could alter the value of *dateok*, and so six data sets are required to test the case labels. In addition, the default case also needs testing. Thus, the program should be tested with values such as the following:

```
      day     month
(a)   31        1      {Tests valid date in first label}
(b)   32        1      {Tests invalid date in first label}
(c)   28        2      {Tests valid date in second label}
(d)   29        2      {Tests invalid date in second label}
(e)   30        4      {Tests valid date in third label}
(f)   31        4      {Tests invalid date in third label}
(g)   20       13      {Test default}
```

In addition, *month* values other than the first ones in the case label lists should be tested. For each such test, two values of *day* will be required to verify that the inequalities work correctly.

Problem 7.3

Problem statement

Modify the design in Problem 7.2 so that it caters for the possibility of a leap year. The user will now input three integers corresponding to the day, month and year in that order. For the purposes of this question a leap year is defined to be one that leaves zero remainder when divided by four.

Design

```
         {Test for valid date including leap years}
1.1      write 'Enter day as an integer '
1.2      read in day
1.3      write 'Enter month as an integer '
1.4      read in month
1.5      write 'Enter year as an integer '
1.6      read in year
1.7      dateok := true
2        select case depending on month
3.1          1, 3, 5, 7, 8, 10, 12   :   if day > 31 then
3.2                                           dateok := false
3.3                                       ifend
3.4          2                      :   if year mod 4 = 0 then
3.5                                       if day > 29 then
3.6                                           dateok := false
3.7                                       ifend
3.8                                     else
3.9                                       if day > 28 then
3.10                                          dateok := false
3.11                                      ifend
3.12                                    ifend
3.13         4, 6, 9, 11            :   if day > 30 then
3.14                                        dateok := false
3.15                                    ifend
3.16         default                :   dateok := false
4        selectend
5.1      if dateok then
5.2          write out 'Date may be valid'
5.3      else
5.4          write out 'Date is not valid'
5.5      ifend
```

Data table

Identifier	Description	Type
day	Day of the month	*integer* variable
month	Month expressed as an integer	*integer* variable
year	Year as an integer	*integer* variable
dateok	Flag set true if date is OK	*Boolean* variable

Test data

To test the alteration to the code we must test February inputs to see if leap years are handled correctly. The following are some suggested test values:

	day	*month*	*year*	
(a)	29	2	1992	{Tests valid value of 29 for day in a leap year}
(b)	29	2	1991	{Tests invalid day in non-leap year}
(c)	28	2	1992	{Tests valid date in a leap year}
(d)	28	2	1991	{Tests valid date in non-leap year}

Problem 7.4

Problem statement

This problem concerns the validation of a user input into an integer variable called *number*. Write a design that prompts a user to input an integer which satisfies the inequality $2 \le number \le 5$, that is, an integer in the range 2 – 5 inclusive. You may assume that the user enters only integer values, but your design should check that the input lies in the required range. If it does, a message should be output saying that an input error has occurred and the user should be repeatedly asked to try again until valid data are input. The dialogue below, in which user responses are underlined, illustrates the prompts that should be issued when an input error occurs.

```
Enter an integer in the range 2 to 5 inclusive ? 1
You must enter an integer in the stated range 2 to 5. Try again ? 6
You must enter an integer in the stated range 2 to 5. Try again ? 3
```

Design

```
        {Validate integer input is in range 2 to 5}
1.1     write 'Enter an integer in the range 2 to 5 inclusive?'
1.2     read in number
2.1     loop while (number < 2) or (number > 5)
3.2        write 'You must enter an integer in the stated range 2 to 5. Try again?'
3.3        read in number
4       loopend
```

Data table

Identifier	Description	Type
number	Integer input by user	*integer* variable

Test data

Clearly, values smaller than 2 and larger than 5 must be included in the test data as well as values between these numbers. The values 2 and 5 themselves should also be included.

Problem 7.5

Problem statement

Write a design that will remove from a string any text from (and including) an opening brace, up to and including the first closing brace that follows. Should only an opening brace be in the string then remove all text from then on. If there is no opening brace then the string should be left unaltered. Your design should enable a user to enter a string and should write out the string resulting from the deletion. You may assume that the input string is not null.

Data table

Identifier	Description	Type
i	Index of character in *given*	*integer* variable
newstr	New string with braces removed	*string* variable
given	Old input string	*string* variable
withinpair	Flag denoting open/closed brace pair	*Boolean* variable

Design

	{Remove text between braces}			{Remove text between braces}
1.1	*i* := 1		1.1	*newstr* := ''
1.2	*newstr* := ''		1.2	write 'Enter text '
1.3	write 'Enter text '		1.3	read in *given*
1.4	read in *given*		2.1	loop for *i* := 1 to *length*(*given*)
2.1	loop while *i* <= *length*[*given*]		3.1	if *withinpair* then
3.1	if *given*[*i*] = '{' then		4.1	if *given*[*i*] = '}' then
4.1	repeat		5	*withinpair* := false
4.2	increment *i*		6	ifend
4.3	until *given*[*i*] = '}' or *i* = *length*[*given*]		7	else
5	else		8.1	if *given*[*i*] = '{' then
6.1	*newstr* := *newstr* + *given*[*i*]		9	*withinpair* := true
7	ifend		10	else
8.1	increment *i*		11.1	*newstr* := *newstr* + *given*[*i*]
9	loopend		12	ifend
10.1	write out 'New string is :', *newstr*		13	ifend
			14	loopend
			15.1	write out 'New string is :', *newstr*

Test data

All allowable combinations of braces need to be tested. Here is a potential list:

input	output
No braces at all	No braces at all
A {single} brace	A brace
{All is in a brace}	
A {no closing brace	A
A }no opening brace	A }no opening brace

Problem 7.6

Problem statement

One of the problems that a compiler has to deal with is to check that brackets within expressions are well formed. A sequence of brackets is well formed if there are equal numbers of opening and closing brackets and the number of closing brackets never exceeds the number of opening brackets. In this problem you are to ask the user to input a string that should consist of an expression which includes brackets only of the type '[' or ']'. The output from the program should be a message reporting whether or not the expression was well formed. If at any stage of the processing the number of closing brackets exceeds the number of opening brackets then the error should be reported immediately, together with the position at which it occurred.

Design

1.1	write out 'Enter an expression '
1.2	read in *expression*
1.3	*moreclosing* := false
1.4	*position* := 1
1.5	*opencount* := 0
1.6	*closecount* := 0
2.1	loop while *position* <= *length*(*expression*) and not *moreclosing*
3.1	if *expression*[*position*] = '[' then
3.2	increment *opencount*
3.3	else
3.4	if *expression*[*position*] = ']' then

3.5	increment *closecount*
3.6	if *closecount* > *opencount* then
3.7	*moreclosing* := true
3.8	write 'Number of closed brackets exceeds number of open brackets '
3.9	write out 'at character ', *position*
3.10	ifend
3.11	ifend
3.12	ifend
3.13	increment *position*
4	loopend
5.1	if not *moreclosing* then
5.2	if *closecount* = *opencount* then
5.3	write out 'The expression is well formed'
5.4	else
5.5	write out 'The expression is not well formed – too many left brackets'
5.6	ifend
5.7	ifend

Data table

Identifier	Description	Type
expression	Expression being tested	*string* variable
moreclosing	True indicates closing bracket error	*Boolean* variable
position	String index	*integer* variable
opencount	Number of opening brackets	*integer* variable
closecount	Number of closing brackets	*integer* variable

Test data

This needs to include data without any brackets, data with a single set of correct brackets, some correctly nested brackets, data with too many left brackets and data with too many right brackets.

Problem 7.7

Problem statement

This problem is concerned with the linear search that was introduced in Section 6.3. An alternative method, which avoids the use of a dummy item in the array to be searched, requires the use of a Boolean operator. This search process has the form:

```
repeat
    search for item
until (item is found) or (the end of the array is reached)
```

Write a design incorporating these design steps that will search an array *names* indexed 1..*maxsize* of base type *string* for an item input by a user. You may assume that the array is initialized and the outcome of the search should form the output of your design.

Design

	{Linear search version 2}
1.1	write 'Enter item to be searched for '
1.2	read in *item*
1.3	*index* := 0
2	repeat
3.1	increment *index*
4.1	*found* := (*item* = *names*[*index*])

5.1   until (*found*) or (*index* = *maxsize*)
6.1   if *found* then
6.2   write out 'Item is at index ', *index*
6.3   else
6.4   write out 'Item is not in list'
6.5   ifend

Data table

Identifier	Description	Type
maxsize	Array index upper bound	*integer* constant
names	Array of names	array[1..*maxsize*] of *string* variable
item	Item being searched for	*string* variable
index	Index to element being examined	*integer* variable
found	True if item is found, false otherwise	*Boolean* variable

Test data
The array names will have to be initialized for test purposes. The value of *maxsize* can be chosen to be small to minimize this process. The array should then be searched for the first and last elements in the array as well as at least one other existing value. A search also needs to be made for a value not in the array.

Problem 7.8

Problem statement
The code fragment below is an attempt to solve Problem 7.7 using a preconditioned loop rather than a postconditioned loop. The declarations are as given in the solution to Problem 7.7. Find the error and correct it.

```
{An erroneous linear search}
write('Enter item to be searched for ');
readln(item);
index := 1;
while (item <> names[index]) and (index <= maxsize) do
  index := index + 1;
if index <= maxsize then
  writeln('Item is at index ', index)
else
  writeln('Item is not in list')
```

Test data
The same sort of test data will be required here as in Problem 7.7. Particular attention needs to be paid to searching for the first and last elements in the array to ensure that the code works properly for them.

Problem 7.9

Problem statement
The specification of Problem 6.1 is modified in this problem so that the initial and final address values input by the user are verified to be in the range 1 to *maxsize* inclusive. As each value is input it should be tested to see if it lies in this range. If it does not, a message should be output reporting the error, and program execution should terminate immediately. The further constraint on the input values described in Problem 6.1 should also be incorporated into this design.

Design

{Fill memory, validating input addresses}

 1.1   write 'Enter initial address '
 1.2   read in *initial*
 2.1   if (*initial* <= 0) or (*initial* > *maxsize*) then
 3.1   write out 'Initial address is not in
               address range '
 4   else
 5.1   write 'Enter final address '
 5.2   read in *final*
 6.1   if (*final* <= 0) or (*final* > *maxsize*) then
 7.1   write out 'Final address is not in
                   address range'
 8   else
 9.1   if *initial* <= *final* then
 9.2   write 'Value to fill memory is? '
 9.3   read in *FillValue*
 9.4   loop for *i* := *initial* to *final*
 9.5   memory[*i*] := *FillValue*
 9.6   loopend
 9.7   else
 9.8   write out 'Initial address is
                       larger than final address'
 9.9   ifend
10   ifend
11   ifend

{Fill memory, validating input addresses}

 1.1   write 'Enter initial address '
 1.2   read in *initial*
 2.1   if (*initial* >= 0) and (*initial* <= *maxsize*) then
 3.1   write 'Enter final address '
 3.2   read in *final*
 4.1   if (*final* >= 0) and (*final* <= *maxsize*) then
 5.1   if *initial* > *final* then
 5.2   write out 'Initial address is
                       larger than final address'
 5.3   else
 5.4   write 'Value to fill memory is? '
 5.5   read in *FillValue*
 5.6   loop for *i* := *initial* to *final*
 5.7   memory[*i*] := *FillValue*
 5.8   loopend
 5.9   ifend
 6   else
 7.1   write out 'Final address is not in
                   address range'
 8   ifend
 9   else
10.1   write out 'Initial address is not in
               address range '
11   ifend

Data table

Identifier	Description	Type
maxsize	Array index upper bound	*integer* constant
memory	Array simulating machine memory	array[1..*maxsize*] of string variable
initial	First address of range to be filled	*integer* variable
final	Last address of memory to be filled	*integer* variable
FillValue	Value to fill range	*integer* variable
i	Loop control variable	*integer* variable

Test data

The following sequence of test data value descriptions will be needed:

(a)   Values of *initial* that are not in the required range (both too big and too small).
(b)   A valid value for *initial*. Values of *final* that are out of range.
(c)   A valid value for *initial* and a valid value for *final* but with *initial* > *final*.
(d)   A valid value for *initial* and a valid value for *final* but with *initial* < *final*.
(e)   A valid value for *initial* and a valid value for *final* but with *initial* = *final*.

Problem 7.10

Problem statement

In Problem 5.20 we looked at the problem of finding the number of occurrences of the pattern 'the' in an input string, assuming that the user inputs at least two characters. Rewrite the design using a single compound Boolean condition instead of the nested *if* statements used in the solution.

Design

> {Count occurrences of 'the' in input string using a compound Boolean}

1.1	*count* := 0
1.2	write 'Enter the string '
1.3	read in *sentence*
1.4	*first* := *sentence*[1]
1.5	*second* := *sentence*[2]
2.1	loop for *current* := 3 to *length*(*sentence*)
3.1	if (*first* = 't') and (*second* = 'h') and (*sentence*[*current*] = 'e') then
3.2	increment *count*
3.3	ifend
3.4	*first* := *second*
3.5	*second* := *sentence*[*current*]
4	loopend
5.1	write out 'Number of occurrences is ' *count*

Data table

Identifier	Description	Type
count	Occurrences of pattern 'the'	*integer* variable
sentence	Input string	*string* variable
first	First character of the 3 currently being examined	*char* variable
second	Second character of 3 currently being examined	*char* variable
current	Index of the third character being examined	*integer* variable

Test data

The same test data as for Problem 5.20 will suffice here.

Problem 7.11

Problem statement

Redefine the array *directory* of Problem 6.16 using appropriate constant and subrange type definitions. You should assume that *year* is an integer of at most two digits, with 0 representing 1980. Cluster numbers are integers in the range 2 to 355 inclusive. You should redefine the *time* field as a record with two fields: hours and minutes, where the latter are defined as an appropriate subrange type.

Design

The data table below gives a partial solution to the new definition. It illustrates how subranges are defined in design.

Data table

Identifier	Description	Type
maxentries	Maximum number of directory entries	*integer* constant value 112
dayRange	Subrange type definition	1..31
monthRange	Subrange type definition	1..12
yearRange	Subrange type definition	0..99
hourRange	Subrange type definition	0..23

Problem 7.12

Problem statement

Using the enumeration type *weekdays* defined in Section 7.7 write down a Pascal definition for a subrange *weekday* that corresponds to the days Monday to Friday inclusive. Hence define an array *weeklywork* of type *real* and indexed on this subrange.

Problem 7.13

Problem statement

A company making machined parts works a three-shift system from Monday to Friday inclusive. The shifts are referred to as the early, late and night shifts, the first shift of the week being the Monday early shift and the last being the Friday night shift. The table below shows the number of parts produced by each shift in a typical week:

	Monday	Tuesday	Wednesday	Thursday	Friday
early	100	132	98	174	211
late	213	169	216	148	196
night	175	221	201	100	75

The company wants to keep a computer record of the number of parts produced each week in a two-dimensional array, indexed by an enumeration type representing the shifts and the days of the week. Write a design that will enable a user at a keyboard to input the production for each shift in a given week and will produce as output a table similar to that above. As data are input the design must provide prompts which tell the user the name of the shift and the day of the week for which input is being requested. You should use suitably defined and initialized parallel arrays for the input and output in the design.

A parallel array is used to handle the output text corresponding to the enumeration types and this array is initialized as part of step 1:

Design

```
        {Weekly production figures}
1.1     dayname[mon] := 'Monday'        1.2   dayname[tue] := 'Tuesday'
1.3     dayname[wed] := 'Wednesday'     1.4   dayname[thur] := 'Thursday'
1.5     dayname[fri] := 'Friday'        1.6   shiftname[early] := 'Early'
1.7     shiftname[late] := 'Late'       1.8   shiftname[night] := 'Night'
2.1     loop for day := mon to fri
3.1        loop for shift := early to night
4.1           write 'Enter production for the ', dayname[day], shiftname[shift], ' shift'
4.2           read in week[day, shift]
5          loopend
6       loopend
7.1     write out ' ', 'Monday', 'Tuesday', 'Wednesday', 'Thursday', 'Friday'   {The table headings}
7.2     loop for shift := early to night
7.3        write shiftname[shift]                                                {The row heading}
7.4        loop for day := mon to fri
7.5           write week[day, shift]
7.6           write out                                                         {Create a new row}
7.7        loopend
7.8     loopend
```

Data table

Identifier	Description	Type
DayType	Enumerated type definition	(*mon, tue, wed, thur, fri*)
ShiftType	Enumerated type definition	(*early, late, night*)
week	Array holding weekly production	array[*DayType, ShiftType*] of *integer* variable
day	Day of the week	*DayType* variable
shift	Shift within a day	*ShiftType* variable
dayname	Array of weekday names	array[*DayType*] of *string* variable
shiftname	Array of shift names	array[*ShiftType*] of *string* variable

Test data
Testing will consist of checking the output of the prompts and that the rest of the output has a tabular form.

Problem 7.14

Problem statement
Small advertisements in newspapers often abbreviate words to save space. Typically, this is done by removing the vowels from the words. For example, the advertisement '3-bedroomed detached house with garden' would be abbreviated to '3-bdrmd dtchd hs wth grdn'. Write a design that enables a user to input a string and produces as output the input string with the all the vowels removed. You may assume that each word of the input string consists of at least one character.

Design

	{Small ads abbreviation}
1.1	write out 'Enter the advert '
1.2	read in *advert*
1.3	*abbreviation* := ''
1.4	*vowels* := ['a', 'e', 'i', 'o', 'u']
2.1	loop for *position* := 1 to *length*(*advert*)
3.1	if not (*advert*[*position*] in *vowels*) then
3.2	*abbreviation* := *abbreviation* + *advert*[*position*]
3.3	ifend
4	loopend
5.1	write out 'Abbreviation is ', *abbreviation*

Data table

Identifier	Description	Type
advert	Input string	*string* variable
vowels	Set of vowel characters	set of *char* variable
abbreviation	Input string with vowels removed	*string* variable
position	Loop control variable	*integer* variable

Test data
This should include words that have vowels together with words that do not. Words that start and end with a vowel should also be included.

Problem 7.15

Problem statement
The method by which the abbreviations were obtained in Problem 7.14 means that words beginning with a vowel have that and all the other vowels removed. This can make it difficult to deduce what the original word was. For example, the word *one* would be abbreviated by this method to *n*. A better method of abbreviation does not remove a vowel if it begins a word. So the advertisement '3-bedroomed flat very good condition inspection anytime' would be abbreviated to '3-bdrmd flt vry gd cndtn inspctn anytm', where the words *inspection* and *anytime* do not have their initial vowels removed. Write a design that enables a user to input a string and produces as output the input string with the vowels removed in the manner just described. You may assume that the words in the input string are separated by single-space characters and that the string contains at least one character.

Design

        {Small ads abbreviation version 2}
1.1   write out 'Enter the advert '
1.2   read in *advert*
1.3   *abbreviation* := "
1.4   *NewWord* := true
2.1   loop for *position* := 1 to *length*(*advert*)
3.1   if *NewWord* then
3.2.1   *abbreviation* := *abbreviation* + *advert*[*position*]
3.2.2   *NewWord* := false
3.3   else
3.4.1   select case depending on *advert*[*position*]
3.4.2   'a', 'e', 'i', 'o', 'u'   : do nothing
3.4.3   '□'   : *abbreviation* := *abbreviation* + *advert*[*position*]
3.4.4   *NewWord* := true
3.4.5   default   : *abbreviation* := *abbreviation* + *advert*[*position*]
3.4.6   selectend
3.5   ifend
4   loopend
5.1   write out 'Abbreviation is ', *abbreviation*

Data table

Identifier	Description	Type
advert	Input string	*string* variable
abbreviation	Input string with vowels removed	*string* variable
position	Loop control variable	*integer* variable

Test data

Data sets need to be generated that have the following properties:

(a)   An initial word that begins with a vowel.
(b)   An initial word that begins with a consonant.
(c)   An initial word beginning with two vowels (only the first should remain after processing).
(d)   Inputs of several words, containing both types of initial letters.

Problem 7.16

Problem statement

This problem is concerned with counting the frequencies of pairs of characters in a string. The count is restricted to lower case letters and within word pairs so that punctuation marks and spaces are not considered. The counts are to be recorded in a two-dimensional array, suitably indexed. Your design should input a string, calculate the pair counts and write out the results in the form of a table. The illustration below shows the first two rows of the type of output required.

```
  a b c d e f g h i j k l m n o p q r s t u v w x y z
a 0 1 0 0 0 0 0 0 0 0 0 0 0 0 0 1 0 0 0 0 0 0 0 0 0 0
b 0 0 0 0 0 0 0 0 0 0 0 0 0 0 0 1 0 0 0 0 0 0 0 0 0 0
```

Design

        {Count the pairs in a string}
1.1   write 'Enter the text to be analysed '
1.2   read in *paragraph*
1.3   *lowercase* := ['a'..'z']

```
1.4      loop for first := 'a' to 'z'
1.5         loop for second := 'a' to 'z'
1.6            paircount[first, second] := 0
1.7         loopend
1.8      loopend
1.9      first := paragraph[1]
2.1      loop for position := 2 to length(paragraph)
3.1         second := paragraph[position]
3.2         if (first in lowercase) and (second in lowercase) then
4.1            paircount[first, second] := paircount[first, second] + 1
5        ifend
6.1         first := second
7        loopend
8.1      write out ' a b c d e f g h i j k l m n o p q r s t u v w x y z'
8.2      loop for first := 'a' to 'z'
8.3         write first, ' '
8.4         loop for second := 'a' to 'z'
8.5            write paircount[first, second], ' '
8.6         loopend
8.7         write out    {go to new line}
8.8      loopend
```

Data table

Identifier	Description	Type
alpha	Subrange type definition	'a'..'z'
lowercase	Set of lower case characters	set of *alpha* variable
paragraph	Input text	*string* variable
first	First character of a pair	*char* variable
second	Second character of a pair	*char* variable
paircount	Array holding the counts	array[*alpha*, *alpha*] of *integer* variable
position	Index to the characters in *paragraph*	*integer* variable

Test data

This should include pairs of characters that are unique as well as pairs that are repeated. The results will need to be evaluated by hand and compared with the output produced by the program.

Problem 7.17

Problem statement

In Problem 7.13 parallel arrays were used to handle the difficulty of input and output related to enumeration types. In this problem you are asked to give an alternative design that avoids their use by exploiting case statements to generate the correct prompts.

Design

```
         {Weekly production version 2}
1        {No initializing required}
2.1      loop for day := mon to fri
3.1         loop for shift := early to night
4.1            write 'Enter production for the '
4.2            select case depending on day
4.3               mon  :  write 'Monday '
4.4               tue  :  write 'Tuesday '
4.5               wed  :  write 'Wednesday '
```

4.6	*thur* : write 'Thursday '	
4.7	*fri* : write 'Friday '	
4.8	selectend	
4.9	select case depending on *shift*	
4.10	*early* : write 'Early shift'	
4.11	*late* : write 'Late shift'	
4.12	*night* : write 'Night shift'	
4.13	selectend	
4.14	read in *week*[*day*, *shift*]	
5	loopend	
6	loopend	
7.1	write out ' ', 'Monday', 'Tuesday', 'Wednesday', 'Thursday', 'Friday'	
	{The table headings}	
7.2	loop for *shift* := *early* to *night*	
7.3	write *shift*	{The row heading}
7.4	loop for *day* := *mon* to *fri*	
7.5	write *week*[*day*, *shift*]	
7.6	write out	{Create a new row}
7.7	loopend	
7.8	loopend	

Data table
The data table is as before, with the exception that the parallel arrays holding the names of the days and shifts are not declared here.

Test data
The only changes here involve output to the screen, and so a test of the new output formats will be required to ensure that they are satisfactory.

Problem 7.18

Problem statement
This problem is based on Problem 7.13. The company notices that the shift which produces the most items in a week is often followed by one whose production is very low. The suspected cause is that the shift following the high-production shift has to spend much of its time on emergency maintenance, replacing parts that have worn on the machines during the previous shift. The company therefore wishes to assess its maintenance policy. The current policy is that all routine maintenance is done by the Friday night shift, which means that shift never produces the best production figures of the week. Write a design that finds and then outputs the shift with the best production for the week. The output should specify the day and the name of the shift, the number of items produced and the number of items produced by the next shift. If the shift producing the largest number of items is not unique, then the last shift of the week producing that largest number of items is deemed to have the best production. An illustration of the output required, based on the data given in Problem 7.13, is:

```
The best production was on the Tuesday night shift.
It produced 221 items.
The next shift produced 98 items.
```

Design

	{Best production shift}
1.1	*bestprod* := 0
2.1	loop for *day* := *mon* to *fri*

2.2	loop for *shift* := *early* to *night*
3.1	if *week*[*day, shift*] >= *bestprod* then
3.2	*bestprod* := *week*[*day, shift*]
3.3	*bestday* := *day*
3.4	*bestshift* := *shift*
3.5	ifend
4.1	loopend
4.2	loopend
5.1	write out 'The best production was on the ', *dayname*[*bestday*], *shiftname*[*bestshift*], ' shift.'
5.2	write out 'It produced ', *bestprod*, ' items.'
5.3	if *bestshift* <> *night* then
5.4	write out 'The next shift produced ', *week*[*bestday, succ(bestshift)*], ' items.'
5.5	else
5.6	write out 'The next shift produced ', *week*[*succ(bestday), early*], ' items.'
5.7	ifend

Data table

Identifier	Description	Type
bestprod	Best production of the week	*integer* variable
bestday	Day on which *bestprod* was produced	*DayType* variable
bestshift	Shift in which *bestprod* was produced	*ShiftType* variable

Test data

Several runs of the program will be required in which the best production occurs in all the possible different shifts. This will then test whether the program correctly calculates what the following shift is.

Problem 8.1*

Problem statement

Write a Pascal procedure to implement the following specification:

menu

{Clear the screen and then write out to the screen the following menu		

{Clear the screen and then write out to the screen the following menu
    1 Enter data
    2 Update data
    3 Print data
    4 Quit
The first character of each menu option should occupy the leftmost position on the screen.}

Design

1	clear screen
2	write out '1 Enter data'
3	write out '2 Update data'
4	write out '3 Print data'
5	write out '4 Quit'

Test data

The procedure needs to be incorporated into a driver program. The simplest driver program is one whose single statement is a call to *menu*.

Problem 8.2*

Problem statement

This problem concerns the implementation and testing of the following procedure in which *string4* is a type identifier representing *string*[4].

GetFourChars

{Prompt for and read in a string of four characters from the keyboard. Inputs which do not have precisely four characters are rejected with a suitable error message and the process is repeated until a valid input is entered.}		
FourChars	Input characters	*string4* parameter

Design

GetFourChars

1.1	write out 'Enter a string of length 4'
1.2	read in *instring*
2.1	loop while *length*(*instring*) <> 4
3.1	write out 'String must have length 4. Please enter again'
3.2	read in *instring*
4	loopend
5	*FourChars* := *instring*

FourChars

Data table

Identifier	Description	Type
instring	Input string to be validated	*string* variable

Test data

To test this procedure it is necessary to write a driver program. The simplest driver program is one which calls the procedure just once, but this would involve executing the program for each data value entered from the keyboard. We shall write a driver program which encloses the call to the procedure in a loop so that we can test without having to re-execute the program each time. The following program design will suffice:

1	write out 'Terminate test program by entering zzzz'
2	repeat
3	*GetFourChars*(*input*)
4	until *input* = 'zzzz'

Data table

Identifier	Description	Type
input	Actual parameter	*string4* variable

Values to be used when executing this program could include strings of length 3, 4 and 5. This will determine whether or not it functions correctly on incorrect data inputs.

Problem 8.3(i)*

Problem statement

Integer data values are stored contiguously in an array. Not all elements of the array may be in use at any given time; the number in use is stored in a variable *size*. A data item is removed by moving up subsequent elements and *size* is decremented by 1. So, if *size* has value 9 and the element at index 6 is to be removed, the data at element 7 are moved to index 6, that at index 8 is moved to index 7 and that at index 9 is moved to index 8. The specification below is for a procedure to carry out this removal process.

Data table

Identifier	Description	Type
maxsize	Array index upper bound	*integer* constant
sizetype	Type definition	0..*maxsize*
indextype	Type definition	1..*maxsize*
arraytype	Type definition	array[*indextype*] of *integer*

remove

data	Array holding the contiguous data	*arraytype* parameter
RemoveIndex	Index of element to be removed	*indextype* parameter
size	Number of elements in use	*sizetype* parameter

{Remove the item at index *RemoveIndex* by moving up subsequent array elements of *data* one position. Decrement *size* by 1. It is the responsibility of the calling program to ensure that *RemoveIndex* has a value that corresponds to an existing element.}

data	Updated array holding the contiguous data	*arraytype* parameter
size	Updated number of elements in use	*sizetype* parameter

Design

Care has to be taken to get the indexes correct when moving the elements. This is particularly the case when there is only one stored item. When this is the case in the design below, step 1 is a loop from 1 to 0, and so the loop body does not execute. With this approach, the loop control variable *i* must be defined to allow it to assume the value 0, and so is defined to be of type *sizetype*. An alternative design is to execute steps 1 to 3 only when *size* has value 1 or more, in which case *i* can be defined to be of type *indextype*.

remove

---

data, RemoveIndex, size

```
1       loop for i := RemoveIndex to size − 1
2           data[i] := data[i + 1]
3       loopend
4       size := size − 1
```

---

data, size

Data table

Identifier	Description	Type
i	Loop control variable	*sizetype* variable

Test data

To test this procedure it will have to be called several times with different parameters. We shall write a driver program which enables it to be called as often as we wish – in other words, we shall include the call in a loop. The design below contains the details. We initialize the array by means of a loop and write out its size and elements after each deletion.

```
1.1     loop for i := 1 to maxsize   {initialize all array elements}
1.2         TestData[i] := 10 + i
```

1.3   loopend
1.4   *TestSize := maxsize*;
1.5   *continue* := 'y';
2   loop while *continue* = 'y'
3.1   write out 'Index of last element is ', *TestSize*
3.2   write out 'Enter index to be removed '
3.2   read in *DeleteIndex*
3.3   *remove(TestData, DeleteIndex, TestSize)*;
4.1   write out 'Index   Value' {write out the array elements}
4.2   loop for *i* := 1 to *TestSize*
4.3   write out *TestData*[*i*]
4.4   loopend
5.1   write out 'Continue y/n '
5.2   read in *continue*
6   loopend

Data table

Identifier	Description	Type
i	Loop control variable	*sizetype* variable
TestData	Actual parameter of array data	*arraytype* variable
TestSize	Actual parameter of elements in use	*sizetype* variable
DeleteIndex	Actual parameter of element to delete	*indextype* variable
continue	Outer loop control variable	*char* variable

To complete the driver program a value for the constant *maxsize* will have to be chosen. A fairly small value will suffice, say, 10. For testing the removals particular attention should be paid to deleting the first and last elements of the array, that is, those with indexes 1 and *TestSize*. Deletions should continue to ensure that an array consisting of only a single item has that item removed correctly.

Problem 8.3(ii)*

Problem statement

This problem is similar to Problem 8.3(i), except that here we change the specification so that the value of *RemoveIndex* is tested to see if it corresponds to an existing element. This means that the type of this parameter is now *integer* and that its value is tested explicitly by the procedure. The actual parameter corresponding to *RemoveIndex* will also be of type *integer*. The procedure also includes an additional results parameter which reports the success or otherwise of the removal. The identifiers used in the specification are those of Problem 8.3(i).

remove

data	Array holding the contiguous data	*arraytype* parameter
RemoveIndex	Index of element to be removed	*integer* parameter
size	Number of elements in use	*sizetype* parameter
{If 1 <= *RemoveIndex* <= *size* then remove the item at index *RemoveIndex* by moving up subsequent array elements of *data* one position. Decrement *size* by 1 and set *success* to true. Otherwise set *success* false and do nothing to the other parameters.}		
data	Updated array holding the contiguous data	*arraytype* parameter
size	Updated number of elements in use	*sizetype* parameter
success	Flag denoting success of operation	*Boolean* parameter

Design

remove
_____

data, RemoveIndex, size
_____

1	if $(1 <= RemoveIndex)$ and $(RemoveIndex <= size)$ then
2.1	loop for $i := RemoveIndex$ to $size - 1$
2.2	$data[i] := data[i + 1]$
2.3	loopend
2.4	$size := size - 1$
2.5	$success :=$ true
3	else
4	$success :=$ false
5	ifend

_____

data, size
_____

Data table

Identifier	Description	Type
i	Loop control variable	*sizetype* variable

Test data

We can use a similar driver program to that of Problem 8.3(i), but here we need to include tests for unsuccessful removals. The design below uses the identifiers of Problem 8.3(i) with the addition of *flag*, which is a Boolean actual parameter corresponding to the formal parameter *success*.

1.1	loop for $i := 1$ to *maxsize* {initialize all array elements}
1.2	$TestData[i] := 10 + i$
1.3	loopend
1.4	$TestSize := maxsize$;
1.5	$continue :=$ 'y';
2	loop while $continue =$ 'y'
3.1	write out 'Index of last element is ', *TestSize*
3.2	write out 'Enter index to be removed '
3.2	read in *DeleteIndex*
3.3	remove(*TestData, DeleteIndex, TestSize, flag*);
4.1	if *flag* then
4.2	loop for $i := 1$ to *TestSize* {write out the array elements}
4.3	write out $TestData[i]$
4.4	loopend
4.5	else
4.6	write out 'Invalid input data – no changes made'
4.7	ifend
5.1	write out 'Continue y/n '
5.2	read in *continue*
6	loopend

Problem 8.4

Problem statement

A procedure is to be written that takes a year as source data and has two results: a Boolean whose value is to be true if the year is a leap year, false otherwise, and the next occurrence of a leap year. You may assume that the source data are represented by an integer and that a leap year is one in which its integer representation is exactly divisible by 4.

leapyear

year	20th century year	*integer* parameter
{If *year* is a leap year assign *currentleap* the value true otherwise set it false. In either event assign to *nextleap* the next occurrence of a leap year.}		
currentleap *nextleap*	True if *year* is a leap year Next leap year occurrence	*Boolean* parameter *integer* parameter

Design

leapyear

year

1	*currentleap* := false
2	select case depending on (*year* mod 4)
3.1	0 : *currentleap* := true
3.2	*nextleap* := *year* + 4
3.3	1 : *nextleap* := *year* + 3
3.4	2 : *nextleap* := *year* + 2
3.5	3 : *nextleap* := *year* + 1
4	selectend

nextleap, currentleap

Test data

A loop which calls *leapyear* for four consecutive years and writes out the status of the results parameters will suffice. In our driver program below, we let the loop execute over a greater number of years than this bare minimum.

1	loop for *currentyear* := 1990 to 1999
2.1	*leapyear*(*currentyear*, *nextleap*, *isleap*);
2.2	if *isleap* then
2.3	write out *currentyear*, ' is a leap year and next one is ', *nextleap*
2.4	else
2.5	write out *currentyear*, ' is not a leap year but next one is ', *nextleap*
2.6	ifend
3	loopend

Data table

Identifier	Description	Type
currentyear *nextleap* *isleap*	Loop control variable Next leap year after *currentyear* Flag denoting current year is a leap year	*integer* variable *integer* variable *Boolean* variable

Problem 8.5

Problem statement

Write a Pascal function corresponding to the specification:

confirm

prompt	A string prompt	*string* parameter
{Write out *prompt* and read in a character from the keyboard. If the character is 'y' or 'Y' assign true to *result* otherwise assign it the value false.}		
confirm	True for 'y' or 'Y'	*Boolean* function value

Design
We have chosen to use the identifier *confirm* for the name of this function.

confirm

prompt

	{Check response for 'y' or 'Y'}
1.1	write out *prompt*
1.2	read in *ch*
2.1	*confirm* := (*ch* = 'y') or (*ch* = 'Y')

confirm

Data table

Identifier	Description	Type
ch	Input character	*char* variable

Test data
A simple driver program design, in which *message* is a string variable, is as follows:

1	if *confirm*('This is a test message. Press y/n to continue.') then
2	write out 'User responded yes to test message'
3	else
4	write out 'User did not respond yes to test message'
5	ifend
6	*message* := 'A string stored in a variable. Press y/n to continue.'
7	if *confirm*(*message*) then
8	write out 'User responded yes to test message'
9	else
10	write out 'User did not respond yes to test message'
11	ifend

Problem 8.6

Problem statement
Write a Pascal function corresponding to the following specification:

Data table

Identifier	Description	Type
maxsize	Array index upper bound	*integer* constant
vector	Array type definition	array[1..*maxsize*] of *integer*
compare	(*first, second*)	*Boolean* function(*vector, vector*)

compare		
first	First array	*vector* parameter
second	Second array	*vector* parameter
{Compare the two arrays element by element. If the arrays have identical corresponding elements assign *result* the value true otherwise assign to it the value false.}		
compare	True if arrays identical	*Boolean* function value

Design

compare
___
first, second
___

	{compare the two arrays}
1.1	*result* := true
2.1	loop while $i <= 20$ and *result*
3.1	if *first*[*i*] <> *second*[*i*] then
3.2	*result* := false
3.3	ifend
3.4	$i := i + 1$
4	loopend
5	*compare* := *result*

___
compare
___

Test data

A driver program is required that will enable both possible outcomes to be tested. The program below will have to be executed for each different set of initial values for the arrays. For this reason, *maxsize* is chosen to be very small.

1.1	loop for $i := 1$ to *maxsize*
1.2	write out 'For arrays enter both values for index ', i
1.3	read in *firstvect*[*i*], *secondvect*[*i*]
1.4	loopend
2.1	write out 'Arrays initialized as follows'
2.2	write out 'Index Array1 Array2'
2.3	loop for $i := 1$ to *maxsize*
2.4	write out i, *firstvect*[*i*], *secondvect*[*i*]
2.5	loopend
3.1	if *compare*(*firstvect*, *secondvect*) then
3.2	write out 'The arrays are the same.'
3.3	else
3.4	write out 'The arrays differ.'
3.5	ifend

Data table

Identifier	Description	Type
firstvect	First array	*vector* variable
secondvect	Second array	*vector* variable
i	Loop control variable	*integer* variable

Sets of values for the arrays could include the following:

	firstvect	*secondvect*	
(a)	1 2 3	1 2 3	{Corresponding elements are the same}
(b)	1 2 3	2 2 3	{Differ in the first element}
(c)	1 2 4	1 2 3	{Differ in the last element}

Problem 8.7

Problem statement

The following specification is an example of a procedure which has no results. Write a Pascal procedure declaration for it.

blanklines

n	Number of blank lines	*integer* parameter
{Output *n* blank lines to the screen.}		

Design

blanklines

n

	{Output *n* blank lines}
1	loop for *i* := 1 to *n*
2	write out
3	loopend

Test data

We need to be able to count the blank lines and to test for different actual parameter values. The following simple program design, in which *n* is an integer variable, caters for both of these:

1 write 'Enter number of blank lines '
2 read in *n*
3 *blanklines*(*n*)
4 write out 'There are ', *n*, ' blank lines above this one'

This program should be executed with input values consisting of 0, 1 and 2.

Problem 8.8

Problem statement

The integer part of a real number is the largest integer that does not exceed the number. For example, the integer part of 23.45 is 23. Negative real numbers are a little more difficult. The integer part of − 3.45 is − 4 and not − 3 as you might at first suppose. This is because − 3 exceeds − 3.45 (it is nearer to zero than − 3.45 is and hence is larger than it). However, − 4 does not exceed − 3.45 and so must be its integer part. You are to write a function to find the integer part of a real number. The specification of the function is:

integerpart

x	A real number	*real* parameter
{Find the integer part of *x*, that is, the largest integer that does not exceed *x*.}		
integerpart	Integer part of *x*	*integer* function value

Test data

A very simple driver program, in which *x* is a real variable, is as follows:

1 write 'Enter a real '
2 read in *x*
3 write out 'Integer part is ', *integerpart*(*x*)

This will need to be executed with positive input values, negative input values, 0, and other positive and negative integers.

Design

integerpart

x

1	*intx* := 0
2.1	if *x* > 0 then
3.1	loop while *x* >= 1
3.2	decrement *x*
3.3	*intx* := *intx* + 1
3.4	loopend
4	else
5.1	loop while *x* < 0
5.2	increment *x*
5.3	*intx* := *intx* − 1
5.4	loopend
6	ifend
7	*integerpart* := *intx*

integerpart

Data table

Identifier	Description	Type
intx	Local variable used in calculation	*integer* variable

Problem 8.9

Problem statement

A large educational establishment employs a large number of tutors, each of whom marks a number of student scripts. Each marked script contains the grade obtained on each question and the overall grade, this being the sum of the individual question scores. The individual scores and the overall grade are entered into a computer, which checks that the overall score is indeed the sum of the individual scores. Write a Pascal function for the specification of this validation process given below.

TotalValid

question1	Score on Question 1	*integer* parameter
question2	Score on Question 2	*integer* parameter
question3	Score on Question 3	*integer* parameter
total	Recorded total grade	*integer* parameter
{If the sum of the three question scores is the same as the recorded total grade then assign true to *valid*, otherwise assign the value false.}		
TotalValid	True if *total* is correct	*Boolean* function value

Design

TotalValid

question1, question2, question3, total

1	*TotalValid* := (*total* = *question1* + *question2* + *question3*)

TotalValid

Test data

The following simple program, in which all variables are of type *integer*, can be used to test the function:

1.1	write 'Enter 3 question scores '
1.2	read in *qu1*, *qu2*, *qu3*
1.3	write 'Enter the sum of the 3 question scores '
1.4	read in *total*
2.1	if *TotalValid*(*qu1*, *qu2*, *qu3*, *total*) then
2.2	write out 'Sum is correct'
2.3	else
2.4	write out 'Sum is not correct'
2.5	ifend

This program needs to be executed with input data that sum correctly and input data that do not sum correctly.

Problem 8.10

Problem statement

Automatic change machines must calculate the number of coins of each denomination to issue before delivering the coins to the customer. This problem is concerned with a design for a procedure for doing this calculation. It is assumed that the only coins in the machine are pound, fifty pence, twenty pence, ten pence, five pence and one pence coins. The procedure is to return the minimum number of coins of each denomination that are required to make up any input sum of money. The amount, 3 pounds 45 pence, is written as £3.45, and this will be passed to the procedure as the integer 345. Write a design for this procedure whose detailed specification is:

change

money	An amount of money in pence	*integer* parameter
{Find the least number of coins of each of the denominations £1, 50p, 20p, 10p, 5p, 2p, 1p to make up the amount represented by *money*. }		
pounds	Number of pound coins	*integer* parameter
fifties	Number of 50p coins	*integer* parameter
twenties	Number of 20p coins	*integer* parameter
tens	Number of 10p coins	*integer* parameter
fives	Number of 5p coins	*integer* parameter
twos	Number of 2p coins	*integer* parameter
ones	Number of 1p coins	*integer* parameter

Test data

In the driver program below we have used the same identifiers for the actual parameters as for the formal ones.

1	write 'Enter an amount of money '
2	read in *money*
3	*change*(*money*, *pounds*, *fifties*, *twenties*, *tens*, *fives*, *ones*)
4	write out *pounds*, ' Pounds'
5	write out *fifties*, ' Fifties'
6	write out *twenties*, ' Twenties'
7	write out *tens*, ' Tens'
8	write out *fives*, ' Fives'
9	write out *ones*, ' Ones'

It is impossible to test all possible combinations of coin outputs here. We should certainly execute this program with the values 1, 2, 5, 20, 50 and 100, as in each case this should result in a single denomination of coin (i.e. all output values except 1 are zero). We should also test 0 and 186, the latter requiring one coin of every denomination.

Design

change
_____

money
_____

1.1	*pounds* := *money* div 100
1.2	*SumLeft* := *money* mod 100
2.1	*fifties* := *SumLeft* div 50
2.2	*SumLeft* := *SumLeft* mod 50
3.1	*twenties* := *SumLeft* div 20
3.2	*SumLeft* := *SumLeft* mod 20
4.1	*tens* := *SumLeft* div 10
4.2	*SumLeft* := *SumLeft* mod 10
5.1	*fives* := *SumLeft* div 5
5.2	*SumLeft* := *SumLeft* mod 5
6.1	*twos* := *SumLeft* div 2
6.2	*SumLeft* := *SumLeft* mod 2
7.1	*ones* := *SumLeft*

_____

pounds, fifties, twenties, tens, fives, twos, ones
_____

Problem 8.11*

Problem statement

Many operating systems only use upper case characters and automatically convert any user inputs of lower case characters to upper case. In this problem you are to use the built-in function *upcase*, which converts a lower case character to its upper case equivalent, to write an analogous procedure for string inputs.

upinput

{Read characters from the keyboard into the string *input*. Before echoing characters to the screen and before storing them convert any lower case alphabetic characters to upper case.}		
input	An upper case string	*string* parameter

Design

The code can be based on the design below in which *ch* is a *char* variable. The <ret> character has ordinal value 13.

upinput
_____

1	initialize input to null string
2	repeat
3	*ch* := *readkey*
4	write the upper case version of *ch* to the screen
5	if input character is not <ret> then
6	concatenate *ch* to input
7	until current character is <ret>
8	write out new line character

_____

input

Test data

This should include both upper and lower case characters as well as non-alphabetic characters.

Problem 8.12*

Problem statement

The procedure in Problem 8.11 did not permit the user to erase erroneous inputs. In this problem we extend the specification to allow the use of the delete key. It has ordinal value 8.

upinput

{Read characters from the keyboard into the string *input*. Before echoing characters to the screen and before storing them convert any lower case alphabetic characters to upper case. Erroneous input characters may be deleted with the delete key.}		
input	An upper case string	*string* parameter

Design

To cater for the delete key we first need to identify when it has been pressed. The actions that have to be taken when it is detected are to move the cursor left by one position, erase the character at that position leaving the cursor in the same place, and then to remove the character from the end of the input string. To move the cursor one position left requires knowledge of its current position. The built-in function *wherex* gives the x co-ordinate of the cursor and the function *wherey* gives its y co-ordinate. Neither of these functions has any parameters. The procedure can be based on the following design:

upinput

```
1      initialize input to null string
2      repeat
3        ch := readkey
4        select case depending on ord(ch)
5.1        32..126 :  write upcase(ch)
5.2                   concatenate ch to input
5.3        8       :  move cursor one position left
5.4                   write ' '
5.5                   move cursor one position left
5.6                   delete last character of input
6        selectend
7      until current character is <ret>
8      write out new line character
```

input

Test data

Similar test data can be used here as in Problem 8.11, but user inputs will have to include the use of the delete key. One test should include the input of some characters followed immediately by their deletion. This test should also try to delete from an empty input sequence.

Problem 8.13*

Problem statement

Integer values are often written out with leading zeros so the same numbers of characters are written out irrespective of the integer value. This problem is concerned with a procedure to write out integers in this form.

StrWrite

value	An integer value	*integer* parameter
space	A field width	*integer* parameter
{Write the integer *value* on a field width of *space* inserting leading zeros if required. If field width is too small then ignore it.}		

Design

The design can exploit the built-in procedure *Str* which converts a numeric value to its string representation. It has two parameters, the first of which in this case will be an *integer* parameter and the second a *string* parameter. The procedure can be based on the following design:

StrWrite

value, space

```
1    convert value to a string
2    if length(valstr) < space then
3        loop for i := 1 to space − length(valstr)
4            write '0'
5    write value
```

Data table

Identifier	Description	Type
i	Loop control variable	*integer* variable
valstr	String equivalent of an integer	*string* variable

Test data

The driver program will have to test that the correct number of leading zeros are inserted and that integers which exceed the given field width are written out correctly. The following design is for a simple driver program in which *i* and *number* are integer variables:

```
1    loop for i := 0 to 4
2        StrWrite(number, 4)
3        number := 10*number
4        write out new line character
5    loopend
```

Problem 8.14

Problem statement

Write a Pascal declaration for the following procedure specification:

swap

a	First number	*real* parameter
b	Second number	*real* parameter
{Exchange the values stored by *a* and *b*.}		
a	Stores the old second number	*real* parameter
b	Stores the old first number	*real* parameter

Design

swap

a, b

1	*temp := a*
2	*a := b*
3	*b := temp*

a, b

Test data

We have used the same actual parameter identifiers in the following driver program:

1 *writeln*('Enter two reals ');
2 *readln*(*a, b*);
3. *writeln*('a has value ', *a*:4:2, ' b has value ', *b*:4:2);
4 *swap*(*a, b*);
5 *writeln*('a has value ', *a*:4:2, ' b has value ', *b*:4:2);

Test values should include those that are the same as well as those that differ.

Problem 8.15

Problem statement

Write a design corresponding to the procedure specification below. The part of the procedure that asks the user to confirm that the input is correct should be designed using the function specification *confirm* of Problem 8.5. However, the design of the function should be modified so that it exploits the built-in function *readkey* at step 1.2.

readstring

{Prompt for a string of characters to be input from the keyboard. Accept the string to the parameter *instring*. Write out *instring* and ask the user if it is correct. Repeat until the user confirms the input is correct.}		
instring	String input by user	*string* parameter

Design

readstring

1	repeat
2.1	write 'Enter a string '
2.2	read in *instring*
2.3	write out 'Your entry was ', *instring*
3	until *confirm*('Press Y to confirm any other key to re-enter :')

instring

Test data
The driver program can consist of a single statement, namely, a call to *confirm*. Testing should include the rejection of the initial input to test that the loop described in the specification functions correctly.

Problem 8.16
Problem statement
Write a function declaration for the following specification:

inrange

start	Lower bound of a *char* range	*char* parameter
finish	Upper bound of a *char* range	*char* parameter
between	Any character	*char* parameter
{Determine whether *between* satisfies *start* <= *between* <= *finish*. If it does, then *inrange* is set to true, otherwise it is set to false.}		
inrange	Result of test	*Boolean* function value

Design

inrange
_____

_____
   1   inrange := (*start* <= *between*) and (*between* <= *finish*)
inrange
_____

Test data
The driver program must be able to test values that are in range and those that are not. The following design enables this to be done on different executions. All variables are of type *char*.

```
 1    write 'Enter the first character of the range followed by <ret> '
 2    read in first
 3    write 'Enter the second character of the range followed by <ret> '
 4    read in last
 5    write 'Enter any character followed by <ret> '
 6    read in middle
 7    if inrange(first, last, middle) then
 8       write out 'Last entry was between the first two'
 9    else
10       write out 'Last entry was not between the first two'
11    ifend
```

Problem 8.17
Problem statement
Write a procedure declaration for the following specification:

newrange

start	Lower bound of *char* subrange	*char* parameter
target	Character within subrange	*char* parameter
finish	Upper bound of *char* subrange	*char* parameter
shot	Any character in subrange	*char* parameter

{Replace the subrange *start..finish* by one of the subranges *start..shot*, *shot..finish* or *shot..shot* determined by whether *shot* comes after *target*, *shot* comes before *target* or *shot* equals *target* respectively. For example, if *start*, *target* and *finish* have values 'a', 'g' and 'z' respectively and *shot* has value 'k' then, since 'k' comes after 'g', the new subrange will be 'a'..'k' so that *start* will be returned with value 'a' and *finish* with value 'k'. Notice that the new subrange still contains *target* but is smaller than the original subrange.}

start	New lower bound of subrange	*char* parameter
finish	New upper bound of subrange	*char* parameter

Design

newrange

start, finish, target, shot

```
1    if shot > target then
2        finish := shot
3    else
4        if shot < target then
5            start := shot
6        else
7            start := target
8            finish := target
9        ifend
10   ifend
```

start, finish

Test data

We have used the same actual parameter identifiers in the driver program.

```
1    start := 'a'
2    finish := 'z'
3    write 'Enter a target character '
4    read in target
5    repeat
6        write 'Enter a guess of the target '
7        read in shot
8        newrange(start, finish, target, shot)
9        write out 'New range is ', start, finish
10   until (shot = target)
```

Given the initialization of *start* and *finish*, at least three values of *target* should be used: 'a', 'z' and some value between. Within the loop the target should be approached both from 'above' and 'below' and a mixture of both. So, for example, if *target* is set to 'm' then the four executions with this value should be carried out with guess inputs as follows:

(a) 'a' 'l' 'm' {Approach from below starting with initial character of range)
(b) 'z' 'n' 'm' {Approach from above starting with last character of range)
(c) 'l' 'n' 'm' {Alternate from above and below}
(d) 'm'   {Get it on first attempt}

Problem 8.18

Problem statement

Write a program that uses the routines in Problems 8.16 and 8.17 to play the following game. Player 1 chooses a letter, which we shall call the target, in the range 'a' to 'z', and player 2 has to discover the target in as few guesses as possible. To help player 2 a prompt is to be given indicating the subrange in which the target letter lies. Initially, this subrange is 'a' to 'z', but after each guess it will be updated by replacing one of the end points by the guess, in such a way that the new subrange contains the target. The game concludes as soon as player 2 guesses the target. When this happens, the number of guesses required is to be output. All input is to be validated, which means that any input which does not lie in the prompted range is to be ignored and does not contribute to the game. Typical output from the program, in which user responses are underlined, would be:

```
First player: Enter a letter in the range a to z r
Second player: Enter a guess in the range a to z c
Second player: Enter a guess in the range c to z b
Guess is not in stated range - guess is ignored
Second player: Enter a guess in the range m to z r
You took 3 attempts
```

Design

1.1	*count* := 0
1.2	*start* := 'a'
1.3	*finish* := 'z'
2	repeat
3.1	write out 'First player: Enter a letter in the range ', *start*, ' to ' , *finish*
3.2	read in *target*
4.1	until *inrange*('a', 'z', *target*)
5	repeat
6.1	write out 'Second player: Enter a guess in the range ', *start*, ' to ', *finish*
6.2	read in *shot*
7.1	if not *inrange*(*start*, *finish*, *shot*) then
7.2	write out 'Guess is not in the stated range – guess is ignored'
7.3	else
7.4	*newrange*(*start*, *finish*, *target*, *shot*)
7.5	*count* := *count* + 1
7.6	ifend
8.1	until *finish* = *start*
9.1	write out 'You took ', *count*, ' attempts'

Data table

Identifier	Description	Type
inrange	(*start*, *finish*, *target*)	*Boolean* function(*char*, *char*, *char*)
newrange	(*start*, *finish*, *target*, *shot*)	procedure(*char*, *char*, *char*, *char*)
count	Number of guesses	*integer* variable
start	Lower bound of subrange	*char* variable
finish	Upper bound of subrange	*char* variable
target	Character to be guessed	*char* variable
shot	The guess of player 2	*char* variable

Test data

Essentially, this problem requires the assembly of the different routines developed in Problems 8.15 and 8.16. Since these routines have already been tested, all that is required here is to check that the screen outputs are satisfactory, guesses outside the stated range are ignored and that the count of the number of attempts is correct.

Problem 10.1*

Write a driver program that will enable all the operations of the abstract data type *tabletype*, as implemented by the unit *uTable1*, to be tested at the same time. Your program should consist of a loop within which the operations can be selected from a menu. The menu should have the following form:

```
1 : Insert data into table
2 : Search table
3 : Test for full table
4 : Display the table
5 : Quit

Enter your choice
```

What changes would have to be made to your program to test the second implementation stored in **unit** *uTable2*?

Problem 10.2

Problem statement

The notation 3:45.6 is often used to denote the period of time 3 minutes 45.6 seconds where .6 is the decimal part of a second. Here, we shall only consider periods of time consisting of minutes and seconds, the latter having at most one decimal place. The notion of negative times is not included, and so all times are positive or zero. A record structure of type *timetype*, consisting of the three fields *minutes*, *seconds* and *decimalpart*, will be used to store time values. These values, together with the operations described below, will make up an abstract data type called *timetype*.

The operations on *timetype* are defined below. You are asked to implement them as a Pascal unit called *uTimADT1*.

readin

{Read in a time expressed in the form m:s.d where m is any number of digits representing minutes, s consists of at most two digits representing seconds and d is a single digit representing the decimal part of a second. No validation is required on the input which may be assumed to be in exactly the correct format and so will always contain a single colon and a single (decimal) point.}		
time	Time read in	*timetype* parameter

writeout

time	Time to be written out	*timetype* parameter
{Write out the time in the format m:s.d where m is the number of minutes, s the whole number of seconds output as two digits and d the decimal part of the number of seconds. A time like 2.5 seconds should be output in the form 0:02.5.}		

add

a	Operand of operator	*timetype* parameter
b	Operand of operator	*timetype* parameter
{Add time *a* to time *b* and assign to *result*.}		
result	Sum of *a* and *b*	*timetype* parameter

Design

First, we give the data table containing the declarations that will go in the interface part of the Pascal unit.

Data table for Pascal unit uTimADT1

Identifier	Description	Type
	PRIVATE	
timetype	Record type definition	
	minutes	*integer* variable
	seconds	0..59 variable
	decimalpart	0..9 variable
	recordend	
	PUBLIC	
timetype	Type definition representing time	private
readin	(*time*)	procedure(*timetype*)
writeout	(*time*)	procedure(*timetype*)
add	(*a, b, result*)	procedure(*timetype*, *timetype*, *timetype*)

Now we give the designs of the individual operations.

readin

```
1    read in input
2    with time do
3        minutes := 0
4        seconds := 0
5        decimalpart := 0
6        i := 1
7        loop while input[i] <> ':'
8            minutes := 10*minutes + ord(input[i])
                 – ord('0')
9            i := i + 1
10       loopend
11       i := i + 1
12       loop while input[i] <> '.'
13           seconds := 10*seconds
                 + ord(input[i]) – ord('0')
14           i := i + 1
15       loopend
16       i := i + 1
17       decimalpart := ord(input[i]) – ord('0')
18   withend
```
time

writeout

```
1    with time do
2        if minutes > 0 then
3            write minutes, ':'
4        else
5            write '0:'
6        ifend
7        if seconds = 0 then
8            write out '00.'
9        else
10           if seconds < 10 then
11               write '0', seconds, '.'
12           else
13               write seconds, '.'
14           ifend
15       ifend
16       write decimalpart
17   withend
```

add

----

a, b

----

1   *total := a.decimalpart + b.decimalpart*
2   *result.decimalpart := total* mod 10
3   *carry := total* div 10
4   *total := a.seconds + b.seconds + carry*
5   *result.seconds := total* mod 60
6   *carry := total* div 60
7   *result.minutes := a.minutes + b.minutes + carry*

----

result

Data table for add

Identifier	Description	Type
total	Sum of components	*integer* variable
carry	Carry resulting from addition	0..1 variable

Test data
To test the abstract data type we need a driver program that will enable us to test all three operators. The simplest program is one that reads in two times, adds them and writes out their sum. The design below, in which all the variables are of type *timetype*, will enable this to be done.

1   write 'Enter first time in the form m:n.p where m, n, p are digits'
2   *readin(time1)*
3   write 'Enter second time in the form m:n.p where m, n, p are digits'
4   *readin(time2)*
5   *add(time1, time2, result)*
6   write 'Sum of the two times is '
7   *writeout(result)*

Test data values need to be chosen to see whether *readin* works as specified, whether *add* sums times correctly, and whether *writeout* produces output in the correct form.

Problem 10.3*

Problem statement
In this problem you are asked to extend the abstract data type *timetype* by including an additional operator, *subtract*, whose specification is given below. The new abstract data type should be implemented in a Pascal unit called *TimeADT2*.

subtract

a	Operand of operator	*timetype* parameter
b	Operand of operator	*timetype* parameter
{If time *b* is after time *a* then assign the difference *b − a* to *result* and set *flag* true. Otherwise set *flag* false.}		
result	The difference *b − a*	*timetype* parameter
flag	Set false if subtraction not allowed	*Boolean* parameter

Design
The simplest design is to convert the representations *a* and *b* into real values and to subtract the real values. This result then needs to be converted back into the representation used in *timetype*. To do this will require the use of the built-in Turbo Pascal procedures *trunc* and

round. Both return values of *integer* type, the former truncating and thereby ignoring any decimal part, the latter rounding to the nearest integer before conversion.

subtract

---

a, b

1.1	with *a* do
1.2	*aseconds* := 60*minutes* + *seconds* + *decimalpart* /10
1.3	withend
2.1	with *b* do
2.2	*bseconds* := 60*minutes* + *seconds* + *decimalpart* /10
2.3	withend
3.1	if *bseconds* < *aseconds* then
4	*flag* := false
5	else
6.1	*flag* := true
6.2	*difference* := *bseconds* − *aseconds*
6.3	with *result* do
6.4	*minutes* := trunc(*difference*) div 60
6.5	*seconds* := trunc(*difference*) mod 60
6.6	*difference* := 10*(*difference* − 60**minutes* − *seconds*)
6.7	*decimalpart* := round(*difference*)
6.8	withend
6.9	ifend

---

result

Data table for subtract

Identifier	Description	Type
aseconds	Time *a* as a real	*real* variable
bseconds	Time *b* as a real	*real* variable
difference	*bseconds* − *aseconds*	*real* variable

Test data

The driver program in Problem 10.2 can be adapted to include a call to *subtract*. This procedure will need more thorough testing than the others because subtraction of times is not straightforward even when doing it by hand!

Problem 10.4

Problem statement

In this problem we shall define and implement an abstract data type *moneytype* to represent amounts of money. The operations below define *moneytype*. The specification of *readin* exploits a real variable to simplify the design of this operation. In *writeout* we use the symbol $ to denote the unit of currency. The abstract data type will be implemented in a Pascal unit *uMoney1*.

readin

{Read in an amount of money to *amount*. The amount is to be entered as a real number having at most 2 decimal places. No validation is to be carried out on this input.}		
amount	Amount of money read in	*moneytype* parameter

writeout

a	An amount of money	*moneytype* parameter
{Write out *amount* together with the appropriately placed symbol $. For example, the amounts 3 units 45 cents and minus 4 units 8 cents should be written out as $3.45 and −$4.08 respectively.}		

add

a	An amount of money	*moneytype* parameter
b	An amount of money	*moneytype* parameter
{Assign to *results* the sum of money $a + b$.}		
result	Sum of a and b	*moneytype* parameter

subtract

a	An amount of money	*moneytype* parameter
b	An amount of money	*moneytype* parameter
{Assign to *results* the difference of money $a - b$.}		
result	The difference $a - b$	*moneytype* parameter

Test data

To test the abstract data type we need a driver program that will enable us to test all four operators. The simplest program is one that reads in two amounts of money, adds them, writes out their sum, subtracts them and writes out their difference. The design below, in which all the variables are of type *moneytype*, will enable this to be done.

1   write out 'Enter an amount of money as a real '
2   *readin(a)*
3   write out 'Enter a second amount of money as a real '
4   *readin(b)*
5   *add(a, b, sum)*
6   write 'Sum of the two amounts is '
7   *writeout(result)*
8   *subtract(a, b, difference)*
9   write 'Difference of the two amounts is '
10 *writeout(difference)*

Design

First, we give the data table containing the declarations that will go in the interface part of the Pascal unit.

Data table for Pascal unit uMoney1

Identifier	Description	Type
	PRIVATE	
moneytype	Type definition for money	*integer*
	PUBLIC	
moneytype	Type definition for money	private
readin	(*amount*)	procedure(*moneytype*)
writeout	(*amount*)	procedure(*moneytype*)
add	(*a, b, result*)	procedure(*moneytype, moneytype, moneytype*)
subtract	(*a, b, result*)	procedure(*moneytype, moneytype, moneytype*)

Now we give the designs of the individual operations.

writeout	
amount	
1	if *amount* >= 0 then
2.1	write '$', *amount* div 100, '.'
2.2	if *amount* mod 100 < 10 then
2.3	write '0', *amount* mod 100
2.4	else
2.5	write *amount* mod 100
2.6	ifend
3	else
4.1	write '–$', (–*amount*) div 100, '.'
4.2	if (–*amount*) mod 100 < 10 then
4.3	write '0', (–*amount*) mod 100
4.4	else
4.5	write (–*amount*) mod 100
4.6	ifend
5	ifend

readin	
1	read in *amount*
2	*amount* := *round*(100*amount)
amount	

add	
a, b	
1	*result* := *a* + *b*
result	

subtract	
a, b	
1	*result* := *a* – *b*
result	

Problem 10.5

Suppose a user had somehow managed to work out that *moneytype* in Problem 10.4 is implemented as *integer* and was trying to circumvent the input operation *readin* provided by the abstract data type. Why would the following attempt fail?

```
program Naughty;
uses uMoney1;
var
  a, b, sum : integer;
begin
  write('Enter an amount of money as a real ');
  readln(a);
  write('Enter a second amount of money as a real ');
  readln(b);
  add(a, b, sum);
    :
```

Problem 10.6

Problem statement

In this problem we contrast the implementation of *moneytype* given in Problem 10.4 with one that uses a totally different representation. Here, dollars and cents are to be represented as integer field values. For positive amounts of money both field values are positive and for negative amounts both will be negative. So, for example, the field values representing – $4.56 will be – 4 and – 56 respectively. The data table below defines the fields. Note that data hiding occurs naturally here because *moneytype* is a record and so cannot be manipulated without a detailed knowledge of its fields. The new implementation should be called *uMoney2*.

Design

First, we give the data table containing the declarations that will go in the interface part of the Pascal unit.

Data table for Pascal unit uMoney2

Identifier	Description	Type
	PRIVATE	
moneytype	Record type definition	
	dollars	*integer* variable
	cents	–99..99 variable
	recordend	
	PUBLIC	
moneytpe	Type definition for money	private
readin	(*amount*)	procedure(*moneytype*)
writeout	(*amount*)	procedure(*moneytype*)
add	(*a, b, result*)	procedure(*moneytype, moneytype, moneytype*)
subtract	(*a, b, result*)	procedure(*moneytype, moneytype, moneytype*)

---

add

---

a, b

---

1   *pence := a.cents + b.cents*
2.1 if *pence* >= 100 then
2.2   *carry := 1*
2.3   *pence := pence – 100*
2.4 else
2.5   if *pence* <= –100 then
2.6   *carry := –1*
2.7   *pence := pence + 100*
2.8   else
2.9   *carry := 0*
2.10   ifend
2.11   ifend
3.1 with *result* do
3.2   *cents := pence*
3.3   *dollars := a.dollars + b.dollars + carry*
3.3   if (*dollars* < 0) and (*cents* > 0) then
            {make both the same sign}
3.4   *dollars := dollars + 1*
3.5   *cents := cents – 100*
3.6   else
3.7   if (*dollars* > 0) and (*cents* < 0) then
                {make both the same sign}
3.8   *dollars := dollars – 1*
3.9   *cents := cents + 100*
3.10   ifend
3.12   ifend
3.13   withend

---

result

---

readin

---

1   read in *moneyin*
2   with *amount* do
3   *dollars := trunc(moneyin)*
4   *cents := round(100*moneyin*
            *– 100*dollars)*
5   withend

---

amount

---

writeout

---

amount

---

1   with *amount* do
2   if (*dollars* >= 0) and (*cents* >= 0) then
3   write '$', *dollars*, '.'
4   else
5   write '–$', *abs(dollars)*, '.'
6   ifend
7   if *abs(cents)* < 10 then
8   write '0'
9   ifend
10   write *abs(cents)*
11   withend

---

subtract

---

a, b

---

1   *b.dollars := –b.dollars*
2   *a.cents := –a.cents*
3   *add(a, b, result)*

---

result

Data table for add

Identifier	Description	Type
pence	Used in cent calculation	−198..198 variable
carry	Carry resulting from addition	−1..1 variable

Data table for readin

Identifier	Description	Type
moneyin	A sum of money	*real* variable

Test data

Exactly the same driver program can be used here as in Problem 10.4, except that the reference to *uMoney1* will have to be changed to *uMoney2*. The program will then have to be recompiled. The new abstract data type will need thorough testing since all the operations have different implementations.

Problem 11.1

Problem statement

A new stack is defined to include a new operation called *print*. This operation takes a stack as source data and writes out its contents to the screen, starting at the top of the stack and working towards the bottom. In other words, the output on the screen will have the top of the stack at the top of the screen. Suitable prompts should accompany the output so that this orientation of the output is clear to the user. The operation has no results. Write a Pascal unit called *uGenStk1* that implements this abstract data type.

Design

Essentially, all the design work is contained in the text. The procedure *display* in the program *TestuchStack* on page 192 can be adapted for use here. This requires a change of procedure identifier and a change to the parameter's type. All that is then required is to assemble it with the code for *uGenStk0* into a single Pascal unit using the new name.

Test data

Again, the program *TestuchStack* on pages 191–3 can be modified to provide a driver program for this abstract data type. The procedure *display* must be removed from the declarations and the call to it be replaced by a call to *print*.

Problem 11.2

Problem statement

The stack in this problem is defined to be the same as that in Problem 11.1, but with the operation *print* replaced by the operation *revprint*. This operation takes a stack as source data and writes out its contents, starting at the bottom of the stack and working towards the top. In other words, the bottom of the stack will appear at the top of the screen. Suitable prompts should accompany the output so that this orientation of the output is clear to the user. The operation has no results. What changes are required to the solution in Problem 11.1? (The unit implementing this change should be called *uGenStk2*.)

Problem 11.3

Problem statement

Write a Pascal unit called *uGenStk3* to implement a stack which is defined to have the operations *push*, *isempty* and *create*, as defined in *uGenStk1*, but which has a different *pop* operation. In addition, there is a new operation called *top*. The specifications of these operations are:

pop

stack	Representation of stack	*genstack* parameter
{Remove the item on top of *stack* and return updated stack. If the stack is empty write out 'stack underflow'.}		
stack	Updated stack	*genstack* parameter

top

stack	Representation of stack	*genstack* parameter
{Return the item at the top of the stack. If the stack is empty write out 'stack underflow'.}		
item	Updated stack	*integer* parameter

Design

pop		*top*	
stack		*stack*	
1	with *stack* do	1	with *stack* do
2	if *isempty*(*stack*) then	2	if *isempty*(*stack*) then
3	write out 'stack underflow'	3	write out 'stack underflow'
4	else	4	else
5	decrement *stacktop*	5	*item* := *stackarray*[*stacktop*]
6	ifend	6	ifend
7	withend	7	withend
stack		*item*	

Test data

The driver program will have to be updated to include an extra option to test *top*. The two routines will have to be tested on an empty stack as well as on one with items on it. Testing *top* will involve checking that the stack is not altered by the operation.

Problem 11.4

Problem statement

In Problem 7.6 we looked at a design for determining whether or not a sequence of brackets of the type '[' or ']' were well formed. We shall now generalize that problem by allowing different sorts of parentheses, including the brackets '[' and ']', to appear in arithmetic expressions. The parentheses may be nested to any level, and the problem is to determine whether an expression is well formed. For example, the expression {1 + (5*[8 + 3])}/4 is well formed and has value {1 + 55}/4, that is 14. Compare it with the following expressions, all of which are invalid: ((2 + 4), 7 + 4], ([2 + 6}*5). If we assume that an expression is scanned from left to right, a stack can be used to carry out this checking process by pushing opening parentheses onto the stack. When a closing parenthesis is encountered it must match the last parenthesis pushed onto the stack. This can be checked by popping the stack and checking for a match. If at any stage what is popped does not match the closing parenthesis then the expression is not well formed. Write a program that requests an expression and reports whether or not it is well formed. Should an expression not be well formed, this is to be reported immediately and no further characters should be examined. Your program should allow for parentheses of the type '(' '{' or '[' together with their closing equivalents. You may assume that the unit *uchStack* is available.

Design

The design will examine each character in turn. If it is an opening bracket then it will be pushed onto the stack. If it is a closing bracket then it will have to be compared with the character popped from the top of the stack. The comparison will be carried out by a function *match* specified below.

match

open	An opening bracket	*char* parameter
closed	A closing bracket	*char* parameter
{If *open* and *closed* are a matching opening and closing pair of brackets from the collection {, [, (then return the value true, otherwise return false.}		
match	True for matching brackets	*Boolean* function value

```
1.1     create(bracketstack)
1.2     valid := true
1.3     write 'Enter an arithmetic expression '
1.4     read in expression
1.5     index := 1
2.1     loop while valid and index <= length(expression)
3.1         select case depending on expression[index]
4.1             '(', '{', '[' :  push(bracketstack, expression[index])
4.2             ')', '}', ']' :  if isempty(bracketstack) then
4.3                                     valid := false
4.4                               else
4.5                                     pop(bracketstack, lastopener)
4.6                                     valid := match(lastopener, expression[index])
4.7                               ifend
5           selectend
6.1         index := index + 1
7       loopend
8.1     if not isempty(bracketstack) then
8.2         valid := false
8.3     ifend
8.4     if valid then
8.5         write out 'Expression is valid'
8.6     else
8.7         write out 'Expression is not well formed'
8.8     ifend
```

Data table

Identifier	Description	Type
bracketstack	Representation of *char* stack	*charstack* variable
match	(open, closed)	*Boolean* function(*char, char*)
valid	Flag denoting well formed expression	*Boolean* variable
expression	Input arithmetic expression	*string* variable
index	Index to current character	*integer* variable
lastopener	Character on top of stack	*char* variable

We leave the design of the function *match* to you.

Test data
This will need to include inputs which have no brackets, single brackets of the same type, single brackets of different types (not well formed) and sets of nested brackets.

Problem 11.5

Problem statement
Write a new version of the Pascal unit *uGenStk1* that uses a pointer-based implementation.

Design
The only operator not so far designed is that of *print*. In the design below, *current* is of type *genstack*.

print	
stack	

1	write out 'Top of stack'
2	*current := stack*
3	loop while *current <> nil*
4	write out *current^.stackitem*
5	*current := current^.link*
6	loopend
7	write out 'Bottom of stack'

Test data
What changes are required to the driver program of Problem 11.1 in order that it can be used here? The same test data as applied to Problem 11.1 can be applied here.

Problem 11.6

Problem statement
Write a Pascal unit called *uGenStk4*, to implement a pointer-based representation of a stack that has the same operations as those in *uGenStk1* together with the operation *count* specified below.

count		
stack	Representation of stack	*genstack* parameter
{Count the number of items in *stack*. If *stack* is empty return the value 0.}		
count	Number of items in *stack*	*integer* parameter

Design
In the design below *i* is an *integer* variable.

count	
stack	

1	*current := stack*
2	*i := 0*
3	loop while *current <> nil*
4	increment *i*
5	*current := current^.link*
6	loopend
7	*count := i*

count	

Test data
The driver program of Problem 11.1 can be modified to include the extra option corresponding to a call to *count*. This should be tested for empty and non-empty stacks.

Problem 11.7
Problem statement
Write a new version of the Pascal unit *uGenStk2* that uses a pointer-based implementation.

Design
All that is required is to replace the operation *print* in *uGenStk1* of Problem 11.5 by *revprint*. However, this is more difficult than the array version. This is because there is no variable that points to the bottom of the stack. The only way to overcome this is to go to the bottom of the stack, write out the element, then go to the penultimate item and write it out, and so on. What information do we require to, say, access the third item from the bottom of the stack? We need to know how many items are in the stack. The function *count* of Problem 11.6 can be used to determine this.

revprint

stack	
1	write out 'Bottom of stack'
1	*noitems* := *count*(*stack*)
2	loop for i := 1 to *noitems*
3	current := *stack*
4	loop for j := 1 to *noitems* − i
5	current := *current^.link*
6	loopend
7	write out *stack.stackitem*
8	loopend
7	write out 'Top of stack'

Data table

Identifier	Description	Type
noitems	Number of items in the stack	*integer* variable
count	(*stack*)	*integer* function(*genstack*)
current	Pointer to a stack item	*genstack* variable
i	Loop control variable	*integer* variable
j	Loop control variable	*integer* variable

Test data
This should be tested for zero and non-zero counts.

Problem 11.8
Problem statement
Write a new version of the Pascal unit *uGenStk3* that uses a pointer-based implementation.

Design
The implementation can be based on the pointer version of *uGenStk1* but with new procedures *pop* and *top*.

pop		top	
stack		*stack*	
1	if *isempty*(*stack*) then	1	if *isempty*(*stack*) then
2	write out 'stack underflow'	2	write out 'stack underflow'
3	else	3	else
4	*stack* := *stack^.link*	4	*item* := *stack^.stackitem*
5	ifend	5	ifend
stack		*item*	

Test data

What changes are required to the driver program of Problem 11.3 so that it can be used here? The same test data as were used in Problem 11.3 can be applied here.

Problem 11.9

What changes would be required if Problem 11.4 was now implemented using a pointer-based representation of the stack?

Problem 12.1

Problem statement

The abstract data type *stringqueue* is to have an additional operation, namely, that of printing a queue as given by the procedure *displayqueue* in Exercise 12.3. Describe the changes that would be required to *uqueue* in order to accommodate this change.

Problem 12.2

In this problem you are to write the interfaces for two different representations of the abstract data type *stock*. Since there are either 31 or 32 cards in the stock at any given time an array can be used to represent the stock. For simplicity, you should define *cardtype* to be the integer subrange 1..52.

(a)   In the first representation index 1 is used to represent the top of the stock and index 32 the bottom of the stock before a card is drawn. If the drawn card was taken from the top of the stock then all subsequent elements would be moved up the array so that the card which was at index 2 now becomes the new top card. This would then mean that the bottom card would have index 31. The player then discards, and this card would be assigned to the element at index 32.

(b)   Moving the array elements can be avoided by using variables to denote the index of the current top and bottom of the stock. This is analogous to the way the top of the array representation of a stack was recorded. Drawing a card from the bottom of the stock would not require the movement of the other array elements, as the draw and subsequent discard only involve the element with index 32. Write an interface for this representation.

Problem 12.3

An alternative representation would be to use a pointer-based system, similar to that of Figure 12.2, using a sequence of linked records with the data field representing a playing card. The same strategy to identify the top and bottom of the stock could be adopted as was used in Figure 12.3. Would it be necessary to include a dummy first item, as in the case of a queue? What problems are associated with drawing a card from the bottom of the stock with this representation, and how might they be resolved?

Problem 12.4
Write an interface for the representation described in Problem 12.3.

Problem 12.5
Problem statement
Write the implementation part for each of the operations *drawtop*, *drawbottom*, *showbottom*
and *replace*, based upon the definitions given in the solution to Problem 12.4.

Design

drawtop
stock
1   with *stock* do
2   *draw := top^.card*
3   *top := top^.link*
4   withend
stock, draw

drawbottom
stock
1   with *stock* do
2   *draw := bottom^.card*
3   *penultimate^.link := nil*
4   *bottom := penultimate*
5   *penultimate := nil*
6   *showbottom(stock)*
7   withend
stock, draw

replace
stock, discard
1   *new(temp)*
2   *temp^.card := discard*
3   *temp^.link := nil*
4   *bottom^.link := temp*
5   *penultimate := bottom*
6   *bottom := temp*
stock

showbottom
stock
1   write out *stock.bottom^.card*
stock, draw

Test data
Before we can write a driver program we will need to implement *makestock*. We shall do so
for purposes of testing by assigning integer values to the 32 cards of the stock. The driver
program itself will need to be able to draw cards from the top and bottom of the stock. Both
of these must then be followed by a call to *replace* so that a discard can be placed on the
bottom of the stock. We would want to be able to do this repeatedly, so a simple loop for
these actions is suggested. In order to see whether the routines are functioning correctly we
will need to be able to see the stock, or at least the top and bottom couple of cards. We shall
write a procedure *print*, whose task is to write out these cards to the screen. Testing will
require removal from the top and the bottom of the stock and checks to see that the discard
goes to the bottom of the stock.

Problem 12.6*
Problem statement
In this problem the specifications of *front* and *remove* are altered so that they return an
additional result status parameter.

front

queue	Representation of string queue	*stringqueue* parameter
{If *queue* is not empty set *success* to true and assign to *item* the value at the head of the queue leaving *queue* unaltered. Otherwise set *success* to false and leave *item* undefined.}		
item	Item at head of queue	*string* parameter
success	Error status flag	*Boolean* parameter

remove

queue	Representation of string queue	*stringqueue* parameter
{If *queue* is not empty remove the item at the head of *queue* and return updated *queue* setting success to true. Otherwise set *success* to false.}		
queue	Updated queue	*stringqueue* parameter
success	Error status flag	*Boolean* parameter

Write an implementation of a queue that uses these new specifications.

Design

The basic designs remain as before. However, they have to distinguish between an empty and a non-empty queue and to assign a value to *success* as appropriate. The driver program will need updating to reflect the fact that these two procedures have additional parameters.

Test data

The same data can be used to test this new implementation as that for the original implementation.

Problem 13.1

Problem statement

An administrator receives memos from colleagues and files them for processing in an in-tray. Each memo has a numerical code identifying its originator, and the administrator files the memos in chronological order of receipt within originator number. So, for example, all files originating from colleague 10 will be filed in order with the oldest memo at the top, all the memos from colleague 10 will precede those originating from colleague 11, and so on. The administrator processes one memo at a time by retrieving it from the pile, reading its contents and implementing any actions required. When this has been done, the memo is discarded. For a given originator, the administrator will deal with the memos in strict chronological order of receipt. Thus, for originator 10, the oldest memo will be dealt with first, followed by the next oldest, and so on. However, the administrator will choose the originator on whose memos to work. The system is to be computerized, and an abstract data type *pileofmemo* is to be designed that models the system described above. The memos consist of two pieces of data: an originator number and text corresponding to the message. The following operations are included in the definition of *pileofmemo*:

insert

pile	A representation of the in-tray	*pileofmemo* parameter
originator	Originator of memo	*integer* parameter
giveninfo	Text of memo	*string* parameter
{Insert the new memo in order of originator number. Within originator number, memos are ordered in chronological order of receipt.}		
pile	Updated memo pile	*pileofmemo* parameter

remove

pile	A representation of the in-tray	*pileofmemo* parameter
originator	Originator of memo	*integer* parameter

{Search for the first occurrence of a memo originating from *originator* in the pile, remove it from the pile and return the text of the memo to *item*. If no such memo exists assign to *item* the value 'No such memo'.}

pile	Updated memo pile	*pileofmemo* parameter
item	Text of memo from *originator*	*string* parameter

create

{Create a new pile of memos.}

pile	A new pile of memos	*pileofmemo* parameter

print

pile	A pile of memos	*pileofmemo* parameter

{Write out the contents of all memos in the in-tray, that is, the originator number and text for each memo in *pile*.}

isempty

pile	A pile of memos	*pileofmemo* parameter

{Return the value true if the pile is empty, false otherwise.}

isempty		*Boolean* function value

A linked representation is to be used for the abstract data type. The type *pileofmemo* will be a record having three fields: the first two corresponding to the originator and memo text and the third being a pointer to the next record. Write a Pascal implementation for this abstract data type and implement a driver program for testing it.

Design

The operations *insert* and *remove* are both going to involve searching, and so a dummy item will be used to avoid problems inserting into an empty pile or deleting to create an empty pile. The same search routine cannot be used for both *insert* and *remove* because that for *insert* will have to find the location of the last existing memo from the originator whereas the search for *remove* is required to find the first of the originator's list of memos. The data table corresponding to the interface of the unit is shown overleaf.

The procedure *insert*

The design of this routine assumes the use of a dummy record, and so the design can be based upon that in the text. The major problem then is specifying and designing an appropriate search routine. This is done by means of a procedure *inwhere*. The result of the search must point to the location of the predecessor to the insertion point because this record has to have its link field updated to point to the new item. An originator may or may not already have memos stored in the pile, so two loops are required. The first loop searches as far as the first of the originator's memos and the second then searches within them to their end.

Data table for Pascal unit uPile

Identifier	Description	Type
	PRIVATE	
pileofmemo	Pointer type definition	pointer to *pilerec*
pilerec	Record type definition	
	from {Originator's number}	*integer* variable
	info {Text of memo}	*string* variable
	link {Link to next record}	*pileofmemo* variable
	recordend	
	PUBLIC	
pileofmemo	A representation of the in-tray	private
insert	(*pile, originator, giveninfo*)	procedure(*pileofmemo, integer, string*)
isempty	(*pile*)	*Boolean* function(*pileofmemo*)
remove	(*pile, originator, item*)	procedure(*pileofmemo, integer, string*)
create	(*pile*)	procedure(*pileofmemo*)
print	(*pile*)	procedure(*pileofmemo*)

inwhere
___

pile, originator
___

  1.1   *pile^.from* := *originator*
  1.2   *lag* := *pile*
  1.3   *lead* := *pile^.link*
  2   loop while *lead^.from* < *originator*
  3.1   *lag* := *lead*
  3.2   *lead* := *lead^.link*
  4   loopend
         {*lag* now points to the predecessor of sequence of originator memos or to the predecessor of the insertion point}
  5   if (*lead^.from* = *originator*) and (*lead* <> *pile*) then
         {Find the end of the originator's sequence of memos}
         {Following search must stop prior to the dummy item}
  6.1   loop while (*lead^.from* = *originator*) and (*lead* <> *pile*)
  6.2   *lag* := *lead*
  6.3   *lead* := *lead^.link*
  6.4   loopend
  7   ifend
  8   *location* := *lag*

location
___

Data table for inwhere

Identifier	Description	Type
lead	Pointer to a memo record	*pileofmemo* variable
lag	Pointer lagging one record behind *lead*	*pileofmemo* variable

The design for *insert* is now very similar to the design developed in the text.

The procedure *remove*

To remove a memo, the user must choose an originator. The pile will then have to be searched for the first record with this originator. A similar routine to *flightsearch* could be specified for the search routine here, but we shall consider a routine called *outwhere*, which will have only one results parameter that must point to the predecessor of the record to be removed because the predecessor's link field has to be updated in order to carry out the deletion.

outwhere

---

pile, originator

1.1	*pile^.from := originator*
1.2	*lag := pile*
1.3	*lead := pile^.link*
2	loop while *lead^.from < originator*
3.1	*lag := lead*
3.2	*lead := lead^.link*
4	loopend
	{*lead* now points to either the first originator memo or to *pile*}
5.1	if (*lead^.from = originator*) and (*lead <> pile*) then
5.2	*location := lag*
5.3	else
5.4	*location := nil*
5.6	ifend

---

location

The same data table applies as for *inwhere*, and the design of *remove* is similar to that in the text.

Test data

The driver program will have to enable all the operations to be tested. In particular, it will have to allow for the testing of insertion, deletion, printing and testing for an empty pile. Since we would want to test these in combinations, a menu-driven program, with these as choices within a loop, would seem to be the simplest approach. Data corresponding to the following situations need to be derived for test purposes:

(a) Does *insert* work correctly on an empty pile?
(b) Insert data for an originator who does not have any memos in the current pile.
(c) Insert data for an originator who does have memos in the current pile. Check that such inserts are entered in the correct order.
(d) Insert a memo immediately after the dummy, that is, preceding all existing data.
(e) Insert a memo after the last existing memo, that is, after all existing memos.
(f) Insert into the 'middle' of existing data.
(g) Delete the memo of a single memo pile.
(h) Delete memos from an originator who has several memos stored. Check that deletions are carried out in the correct order.
(i) Delete the first memo on the pile, that is, the one just after the dummy.
(j) Delete the last memo on the pile.

Problem 14.1

Problem statement

Write a driver program that will enable the abstract data type *stringtree*, developed in the text, to be tested.

Design

The driver program will have to permit the testing of the operations. In particular, repeated tests will be required on *isempty*, *insert*, *isthere* and *print*, and so a menu-driven design within a loop is suggested. We can exploit the general design of the driver program for sequences here.

Test data

Data corresponding to the following situations should be generated in order to test the implementation:

(a) Does *insert* work correctly on an empty tree?
(b) Insert data which alphabetically precede all existing data.
(c) Insert data which come alphabetically after all existing data.
(d) Insert data which are in the 'middle' of existing data.
(e) Find data which appear alphabetically first in the tree.
(f) Find data which appear alphabetically last in the tree.
(g) Find data which appear alphabetically in the middle of the data in the tree.
(h) Find the data which were inserted first in the tree.
(i) Find the data which were most recently inserted into the tree.
(j) Attempt to find data which are not in the tree.

Problem 14.2

Problem statement

The concordance will be represented by a binary tree whose nodes will be records having four fields: two link fields for the left and right subtrees, one field for the word and one for its frequency. Write down the interface for a Pascal unit *uconcord* that makes suitable declarations for the nodes and operations.

Problem 14.3

Problem statement

The operations *insert* and *howmany* are both required to search the concordance. A procedure *findwhere* will be developed for this purpose. Write a procedure corresponding to the following specification:

findwhere

concordance	A representation of the concordance	*concordtype* parameter
inword	Word whose location is sought	*string* parameter
{If *inword* is in the concordance then set *exists* true and return the pointer value *location* that identifies the node containing *inword*. If *inword* is not in the concordance, set *exists* to false and return *location* with pointer value that identifies the node which would be the parent node of *inword*.}		
location	Pointer to a node	*concordtype* parameter
exists	True if *inword* is in concordance	*Boolean* parameter

Design

Data table for findwhere

Identifier	Description	Type
lead	Pointer to a node record	*concordtype* variable
lag	Pointer lagging one record behind *lead*	*concordtype* variable

findwhere

---

concordance, inword

1.1	*exists* := false
1.2	*lead* := *concordance*
1.3	*lag* := *nil*
2	loop while *lead* <> *nil*
3.1	*lag* := *lead*
3.2	if *inword* < *lead^.word* then
3.3	*lead* := *lead^.left*
3.4	else
3.5	if *inword* > *lead^.word* then
3.6	*lead* := *lead^.right*
3.7	else
3.8	*lead* := *nil*
3.9	*exists* := true
3.10	ifend
3.11	ifend
4	loopend
5	*location* := *lag*

---

location, exists

Test data
This procedure will be tested when we have implemented the complete data type.

Problem 14.4

Problem statement
Write the implementation part of the unit *uconcord*.

Data table for the routines

Identifier	Description	Type
temp	Pointer to new node	*concordtype* variable
location	Pointer to insertion point	*concordtype* variable
exists	Flag denoting existence of word	*Boolean* variable

Test data
The driver program simply needs to allow for insertions and counts. Data corresponding to the following situations should be generated in order to test the implementation:

(a) Does *insert* work correctly on an empty concordance?
(b) Insert a single word into an empty concordance and check its count.
(c) Insert two copies of a single word into an empty concordance and check its count.
(d) Insert a word which precedes all words in the concordance and check its count.
(e) Insert a word which comes after all words in the concordance and check its count.
(f) Count occurrences of a word given in an empty concordance.
(g) Count occurrences of a non-existent word in a non-empty concordance.
(h) Count occurrences of an existing word in a concordance.

Design

insert
concordance, inword

1	if *isempty(concordance)* then
2.1	*new(concordance)*
2.2	*concordance^.word := inword*
2.3	*concordance^.count := 1*
2.4	*concordance^.left := nil*
2.5	*concordance^.right := nil*
3	else
4	*findwhere(concordance, inword,*
	location, exists)
5	if *exists* then
6	*location^.count := location^.count + 1*
7	else
8.1	*new(temp)*
8.2	*temp^.word := inword*
8.3	*temp^.count := 1*
8.4	*temp^.left := nil*
8.5	*temp^.right := nil*
8.6	if *inword < location^.word* then
8.7	*location^.left := temp*
8.8	else
8.9	*location^.right := temp*
8.10	ifend
9	ifend
10	ifend

location

create

1	*concordance := nil*

concordance

howmany

1	*findwhere(concordance, inword,*
	location, exists)
2.1	if *exists* then
2.2	*howmany := location^.count*
2.3	else
2.4	*howmany := 0*
2.5	ifend

concordance

Problem 15.1

Problem statement

Write a recursive procedure, *binary*, corresponding to the following specification:

binary

number	An integer	*integer* parameter
{Write out the binary equivalent of the integer.}		

Design

binary
number

1	if (*number* = 0) or (*number* = 1) then
2	write *number*
3	else
4	*binary(number* div 2)
5	write *number* mod 2
6	ifend

Test data
A simple driver program that requests an integer input and then calls *binary* will suffice.
Testing with the integers 0, 1, …, 16 should suffice.

Problem 15.2

Problem statement
Hexadecimal numbers are numbers to the base 16, and are extensively used in low-level and
machine-language programming. The digits for hexadecimal numbers are the digits 0 – 9,
together with the letters A, B, C, D, E, F which correspond to the decimal numbers 10 – 12
respectively. Hexadecimals often have the letter H written after them to denote the fact that
they are hexadecimal and not base 10 numbers. Hence 13H denotes the hexadecimal
number 13, that is $1 \times 16 + 3$ to base 10. Similarly, 3DH is $3 \times 16 + 13$ to the base 10. Write
a recursive procedure, *hex*, that converts base 10 numbers to their hexadecimal equivalent.

hex

number	An integer to the base 10	*integer* parameter
{Write out the hexadecimal equivalent of the integer.}		

Design

hex

number

1	if (*number* >= 0) and (*number* <= 15) then
2.1	if *number* <= 9 then
2.2	write *number*
2.3	else
2.4	select case depending on *number*
2.5	'10' : write 'A'
2.6	'11' : write 'B'
2.7	'12' : write 'C'
2.8	'13' : write 'D'
2.9	'14' : write 'E'
2.10	'15' : write 'F'
2.11	selectend
2.12	ifend
3	else
4	*hex*(*number* div 16)
5	*remainder* := *number* mod 16
6.1	if *remainder* <= 9 then
6.2	write *remainder*
6.3	else
6.4	select case depending on *remainder*
6.5	'10' : write 'A'
6.6	'11' : write 'B'
6.7	'12' : write 'C'
6.8	'13' : write 'D'
6.9	'14' : write 'E'
6.10	'15' : write 'F'
6.11	selectend
6.12	ifend
7	ifend

Data table

Identifier	Description	Type
remainder	Remainder from integer division	0..15 variable

Test data

A simple driver program that requests an integer input and then calls *binary* will suffice. Testing with the integers 0, 1, 9, 10, ..., 16, 17 and then some larger values should be all that is required.

Problem 15.3

Problem statement

Write a recursive routine for the tree operation *isthere* specified in Section 14.2.

Design

isthere
_____

tree, item
_____

```
 1    if isempty(tree) then
 2       found := false
 3    else
 4       if item < tree^.data then
 5          found := isthere(tree^.left, item)
 6       else
 7          if item > tree^.data then
 8             found := isthere(tree^.right, item)
 9          else
10             found := true
11          ifend
12       ifend
13    ifend
14    isthere := found
```
_____

isthere
_____

Data table

Identifier	Description	Type
found	Flag to denote item found	*Boolean* variable

Test data

The implementation corresponding to this design replaces the code for *isthere* in the implementation part of the Pascal unit *utree*. No other changes are required to this unit which can then be recompiled. The original driver program given in the solution to Problem 14.1 can be used here to test this new implementation because no changes have been made to the interface part of *utree*. However, it will need to be recompiled.

Problem 15.4

Problem statement

Write a recursive print procedure that writes out the data using a postorder traversal to replace the tree operation *print* in *utree*.

Design

print

tree
1   if *tree = nil* then
2   do nothing
3   else
4   print(*tree^.left*)
5   print(*tree^.right*)
6   write out *tree^.data*
7   ifend

Test data

The same comments as in Problem 15.3 apply here.

Problem 15.5

Problem statement

Write a recursive print procedure that writes out the data using a preorder traversal to replace the tree operation *print* in *utree*.

Design

print

tree
1   if *tree = nil* then
2   do nothing
3   else
4   write out *tree^.data*
5   print(*tree^.left*)
6   print(*tree^.right*)
7   ifend

Test data

The same comments as in Problem 15.3 apply here.

Problem 15.6

Problem statement

An additional operation of counting the number of nodes of a binary search tree is to be added to the abstract data type *stringtree*. The new data type is to be implemented in a Pascal unit *utree1*. Write a recursive function for this operation to the following specification:

countnodes

tree	Representation of a tree	*stringtree* parameter
{Count the number of nodes in *tree*.}		
countnodes	Number of nodes in tree	*integer* function value

Design

countnodes

tree	
1	if *isempty*(*tree*) then
2	count := 0
3	else
4	leftcount := countnodes(tree^.left)
5	rightcount := countnodes(tree^.right)
6	count := leftcount + rightcount + 1
7	ifend
8	countnodes := count

countnodes

Data table

Identifier	Description	Type
count	Number of nodes in total	*integer* variable
leftcount	Number of nodes in left subtree	*integer* variable
rightcount	Number of nodes in right subtree	*integer* variable

Test data

The driver program will need to be expanded to include this extra option. Its **uses** statement will also have to be altered to reference *utree1*. The count should be tested for both zero and non-zero numbers of nodes.

Problem 15.7

Problem statement

An alternative specification for the operation of insertion into a binary tree would allow duplicate entries. The specification below allows for this. Write a recursive procedure to implement this specification. Your implementation should replace the procedure *insert* in unit *utree1* of Problem 15.6.

insert

tree	Representation of a tree	*stringtree* parameter
item	Item to be inserted	*string* parameter
{Insert *item* in *tree*. The item is inserted in the left subtree of a node if it strictly precedes the data in that node. Otherwise it is inserted in the right subtree.}		
tree	Updated string tree	*stringtree* parameter

Design

See opposite page.

Data table

Identifier	Description	Type
temp	Pointer to current node	*stringtree* variable

Test data

The same driver program can be used here as in Problem 15.6.

insert

tree, item	
1	if _isempty(tree)_ then
2.1	_new(temp)_
2.2	_temp^.left := nil_
2.3	_temp^.right := nil_
2.4	_temp^.data := item_
2.5	_tree := temp_
3	else
4.1	if _item < tree^.data_ then
4.2	_insert(tree^.left, item)_
4.3	else
4.4	_insert(tree^.right, item)_
4.5	ifend
5	ifend

tree

Problem 15.8

Problem statement

In this problem you should assume that the insertion of items into a tree allows for duplicate entries, as described in Problem 15.7. A different node-counting operation is to be provided that replaces the function _countnodes_ in _utree1_ and enables the number of occurrences of a particular item to be counted. Write a recursive procedure to the specification given below.

countnodes

tree	Representation of a tree	_stringtree_ parameter
item	Item to be inserted	_string_ parameter
{Count the number of occurrences of _item_ in _tree_.}		
countnodes	The number of occurrences	_integer_ function value

Design

This problem is similar to Problem 15.6 except that a node is included in the count only if its data match those of the source parameter.

countnodes

tree, item	
1	if _isempty(tree)_ then
2	_count := 0_
3	else
4	_leftcount := countnodes(tree^.left)_
5	_rightcount := countnodes(tree^.right)_
6	if _tree^.data = item_ then
7	_count := leftcount + rightcount + 1_
8	else
9	_count := leftcount + rightcount_
10	ifend
11	ifend
12	_countnodes := count_

count

Data table

Identifier	Description	Type
count	Number of nodes in total	*integer* variable
leftcount	Number of nodes in left subtree	*integer* variable
rightcount	Number of nodes in right subtree	*integer* variable

Test data

The same driver program as that used in Problem 15.6 can be used here. Test data will have to include node values that occur more than once.

APPENDIX I : COLLECTED PASCAL SYNTAX

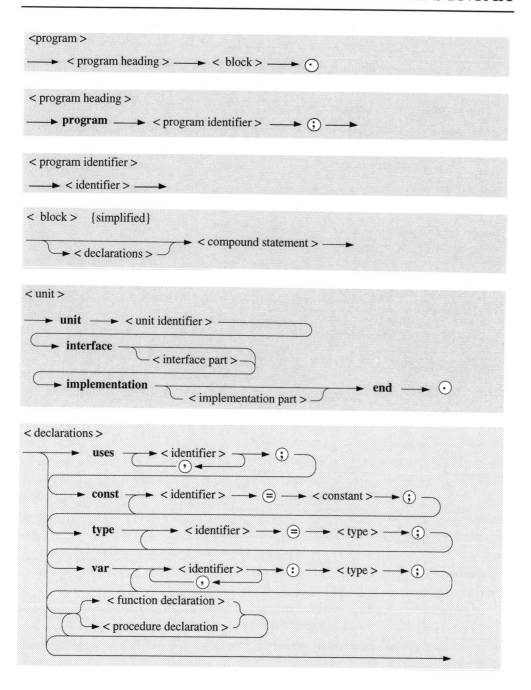

< interface part >

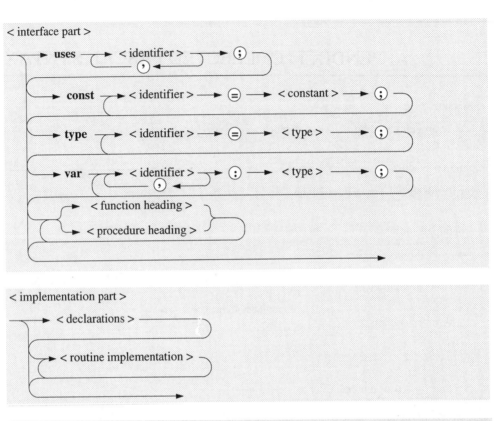

< implementation part >

< routine implementation >

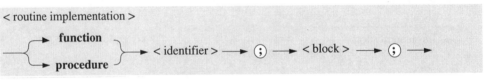

< identifier >

< constant >

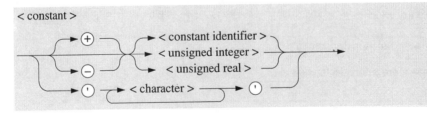

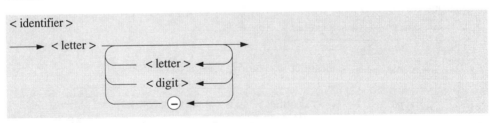

< unsigned integer >

< unsigned real >

< type >

< ordinal type >

< subrange type >

< enumeration type >

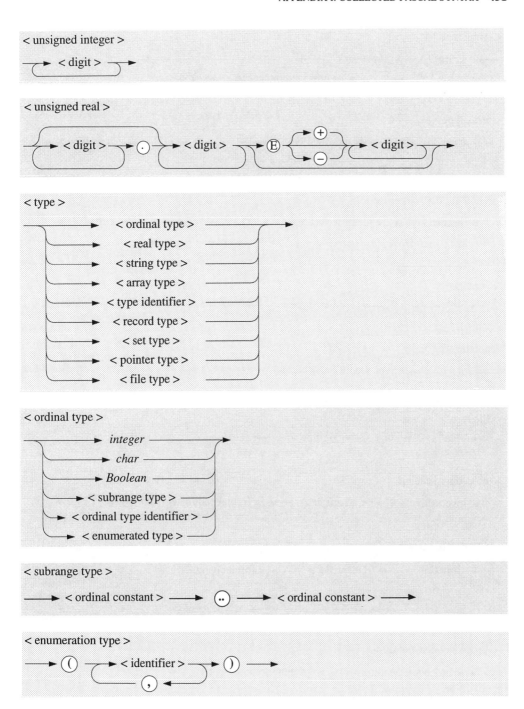

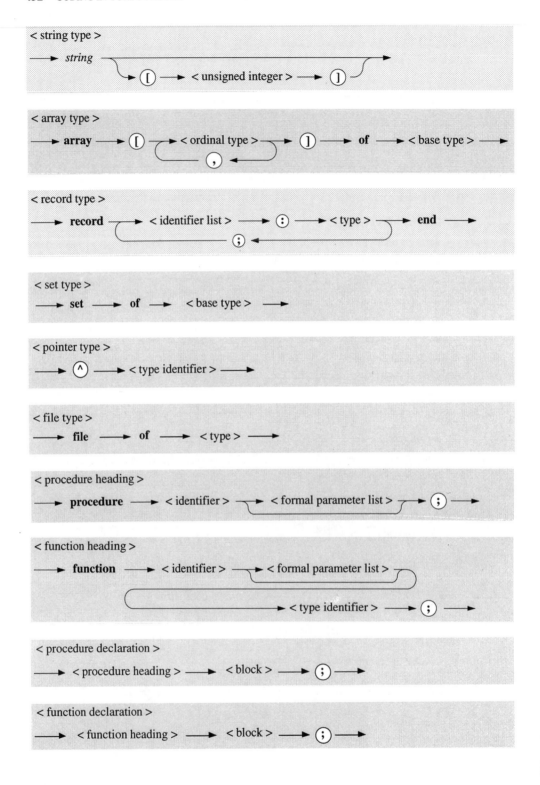

< formal parameter list >

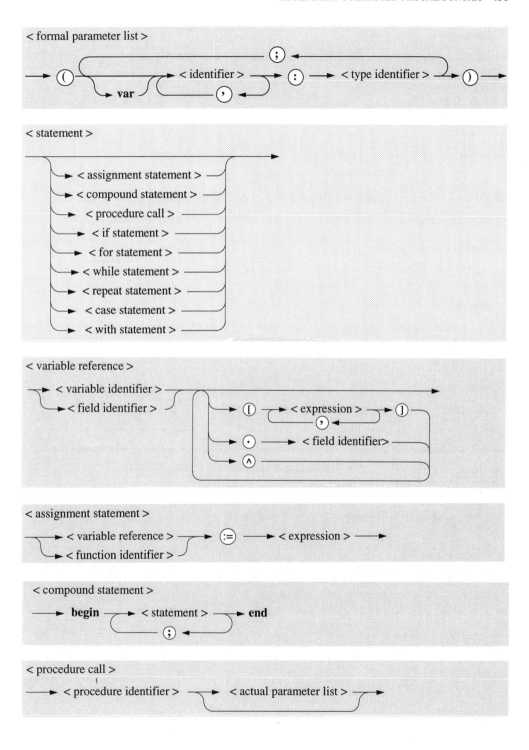

< statement >

< variable reference >

< assignment statement >

< compound statement >

< procedure call >

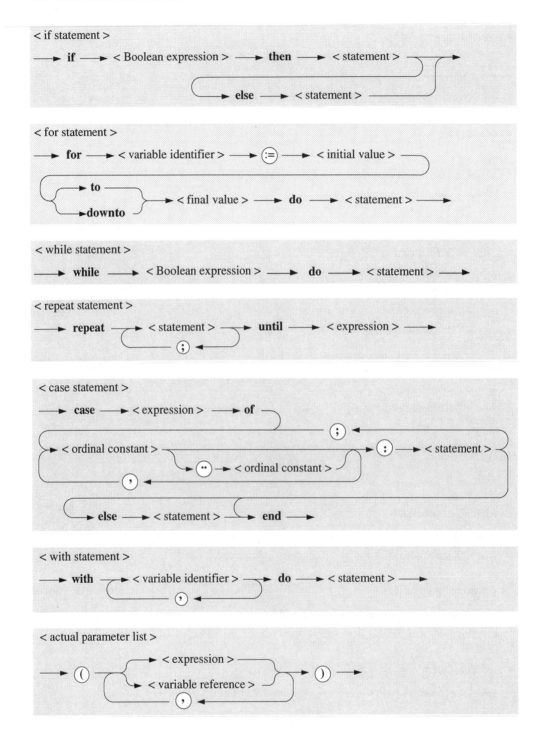

< term >

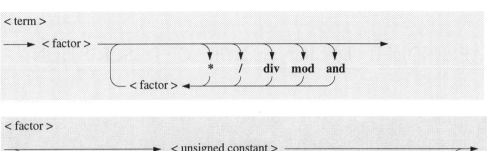

< factor >

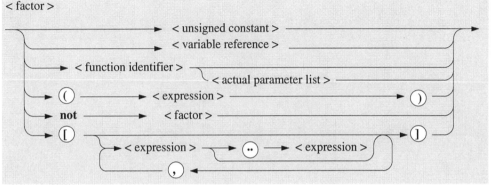

< expression >

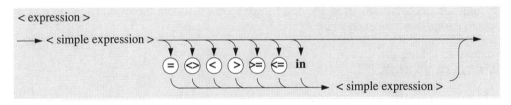

< simple expression >

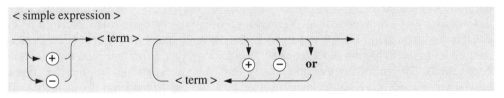

APPENDIX II : DESIGN LANGUAGE DESCRIPTION

This appendix gives an informal account of the design language used in this book. It includes the conventions used for declaring variables in data tables and the method by which design steps are expressed.

A.1 DATA TABLES

All variables which are used in a design must be declared in a data table. The description column is intended to give the reader an idea of the purpose of the identifier. The descriptions here are hypothetical. Variables of structured type are often declared using constant and type definitions. We shall adopt the convention that identifiers are declared in data tables in the following order: constant declarations, type definitions and then variable declarations. The following example shows how subranges, strings, enumerated types, arrays and records may be declared. Notice how the field identifiers for a record are declared in the description column, with the field type being given in the type column.

Data table

Identifier	Description	Type
maxsize	Constant definition	*integer* constant
range	Subrange type definition	1..*maxsize*
monthtype	Enumeration type definition	(*dec, jan, feb, mar*)
recordtype	Record type definition	
	authorname {Name of author}	*string* variable
	date {Title of book}	*monthtype* variable
	recordend	
namearray	An array of surnames	array[*indexrange*] of *string* variable
number	A user input value	*integer* variable
average	Average of user inputs	*real* variable
author	Author details	*recordtype* variable

456

A.2 PROCEDURE AND FUNCTION SPECIFICATIONS

A routine, that is, a procedure or function, consists of four parts: the identifier of a routine, its source data, the process which transforms the source data into results, and the results themselves. The style of presentation is illustrated below. A routine which is to be designed as a function will have a single result, having the same identifier as the routine itself, and which will be of type *integer, real, char* or *Boolean* (or a subrange of these types). Source data and results, which are of structured type, are declared using type identifiers as illustrated below.

minimax

first	An integer	*range* parameter
second	An integer	*range* parameter
third	An integer	*range* parameter
{Return to *smallest* the smallest of the three source parameters and to *largest* the largest of the three source parameters.}		
smallest	Smallest of the inputs	*range* parameter
largest	Largest of the inputs	*range* parameter

A routine must be declared in the data table of the program which calls it. The declaration comes before the variable declarations and after the type definitions. To declare a *procedure* its identifier is listed in the identifier column and its formal parameters are listed, enclosed in brackets, in the description column. In the type column, the word *procedure* precedes the list of parameter types which must match, in order and number, the formal parameters already mentioned. The declaration of a *function* is similar except that the type column specifies the type of function result and uses the word *function* instead of *procedure*. Parameters which are both source data and results are declared only once in the data table. Programs which call many routines must declare them one after the other, and the order in which they are declared will affect their referencing environments. The declaration for the procedure specification above is:

Data table

Identifier	Description	Type
maxsize	Constant definition	*integer* constant
range	Subrange type definition	1..*maxsize*
minimax	(*first, second, third, smallest, largest*)	procedure(*range, range, range, range, range*)

Abstract data types may be designed so that the details of the representation are hidden from the user. The term 'module' is used for the design corresponding to an abstract data type and its data table has two parts: one public and one private. Typically, module data tables declaring an abstract data type will include pointer variables. The type to which a pointer variable points appears after the definition of the pointer itself. Private procedures which are required in the design of the public routines should be declared to be private, as illustrated below for the module *adtmodule*. In this illustration, *find* can be called by *operation* (because its declaration precedes that of *operation*) but it may not be called by the user of the module because it is declared to be private.

Data table

Identifier	Description	Type
	PUBLIC	
adttype	Type definition representing ADT	private
create	(*adtobject*)	procedure(*adttype*)
find	(*adtobject*, *search*)	private procedure(*adttype*, *string*)
operation	(*adtobject*, *adtobject*)	procedure(*adttype*, *adttype*)
	PRIVATE	
adttype	Type definition	pointer to *nodetype*
range	Record type definition	
	word {Data}	*string* variable
	link {Pointer to next item}	*nodetype* variable
	recordend	

A.3 DESIGN STATEMENTS

The design fragments in this section are for illustration and do not form a coherent piece of design. Identifiers used in designs are italicized, whereas all other design words are not.

A.3.1 Sequence

Design steps are numbered as illustrated below:

1   step 1
2.1 first step in refinement of step 2
2.2 second step in refinement of step 2
2.3 third step in refinement of step 2
3   step 3

A step may be a comment, in which case it is enclosed in braces and does not have a step number. Other basic steps are illustrated below:

1	write out 'Enter a number '	{Data output: text in quotes}
2	read in *number*	{Data input statement}
3	increment *number*	{This means by 1 unless stated otherwise}
4	decrement *number*	{This means by 1}
5	increment *number* by 2	
6	write out 'The value is ', *number*	{Variables are not in quotes in write out steps}
7	*number* := 10	{Assign 10 to number}
8	do nothing	{A dummy statement}

A.3.2 Conditional statements

The *if* statement

1 if *condition* then
2   steps
3 else
4   steps
5 ifend

The steps which occur in step 2 (and its subsequent refinements) are collectively referred to as the *then* clause. Those which form step 4 are called the *else* clause. If step 4 is *do nothing* then steps 3 and 4 may be omitted. A collection of *if* statements may be nested to any level, but each one must have an *ifend*.

The *case* statement

This enables a choice to be made from several possibilities. The case statement executes the statement prefixed by the case label, or case range, which is equal to the value of the selector. If no such match exists and the default statement is present, the statement following the default is executed. Case selectors must be of enumerated type. In the example below *ch* is a *char* variable which is used as a selector.

```
1   select case depending on ch
2       'A'    :  write out 'Letter is upper case A'
3       'B'..'D' :  write out 'Letter is upper case and lies between B and D inclusive'
4       'E'    :  write out 'Letter is upper case E'
5       default :  write out 'Letter is none of A to E'
6   selectend
```

A.3.3 The *with* statement

The *with* statement is shorthand for referencing fields of a record. Within a *with* statement, the fields of one or more specific record variables can be referenced using their field identifiers only.

```
1   with author do
2       authorname := 'Sargent'
3       title := 'An Introduction to Program Design'
4   withend
```

A.3.4 Repetitive statements

There are three kinds of design loops:

The *for* loop

```
1   loop for i := 1 to 20
2       step(s) within loop body
3   loopend
```

A *for* loop is executed a predetermined number of times, and the loop control variable, *i* in the example above, must not be updated within the body of the loop. Variables referenced within the loop must be initialized outside it.

The *while* loop

```
1   initialize variables
2   loop while expression
3       step(s) within loop body
4   loopend
```

The expression controlling the repetition must be of type *Boolean*. The body of the loop must contain a statement which enables the value of the expression to be updated in order to ensure that the loop eventually ceases execution. Variables which appear in the expression must be initialized prior to the loop statement.

The *repeat* loop

```
1   repeat
2       step(s) within loop body
3   until expression
```

The expression controlling the repetition must be of type *Boolean*. The body of the loop must contain a statement which enables the value of the expression to be updated in order to ensure that the loop eventually ceases execution. A *repeat* loop is always executed at least once.

A.3.5 Design indentation

The steps occurring between any of the following matching pairs should be indented:

```
loop – loopend
repeat – until
select – selectend
with – withend
```

The steps in the *then* and *else* clauses of an *if* statement should be indented.

A.4 PROCEDURE DESIGNS

Procedure designs are presented in a similar way to their specification except that the process part is replaced by a design showing how the results are to be obtained from the source data. The format of the design is the same as that for a program. The source data are listed one after the other as a formal parameter list. The type of each parameter is as given in the specification of the routine. Results are listed in a similar way.

minimax

first, second, third

```
1.1   largest := first
1.2   smallest := first
2.1   if second > largest then
2.2       largest := second
2.3   ifend
3.1   if third > largest then
3.2       largest := third
3.3   ifend
4.1   if second < smallest then
4.2       smallest := second
4.3   ifend
5.1   if third < smallest then
5.2       smallest := third
5.3   ifend
```

largest, smallest

A.5 PROCEDURE CALLS

The general form of a procedure call is illustrated by

> *minimax(initial, middle, last, max, min)*

where *initial*, *middle* and *last* are the actual parameters corresponding to the formal source data parameters and *max*, *min* are the actual parameters corresponding to the results. The actual parameters would have to be declared in the data table of the calling program.

A.6 FUNCTION DESIGNS

The same design notation is used as for procedures, but a function result always has the same identifier as the function.

A.7 FUNCTION CALLS

Functions are always called in expressions. For example, if *name* is a string variable:

> loop for $i := 1$ to *length(name)*;
> if *length(name)* > 10 then

A.8 ASCII CODES

The following values are the ASCII codes for the alphanumeric keys on a keyboard:

32	space	51	3	70	F	89	Y	108	l
33	!	52	4	71	G	90	Z	109	m
34	"	53	5	72	H	91	[	110	n
35	#	54	6	73	I	92	\	111	o
36	$	55	7	74	J	93	]	112	p
37	%	56	8	75	K	94	^	113	q
38	&	57	9	76	L	95	_	114	r
39	'	58	:	77	M	96		115	s
40	(	59	;	78	N	97	a	116	t
41	)	60	<	79	O	98	b	117	u
42	*	61	=	80	P	99	c	118	v
43	+	62	>	81	Q	100	d	119	w
44	,	63	?	82	R	101	e	120	x
45	-	64	@	83	S	102	f	121	y
46	.	65	A	84	T	103	g	122	z
47	/	66	B	85	U	104	h	123	{
48	0	67	C	86	V	105	i	124		
49	1	68	D	87	W	106	j	125	}
50	2	69	E	88	X	107	k	126	~

APPENDIX III : PROGRAMMING GUIDELINES

Guideline (program)

    Every program must have a heading of the form

    program *identifier*;

Guideline (declarations part)

    Immediately following the program heading come the variable declarations (if there are any) indicated by the reserved word **var**. The declarations part corresponds to the implementation of the design data table.

Guideline (declarations)

    Each declaration has the form: identifier list, colon, variable type, in which the list consists of identifiers separated by commas. Every declaration must be followed by a semicolon.

Guideline (end)

    A semicolon should never immediately precede the word **end**.

Guideline (if then else)

    When the *then* clause consists of a single design construct, its implementation is a single statement not followed by a semicolon. When the *then* clause consists of two or more design constructs (or is a single *if then* construct without an *else*) then it must be implemented as a compound statement, where the **end** is not followed by a semicolon. When the design of the *else* clause consists of a single construct, its implementation is a single statement followed by a semicolon (provided the next word is not **end**). When the *else* clause consists of two or more design constructs it must be implemented as a compound statement. The **end** corresponding to this compound statement should be followed by a semicolon provided it does not immediately precede the word **end**.

Guideline (while)

    When a *while* loop body consists of a single construct, its implementation is a single statement followed by a semicolon (provided the next word is not **end**). When a *while* loop body consists of two or more design constructs then it must be implemented using a compound statement. The statement preceding the **end** that terminates the compound statement should not be followed by a semicolon. Whether the **end** itself is followed by a semicolon is determined by what follows on.

Guideline (comment)

    Any text appearing between braces is a comment and is ignored by the compiler. A comment may extend over many lines.

Guideline (declare before use rule)

    An identifier must be declared (or defined) before it is referenced.

Guideline (for)

When a *for* loop body consists of a single construct, its implementation is a single statement followed by a semicolon (provided the next word is not **end**). When a *for* loop body consists of two or more design constructs then it must be implemented using a compound statement followed by a semicolon (unless the following word is **end**).

Guideline (repeat)

All the construct(s) in the implementation of a *repeat* loop are followed by a semicolon except the one that immediately precedes the word **until**. The line containing **until** is also followed by a semicolon unless it is the penultimate statement of a compound statement.

Guideline (with)

If a **with** construct contains more than one design construct then a compound statement is required – otherwise it is not.

Guideline (case statement)

A **case** statement begins with the word **case** and terminates with the word **end**. Each case except the last one listed has the form: case list, colon, statement, semicolon. The last case listed has the form: case list, colon, statement. The default case is implemented using **else**, which has the same syntax as the **else** of an **if** statement.

Guideline (case labels)

Case labels must be of ordinal type and must match the type of the case selector. They can consist of single items, multiple items separated by commas, subranges or a combination of all three. However, the labels should be unique and non-overlapping.

Guideline (case)

If more than a single construct is to be executed corresponding to a particular case label then they must be implemented using a compound statement.

Guideline (function)

If a routine has a single result of simple type then it should be implemented as a function. (Routines having string results may be implemented as functions.)

Guideline (procedure heading)

The form of a procedure heading is the reserved word **procedure**, followed by the procedure's identifier, followed by the formal parameters enclosed in braces, followed by a semicolon.

Guideline (procedure formal parameters)

Parameters are declared in a list, the components of which are separated by semicolons. Each component has the form: an identifier list (each identifier being separated by a comma), followed by a colon, followed by a type identifier. Parameters of structured type must be declared using a type identifier. Results parameters must be preceded by the word **var**.

Guideline (function heading)

The form of a procedure heading is the reserved word **function**, followed by the procedure's identifier, followed by the formal parameters enclosed in braces, followed by a colon, followed by a simple type.

Guideline (formal parameters)

Parameters are declared in a list, the components of which are separated by semicolons. Each component has the form: an identifier list (each identifier being separated by a comma), followed by a colon, followed by a type identifier. Parameters of structured type must be declared using a type identifier. **var** should not be used.

Guideline (routine declaration)

Routines are declared immediately after the **var** declarations. A routine declaration consists of a routine heading followed by the local declarations in the usual order **const**, **type**, **var** (and, potentially, procedure). Finally, there is the compound statement corresponding to the procedure body. The word **end** of this compound statement is followed by a semicolon.

Guideline (pointer type definition)

Pointer type definitions have the form: identifier, equals sign, circumflex and then the identifier of the type to which it points. Note that the circumflex precedes the type being pointed at.

Guideline (pointer variable)

The variable pointed to by a (pointer) variable whose identifier is *ptr* is denoted by *ptr^*. Here, the circumflex follows the identifier.

Guideline (*new*)

This reserves enough memory in the heap for the value of the type to which the pointer variable is bound, and then assigns to the pointer variable the start address of this range. (This address cannot be accessed directly by the user.)

Guideline (unit declaration)

A unit declaration consists of two parts: an interface part and an implementation part. The interface part must contain declarations for all the identifiers which are to be exported, but it should contain only routine headings (not bodies). The implementation part may declare any identifiers required in the implementation of the routines declared in the interface. A unit always terminates with **end.** which must be preceded by a semicolon.

Guideline (unit compilation)

A unit must be compiled before a program which uses it is compiled.

Guideline (structured file)

A data value of structured type must be written to a file using *write*. The first parameter of *write* must be the internal file identifier; the second must be an identifier of the variable of the type being stored. It is an error to attempt to use *writeln* for this purpose.

Guideline (abstract data types)

The components forming the representation of the data being modelled should be encapsulated in a record whose identifier will represent the type.

Guideline (abstract data type operations)

The operations should be implemented using routines whose parameters are expressed in terms of the abstract data type identifier referred to above.

Guideline (exported identifiers)

Implementation details which have to be declared in the interface part should remain private to the implementor, even though Pascal has no way of enforcing this.

INDEX